Utilitarianism and Empire

Utilitarianism and Empire

Edited by
Bart Schultz and Georgios Varouxakis

LEXINGTON BOOKS

A Division of
ROWMAN & LITTLEFIELD PUBLISHERS, INC.
Lanham • Boulder • New York • Toronto • Oxford

LEXINGTON BOOKS

A division of Rowman & Littlefield Publishers, Inc.
A wholly owned subsidary of The Rowman & Littlefield Publishing Group, Inc.
4501 Forbes Boulevard, Suite 200
Lanham, MD 20706

PO Box 317
Oxford
OX2 9RU, UK

British Library Cataloguing in Publication Information Available

Library of Congress Cataloging-in-Publication Data

Utilitarianism and empire / edited by Bart Schultz and Georgios Varouxakis.
    p. cm.
    Includes index.
    ISBN 0-7391-0575-2 (alk. paper)—ISBN 0-7391-1087-X (pbk. : alk. paper)
    1. Great Britain—Colonies—History—19th century. 2. Great Britain—Colonies—
Administration—History—19th century. 3. Imperialism—Government policy—
Great Britain—History—19th century. 4. Race relations—Government policy—
Great Britain—History—19th century. 5. Utilitariansim—Great Britain—Colonies—
History—19th century. 6. Slave-trade—Government policy—Great Britain—
History—19th century. 7. Mill, James, 1773–1836. History of British India. 8. Mill,
John Stuart, 1806–1873—Influence. 9. Bentham, Jeremy, 1748–1832—Influence. I.
Schultz, Bart. II. Varouxakis, Georgios, 1966
DA16.U87 2005
325'.32'0941—dc22   2005008501

Printed in the United States of America

∞™ The paper used in this publication meets the minimum requirements of
American National Standard for Information Sciences—Permanence of Paper for
Printed Library Materials, ANSI/NISO Z39.48–1992.

To Jerry Schneewind

Contents

Acknowledgments   ix

1   Introduction   1
Bart Schultz and Georgios Varouxakis

2   Jeremy Bentham on Slavery and the Slave Trade   33
Frederick Rosen

3   Jeremy Bentham: Legislator of the World?   57
Jennifer Pitts

4   James Mill's *The History of British India*: The Question of
Utilitarianism and Empire   93
Javed Majeed

5   Mill on Happiness: The Enduring Value of a Complex Critique   107
Martha C. Nussbaum

6   Liberalism's Limits: Carlyle and Mill on "The Negro Question"   125
David Theo Goldberg

7   Empire, Race, Euro-centrism: John Stuart Mill and His Critics   137
Georgios Varouxakis

8   Chairing the Jamaica Committee: J. S. Mill and the
Limits of Colonial Authority   155
J. Joseph Miller

9   The Early Utilitarians, Race, and Empire:
    The State of the Argument   179
    H. S. Jones

10 Imagining Darwinism   189
    David Weinstein

11 Sidgwick's Racism   211
    Bart Schultz

Index   251

About the Contributors   261

Acknowledgments

The two editors of this book wish to thank, first of all, the contributors for having written and offered the outstanding articles that are included in the volume. Georgios Varouxakis would like to express his deep gratitude to Bart Schultz for having conceived of this volume, then for having invited him to participate as a contributor and then for having invited him to co-edit the book, and for having been so patient yet firm throughout the process; and, last but not least, for his remarkably contagious enthusiasm. Bart Schultz would like to express his heartfelt thanks to Georgios Varouxakis for his invaluable collaborative work, without which this volume would not have come to fruition.

The two editors gratefully acknowledge Blackwell Publishing for permission to reprint David Theo Goldberg's "Liberalism's Limits," the MIT Press and *Daedalus* for permission to reprint Martha Nussbaum's "Mill on Happiness," *Political Theory* as well as Princeton University Press for permission to reprint Jennifer Pitts's "Jeremy Bentham: Legislator of the World?" (an essay based on chapters 4 and 5 of her forthcoming book *A Turn to Empire: The Rise of Imperial Liberalism in Britain and France*), and the *Stanford Encyclopedia of Philosophy* for permission to reprint parts of David Weinstein's entry on "Herbert Spencer." The essays by Nussbaum, Pitts, and Weinstein have all been revised by their authors for publication in this volume. Parts of Bart Schultz's "Sidgwick's Racism" are adapted from chapter 8 of his *Henry Sidgwick: Eye of the Universe* (New York: Cambridge University Press, 2004); these are reprinted with permission, and grateful acknowledgement is made to Cambridge University Press.

1

Introduction

Bart Schultz and Georgios Varouxakis

CLASSICAL UTILITARIANISM, RACE, AND EMPIRE

In a wonderful, sarcastic little essay titled "The Harm That Good Men Do," Bertrand Russell wrote that "it is the fashion to decry the Victorians, but I wish our age had half as good a record as theirs." Russell was referring to the record of Bentham and the Benthamites on the reformism that reached fruition in the early and middle Victorian period:

> At the beginning of the period comes the Reform Act, which made Parliament representative of the middle-class, not, as before, of the aristocracy. This Act was the most difficult of the steps towards democracy in England, and was quickly followed by other important reforms, such as the abolition of slavery in Jamaica. At the beginning of the period the penalty for petty theft was death by hanging; very soon the death penalty was confined to those who were guilty of murder or high treason. The Corn Laws, which made food so dear as to cause atrocious poverty, were abolished in 1846. Compulsory education was introduced in 1870.[1]

For Russell, this record of social improvement had everything to do with the classical utilitarianism of Bentham and his followers: "A very large proportion of the progress during those years must be attributed to the influence of Bentham. There can be no doubt that nine-tenths of the people living in England in the latter part of last century were happier than they would have been if he had never lived." However, cognizant of the antipathy so often directed at utilitarianism, Russell added the sarcastic twist: "So shallow was his philosophy that he would have regarded this as a vindication of his activities. We, in our more enlightened age, can see that such a view is preposterous;

but it may fortify us to review the ground for rejecting a groveling utilitarianism such as that of Bentham." There follows a characteristically Russellian lampoon of religious conceptions of moral goodness, which generally consider "it the business of the authorities to safeguard the young against those who question the wisdom of the views generally accepted by middle-aged successful citizens."[2]

Russell, who was the "secular" (but literal) godson of John Stuart Mill and one of Henry Sidgwick's Cambridge students, clearly had classical utilitarian sympathies, at least after his early Idealistic phases. For most of his life, he held that the greatest happiness of the greatest number was a standard for moral and political evaluation that made much more sense than conventional, received opinion, with its usual mix of superstition, complacency, and hypocrisy. And interestingly, the Victorian-born Russell unflinchingly bore this standard through a very long life of re-formist agitation, in a career that carried him all the way from work for the enfranchisement of women to protests against the nuclear arms race and the ongoing imperialism of the western powers. J. S. Mill's godson was, at the end of his activist life, busily agitating against the imperialist ventures of the United States and its allies in Vietnam, finding himself at home in the student protests of the sixties.[3]

Russell's case is illustrative of the paradoxes that inform the present collection of essays. After all, most of Russell's fellow dissidents in the 1960s—from Sartre to Habermas, from Foucault to Bill Ayers—would have urged that classical utilitarianism was the friend, not of the new politics of protest but of the administrative rationality that they were in one form or another protesting. As Foucault famously put it:

> Panopticism is one of the characteristic traits of our society. It's a type of power that is applied to individuals in the form of continuous individual supervision, in the form of control, punishment, and compensation, and in the form of correction, that is, the molding and transformation of individuals in terms of certain norms. The threefold aspect of panopticism—supervision, control, correction—seems to be a fundamental and characteristic dimension of the power relations that exist in our society.[4]

As Foucault elaborates, in "panopticism, the supervision of individuals is carried out not at the level of what one does but of what one is, not at the level of what one does but of what one might do." And at the start of the nineteenth century, pace Russell, "there dawns an age of panopticism, a system that was to spread over the whole practice, and, to a certain degree, the whole theory of penal law." This is the real legacy of Bentham—Foucault's term being of course meant as homage to Bentham, whose "Panopticon" scheme for prison reform encapsulated the notion. If the tribute is back-handed, it is nonetheless extreme:

Among the theorists I cited earlier, there was one who in a sense foresaw and presented a kind of diagram of this society of supervision [*surveillance*], of this great social orthopedics—I'm thinking of Jeremy Bentham. I hope historians of philosophy will forgive me for saying this, but I believe that Bentham is more important for our society than Kant or Hegel. All our societies should pay homage to him. It was he who programmed, defined, and described in the most exact manner the forms of power in which we live, and who presented a marvelous and celebrated little model of this society of generalized orthopedics—the famous Panopticon, a form of architecture that makes possible a mind-over-mind type of power; a sort of institution that serves equally well, it would seem, for schools, hospitals, prisons, reformatories, poorhouses, and factories. The Panopticon is a ring-shaped building in the middle of which there is a yard with a tower at the center. The ring is divided into little cells that face the interior and exterior alike. In each of these little cells there is, depending on the purpose of the institutions, a child learning to write, a worker at work, a prisoner correcting himself, a madman living his madness. In the central tower there is an observer. Since each cell faces both the inside and the outside, the observer's gaze can traverse the whole cell; there is no dimly lit space, so everything the individual does is exposed to the gaze of an observer who watches through shuttered windows or spy holes in such a ways as to be able to see everything without anyone being able to see him. For Bentham, this marvelous little architectonic ruse could be used by a variety of different sorts of institutions. The Panopticon is the utopia of a society and a type of power that is basically the society we are familiar with at present, a utopia that was actually realized. This type of power can properly be given the name panopticism. We live in a society where panopticism reigns.

Panopticism is a form of power that rests not on the inquiry but on something completely different, which I will call the "examination."[5]

If, as James Miller has urged, the protests of the sixties were the politics of Foucauldian transgression, of subversion, not conversion, then it ought to seem that Russell's utilitarianism was as out of joint with the movement as a reincarnated Bentham's would have been.[6] But of course, this was not the case, and Russell was in fact as attuned to the insidious forms of power and surveillance embedded in twentieth-century technocracy as Foucault. The contested terrain of politics only brought such public intellectuals into harmony. When it came to sixties oppositional politics, there was little to divide Russell (and his follower Noam Chomsky) from Foucault, just as in earlier decades there had been little to divide Russell from the participatory democracy of John Dewey. One of the main differences was, ironically, that Russell managed to be a much more powerful critic of the institutions of higher education, whereas Foucault resolutely avoided biting the hand that fed him.

Curiously enough, in the decades since Russell and Foucault found themselves strange bedfellows, the paradoxes swirling about the legacy of classical utilitarianism have only deepened, to the point where it sometimes seems that here is another case of "two cultures"—one at least somewhat sympathetic to the legacy, the other implacably hostile. Or perhaps this is the last, lingering vestige of the hoary old "analytical v. Continental" philosophical divide. At any rate, with the success of so much academic work in Foucauldian constructionism, especially in the area of gender and gay studies, and with that of the often related work on orientalism and postcolonialism, it often goes without saying in various academic disciplines that the only serious interest one could have in this legacy is more or less the one defined by Foucault, adapted perhaps to the concerns of Edward Said, Homi Bhaba, and Gayatrai Spivak. To be sure, philosophy departments might allow that classical utilitarianism can continue to serve as a useful foil, a good way to bring out the superior wisdom of Kantianism, Rawlsianism, virtue ethics, or whatever. But the reigning "serious alternatives"—unless one is a philistine hopelessly perverted by economistic conceptions of rationality—are always of the form Kant v. Nietzsche, Aristotle v. Kant, Foucault v. Habermas, Habermas v. Rawls, Nussbaum v. Butler, Derrida and Rorty v. everyone, etc., with the younger Mill sometimes entering the arena only by virtue of his supposed magnificent inconsistency, such that he was really more Aristotelian than Benthamite. Intellectually dead, but socially alive and now playing the role that orthodox Christianity once played—that is the implied verdict.

The contributors to this volume are not united by much, but they are at least united by a sense that the construction of the classical utilitarian legacy in recent decades is profoundly unsatisfactory, sharing many of the same reductionistic crudities of the construction of "Victorianism." There is here no sweeping dismissiveness toward recent academic trends; indeed, some of the contributors, such as Schultz, are quite in sympathy with, for example, Said's work. But all share a sense that valuable as, say, the debates over orientalism have been, they have often failed to do justice to the complexities and potentialities of the classical utilitarian legacy. It will no longer do to chalk up the better sides of Mill or Russell—or Bentham for that matter—as marvelous inconsistencies, in which their intelligence triumphed over their explicit theorizing. Nor is it enough to set up the debate with a stock bit of James Mill on India, as Alexander Macfie does in his *Orientalism: A Reader*, breezily noting that "Mill betrays many of the preconceptions and prejudices later associated by its critics with orientalism."[7] Utilitarianism cannot be so encapsulated; it was a rich, complex, and conflicted historical movement that changed considerably even in the space from Bentham to James Mill, much less that from Bentham to Henry Sidgwick. Even Said, in *Orientalism*, started out by insisting that if "nearly every nineteenth-century writer . . . was extraordinarily well aware of the fact of empire," this "is a subject not very well studied," as readily as the "modern Victorian specialist" might admit that "liberal cultural heroes like John Stuart Mill, Arnold, Carlyle, Newman, Macaulay, Ruskin, George Eliot, and even Dickens had definite views on race and imperialism, which are quite easily to be found at work in their writing."[8] Like Foucault, Said tended to speak of Victorian liberalism rather than utilitarianism, which on this count remains "a subject not very well studied."

Thus, our aim is to bring out, to engage with, the different aspects of the utilitarian legacy that bear directly on questions of race and empire in a way that recognizes this historical complexity, how, in particular, there was no single construction of "race" or the "Orient" or "empire" informing the work of Bentham, the Mills, Spencer, and Sidgwick. To the best of our knowledge, no such comprehensive effort at understanding the classical utilitarian tradition on these crucial topics has previously been attempted, and even many of the piecemeal studies, pro or con, have tended to avoid the perplexing details. Works that ought to be helpful on this score—whether George Stocking's *Victorian Anthropology* or Spivak's *Critique of Postcolonial Reason*—turn out to have very little to say about the most famous of the utilitarians. As popular as Bernard Williams's gibe at "Government House" utilitarianism has been in philosophical circles, neither Williams nor anyone else has so much as tried to come to terms with the historical realities that such a phrase suggests.[9] And if the contributions to this volume are any indication, the phrase itself is more of a slur than a witticism. Subject populations would often have been better off with more utilitarians in government and fewer Platonists, Kantians, and Idealists, though again, much would have depended on precisely which utilitarians were involved. There was no one vision of the social realization of the utilitarian perspective.

Hence, this collection, featuring many of the most illustrious scholars connected with utilitarian studies, ought to prove uniquely valuable, not only to those with a sympathetic interest in the utilitarian legacy, but also to those who side with its many critics. It is a paradox worthy of the twenty-first century that so many of these critics should be more familiar with and solicitous of Nietzsche's views on race—and scorn for happiness—than with the views that supposedly make up the fabric of "the power relations that exist in our society."

JEREMY BENTHAM, JAMES MILL, AND JOHN STUART MILL

Reform the world by example, you act generously and wisely: reform the world by force, you might as well reform the moon, and the design is fit only for lunatics.[10]

It should become clear from a perusal of the texts published in this volume that there was no *one* single "utilitarian" position on issues of empire and colonies. As Jennifer Pitts puts it aptly in one of the chapters of this volume: "With regard to colonies, there was no unitary utilitarian logic but rather a transformation of the tradition that reflected a broader shift in European thought on empire from the late eighteenth to the early nineteenth century, away from profound doubts about colonial aspirations and toward increasingly emphatic support for them." Not only the different thinkers of the classical utilitarian tradition appear to have adopted different positions on colonies and empire. Moreover, even in the thought and writings of each one of the thinkers in question there is not always a single, coherent line on such issues throughout their lifetime; rather, there are tensions, if not contradictions, as a number of considerations seem to have affected the stance they adopted in each case. However, some conclusions can be drawn relatively safely. As regards particularly the three first thinkers in the classical utilitarian tradition covered in this volume, Jeremy Bentham, James Mill and John Stuart Mill, one of the major contributions of the concentration and juxtaposition in this volume of a number of different studies of their respective attitudes toward issues of race, slavery, colonies and empire is the emergence of Jeremy Bentham as a much more enlightened and open-minded thinker than conventional academic wisdom would have one believe. The combined effect of the chapters contributed by Jennifer Pitts, Fred Rosen, and Javed Majeed is to offer a new and unconventional reading of the utilitarian tradition in which Bentham stands out as a particularly enlightened and broad-minded thinker, free from a number of blemishes with which the British utilitarians in the lump have been charged by later scholarship.

Jeremy Bentham

Fred Rosen, in an ambitious and far-reaching article, sets out to challenge a number of criticisms that have been raised against Bentham's approach to the institution of slavery and the slave trade. Though he discusses other criticisms as well, his main target is Lea Campos Boralevi's claims in *Bentham and the Oppressed*.[11] It is the least of Boralevi's criticisms that Bentham failed to write at length on the issue of slavery. What is more, according to her, the paucity of writings on slavery which she attributes to Bentham is itself probably due to the fact that the issue of slavery exposed what she calls an "ambiguity" or even "contradiction" in Bentham's philosophy. Thus, the stakes are high, as it is not just Bentham's attitude toward slavery that is the issue, but, moreover, the very coherence of his overall philosophy. Boralevi claims that Bentham was not able to ever reconcile his emphasis on security, and particularly security of property, with a similar emphasis on equality as ends of legislation. She claims that the same applies to his utilitarian emphasis on happiness with that on securing rights to property—in other words, that he was never able to reconcile them. Finally, Boralevi criticizes Bentham for denying the reality and validity of natural rights. As he promises in the beginning of the article, Rosen does indeed offer a complex challenge at three mutually reinforcing levels:

partly historical, by linking up Bentham's scattered remarks on slavery to the political contexts to which they were associated; partly textual, by examining a number of passages in the context of the works in which they appeared; and partly philosophical, by exploring Bentham's overall consistency and the coherence of his thought and showing that the alleged contradictions are only apparent. Rosen makes good use of material that seems to have been unknown to earlier commentators, including the critics whose views he sets out to refute. He convincingly challenges the widespread view that the impetus for the abolition of the slave trade between 1787 and 1807 and then for the gradual abolition of slavery during the 1820s (culminating in the abolition of slavery in British colonies from 1833) had come almost exclusively from religious circles (Quakers, Evangelicals, and Methodists); side by side (and often in cooperation) with those, Rosen maintains, "there was another strand of activity at this time, based in the Lansdowne circle, that also attacked slavery and the slave trade, and this strand included Bentham." In that context he fruitfully highlights the relevance of Bentham's involvement with France at the time of the French Revolution and the numerous works which he wrote on, and for France, which, among other things, earned him honorary French citizenship in 1792 (a relevance that, as so many other themes, becomes obvious and accessible thanks to the superb new edition of Bentham's *Collected Works* by the Bentham Project at University College London).[12] To Boralevi's argument that the fact that Bentham failed to discuss slavery and the slave trade in his correspondence with William Wilberforce must be taken to show his lack of interest in the issue, Rosen juxtaposes Bentham's close cooperation with some of the most important other participants in the antislavery campaign, notably Samuel Romilly and the Genevan Etienne Dumont,[13] both of whom he knew well through the Lansdowne circle. The chapter is also very well informed and informative concerning the historical context within which all these activities were taking place and depicts the complexity of the problem of slavery succinctly and to great effect.

But though very important and sufficient in themselves to sustain a challenge against most of the charges leveled against Bentham by late-twentieth-century commentators, the meticulous historical contextualization and the evocation of hitherto unnoticed material by no means exhaust the significance of Rosen's chapter. Far more important and ambitious is his textual and philosophical analysis. To start with, Rosen shows that there was a shift in Bentham's use of the term "slavery," corresponding to a growing politicization of the issue of slavery on his part and, more generally, to a clear radicalization of his thinking. In his earliest writings on slavery, particularly the civil law writings, drafted in the 1770s and early 1780s, Bentham emerges as unequivocally opposed to slavery and committed to liberty. According to Rosen, Bentham's discussion there consisted of the development of two themes. "The first was concerned with arguments to establish that the institution of slavery was not beneficial to the master or the slave, and the second, with a strategy for emancipation." The latter was "a strategy for gradual emancipation that attempted to avoid violent revolution." What is interesting in terms of how Bentham used the term "slavery" in different periods is that in his early writings what distinguished slavery was *its perpetuity*. Now, as Rosen shows using numerous examples, in Bentham's later, "more political" writings, his attitude toward slavery seems to have changed in one important way. While in his early writings he had endeavored to define slavery more precisely in terms of the perpetuity of subjection, in his later writings Bentham used the term "slavery" rather more broadly to refer to "numerous conditions of subordination where power was exercised unjustly." Rosen sees this as a "'politicization' of the term 'slavery' to include virtually all instances of persistent unjust oppression or even exploitation." What is more: "But at the same time it followed from his belief that subjection was characteristic of the human condition and persisted everywhere. When he began to assert the importance of radical reform, he also asserted that certain conditions, analogous to slavery, could both be defined in these terms and then remedied. It was as if by calling these conditions those of servitude and slavery, Bentham was attempting to arouse interest in reform by showing how degrading numerous existing political and legal institutions were to the mass of the people." And, at the same time, "he seemed to have implicitly adopted the view, or, at least, the rhetoric attached to it, that there was a remedy for all slavery."

One of the commonplace criticisms of Bentham's approach to slavery is that he only used economic arguments—to the effect that free labor was far more productive than slave labor, an argument that had been used earlier by Adam Smith and readily adopted by Bentham in his economic writings. But that was not all—far from that, in fact. For Rosen demonstrates that Bentham's arguments with regard to slavery were much more concerned with virtue and justice than his critics would have one believe. In *Emancipate Your Colonies*, Bentham kicked off by reminding the French that only some years earlier they had gone to war on the side of the Americans, who were fighting for their independence against Britain on the grounds of justice: "You abhor the subjection of one nation to another: You call it slavery. You gave sentence in the case of Britain against her colonies: Have you so soon forgot that sentence?"[14] This link between justice, slavery, and colonies was not confined to *Emancipate Your Colonies*. As Rosen notes, it appears elsewhere in Bentham's writings at this time, "as, for example, when he wrote: 'Colony-holding is a species of slave-holding equally pernicious to the tyrant and the slave.' This remark brings out vividly the way Bentham thought about slavery, in so far as black slavery was regarded as one case in a general concept of slavery which included colony-holding as another." Thus, for Bentham, the abolition of the slave trade would not, in itself, eventually lead to the abolition of slavery, unless the colonies themselves were also abolished. Even more importantly, Rosen remarks that "Bentham developed this idea of the inconsistency of the French in later attacking the French Declaration of Rights which proclaimed that all men were born free and equal and remained so, but did so in a world in which many people were born slaves. How could anyone, Bentham asked, be both free and a slave at the same time. Only by denying that what is, is not." According to Rosen, "Bentham would be misunderstood if he is interpreted simply as denying the validity of the doctrine of moral and natural rights," as Boralevi and others have accused him of doing.[15] The issue is quite different, for Rosen: "However, Bentham was insisting on the importance of truth, and the truth was that all people were born as helpless infants in a state of subjection and most people at most times lived in various degrees of legal, political, economic, and social subjection. To pretend that such subjection did not exist or to insist that it must not exist was both a denial of the truth and an encouragement to pointless violence and chaos that would never lead to a condition of freedom and equality." Thus, Rosen argues that Bentham employed the term "slavery" in these contexts in "a serious attempt to define the human condition in terms of varying degrees of subjection." According to Bentham, progress toward human happiness could not be made without an admission of this truth about the human condition. However, accepting such a truth did not entail "a denial that black slavery and the slave trade were great evils and should not continue." But it "affected how one perceived these evils and how one engaged politically against them."

Rosen also addresses Boralevi's strong objections to Bentham's argument for gradual abolition of slavery, objections which, as he notes, "go to the heart of his theory." What Boralevi reads in Bentham's argument for gradual abolition is a clash between the increase in general happiness (that would result from the liberation of the slaves) with the loss of property suffered by the masters. According to Boralevi, "the conflict is resolved by Bentham with a compromise which appears distinctly to be more in favour of property than of the slaves. According to the priority always given to security over the other 'subsidiary ends' of abundance and equality, Bentham's plea for gradual abolition is the best deal he has to offer to the slaves."[16] In other words, Boralevi claims that the reason for Bentham's failure to make a straight utilitarian calculation of happiness and conclude that slavery should be immediately abolished on account of the great pain it generated, was his emphasis on security and in particular security of property; this is what dictated that emancipation should be gradual, Boralevi thinks. Thus she saw Bentham in a line starting from Hobbes's emphasis on security and continuing with Locke's defense of property.[17] Rosen refutes this association of Bentham with a Lockean view in which property rights were paramount. First of all, Rosen notes, in his "Article on Utilitarianism" Bentham had specifically rejected such a position. Rather, "Bentham fully understood that a Lockean emphasis on security of property might well conflict with his principle of utility. For Bentham, as I have argued, on numerous occasions, security against being harmed was a form of liberty and in itself generated happiness.[18] On this view slavery was an evil and should be abolished." Why, then, did Bentham oppose immediate emancipation? Rosen's reply to this fundamental question is that "Bentham was far more concerned with protecting the slaves than the masters and would have favored immediate abolition, if he could have been confident that such abolition would enhance the well-being of the slaves." He adduces evidence from Bentham's later writings on Spanish colonies, where, in a chapter on slavery and the slave trade (in which he described the slave trade as "this foulest of all political and moral leprosies")[19] Bentham explicitly and unequivocally distinguished between the challenges involved in abolishing slave trading and slaveholding respectively. The abolition of the slave trade would require only a negative act of abolition and its enforcement, and Bentham was adamant that no compensation need be paid to the slave traders. "But to abolish slave holding, another social and economic system must be put in its place, one that provided subsistence and security for the newly freed slaves and did not leave them in a worse position in relation to their former masters. The masters also required protection. It was mainly for these reasons that Bentham emphasized gradual emancipation."

As Rosen concludes, unlike what some recent scholarship—which takes him out of context—has claimed, "Bentham might easily stand with Wilberforce and Romilly as an opponent of slavery and the slave trade." Furthermore, Rosen stresses that there is "no evidence that he emphasized security of property *over* abolition." The issue was rather more complex: "Security was a complex idea and tended to preclude reform by force and violence. Bentham believed that 'to reform the world by force, you might as well reform the moon, and the design is fit only for lunatics.' Bentham apparently adhered to this view throughout his life. It stood behind his strategy of gradual reform, which included the abolition of slavery and other forms of injustice and oppression." For these reasons Rosen calls Bentham "a *comprehensive* abolitionist, one who might have foreseen that the bloody struggle in America could produce a kind of abolition, but not one that would establish well being among the newly liberated slaves." Bentham's main object was "to show which forms of servitude were part of the human condition itself and which formed the basis of oppression and injustice. The remedy then remained with humanity, and Bentham attempted to design the institutions and laws that would enable human beings to progress towards happiness. Slavery and the slave trade, together with numerous other activities, would thus have to be abolished as part of this journey towards human happiness." Finally, and to come to the core of Rosen's argument: "In this journey the issue of rights versus utilitarianism remained important, but mainly as part of an account of truth rather than one concerning human entitlements. If rights theory obscures the basic truth about subordination and leads one to proclaim one's freedom where there is none and will not be any for the foreseeable future, its relevance to human happiness will at best be consigned to a rhetorical flourish and at worst to useless conflict and even war."

A convincing argument shared by Rosen and Pitts in their respective contributions to this volume is that Bentham refrained from publicly endorsing certain causes if he was convinced that they had no chances of success for the time being. This is how Pitts accounts for Bentham's failure to address to the British government the equivalent of *Emancipate Your Colonies* (addressed to the French in the 1790s) and "Rid Yourselves of Ultramaria" (addressed to the Spaniards in the 1820s). And Rosen, analyzing Bentham's comments on slavery in the North-African state of Tripoli in *Securities against Misrule*, argues that "he seemed to make action to abolish [slavery] depend on a prospect of success."

To come to colonies and empire, then, as with the rest of the thinkers discussed in this section of the introduction, it is the case with Bentham that his "views on conquest, expansion, and colonial rule were not entirely consistent" and "any conclusions about his writings on colonies must therefore be somewhat tentative" (Pitts, infra). This having been said, however, Jennifer Pitts shows convincingly that "it is important not to settle the ambiguities in Bentham's own writings by reading back onto him the views of his successors, as many recent interpretations have done." Thus, if one reads Bentham "without attributing to him the arguments of later utilitarians and 'Benthamites,'" what emerges is "a thinker deeply skeptical about European colonial rule and much less presumptuous than he has widely been taken to be" (Pitts, infra). Thus, Pitts's article retrieves Bentham's critical stance toward colonial rule.[20]

Why, then, is the prevalent view of Bentham as confused as it turns out to be? Here Pitts has a conclusive answer. As she argues, "The selective reading of Bentham's views on colonies began with his own disciples, and they indeed bear considerable responsibility for the distorted view of Bentham that has become so widespread." It was James Mill that proved to have been "most influential in this regard, for it was he who took the greatest interest in governing India, and who attached the utilitarian name to his closed-minded descriptions of Indian civilization and to his own projects for the country's domination and improvement." It is quite characteristic that, as Pitts again notes very aptly, even John Bowring, who reported quite explicitly the serious differences between Bentham and James Mill, still "believed that [James] Mill's views on international politics represented a fair approximation of Bentham's own." According to Pitts, "Unfortunately for Bentham, and for our understanding of the history of utilitarianism (and British liberalism more broadly), James and J. S. Mill's versions of the story of utilitarianism and empire have largely prevailed." And yet, as Pitts's article shows, Bentham's writings abound with remarks on the dangers and immorality of colonial rule. Much of the responsibility must also rest with Elie Halévy, who elided the distance between Bentham and later utilitarians and led to the impression that those later utilitarians were continuing a colonial project initiated by Bentham. One more major culprit was Eric Stokes. It is quite characteristic that, as Fred Rosen shows in another work, Stokes took a thinker as idiosyncratic as James Fitzjames Stephen to represent the mainstream classical utilitarian position and, by so doing, attributed to Bentham all sorts of positions that would have been anathema to him.[21] Unlike what Halévy (and, following him, Stokes) would have us believe, Bentham did not capitulate before the tempting prospect of India as a captive legislative laboratory for his ideas, stresses Pitts.

One of the many significant contributions of Pitts's article is the extent to which it highlights Bentham's insistence on arguments and criteria not considered "utilitarian" necessarily, such as justice, real glory, as well as his vehement deprecation of motives of national vanity. This is an extremely important theme, not only in Bentham but also in J. S. Mill, as we will try to show further on in this part of the introduction. As Pitts stresses, "It is this complex assortment of arguments that is wholly missing from James Mill's critique of colonies, which adopted the Benthamite economic position and ignored the rest of Bentham's views." It is characteristic how Bentham opened the essay he addressed to the French National Assembly at the time of the French Revolution: "*Emancipate your Colonies.* Justice, consistency, policy, economy, honour, generosity, all demand it of you: all this you shall see. Conquer, you are still but running the race of vulgar ambition: emancipate, you strike out a new path to glory. Conquer, it is by your armies: emancipate, the conquest is your own, and made over yourselves. To give freedom at the expense of others, is but conquest in disguise: to rise superior to conquerors, the sacrifice must be your own."[22] Bentham revived these arguments in the early 1820s in an attempt to persuade the new liberal government in Spain to emancipate its colonies.

Pitts has a clear reply to those who argue that Bentham may have advised the French and the Spaniards to emancipate their colonies but did not think the same when it came to Britain's own colonies. According to her, not only did he criticize the possession of colonies by Britain, but, moreover, "he criticized the entire British political system that had fostered the empire." Thus, Bentham talked of British colonialism with equal disapproval as he did of French or Spanish colonialism. We have already mentioned that Pitts suggests that the main reason why Bentham did not write entire works dedicated to convincing the British governments to emancipate their colonies was his conviction (after the sobering experiences he had had with his attempts to convince them to adopt his *Panopticon* plan) that there was no realistic chance of success. And, in any case, as Pitts notes, Bentham did appeal to the British government to give up its colonial ambitions in his "Plan for an Universal and Perpetual Peace."

Now, all this having been said, Pitts makes no secret of the existence of tensions or even contradictions in Bentham's writings. It is clear that Bentham never adopted the ardor for despotic colonial rule for the benefit of the ruled "natives" that James and J. S. Mill displayed, and yet "his views about whether Indians—as well as American colonists—could benefit from British rule remain somewhat enigmatic and indeed contradictory." This is because "[s]everal passages scattered throughout his work . . . conflict rather starkly with his many strong claims about the damage and injustices colonial rule inflicted on the colonized." However, Pitts is right in stressing that in the passages from the "Institute of Political Economy" (of 1801-1804) which she refers to, and in which Bentham claimed that both Egypt and America would have benefited from British government, it is important that Bentham "makes the same claims about non-European populations as about European settlers in America, so that his scattered pro-colonial arguments are not based, as the Mills' would be, on the peculiar backwardness of non-European societies." In Bentham, "The suggestion . . . is not that Indians were singularly unsuited to self-government by their low place in the scale of development but rather that at times Bentham was inclined to believe that British rule benefited its many subjects, European and non-European alike." In any case, there was, in Bentham's thought, no such thing as the "fully articulated argument for the benefits of colonial rule for the conquered" that one finds in the works of both James and John Stuart Mill, nor anything like the sort of theory of progress the Mills expounded in order to support their argument for the benefits of colonial rule.

Pitts demolishes one by one the (three) pieces of evidence usually adduced by those who argue that Bentham supported the British empire as a vehicle for his aspirations to legislate for the world. She pays particular attention to Bentham's "Essay on the Influence of Time and Place in Matters of Legislation," which examines the importance of culture and climate in law and society and explores what modifications would be necessary if British laws were to be made suitable for application to Bengal. As Pitts puts it: "Bentham's apparent insensibility to cultural particulars, his arrogant confidence in his own ability to legislate for the world, is still considered one of his great failings, so this essay is of particular interest, for it directly addresses the question of how feasible it might be to legislate universally." According to Pitts, "[t]he essay demonstrates Bentham's awareness of the problem, as well as the limits of his understanding." She dispels a number of misunderstandings surrounding this text and Bentham's ambitions in it. She correctly points out that Bentham showed himself very far from content with British law as it was, in the essay in question (or indeed anywhere else). Thus: "The restrained and indeed pessimistic tone of the essay, however, is far from that of the crusading legislator." Moreover, Bentham "made no strong claims for the applicability of his analysis in this essay to the production of actual legislation. 'Time and Place' is in large part a theoretical exercise and should not be taken as evidence of Bentham's own desire to become an 'Indian Solon.'" Rather, as Pitts explains, "Bentham's more limited goal in this essay, then, would be to sketch some of the considerations a legislator would have to take into account" when attempting the task of trying to adapt and translate institutions and a legal system developed in one country to the purposes of governing another country, as the British had to do in a distant colony as different in all sorts of respects form Britain as India was. Bentham by no means shared the Mills' confidence in the impartiality and integrity of East India Company servants. Nor was he anywhere near as convinced as the Mills were that Indians were "barbarous" or unfit for self-rule, and "indeed he criticized the easy move made by many Europeans of assuming, when they observed bad laws, that the people they were designed for must be inferior."

It is also important to note, as Pitts does, that the scope of the concrete reforms Bentham envisaged for India was quite limited indeed: "Reform of the judicial structure (including the inclusion of more Indians throughout the judicial ranks) and the introduction of the panopticon." In other words, Bentham "made no grand claims about civilizing India but instead proposed reforms just as he did for England, Spain, France, Latin America, Greece, and Tripoli."

Pitts is also at her most convincing when she analyzes the merits of Bentham's suggestion for jury trials in India, in his *Principles of Judicial Procedure*. The way Bentham proposed to go about it illustrates, according to Pitts, the gap between his conception of education and development and those of James and John Stuart Mill. For "although Bentham believed that the level of education among the general Indian population was too low to enable the proper function of juries selected from the whole population, he made no claims that Indian society as such was so rude or barbarous as to prevent the possibility of juries altogether." Showing clearly how far Bentham was from the kind of scale of civilization adopted by James Mill, Pitts notes: "Importantly, in discussing these different 'ages' of society, Bentham always compared particular societies with their own pasts, European with the European past and Muslim societies with the age of Mohamed, rather than positing, as both Mills did, that India or Asia generally represented the 'rude' age of humanity." In this way, "his jury proposal shows Bentham discussing India not as a characteristically 'barbarous' society but rather simply as one in which there was not a large pool of people educated enough to serve usefully on juries. The 'general complexion of the public mind,'

Bentham wrote, was too uninformed to make feasible a regular supply of competent jurors from the general population."

Finally, Pitts opines: "Although 'Time and Place' indicates that Bentham was far more aware of the problems with attempting to legislate for all people than his detractors suggest, Bentham's method—his assumption that the way to go about legislating is to produce general codes and then tailor them to circumstances—remained problematic or, at the very least, easily subject to abuse." According to Pitts, this method became particularly dangerous when applied by Bentham's less open-minded disciples or followers.[23]

James Mill

What is the conclusion then? Is James Mill the main culprit? Pitts seems to think so, although she splits the blame between him and his son, John Stuart Mill (who, one senses, should have known better, given the extent to which his views on all sorts of other matters were incomparably more open-minded than his father's). James Mill, Pitts maintains, "combined elements of various strands of thought, most notably utilitarianism and Scottish conjectural history, whose main expositors had questioned the justice of colonization; in combining these strands Mill developed a case for civilizing empire that had not existed in Bentham's thought." Although there was a lot of Bentham's thinking lurking behind several articles James Mill wrote to show that colonies offered no benefit to the conquering country but were rather foisted on metropolitan nations by "sinister private interests," the elder Mill also wrote the *History of British India*, "a work . . . remarkable even for its time in its disparagement of Indians' intellectual and moral capacities." According to Pitts, among these two divergent attitudes that characterized his writings on empire, the one had the upper hand where it mattered most: "When recommending policies toward India, the elder Mill was driven more by his ideas about Indians' mental and cultural deficiencies than by his doubts as a political economist about the colony's benefit to Great Britain."[24]

Javed Majeed also attributes such a somehow schizophrenic attitude toward empire to James Mill in his chapter. Majeed argues that "the tensions in James Mill's project stem from his ambivalent stance on empire." On the one hand, he explains, Mill "took an economic view of imperialism in India and argued that the expense of government, administration, and wars meant that Britain had not derived any economic benefits from India." Thus, in his economic writings, the elder Mill did not accord colonies any importance as markets and insisted that they did not offer any economic benefits to the metropolis. He also argued that colonies offered power and patronage to the ruling elite and were thus used by the latter for the purposes of perpetuating their position. But, as Majeed shows, "Mill's History was divided between this negative view of contemporary imperialism and the possibilities that empire opened up as the testing ground for new bodies of thought which had emerged in the metropolis and which had as their aim the critique and reform of the establishment in Britain itself."

Now, with regard to the inspiration of his thinking on colonies, Pitts argues that James Mill "saw himself at once as a utilitarian and as a heir to the philosophical historians of the Scottish Enlightenment. Mill adopted a notion of the standard of utility from Bentham and an idea of progressive social development from Scottish thinkers such as Smith and Ferguson, and thereby produced a problematic fusion: an index of progress in which utility is the sole standard against which any nation can be measured." It is well known and often adduced against him that in the *History of British India* Mill argued that:

> In looking at the pursuits of any nation, with a view to draw from them indications of the state of civilization, no mark is so important, as the nature of the *End* to which they are directed. Exactly in proportion as *Utility* is the object of every pursuit, may we regard a nation as civilized. Exactly in proportion as its ingenuity is wasted on contemptible or mischievous objects . . . the nation may safely be denominated barbarous.[25]

This, according to Pitts, was "a notion that did justice to neither tradition (not to mention the nations deemed barbarous). In addition to abandoning Bentham's moral objections to colonial rule, Mill transformed what was, in Smith and Ferguson, a broad-minded description of social development into a 'scale of excellence or defect.'"

Now, as Javed Majeed argues in his contribution to this volume, "James Mill's *The History of British India*, published in 1817, had been described as transforming utilitarianism into a militant faith." But, he adds, crucially, "Mill's critique of Indian civilization and its representations by British orientalists was part of a larger critique of the conservatism of British institutions in Britain itself." Majeed is convincing in highlighting the importance of Mill's grasp and exposure of the conservative implications of the orientalist thinking of his time. As he explains, "[William Jones's] views became part of the revitalized conservatism of British institutions both at home and abroad, which emerged in response to the Jacobin threat of the French revolution." However, Majeed maintains, "it was James Mill who in his 1817 History first clearly defined Jones' views as conservative. In doing so, he was to grapple with the problems which were implicit in Jones' own work." These problems were fundamental:

> In general terms, these problems might be defined as the questions of whether it is possible to arrive at an idiom in which different societies and their cultures might be compared and contrasted; whether it is possible to find a language which secures a consistency (and resolves the tensions) between one's political

views on Britain and on India; and the question of the precise role of the practices of the past in the defining and advocating practices for the present day. At the heart of both Jones' work and Mill's attempt to articulate Utilitarianism is this grappling with the general problems of what might be called comparativism, which by its very nature is unstable and provisional.[26]

Majeed shows most interestingly how and why James Mill was particularly negative towards what Majeed calls the politics of the imagination—which Mill saw his opponents indulging in. A major reason for Mill's distrust of the politics of the imagination, according to Majeed, "stemmed from the way in which such notions of the imagination could play a role in redefining cultural and national identities. On the whole, Mill's History paid little attention to cultural, religious, and linguistic differences. It embodied a version of what Ernest Gellner called 'world-leveling, unificatory epistemologies.'" While he says that, "to a certain extent, this aspect of the History was in keeping with the greatest happiness principle, which was universalistic in character," Majed hastens to differentiate Bentham from James Mill, thus finding himself in agreement with what we have seen Jennifer Pitts argues in her chapter: "But Mill lacked Bentham's attention to the importance of circumstances influencing sensibility as data which the legislator should take into account."[27]

Majeed is also lucid in showing the importance of aesthetic categories and the part they played in Mill's formulation of Utilitarianism, "much of which was defined against what Mill saw as the collusion between aesthetic philosophies and politics in the revitalized conservatism of British institutions at home and abroad."

Is James Mill's record an unmitigated series of prejudiced and unpalatable statements and claims, then? Not necessarily, according to Majeed. As he argues, "despite the harsh strictures in the History about the 'Muslim' and 'Hindu' cultures of India, it is also important to draw attention to fragments of another discourse in Mill's project which may have an important resonance in contemporary South Asia." Majeed does find redeeming features in Mill's enterprise. There is no gainsaying that "there is much that is repugnant in Mill's History." Nonetheless, "the questions Mill raises about the relationship of the past to current political practices, and in particular, the possibility of opening up a space for self-definition which is rooted in a provocative disrespect of the ways in which the past has been constructed, might be revisited again." All the more so in the case of South Asia, says Majeed, "given the centrality of communalism" in that region, and "the growth of 'Muslim' and 'Hindu' militancies which rely on the invocation of ready made pasts and ready made origins." Furthermore, Majeed reminds us that James Mill was "equally harsh about British society at the time; it is clear that his History was a matrix in which a critique of British society itself was shaped. It was because Mill saw empire as buttressing powerful groups at home that his History was a critique of the legal, political, and religious institutions in Britain, and of their influence on British rule in India." This is why his *History* is replete with "extensive Benthamite criticisms of the English legal system, it was against the background of India that the ideology of the British establishment was clearly marked out. It also gave Mill the distance necessary to fashion the tools and principles to critique this ideology." In other words, "there was a self-critical and self-reflexive aspect to Mill's History which reflected an attempt to formulate an idiom in which societies might be not just compared and contrasted but also criticized. Both Bentham and Mill made it clear that any critique of another society necessarily involved a critique of one's own society."[28]

John Stuart Mill

In a far-reaching and most interesting chapter contributed to this volume Martha Nussbaum offers us an interpretation of John Stuart Mill's understanding of happiness that highlights the continuing relevance of his philosophy for contemporary anti-hierarchical thinking. Mill's profound commitment to equality is the overarching consideration that affected decisively his attitude towards all sorts of issues, and Nussbaum is right in pointing out that this has particular relevance not only for feminist thinking but also for thinking about ethnicity and race.

This does not mean that there is agreement on how Mill delivered, even if we assumed agreement that his intentions were egalitarian and anti-hierarchical. In fact, one of the features of this volume is that, within it, at least two different readings of J. S. Mill's attitude toward race and racism emerge, mainly in the respective chapters contributed by David Theo Goldberg and Georgios Varouxakis. It is probably not particularly appropriate to comment on that disagreement in an introduction coauthored by one of the participants in the debate. In any case, there is no need for much to be said here, as we are fortunate to have a thorough and sharp commentary on the debate in question in the contribution to this volume by H. S. Jones.[29] Thus, suffice it to say here that the issue is treated in this volume from more than one angle, and we hope that the result is to the benefit of the reader's understanding of different approaches to the subject.

As on so many other subjects, a discussion of the younger Mill's views on colonies and empire cannot fail to include a comparison between him and Bentham. That comparison is pursued fruitfully in this volume in the chapter contributed by Jennifer Pitts. Pitts finds that Mill followed his father more than Bentham with regard to colonies, and that that renders his thought less attractive than Bentham's. As she puts it: "John Stuart Mill, in so many arenas a great critic of his father, adopted many of James Mill's central claims about

India and British government there: most importantly, that there was a sharp dichotomy between civilized and uncivilized nations, that Indians were barbarians incapable of self-government, and that British 'despotism' was the most appropriate form of government for the country for the foreseeable future." Pitts also maintains that J. S. Mill "criticized Bentham's lack of interest in distinctions between civilized and barbarous peoples as a lack of historical understanding and . . . believed that one of his most important departures from Bentham's thought was his theory of character."

As Mill's views on "character" and "national character" in particular are quite a complex issue, a few comments might facilitate the discussion. It has to be clarified that Mill talked of "national character" in two different—though interconnected—senses. In the first place, he spoke of the importance of national character as an end in legislation and social reform. Institutions could not be considered advisable if they did not provide for the improvement of the collective character of the people who were to live under them. In the second place, he spoke of differences of national character between different portions of mankind as an existing fact and of the need for legislators or social reformers to take them into account in the calculation of the means they were to employ in order to achieve their goals (attaining to a better collective or "national" character being one of the main goals). These two senses in which Mill employed the term are not always sufficiently differentiated. An instance where the two senses in which Mill used the term need to be discerned from each other occurs in F. E. L. Priestley's comments on Mill's article "Whewell on Moral Philosophy." Priestley presents Mill's defense of Bentham against Whewell's reproach that Bentham had not sufficiently recognized "what Dr. Whewell calls the historical element of legislation" as somewhat contradictory in view of Mill's own censure that Bentham had ignored national character. The instances in which Mill complained of Bentham's ignoring national character Priestley alludes to were those in his "Remarks on Bentham's Philosophy" (1833) and in "Bentham" (1838). But the two criticisms (Mill's in the 1830s and Whewell's later) were not identical. Mill's main quarrel with Bentham had been that by taking "next to no account of national character and the causes which form and maintain it, he was precluded from considering . . . the laws of a country as an instrument of national culture"[30] or, as he put it elsewhere, "as the great instruments of forming the national character; of carrying the members of the community towards perfection, or preserving them from degeneracy."[31] He reproached Bentham that the latter had not sufficiently attended to the educative function of institutions and laws, their potential use as instruments of national education and culture, as vehicles for the promotion of the national character from the point where it was to the next possible point. Bentham, Mill wrote, had taken great pains to "teach the means of organizing and regulating the merely business part of the social arrangements" but had not proposed any means of ameliorating the character of the people who would live under the institutions in question.[32] This is the meaning of his complaint about national character in his essays on Bentham. Now, it was only as a means to this goal that the existing differences of national character or stage of civilization counted. In order for the legislator to be able to prescribe institutions appropriate for the improvement of the national character of a people, they had to be fully conversant with the stage of civilization at which the people in question found themselves and their character (two separate things, in Mill's mind, as has been argued elsewhere).[33] Given that these differed among different nations, the means through which the improvement would be pursued could not be the same for all cases. But Mill conceded that Bentham did recognize the need for existing differences to be taken into account. The stance John Mill adopted in 1852 in defending Bentham against Whewell's strictures was not new, in any case. He had come to the defense of Bentham against accusations that he ignored existing differences already in 1838 (in the essay "Bentham") by pointing to Bentham's essay "On the Influence of Time and Place in Matters of Legislation" (1782).[34] The main problem with Bentham's approach was not that he did not recognize the need to modify his means in order to achieve his goals but that his goals were insufficiently ambitious in Mill's opinion. As Mill saw it, Bentham recognized the need for adjustments according to differences of time and place in order to promote "the merely business part of the social arrangements."

In other words, in his essays on Bentham, Mill spoke of national character as the aim to be promoted, its improvement being the goal legislation should have in view. This use of the concept of national character is quite different from what Whewell and conservative critics of reformers like Bentham meant by the term. National character was for such people the constant in legislation. Legislation had to be determined by the national character, it should not contradict it. On the other hand, the sense in which Mill spoke of national character in the essay on Bentham was that national character was, or rather should be, the malleable element in legislation. He did, of course, as has already been noted, speak of differences of existing national characters as a factor that had to be taken into account, but only in the choice of the means through which the major consideration, the improvement of the national character, would be achieved.

Now, to come to Mill's views on colonies and empire more directly, in his contribution to this volume J. Joseph Miller sets about shedding light on Mill's attitude toward the possession of colonies and his criteria for good colonial government through an analysis of Mill's stance during the notorious Governor Eyre controversy of 1865-68. Miller engages fruitfully with an argument advanced by Jennifer Pitts in a paper entitled "Empire and Social Criticism: Burke, Mill, and the abuse of colonial power" (2002).[35] In that article Pitts focuses her analysis on a comparison between the respective attitudes displayed by Edmund Burke in the impeachment trial of Warren Hastings for corruption and despotism (1788-1794), and by J. S. Mill during his involvement in the effort to prosecute Governor Eyre of Jamaica in the late 1860s. According to Pitts, unlike Burke, Mill "by avoiding any reference to the racial and colonial context of the abuses, chose throughout the Eyre trial largely to avoid confronting the question of whether colonial rule was prone to abuse. Indeed, he pursued Eyre with such vehemence precisely to exonerate the system by pinning blame on what he insisted were the *criminal* actions of a few individuals."[36] As he puts it himself, Miller in his paper included in this volume suggests "a more charitable reading of Mill's colonialism." To Miller's mind, "Mill pursues Eyre not simply because Eyre threatens a colonial system whose weaknesses Mill refuses to acknowledge. Rather, Eyre represents a particular vision of colonialism (arbitrary despotism wielded only to the advantage of the colonizer) that is fundamentally at odds with Mill's considered conception of colonialism." According to Miller, what incensed Mill is that Eyre carried with him the authority of the British crown, and with that authority he set a precedent that was anathema to Mill's conception of the proper treatment of inhabitants of colonies and British citizens more generally. According to Miller, "Mill was . . . moved to his relentless prosecution of Eyre not so much out of a sense of justice to those whom Eyre wrongly killed and flogged, but rather as a matter of foreign policy." To corroborate his claim Miller quotes from a letter written by Mill at the time of the Eyre controversy, and the quotation needs to be cited here as well:

> At all events, while the world is as full of crime as it is, I do not suppose that however strong my feelings about it, I sh[ould] have considered myself as peculiarly called upon to interfere against him [Eyre]. *But I do consider myself as an Englishman called upon to protest* against what I believe to be an infringement of the laws of England; against acts of violence committed by Englishmen in authority, *calculated to lower the character of England in the eyes of all foreign lovers of liberty*; against a precedent that could justly inflame against us the people of our dependencies; and against an example calculated to brutalize our own fellow countrymen.[37]

After quoting this passage, Miller comments: "Here Mill argues that prosecuting Eyre is not simply a matter of bringing the Governor to justice; rather, for Mill the Eyre case serves as a *casus belli* for reforming British foreign policy." Although we would not use the term "foreign policy," as this is an issue that involves at the same time constitutional (as Miller himself mentions elsewhere in the article), colonial, foreign, as well as domestic policy concerns,[38] the thrust of Miller's argument appears convincing, in that Mill was infuriated by how Eyre's actions would present Britain/England in the eyes of "foreign lovers of liberty" (and, no less importantly, would create "a precedent that could *justly*[39] inflame against us the people of our dependencies"). How foreigners perceived

England/Britain was always of paramount importance to Mill, and he endeavored strenuously and earnestly all his life to elevate this question to the status of a major criterion of the actions and choices of British governments and citizens. But it was not just a matter of foreign policy. As Georgios Varouxakis has argued elsewhere, making his fellow countrymen solicitous of the perception of their country abroad and eager to see it admired and loved for the right reasons was one of the major elements in his conception of what constituted the right kind of patriotism. Varouxakis has called this "cosmopolitan patriotism." One of the senses in which this patriotism is "cosmopolitan" (not the only sense) is that it is a patriotism that feeds on making sure that one acts in a way that conduces to one's country's doing what is best for mankind as well as its being seen to be doing so by relatively impartial observers in a kind of international tribunal of public opinion.[40] The statement that he "consider[ed] [himself] as an Englishman called upon to protest" against "acts of violence committed by Englishmen in authority, calculated to lower the character of England in the eyes of all foreign lovers of liberty; against a precedent that could justly inflame against us the people of our dependencies" is of a piece with the whole theory Mill had developed regarding how vigilant good citizens and patriots should be against wrongdoing on the part of their own government or authorities acting in their name (as Eyre had done in this case). It is worth quoting here what he had to say on the matter in his *Inaugural Address Delivered to the University of St. Andrews* in 1867, the year before he wrote the lines quoted above in a letter. In the *Inaugural Address*, Mill had included in the ideal university curriculum he was proposing the study of international law, which he "decidedly" thought "should be taught in all universities, and should form part of all liberal education." His reasons for thinking so are instructive:

> The need of it is far from being limited to diplomatists and lawyers; it extends to every citizen. . . . Since every country stands in numerous and various relations with the other countries of the world, *and many, our own among the number, exercise actual authority over some of these,*[41] a knowledge of the established rules of international morality is essential to the duty of every nation, and therefore of every person in it who helps to make up the nation, and whose voice and feeling form a part of what is called public opinion. Let not any one pacify his conscience by the delusion that he can do no harm if he takes no part, and forms no opinion. Bad men need nothing more to compass their ends, than that good men should look on and do nothing. *He is not a good man who, without a protest, allows wrong to be committed in his name, and with the means which he helps to supply, because he will not trouble himself to use his mind on the subject.*[42] It depends on the habit of attending to and looking into public transactions, and on the degree of information and solid judgment respecting them that exists in the community, whether the conduct of the nation as a nation, *both within itself and towards others,*[43] shall be selfish, corrupt, and tyrannical, or rational and enlightened, just and noble.[44]

This is impressive indeed: the thinker who is associated (wrongly)[45] with so-called elitism, asserts that as complex an area of policy as foreign and international policy should be under the close scrutiny of the citizens and that it is a gross dereliction of duty if citizens fail to scrutinize their country's foreign policy and international comportment using as an excuse that international law is too complicated to understand. This is a really demanding conception of citizenship and a lofty and high-minded perception of what constitutes a good citizen and a good patriot. Note also that this is not the youthful and—supposedly—starry-eyed Mill but the mature Mill. Mill was involved in a life-long struggle to improve his compatriots by using sentiments of pride or honor (pride or honor *bien entendu*, but by no means the vainglory associated with flag-waving patriotism) and shame in equal measure.[46] It is in this context that his reaction to Eyre's actions makes sense, and Miller's paper is most useful in leading toward this direction.

HENRY SIDGWICK AND HERBERT SPENCER

"Our Army of Martyrs"
For what have all the martyrs died
 On India's crimson plains,
Now streaming with the generous tide,
 Outpoured from heroes' veins,
Where gallant NICHOLSON and NEILL
 Have found a soldier's grave,
And though unscathed by shot or steel,
Fell HAVELOCK good and brave?

Were they whom hosts of orphans weep,
 Whom crowds of widows mourn,
In peace that we may eat and sleep
 From friends and kinsfolk torn?
Their toils, their pains, did they endure,
 And were their lives but sold,
That we might life enjoy secure,
 Whilst they in death are cold.

That we might safely count our gains,
 Increasing day by day,
Only for that, are their remains
 Now mouldering into clay?
That wealth, with unabated flood,
 To England's shores might flow,
Shed they alone their noble blood,
 And are they lying low?

Laid they their lives down but for this,
  That Commerce might pursue
Her thriving course, and rich men miss
  No doit of revenue?
Of pompous wealth, of mere purse-pride
  The champions, did they fall?
If so, they martyrs only died
  To Mammon after all.

Not so; those martyrs' blood, we trust,
  To better purpose sown,
Will not have sunk in Indian dust,
  To bear such fruit alone:
The blood of martyrs is a seed
  Whence springs another crop,
Our heroes were designed to bleed
  For something more than Shop.
Punch (1858)[47]

When it appeared in that oracle of middle-class opinion, *Punch*, "Our Army of Martyrs" marked the difficult birth throes of the true age of imperialism. It was deeply suggestive, with the appropriate alluring vagueness, of the newer modes of ethical uplift in the public sphere. Indeed, the late Victorian world would come to be revealed as a fundamentally different creature even from the world of John Stuart Mill, and the forms of utilitarianism so prominent within it were even more conflicted and paradoxical than those of the great founding fathers, Bentham and the two Mills.

What the poem reflected, of course, was the aftermath of the sepoy uprising—the "Indian Mutiny," as the British called it. In May of 1857, the native Indian troops in Meerut rebelled; they killed their (British) officers and fanned a wider revolt that turned into a struggle for independence that quickly spread across Hindustan, wiping out the British strongholds and leading to the capture of Delhi. The violence of the conflict spiraled out of control, with the British leading the way. As Brooks and Faulkner observe, in their remarkable work *The White Man's Burden: An Anthology of British Poetry of the Empire*: "The British response was savage; mass executions in the name of order prompted Indian reprisals, most notoriously at Cawnpore; military action to contain the rising became a racist vendetta, and the rising was suppressed in what was at times a frenzy of blood-letting." The resulting "profound shock to public opinion" resulted not only in the end of the East India Company, which was blamed for the tragedy, and the crowning of Victoria as Empress of India, but also in an engagement of "the public imagination with the issue of empire as never before." Prior to this event, *Punch*, founded in 1841, had scarcely addressed the matter of empire; afterward, "its pages are full of items on imperial issues."[48] As Brooks and Faulkner rightly argue, here "was the context in which British imperialism came to full consciousness: direct rule over millions of subject people; indirect rule over millions more; the settlement of vast, supposedly empty tracts of the earth's surface. What did such unparalleled dominion mean? What was it for?"[49]

Later utilitarians such as Henry Sidgwick, whose entire life fell within the reign of Victoria, were as emphatic as T. H. Green and the idealists that whatever the British were about, it was "something more than Shop." Sidgwick, as Bart Schultz argues in his contribution to this volume, brought a host of Millian and Benthamite concerns into contact with the post-Millian project of grappling with large-scale social organizations both at home and abroad, within the state and without, and trying to make philosophical sense of them. Shaped by a classicist education that had him even more steeped in Plato and Aristotle than the younger Mill, caught up in university reform and academic liberalism such that his activism was of a piece with the "rise of professional society," Sidgwick was more or less destined to advance the transformation of the utilitarian legacy that Mill had begun, taking it from outside the establishment to inside.

The story has been told from many different angles. Sidgwick's younger contemporary, D. G. Ritchie, wittily observed that if Sidgwick was a Benthamite, then Benthamism had "grown tame and sleek" and lost its antagonism to the status quo.[50] J. B. Schneewind, writing almost a century later, argued at length that the younger Mill had set the stage for Sidgwick by demonstrating utilitarianism's potential respectability to its critics, including such intuitionists as William Whewell:

> Intuitionists could carry on serious philosophical discussion only with opponents who were prepared to take common-sense morality seriously. The earlier utilitarians plainly did not meet this condition, and the interest showed by Austin and James Mill in rules was not an interest in the rules accepted already by common sense. John Stuart Mill convinced the intuitionists that he did take common sense seriously, largely because of his incorporation of it into his theory but also because of his much-mocked distinction between higher and lower pleasures. His views on this topic caused his critics to doubt his logical abilities, but persuaded them of what Thayer called his 'noble qualities of mind.' The usual explanation the critics gave of his use of the distinction was that Mill shared with every decent man certain values incompatible with the older hedonism, and was trying to adapt his theory to take them into account. Thus reassured of Mill's moral soundness, they could allow him to be earnest in granting weight to common sense moral convictions and in seeking a theory which would accommodate them.[51]

At a philosophical level, Sidgwick struggled with Mill's (supposedly) inconsistent hedonistic account of good, but such was his knowledge of and engagement with commonsense morality that even his religious heterodoxy was not enough to allow serious critics to charge him with want of respectability. Particularly in his mature position, with one brother-in-law ensconced as Archbishop of Canterbury and another one on his way to becoming a Tory prime minister, Sidgwick, one could say, represented the utilitarian wing of respectable opinion, at least in his public presentations. And, moreover, this representative function covered the emerging imperial concerns. Sidgwick's circle included many of the leading lights of the effort to define the "something more than Shop" that the British imperial exploits supposedly involved. His Cambridge colleague Sir John Seeley produced one of the textbooks for the new imperialists, with his work *The Expansion of England* (one of the chief objects of Edward Said's analysis of the culture of imperialism). His friend and rival T. H. Green carried on the work of Jowett's Balliol in making Oxford a training ground for imperial statesmen, from Curzon to Milner. His friend and collaborator James Bryce was instrumental in forming the "Imperialist League" and theorizing the meaning of "race" for the new world of the late Victorians. And the list goes on and on—Charles Henry Pearson, Sir Henry Sumner Maine, the Trevelyan family, the Balfour clan. It was Sidgwick's lifelong friend George Trevelyan who sought to immortalize the British at Cawnpore:

> On the summit of the tottering dome, at a height of some twelve feet from the soil, presides a Hindoo idol with an elephant's head. There he sits, a stupid little god, with arms reposing on his knees, gazing across the valley at the minarets of the ancient capital, as though he had never seen any stranger sight than the tourist in his white dress and dust-coloured helmet, or heard any sounds more wild and maddening than the chirping of the grasshoppers, and the lowing of the belated cattle as they stray homeward to their stalls. Not urn, nor monolith, nor broken column is so fit a monument for brave men as the crumbling breastwork and the battered wall. And in like manner the dire agony of Cawnpore needs not to be figured in marble, or cut into granite, or cast of bronze. There is no fear lest we should forget the story of our people. The whole place is their tomb, and the name thereof is their epitaph. When the traveler from Allahabad, rousing himself to learn at what stage of his journey he may have arrived, is aware of a voice proclaiming through the darkness the city of melancholy fame—then those accents, heard for the first time on the very spot itself which they designate, recall, more vividly than written or engraven eloquence, the memory of fruitless valour and unutterable woe."[52]

Yet Sir George, son of Sir Charles, had "no doubt that the Indian Civil Service was a fine career, which held out splendid prospects to honourable ambition . . . better far than this, there was no career which so surely inspired men with the desire to do something useful in their generation; to leave their mark upon the world for good, and not for evil."[53] Sir George and his Cambridge colleague, Professor Sidgwick, were entirely at one in this conviction.

If Sidgwick was the more literary and pessimistic of the two, it was a pessimism in a Tennysonian mode, in which the decline of religion imparted that much more urgency to constructing a mythology of empire. Sidgwick and his friends were no jingoists—jingoism was, indeed, a rather demythologizing thing, crasser even than "Shop." For Sidgwick, Lord Lytton, the poet, novelist and political figure who became one of India's more disastrous British rulers, was the type of expert to be consulted when writing a book on *The Elements of Politics*.[54] This was not quite yet Kipling's conversion of the British "paternalist mission into a racial crusade,"[55] but it was the beginning, an unnerving worry about the issue of race that weaves its way in and out of everything from the analysis of who will perform manual labor in the tropical zones to the perils of decadence in London. The Millian "age of transition" was now discussed—often in a nervously evasive manner—in terms of race and rule, and this so pervasively that Sidgwick could scarcely sit down to dinner with friends without the issue somehow being present, though it was not one that he wanted to see inflaming party debates.

And yet Sidgwick is justifiably regarded as the most sophisticated and the most skeptical of the great nineteenth-century utilitarians—as the philosopher who in intellectual terms most coolly distanced himself from the missionaries' tendency to "rush on to preach what they do not know."[56] Having left the foundations of ethics in tatters with his "dualism of the practical reason"—the irreducible conflict between rational egoism and utilitarianism—Sidgwick was hardly in a position to service the empire after the manner of Seeley and Green. Arguably, at least, his deeper thinking was at odds with his imperialist tendencies, and he presented an undogmatic utilitarianism as potentially affording greater resistance to imperialism than the neo-Kantianism and neo-Hegelianism of Green and the Idealists.

The career of Herbert Spencer, as David Weinstein so compellingly shows, provides in many respects a baffling counterpoint to the transitions embodied in Sidgwick. Arguably, at some elevated philosophical level, there was little separating them. But even though Spencer would outlive him by three years, Sidgwick regarded the much older man as in many respects the voice of the old guard, and he sought, in his very extensive writings on Spencer, to distance himself from the man whose name would become intimately linked to "Social Darwinism." Weinstein makes a powerful case for rereading Spencer as something other than a crude Social Darwinist, and he rightly notes how Sidgwick may have found Spencer too dogmatic on such matters as indefeasible moral rights even while sharing a broadly utilitarian perspective. But the complexities and paradoxes of the utilitarian legacy are driven home with his statement that "nowhere does Spencer's dogmatism divulge itself more strikingly than in his uncompromising opposition to imperialism. . . . Spencer detested imperialism whereas Sidgwick and J. S. Mill embraced it however reluctantly and however much in keeping, despite themselves, with the disciplining spirit of their times." Weinstein provocatively suggests that the liberal utilitarian tradition has itself been reduced and stereotyped, rendered "Other," but he also points to the troubling question of whether, in the late Victorian context of Sidgwick and Spencer, one had to be "dogmatic" simply to resist the imperialist cultural current. Spencer, along with such figures as the old Benthamite A. V. Dicey, another friend of Sidgwick's, had by the turn of the century become dinosaurs to the dinosaurs.

Those who would usher utilitarianism well into the twentieth century—including Bertrand Russell and G. E. Moore—were at this point concerned with questions of race and eugenics simply as a matter of course, no matter where they fell out on the political spectrum. Russell, at least, would live long enough to repent, and return to the vision of his godfather but with a greater enthusiasm for democracy.

One is tempted, at this point, to say "but that is another story," one carrying us beyond "classical utilitarianism." But that would be an odd concluding note for an introduction to a volume pointing up just how messy the notion of "classical" utilitarianism really is, a dysfunctional family resemblance term at best. The apparent villains, the supposed orientalists, Social Darwinists, panopticists, etc., turn out not to be the real ones, or only complexly so. After all, if Said can find Kipling himself filled with ironies, ambivalences, and ambiguities, why should it come as a surprise that thinkers as subtle as Mill and Sidgwick, not to mention Bentham and Spencer, should also turn out to be stranger than one ever suspected? Hardly a contributor to this volume would dissent from Said's pleas for "greater crossing of boundaries, for greater interventionism in cross-disciplinary activity, a concentrated awareness of the situation—political, methodological, social, historical—in which intellectual and cultural work is carried out."[57] Perhaps we would only join with many other commentators on Said's work in urging that he initiated a critical project that has been carried to places he never dreamed of. One cannot know in advance what is on the Other side, or even one's own.

NOTES

1. Bertrand Russell, "The Harm That Good Men Do," in *Skeptical Essays*, ed. Bertrand Russell (New York: Barnes and Noble, 1961), 76–77.

2. Russell, "Good Men," 77.

3. See Bart Schultz, "Bertrand Russell in Ethics and Politics," *Ethics* 102, no. 3 (April 1992) for an overview of Russell's ethical and political development.

4. Michel Foucault, "Truth and Juridical Forms," in *Power: Essential Works of Foucault, 1954–1984*, ed. Paul Rabinow (New York: The New Press, 2000), 70.

5. Foucault, "Truth," 57–58.

6. James Miller, *The Passions of Michel Foucault* (New York: Simon and Schuster, 1993), provides an extremely valuable account of Foucault's politics.

7. Alexander Lyon Macfie, ed., *Orientalism: A Reader* (New York: New York University Press, 2002), 11.

8. Edward Said, *Orientalism* (New York: Vintage Books, 1979), 14.

9. See Bernard Williams, "The Point of View of the Universe: Sidgwick and the Ambitions of Ethics," in *Making Sense of Humanity*, ed. Bernard Williams (New York: Cambridge University Press, 1995), 153–71. Williams's work, and Margaret Urban Walker's *Moral Understandings* (New York: Routledge, 1998), afford good examples of philosophical critiques of utilitarianism that fail to engage with the historical realities involved, despite allusions in that direction. Many of the contributions to the excellent collection, *Philosophers on Race: Critical Essays*, ed. Julie K. Ward and Tommy L. Lott (Oxford: Blackwell Publishers, 2002) provide fine counterexamples, demonstrating how philosophical sophistication need not be conjoined to historical ignorance.

10. Jeremy Bentham, *Emancipate Your Colonies! Addressed to the National Convention of France, 1793, Shewing the Uselessness and Mischievousness of Distant Dependencies to an European State*, in Jeremy Bentham, *Rights, Representation, and Reform: Nonsense upon Stilts and Other Writings on the French Revolution*, ed. Philip Schofield, Catherine Pease-Watkin and Cyprian Blamires [part of: *The Collected Works of Jeremy Bentham*] (Oxford: Clarendon Press, 2002), 310.

11. Lea Campos Boralevi, *Bentham and the Oppressed* (Berlin and New York: Walter de Gruyter, 1984).

12. For an analysis of Bentham's involvement with France at the time of the French Revolution see: J. H. Burns, "Bentham and the French Revolution," *The Transactions of the Royal Historical Society*, 5th series, xvi (1966), 95–114.

13. Dumont's significance for Bentham's influence and reputation can hardly be overestimated. It was he who made the British recluse famous worldwide thanks to his many translations or recensions of works by Bentham which, through the medium of the then major international language, French, spread Bentham's ideas from Latin America through France to Greece and even further.

14. Bentham, *Rights, Representation, and Reform*, 291.

15. Boralevi accused Bentham "of failing to be an abolitionist, because he rejected this doctrine," as Rosen has put it.

16. Boralevi, *Bentham and the Oppressed*, 150–51.

17. Boralevi, *Bentham and the Oppressed*, 157–58.

18. See Fred Rosen, *Bentham, Byron and Greece: Constitutionalism, Nationalism, and Early Liberal Political Thought* (Oxford: Clarendon Press, 1992), 25–76; and Fred Rosen, *Classical Utilitarianism from Hume to Mill* (London: Routledge, 2003).

19. J. Bentham, *Colonies, Commerce, and Constitutional Law: Rid Yourselves of Ultramaria and Other Writings on Spain and Spanish America*, ed. P. Schofield (*CW*) (Oxford: Clarendon Press, 1995), 128.

20. For an excellent recent study that charts the critical attitude toward empire of a number of other major Enlightenment figures see: Sankar Muthu, *Enlightenment against Empire* (Princeton and Oxford: Princeton University Press, 2003).

21. See Fred Rosen, "Eric Stokes, British Utilitarianism, and India," in *J. S. Mill's Encounter with India*, ed. Martin I. Moir, Douglas M. Peers, and Lynn Zastoupil (Toronto: University of Toronto Press, 1999), 18–33.

22. Bentham, "Emancipate Your Colonies," *Rights, Representation, and Reform*, 291.

23. John W. Burrow has argued that the importance of Bentham's essay on the influence of time and place should not be overestimated and that though it may show that Bentham was aware of the possible significance of differences of circumstances he did not translate such awareness into any modification of his basic theories: John W. Burrow, *Evolution and Society: A Study in Victorian Social Theory* (Cambridge: Cambridge University Press, 1968), 24–42.

24. Thus, for Pitts, James Mill "occupies a peculiar place in the history of utilitarian arguments about empire, a position whose oddities and potential contradictions have not fully been explored in the literature on the subject." More precisely, "the peculiarity of Mill's position is most evident in the combination that he managed to sustain of strident criticism of colonies from the colonizer's perspective, primarily on classic political economy grounds, and his disdain for non-European societies and conviction that India, in particular, should be governed by a British despotism with no participation by Indians themselves." And while Mill's economic critique of colonies was reminiscent of that of Bentham, it should be remembered that James Mill did not express any of the moral concerns present in Bentham's work.

25. James Mill, *The History of British India*, abridged and with an introduction by William Thomas (Chicago: Chicago University Press, 1975), 228–29.

26. Javed Majeed, "James Mill's *The History of British India*: The question of Utilitarianism and Empire," infra in this volume.

27. Majeed, infra. In order to substantiate his claim about Bentham's sensitivity Majeed gives reference to: Jeremy Bentham, *An Introduction to the Principles of Morals and Legislation* [in *The Collected Works of Jeremy Bentham*], ed. J. H. Burns and H. L. A. Hart (London: The Athlone Press, 1970), 51–72; and, Bentham, "Essay on the Influence of Time and Place in Matters of Legislation," in *The Works of Jeremy Bentham*, ed. by John Bowring (Edinburgh: William Tait, 1843), 1: 173.

28. Majeed, infra.

29. See H. S. Jones, infra.

30. Emphasis added: J. S. Mill, *Collected Works*, X, 105 ("Bentham" [1838]).

31. J. S. Mill, "Remarks on Bentham's Philosophy" (1833), *Collected Works*, X, 9. This early essay was published (anonymously) as an appendix to Edward Lytton Bulwer's book *England and the English* (now to be found in *Collected Works*, X, 3–18). This essay constituted the apogee of J. S. Mill's apostasy from Bentham and James Mill. On the younger Mill's "seesaw" with regard to his attitudes toward Bentham see: John M. Robson, "John Stuart Mill and Jeremy Bentham, with some Observations on James Mill," in *Essays in English Literature from the Renaissance to the Victorian Age presented to A. S. P. Woodhouse*, ed. Millar MacLure and F. W. Watt (Toronto: University of Toronto Press, 1964), 245–68, at 259–60.

32. J. S. Mill, "Bentham,," *CW*, X, 75–115, at 99.

33. See more on this issue in: Georgios Varouxakis, "National Character in John Stuart Mill's Thought," *History of European Ideas* 24, no. 6 (1998): 375–91.

34. Mill, "Bentham," *CW*, X, 104–5. Hereafter Bentham's essay will be referred to as: "Time and Place." J. S. Mill had read the essay in question (and defended it in a debating speech in 1829). See: John M. Robson, "Which Bentham Was Mill's Bentham?" *The Bentham Newsletter* 7 (May 1983): 15–26, at 17. "Time and Place" has been published in: *The Works of Jeremy Bentham*, ed. John Bowring, 11 vols., Edinburgh, 1838–43), I, 169–94.

35. Jennifer Pitts, "Empire and Social Criticism: Burke, Mill, and the Abuse of Colonial Power," paper presented to the 2002 Annual Meeting of the American Political Science Association, August 29–September 1, 2002. We are most grateful to Jennifer Pitts for having sent us the paper in question and for having given us permission to refer to it and quote from it here.

36. Pitts, "Empire and Social Criticism."

37. Emphasis added: J. S. Mill, *Collected Works*, XVI, 1411 (letter to William Sims Pratten, 9 June 1868)—quoted in Miller, "Chairing the Jamaica Committee," infra.

38. This combination of different concerns is obvious, to our mind, in the very passage quoted by Miller: Mill was determined to protest "against an infringement of the laws of England" (constitutional concerns); "against acts of violence committed by Englishmen in authority, calculated to lower the character of England in the eyes of all foreign lovers of liberty" (foreign policy concerns, and not just that, as will be argued further on); "against a precedent that could justly inflame against us the people of our dependencies" (colonial/imperial concerns); "and against an example calculated to brutalize our own fellow countrymen" (concerns related to the—ever so important in Mill's mind—educating and character-forming consequences of every action or failure of public men in positions of authority).

39. Emphasis added.

40. See more in: Georgios Varouxakis, *Mill on Nationality* (London and New York: Routledge, 2002), 111–27. Also: Georgios Varouxakis, *Victorian Political Thought on France and the French* (Basingstoke, England, and New York: Palgrave, 2002), 21–30.

41. Emphasis added.

42. Emphasis added.

43. Emphasis added.

44. *Collected Works*, XXI, 246–47.

45. For a recent succinct refutation of the imputation of elitism to Mill's thought see: Dale E. Miller, "John Stuart Mill's civic liberalism," *History of Political Thought* 21, no. 1 (2000): 88–107.

46. It may be appropriate to try to see in this context an attitude of Mill's that has recently been criticized. The case in question is a recently raised criticism against Mill's stance with regard to the Irish Question, to the effect that the stance in question was rather Anglo-centric. According to Bruce Kinzer, "The moral thrust of Mill's pamphlet, however, has more to do with England than with Ireland. In response to Fenianism Mill's mind seized upon Irish land as the critical test of English moral will. Failure to act would invite a degrading and ultimately fruitless struggle to hold a people bent upon independence. Separation would signify an inadequacy on England's part far more serious than stark political ineptitude. Dishonor, obloquy, shame—such would be the price exacted by failure. Mill's fecund and radical moral consciousness spawned England and Ireland. Unmistakable signs of this sensibility had been displayed long before 1868: 'We want something which may be regarded as a great act of national justice—healing the wounds of centuries. . . . We want England to have the credit of doing something in love to Ireland, or in duty to her' (1846); 'separation is better than bad government' (1848); 'The social condition of Ireland, once for all, cannot be tolerated; it is an abomination in the sight of mankind' (1848?); 'When the inhabitants of a country quit the country en masse because its Government will not

make it a place fit for them to live in, the Government is judged and condemned' (1852); 'The loss, and the disgrace, are England's: and it is the English people and government whom it chiefly concerns to ask themselves, how far it will be to their honour and advantage to retain the mere soil of Ireland, but to lose its inhabitants' (1865). The only Union worth having was one in which England proved her capacity for upright, responsible leadership. The time had come for England to supply that leadership or get out of Ireland." (Bruce L. Kinzer, *England's Disgrace? J. S. Mill and the Irish Question* [Toronto: University of Toronto Press, 2001], 185). Another reading of the arguments used by Mill to convince his fellow-Englishmen to take the measures he was proposing would be that he was trying to shame them into a better policy for Ireland.

47. Reproduced from *The White Man's Burden: An Anthology of British Poetry of the Empire*, ed. Chris Brooks and Peter Faulkner (Exeter: University of Exeter Press, 1996), 185–86. This collection is an excellent resource for considering the various elements of imperialist thinking in the late Victorian cultural context.

48. Brooks and Faulkner, *White Man's Burden*, 19.

49. Brooks and Faulkner, *White Man's Burden*, 20.

50. D. G. Ritchie, "Review: *The Elements of Politics*," *International Journal of Ethics* 2 (1891–92), 254–55.

51. J. B. Schneewind, *Sidgwick's Ethics and Victorian Moral Philosophy* (Oxford: Oxford University Press, 1977), 187.

52. Sir George Trevelyan, *Cawnpore* (London: Macmillan, 1865), 280.

53. Humphrey Trevelyan, *The India We Left* (London: Macmillan, 1972), 103. This work gives a vivid picture of the attitude toward India of some of Sidgwick's closest friends. In some intriguing comments that George Trevelyan jotted on the proofs of *Henry Sidgwick: A Memoir* (the biography of Sidgwick assembled by his widow Eleanor and brother Arthur), he recalled some remarks of Sidgwick's in the early 1860s, concerning the cant of people worrying about the "poor peers": "'I wish I were a poor peer,' he said, 'with the power of speaking in the House of Lords; the certainty of early office or getting a Colonial Governorship at five and thirty; and a twenty to one chance, as against Commoners, of being Governor General of India.'" Sidgwick Papers, Trinity College, Cambridge University, Add.Ms.b.71.

54. See the discussion in Bart Schultz, *Henry Sidgwick, Eye of the Universe* (New York: Cambridge University Press, 2004), chapter 7.

55. Brooks and Faulkner, *White Man's Burden*, 39.

56. The lines, originally from Walter Bagehot's account of Sidgwick's favorite poet, A. H. Clough, came from his reflections on an upbraiding given him by Alfred Marshall, the economist, who blasted Sidgwick for, among other things, failing to attract a large, devoted following after the manner of T. H. Green at Oxford. See Eleanor Sidgwick and Arthur Sidgwick, eds., *Henry Sidgwick: A Memoir* (London: Macmillan, 1906), 395.

57. Edward Said, "Orientalism Reconsidered," in *Orientalism*, ed. Macfie, 359.

2

Jeremy Bentham on Slavery and the Slave Trade

Frederick Rosen

I

Recent scholarship has not generally approved of Bentham's approach to the institution of slavery. According to Paul Kelly, Bentham's treatment of slavery is an example of a serious difficulty in his account of distributive justice, as the recognized evil of slavery must be reconciled with obligations to secure the property of the masters and the future expectations of the freed slaves.[1] In effect, Bentham rejected the institution of slavery while at the same time recognizing the validity of a number of obligations to sustain it. Kelly contrasts Bentham's approach with that of Rawls, whose contractarian theory of rights does not "acknowledge the legitimacy of any conception of the good which is inconsistent with the principle of right." "Any such institution or practice," Kelly continues, "has no normative force and ought not to be considered in practical decision-making."[2] As long as Bentham and utilitarianism do not rule out practices that violate rights, Kelly believes, this creates "intuitive difficulties" for Bentham's theory.[3] While he acknowledges that Bentham was hostile to the institution of slavery and to the slave trade, he feels that Bentham could have called for immediate abolition with compensation to the slave owners for their loss of property.

Douglas Long makes a similar argument regarding rights from the perspective of liberty and condemns Bentham's approach to slavery for its failure (in writings on political economy) to refer to "dignity, humanity, or rights" and rely only on "the superior capital value and productivity of free labour."[4] For Long, "his dispassionate analysis of the slave's lot must surely constitute one of his most repulsive applications of security for expectations and the avoidance of disappointment."[5]

33

The most extensive critique of Bentham on slavery appears in Lea Campos Boralevi's *Bentham and the Oppressed*.[6] Boralevi begins by noting that slavery was not a major theme in Bentham's writings and wonders why he never wrote at length on so important a topic and never declared himself a clear abolitionist.[7] But she criticizes Long and others for dwelling on a position that is external to Bentham's philosophy and not appreciating a greater failing, depicted at times as an "ambiguity" and at other times as a "contradiction."[8] The theme of slavery brings to light these ambiguities and contradictions and hence may be one reason for Bentham's apparent avoidance of the topic. The contradictions to which she refers are not too different from those later developed by Kelly in terms of Rawlsian contractarianism. Bentham never reconciled his emphasis on security, and particularly security of property, with a similar emphasis on equality as ends of legislation. Nor did he reconcile his utilitarian emphasis on happiness with that on securing rights to property. These problems might be resolvable in numerous contexts but not in the context of slavery, where the oppression and misery caused by this institution could never be balanced against property rights. She also criticizes Bentham for his denial of the reality and validity of natural rights: "Bentham is therefore not opposed to the institution of slavery in itself, but considers it evil only on the basis of its effects. This attitude is a coherent consequence of his denial of any theory of natural rights."[9]

My object in this chapter will be to challenge these views of Bentham's account of slavery. This challenge will be partly historical, to link up Bentham's scattered remarks on slavery to the political contexts to which they were associated, partly textual in seeing various passages in the context of the works in which they appeared, and partly philosophical in exploring more generally Bentham's consistency and the so-called contradictions within his thought.

To introduce this discussion let us turn first to a brief letter concerning the slave trade, written by Bentham, which was published in the *Public Advertiser* on June 6, 1789.[10] Apparently unknown to most Bentham scholars (including those I have just cited) this letter is unique in being his only writing directed specifically at the issues of slavery and the slave trade. He was writing in the midst of the first major parliamentary debate over the slave trade, which followed William Wilberforce's speech and motion for its abolition on May 12, 1789, and dealt with the issue of whether or not the Liverpool slave traders should receive compensation if the trade were abolished. The debate was remarkable not only for the quality of the speeches but also for the unanimity among leading politicians, like Pitt, Fox, and Burke, for abolition. Burke and Pitt specifically discussed the question of compensation, and both rejected it. Burke argued that there was no real problem concerning compensation, as the Liverpool traders might simply employ their capital elsewhere.[11] Pitt rose in the House for a second time during the debate to correct any impression that he might support compensation, just because he was concerned with British resolve after abolition in dealing with other nations that took up the trade Britain would have abandoned, or with clandestine British traders.[12]

Bentham wrote his letter to support Pitt on the subject of compensation and to oppose any indemnification of those currently engaged in the slave trade. His letter was direct, passionate, and stated his position clearly. He referred to slaves as "*sensible* and *rational* beings, whose necks by length of time have been moulded to the yoke." On the subject of indemnification, he wrote:

> I observe the traders in human flesh claim an indemnity for the loss of their trade. Might not the same indemnity have been claimed with the same justice by the receivers of stolen goods? Is it worse to steal handkerchiefs and snuff-boxes than to steal men?

It is important to appreciate Bentham's arguments and his rhetoric, as in the following passage:

> What forced them to give their time and money to this employ? Were there no innocent callings to resort to? Is the word *trade* to be a license for every crime? Do murder and oppression put off their nature by being made a trade? Is it a property in crimes to lose their guilt by repetition? Does the perseverance of the tormentor, and the insensibility which is the consequence, deaden the feelings of the tormented? By shutting our eyes against cruelty, can we change its nature?

When Bentham calculated, as in weighing up the claims for compensation or the grounds of it being payment for the diminution of suffering following the abolition of the slave trade, he still rejected such compensation: "Those only are entitled to indemnification, to those only is indemnification wont to be given who ask for it with clean hands." In this "clean hands" category he placed claims by the American loyalists for indemnification following the War of Independence, but not the slave traders.

Bentham saw little difference between those who killed others with their own hands and those who brought about the death of slaves for the purpose of gain. He objected to being taxed to help pay for such crimes and suggested that those who approved of the slave trade might raise funds to compensate the slave traders. He also rejected the idea of allowing the slave trade to continue for a limited period.

It is worth noting that Bentham rejected the sort of solution that Kelly believes will overcome the "intuitive difficulties" in his theory. He flatly opposed compensation of the slave traders. Nor was he particularly concerned with security of property in this evil trade in human flesh. Although he did not explicitly invoke human rights or talk about liberty, except to deny that slave trading could be defended on the principles of free trade (in the analogy with trade in stolen goods), he could easily have done so. Nor did he see any conflict between property and happiness within his system. For Bentham the slave trade was clearly morally criminal involving murder and oppression on a massive scale and should be abolished by act of parliament.

Despite this clear example of Bentham's public opposition to the slave trade, the question of the paucity of his writings on slavery and the lack of evidence concerning a clear position on the abolition of slavery itself might still be raised. Furthermore, it might be argued that, however he dealt with compensation for the slave trade in this brief essay, problems might remain in his system concerning the application of the principle of utility which have a bearing on slavery and the slave trade. But as we shall see in the next sections, slavery was a highly complex institution and practice, and few in the eighteenth and early nineteenth centuries thought the theoretical and particularly the practical issues raised by slavery might be resolved simply by legislating for its abolition.

II

Until the eighteenth century most traditional religions and philosophies accepted the legitimacy of slavery in one form or another. Hugh Thomas relates a story of the King of Ashanti, who in 1820, following the abolition of the slave trade by Britain, asked a British official why the Christians no longer wanted to buy slaves:

> Was their God not the same as that of the Muslims, who continued to buy, kidnap, and sell slaves just as they had always done? Since the Koran accepted slavery, some Muslims even persuaded themselves that the new Christian behavior was an attack on Islam.
>   Further, French, Portuguese and even Spanish traders still acted as if they thought that slavery was ordained by God, just as the Anglo-Saxons had done up till 1807.[13]

Thus, it seemed odd to this African king that the slave trade should be suddenly abolished on religious grounds at this particular time.

When Thomas Clarkson, the founder of the Society for the Abolition of the Slave Trade in 1787, published his history of the abolition in 1808, he nonetheless could declare:

> To Christianity *alone* we are indebted for the new and sublime spectacle of seeing men going beyond the bonds of individual usefulness to each other—of seeing them associate for the extirpation of private and public misery—and of seeing them carry their charity, as a united brotherhood, into distant lands.[14]

The reader of this passage might be excused for feeling as confused as the King of Ashanti, as we recall the general view within Christianity, often based on ancient philosophies that underpinned Christian doctrine (particularly that of Aristotle), that justified the institution of slavery over many centuries. The standard moral justification for the enslavement of fellow human beings was either that it was natural and of mutual benefit between masters and slaves, or that having been captured in a "just" war, the slaves were being given a lesser punishment and spared a painful death.[15]

Neither Clarkson nor the King of Ashanti provide an answer as to why in the late eighteenth century Christians began to support an abolitionist agenda. Another answer might come from the influence of the Enlightenment. If human beings are born free and equal, slavery would appear to be difficult to justify. Nevertheless, John Locke, for example, was a stockholder in the Royal African Company and also managed to provide a theoretical justification for slavery based on the forfeiture of one's life and thus one's liberty in committing an unjust act of fighting in an unjust war. It is worth noting that only the combatants (and not their wives and children) might be enslaved. The just victor appears to acquire slaves because the unjust combatants have forfeited their right to be free. They become subhuman and are only freed when the just victor receives adequate reparations, although the slave has no "rights" to such freedom.[16]

As in Locke, most of the leading figures of the Enlightenment provided both the grounds for opposing slavery (as in an original natural freedom and equality) and some grounds for delaying immediate abolition of the practice.[17] Montesquieu's *The Spirit of the Laws* contains a number of books and chapters concerned with servitude generally and black slavery in particular.[18] His approach was characteristically witty and urbane, but it also exhibits a moral seriousness beneath its irony and humor. For example, in compiling a list of supposed arguments in defense of black slavery, he wrote: "It is impossible for us to assume that these people are men because if we assumed they were men one would begin to believe that we ourselves were not Christians."[19] Montesquieu was clearly opposed to slavery, which was animated by greed and a desire for luxury rather than a "love of public felicity."[20] And where it existed, he argued, the civil law should attempt to minimize the abuses and dangers of such an institution.[21]

It would be difficult, however, to call Montesquieu a clear abolitionist. Slavery seemed appropriate for a despotism, if not for a monarchy or republic.[22] Climate also was an important factor, although, here too, Montesquieu was highly ambivalent about the effects of a hot climate as grounds for slavery.[23] Furthermore, he took the view that slaves should not be freed in large numbers by a general law and considered the problems that would arise with the immediate abolition of slavery in different constitutions, and, in particular, in republics.[24] Finally, Montesquieu considered African slavery in a larger context of servitude in numerous shapes, from serfdom and ancient domestic slavery to the status of women in different societies and within different practices, such as polygamy and monogamy.[25] Thus, for Montesquieu and for many writers of the Enlightenment slavery was clearly an evil, but a complex evil, and one not susceptible to simple solutions like immediate abolition.

There were exceptions, and we may briefly mention here Rousseau and Voltaire. Rousseau criticized Grotian and Lockean arguments regarding the legitimacy of slavery based on war, found no natural basis for slavery, and insisted that a right of slavery was a contradiction in terms.[26] In *Candide* Voltaire evoked the feelings of the terrible inhumanity of slavery when Candide and Cacambo came upon a slave in Surinam lying on the ground virtually naked with his left leg and right hand missing.[27] That Candide wept at the sight of the slave confirmed the humanity of both. In addition to this sense of humanity that led to some of the Enlightenment opposition to the slave trade, there was a growing economic argument, developed most strongly by Adam Smith, that free labor was far more productive and efficient than slave labor.[28] This was an argument that Bentham fully accepted and developed in his own economic writings.[29]

For the most part, the language and rhetoric of the Enlightenment was directed against the institution of slavery. But even the French revolutionaries exhibited a considerable reluctance to state simply that slavery should be immediately abolished, or, for that matter, that universal suffrage should be immediately instituted.[30] To proclaim that all humans were free and equal by nature did not lead to policies that directly implemented the abolition of slavery.

III

In Britain, when the small group of Quakers and their allies decided to act against slavery, they decided on prudential grounds to campaign against the slave trade rather than take a purely abolitionist stance. As Clarkson put it, "I have no doubt that this wise decision contributed greatly to their success; for I am persuaded that, if they had adopted the other object, they could not for years to come, if ever, have succeeded in their attempt."[31] It was thought that if the slave trade were abolished, slavery would eventually wither away.

The Committee for the Abolition of the Slave Trade was established in May 1787. At an early stage William Wilberforce and Samuel Romilly, close friends and allies of Bentham, became involved in its activities.[32] When Wilberforce initiated the debate over the slave trade in 1789, Bentham, as we have seen, provided strong support in his letter to the *Public Advertiser*. The first vote on the issue in the House of Commons took place in 1791; Wilberforce's bill was defeated by 163 to 88. By the mid-1790s those in favor of the abolition of the slave trade were often labeled "Jacobins," and despite widespread sympathy with the cause of abolition, little happened until 1807, when the bill to abolish the slave trade was successful. The bill was introduced by Wilberforce, but Romilly, who had recently entered parliament and was then Solicitor-General in the Ministry of All the Talents, was instrumental in its success. The final debate in February 1807, when the bill passed by a substantial majority of 283 to 16, culminated with a speech by Romilly comparing the respective contributions of Napoleon and Wilberforce to mankind. Wilberforce wept, as the House unusually rose to applaud his efforts on behalf of humanity in attempting, now successfully, to abolish this evil trade.[33]

Bentham's relationships with both Wilberforce and Romilly are of some significance in clarifying his attitude toward slavery and the slave trade. Boralevi has observed that although Bentham knew Wilberforce at least from 1795 and they corresponded frequently between 1796 and 1811, most of the correspondence concerned the panopticon project and poor-law reform rather than the slave trade. This "strange fact" is then used by Boralevi to suggest that Bentham did not become an "abolitionist" and was indifferent to the abolitionist movement due to the weakness of his belief in liberty.[34] Otherwise, his extensive correspondence with Wilberforce would have been full of discussions concerning progress and failure to abolish slavery and the slave trade.[35]

Boralevi omits to consider Bentham's close friendship with Romilly, with whom he became acquainted as early as 1784 through George Wilson, a barrister and close friend, whom Bentham had known since the 1770s. After Bentham returned from Russia in 1788 and became a member of Lansdowne's coterie of intellectuals, he renewed his friendship with Romilly and, through Lansdowne and Romilly, established a friendship with the Genevan Etienne Dumont, later his editor, whose recensions would make Bentham famous throughout the world.[36] Romilly, as we have noted, had taken a passionate interest and became active in the Committee for the Abolition of the Slave Trade soon after its founding. At this time he became friends with Wilberforce, although when Wilberforce approached him in 1806 to take the leading role in the debate over the abolition of the slave trade, Romilly remarked in his diary, they had not met for nine or ten years. In writing this, he gave no indication that the renewal of their friendship was not welcome on both sides, though he indicated that the break was not due to any fault on his part.[37]

At the time of his letter to the *Public Advertiser* and during the early years of the French Revolution, Bentham was working closely with Lansdowne, Romilly, and Dumont, using the libraries at Bowood and Lansdowne House, and exploiting contacts in France that were initially developed through

Lansdowne but were actively cultivated by Romilly and Dumont.[38] Romilly's keen interest in the movement to abolish the slave trade was connected to his interest in developments in France, particularly as he had numerous contacts and was in regular correspondence with Dumont, who was then in Paris. On May 22, 1789, Dumont wrote to Romilly that he had joined the Société des Amis des Noirs in Paris, which at that time had approximately a hundred members.[39] In October Dumont reported cautiously: "The question of the negroes is not yet ripe, but I assure you that it is kept alive; and I still think it likely that it will be discussed even this session. The Duke de la Rochefoucauld is very earnest about it."[40] On January 26, 1790, Romilly wrote in despair to Dumont about the lack of progress among the French:

> I grieve beyond measure that the National Assembly does nothing respecting the slave trade. The question has been revived here, the first day that the House met on business. If there were any prospect of the French giving up the trade, I think it certainly would be abolished here. I cannot conceive why it is delayed. If the subject were merely introduced, and the temper of the French seen, it would be sufficient.[41]

The British opponents of the slave trade did try to influence developments in France. Clarkson relates his mission to Paris around July 1789 at the suggestion of Wilberforce to see if the French would abolish the slave trade. When he arrived there, he soon met the leading political figures opposed to the slave trade: Rochefoucauld, Condorcet, Villeneuve, Claviere, Brissot, and Lafayette, most of whom were well known to the Lansdowne circle.[42] He noted, however, that a meeting of the Société to which he went was not well attended, as the French seemed more concerned with the revolution than the slave trade. Many thought that if the former was secured, the latter would soon be abolished.[43] Clarkson then provided a long account of his supplying extensive information for an important speech that Mirabeau was to have given in the National Assembly.[44] In this account of laborious research for Mirabeau, Clarkson makes no reference to Dumont and seems wholly unaware of his role in Mirabeau's speech. In fact, Dumont was setting the questions that Clarkson was attempting to answer, and he, rather than Mirabeau, played the main role in drafting the discourse that Mirabeau was going to use.[45] Nor did Clarkson call attention to the importance of Romilly, except later in the debate over abolition in 1805–1807.[46]

The significance of Clarkson's omissions is that the movement for the abolition of the slave trade appears to have been and has often been perceived as a largely Christian affair, with the campaign organized and fought mainly by Quakers and Evangelicals and led by Clarkson, Wilberforce, and Granville Sharp. But there was another strand of activity at this time, based in the Lansdowne circle, that also attacked slavery and the slave trade, and this strand included Bentham. With encouragement and practical assistance from Lansdowne and with Romilly and Dumont serving as intermediaries between Bentham and Mirabeau, Bentham wrote numerous works for France, extracts from some of which, prepared by Dumont, appeared in Mirabeau's *Courier de Provence.* Dumont also prepared a French version of part of Bentham's *Panopticon*, and it constituted the first of many recensions of Bentham's writings.[47] With the publication of a number of these works in the new edition of *The Collected Works of Jeremy Bentham*, it is now possible to survey the numerous topics, from legislative procedure to judicial organization, constitutional law, economics, prisons, and colonies that Bentham covered at this time and formed the basis of his receiving honorary French citizenship in 1792.[48] It is significant that he did not (after his letter to the *Public Advertiser*) write specifically on slavery or the slave trade. This may well have been due to a division of labor between himself and Romilly or to his having received the same intelligence as Romilly and Dumont, that the time was not ripe to pursue this cause. Nevertheless, he occasionally alluded to slavery and the slave trade in the material written at this time. In *Emancipate Your Colonies*, probably written in December 1792 and printed in early 1793 (though not published until 1830), Bentham was possibly attempting to defuse tensions leading to war between France and Britain by arguing that were they to give up their colonies, one source of tension and competition would no longer exist.[49] But when we consider the passage on slavery, another dimension appears:

> Great differences of opinion, and those attended with no little warmth, between the tolerators and proscribers of negro slavery:—emancipation [of colonies] throws all these heart burnings and difficulties out of doors; it is a middle term in which all parties may agree. Keep the sugar islands, it is impossible for you to do right:—let go the negroes, you have no sugar, and the reason for keeping these colonies is at end; keep the negroes, you trample upon the declaration of rights, and act in the teeth of principle.—Scruples must have a term: how sugar is raised is what you need not trouble yourselves about, so long as you do not direct the raising of it. Reform the world by example, you act generously and wisely: reform the world by force, you might as well reform the moon, and the design is fit only for lunatics.[50]

At first glance one might see in Bentham's argument ample confirmation of some of Boralevi's objections to Bentham's refusal to urge the abolition of slavery. Indeed, he apparently saw the absence of colonies as a greater source of virtue than the abolition of slavery, in so far as he proposed the abolition of colonies as a way of avoiding the issue of slavery. If France gave up its colonies the country no longer was responsible for the institution of slavery there. With the abolition of colonies, slavery could continue, but it would be of no concern to the mother country. Bentham seems close to denying any sense of humanity and human feeling.

On the other hand, it is worth recalling that even Clarkson and the Committee did not seek to abolish slavery (as it was considered to be an impossible task) but believed (wrongly, as it turned out) that by prudentially concentrating on the slave trade, slavery itself would also decline. They knew that the direct abolition of slavery probably could not be achieved without force, and Bentham provided the reason for avoiding reform by force in the passage above. Furthermore, Bentham's argument is more concerned with virtue than first appears. At the beginning of the essay, from which the above quotation is taken, Bentham raised the issue of justice regarding colonies, reminding the members of the National Convention that France had earlier made the question of colonies a matter of justice in going to war against Britain on the side of the American colonists fighting for their independence. "You abhor the subjection of one nation to another," wrote Bentham, "You call it slavery."[51]

The link between justice, slavery, and colonies appears elsewhere in Bentham's writings at this time, as, for example, when he wrote: "Colony-holding is a species of slave-holding equally pernicious to the tyrant and the slave."[52] This remark brings out vividly the way Bentham thought about slavery, in so far as black slavery was regarded as one case in a general concept of slavery which included colony-holding as another. For Bentham, to abolish the slave trade, as Clarkson, Wilberforce, and others were contending, would not eventually lead to the abolition of slavery, unless the abolition of the colonies themselves was also undertaken. This belief was not simply a matter of choosing the best means to an end but one of morality itself. The French were showing themselves woefully inconsistent in recognizing the injustice of colonies at one level but in being unwilling to abandon its colonies even where such colonies were shown to be disadvantageous to France.

Bentham developed this idea of the inconsistency of the French in his later attack on the French Declaration of Rights which proclaimed that all men were born free and equal and remained so, but he did so in a world in which many people were born slaves.[53] How could anyone, Bentham asked, be both free and a slave at the same time? Bentham would be misunderstood if he is interpreted simply as denying the validity of the doctrine of moral and natural rights. Boralevi seems to take this view when she accuses him of failing to be an abolitionist because he rejected this doctrine. However, Bentham was insisting on the importance of truth, and the truth was that all people were born as helpless infants in a state of subjection and that most people at most times lived in various degrees of legal, political, economic, and social subjection. To pretend that such subjection did not exist or to insist that it must not exist was both a denial of the truth and an encouragement to pointless violence and chaos that would never lead to a condition of freedom and equality.

That Bentham employed the term "slavery" in these contexts was not meant to be an exercise in rhetorical excess but a serious attempt to define the human condition in terms of varying degrees of subjection. It is important to note here that, for Bentham, progress toward human happiness could not take place unless there was a willingness to accept this truth about the human condition. To accept such a truth did not entail a denial that black slavery and the slave trade were great evils and should not continue. But it affected how one perceived these evils and how one engaged politically against them.

IV

In *An Introduction to the Principles of Morals and Legislation*, Bentham raised the question of whether or not slavery or other modes of servitude ought to be established or maintained. His answer was to refer the question to "the civil branch of the art of legislation."[54] The civil law writings, drafted in the 1770s and early 1780s, appeared in print in Dumont's first recension, published in 1802, and were eventually translated into English.[55] No one could doubt Bentham's opposition to slavery and commitment to liberty, as when he wrote in almost Rousseauian terms: "No one who is free is willing to become a slave; no one is a slave but he wishes to become free." A few lines later he added: "this condition is never embraced from choice, but, on the contrary, that it is always an object of aversion."[56] Bentham's discussion consisted of the development of two themes. The first was concerned with arguments to establish that the institution of slavery was not beneficial to the master or the slave, and the second, with a strategy for emancipation.

As for the first, Bentham began by stating that slavery took many different forms. Ancient slavery differed, he believed, in Athens and Sparta, and there were major differences between the Russian serf and the plantation slave in the southern states of America.[57] But in drawing the line between slavery and freedom, the distinguishing feature of slavery rested with its perpetuity. With this feature alone, the odious character of slavery was fully revealed; the hopelessness engendered by the perpetuity of slavery destroyed character, ambition, love of life, and every element in human life that was forward-looking and productive. Nevertheless, the masters profited greatly from slavery; if not, they would have abolished it. Bentham, however, believed that there were numerous arguments in favor of abolition. First, no slave would choose slavery, and abolition would bring more happiness to the slaves than unhappiness to the small number of masters. Second, the superiority of free to slave labor could easily be established, as the former had the stimulus of reward and a much greater security of condition to encourage them to work for themselves as well as for their employers. A free man, Bentham believed (following Smith), produced more than a slave who was denied the stimulus of reward and only faced punishment, which failed to have a similar effect, and, in fact, took their minds off the products of their labor. A humble day laborer who received a small wage to maintain himself and his family was still in a superior position to a slave, since the day laborer retained the motive of reward, his or her honor would matter (for in a free society shame at being idle operated as a powerful sanction), and everything a day laborer acquired remained his or her own.

Bentham then turned to develop a strategy for gradual emancipation that attempted to avoid violent revolution. This strategy included suggestions such as fixing a price at which a slave could purchase his or her freedom. Although this might delay liberation, it also could be seen to serve the interests of the master in providing incentives to more productive labor and hence lead to greater sympathy with abolition. Another suggestion offered several different proposals affecting hereditary succession so that the prospect of inheriting slaves after the death of the masters was limited. Bentham believed in gradual progress and, like those who sought to abolish the slave trade, thought that full emancipation would eventually take place.[58]

Boralevi has strong objections to Bentham's argument, which go to the heart of his theory:

> Here the increase in general happiness clashes with the loss of property suffered by the master. The conflict is resolved by Bentham with a compromise which appears distinctly to be more in favour of property than of the slaves. According to the priority always given to security over the other "subsidiary ends" of abundance and equality, Bentham's plea for gradual abolition is the best deal he has to offer to the slaves. On the other hand, it is quite clear that he was aware that a different solution could be adopted, if equality was given priority over the other ends.[59]

Boralevi argues that on any straight utilitarian calculation of happiness, and especially one that weighs individuals equally, slavery would be seen as an institution that generated great pain and should be immediately abolished. What stopped Bentham from making this argument was his well-known emphasis on security and in particular security of property, which dictated that emancipation should be gradual. For Boralevi, Bentham was linked with Hobbes's emphasis on security and Locke's defense of property, and it is the institution of slavery that brings to light the contradictions in Bentham's theory.[60]

Did Bentham actually subscribe to what might be called a Lockean view in which property rights were paramount? In his "Article on Utilitarianism" he specifically rejected such a position.[61] Not only did he criticize Locke for too narrow a notion of property in not including all exemptions from pain, which might be the subject of law, as security, but he also accused Locke of devising a theory that would enslave the poor and justify West Indian slavery. Thus, Bentham fully understood that a Lockean emphasis on security of property might well conflict with his principle of utility. For Bentham, as I have argued on numerous occasions, security against being harmed was a form of liberty and in itself generated happiness.[62] On this view slavery was an evil and should be abolished. But if Bentham was not overly concerned with securing the master's property, why did he oppose immediate emancipation? As opposed to Boralevi, I believe that Bentham was far more concerned with protecting the slaves than the masters and would have favored immediate abolition, if he could have been confident that such abolition would enhance the well-being of the slaves.

In his later writings on Spanish colonies in a chapter on slavery and the slave trade, in which he described the slave trade as "this foulest of all political and moral leprosies,"[63] he distinguished between the challenges involved in abolishing slave-trading and slave-holding respectively:

> To abstain from the traffic in slaves, nothing more is necessary than the mere negative act of not engaging in it. . . . To abstain altogether from *Slave-holding* is a course of conduct, which, though *negative* in the expression, would require *positive* acts: acts which, for the formation of an adequately comprehensive, effective and preponderantly beneficial system, would require to be woven into a chain of such intricacy, that upon a cursory view, the mind is bewildered in the contemplation of it. Be the man who he may, freedom to him is no means of well-being, nor so much as of *being*, except so far as accompanied with subsistence and security: subsistence for others as well as for himself: security for others: against him, as well as for him against others.[64]

The abolition of the slave trade would require only a negative act of abolition and its enforcement. As we have seen, for Bentham no compensation need be paid to the slave traders as they dealt with the human equivalent of stolen goods. But to abolish slave-holding, another social and economic system must be put in its place, one that provided subsistence and security for the newly freed slaves and did not leave them in a worse position in relation to their former masters. The masters also required protection. It was mainly for these reasons that Bentham emphasized gradual emancipation, particularly for those who had been born slaves or who had been enslaved for a long period.

V

In *Securities against Misrule*, where Bentham attempted to introduce a variety of practices into an absolute Muslim state to produce good government or at least to limit bad government, he raised the question of the relevance of his discussion to the existence of slavery in the state (Tripoli):

> In the country in question one deplorable and deplorably extensive case—the case of slavery—has been seen alone presenting a particular demand for attention. For, though in the here proposed arrangements it is not on any occasion mentioned, it has not, on any occasion, been overlooked. Not knowing what chance there may be that assistance would be given to any endeavors towards the placing this part of the population of the country upon a footing in any respect superior to that of the brute creation, I must leave it to those to whom it belongs to determine what, if any thing, can be attempted in this view with any prospect of success.[65]

There are three important elements in this passage, written in the early 1820s. First, there is no doubt that slavery was an evil condition and should not exist. Second Bentham made it clear that although he did not discuss slavery, it had not been overlooked. Third, he seemed to make action to abolish it depend on a prospect of success. Note, in addition, that security of property was not mentioned.

The second point is of particular interest, as it deals with the issue of why Bentham did not write at length on the topic of slavery. His response is that slavery, though perhaps not mentioned, was not overlooked. Was Bentham being overly timid in not directly addressing this important subject, which forty years later would lead to one of the bloodiest wars in human history? Bentham may be saying simply that slaves were to be treated in his scheme of legislation the same as any other human being. In *An Introduction to the Principles of Morals and Legislation*, for example, he had no exemptions in the offences against the person that allowed slaves to be harmed by their masters because they were slaves.[66] In *Securities against Misrule*, he similarly expressed the hope that the law of homicide might apply to free and enslaved persons, since one could not easily tell if a dead body was a slave. But in areas where the ruler was the author of decisions, such impartiality would be difficult to establish.[67]

In saying that he had no idea of what reform of slavery might be attempted in this state, Bentham was not being timid but rather revealing his strategy of reform.[68] This strategy, if implemented, might well lead to increased liberty and equality and obviate the need for slavery or other forms of servitude. The strategy was not based on force, so that the abolition of slavery by force was not anticipated. Bentham emphasized the importance of liberty (as security) to good government, so that freedom of expression and the press, free trade, representative government, education, the rule of law, etc. would lead to a condition where slavery would be replaced by free labor and free institutions to the benefit of both slaves and masters. Thus, the issue of slavery might diminish in importance and be conceived as an outmoded institution increasingly belonging to a past age.

In Bentham's more political later writings his attitude toward slavery seemed to change in one important rhetorical, if not theoretical, way. If he attempted in his early writings to define slavery more precisely in terms of the perpetuity of subjection, in his later writings he used the word "slavery" to refer to numerous conditions of subordination where power was exercised unjustly.[69] For example, in *Constitutional Code* he wrote in ringing tones that "*power without obligation* is the very definition of despotism: *slavery*, the condition of those who are subject to it."[70] The context for these remarks was his condemnation of legislators who failed to attend legislative sessions. Later in an attack on monarchy the monarch was referred to as "this universal slave-holder," albeit subjecting the people to political rather than domestic slavery.[71] In an attack on the current mode of remunerating judges that oppressed ordinary people, Bentham, in *Official Aptitude Maximized; Expense Minimized* referred to those who suffered this injustice as slaves who were distinguished from black plantation slavery and that of Catholics under Protestants in Great Britain and Ireland only in that under judicial oppression no clear line of demarcation between masters and slaves existed.[72] In *First Principles Preparatory to Constitutional Code*, Bentham wrote that "every Monarch is a Slaveholder upon the largest scale."[73] In a reference to the British constitution in *Colonies, Commerce and Constitutional Law*, the condition of those who lacked suffrage was depicted as one of slavery to those who had it.[74] The depiction of Roman Catholics as slaves to Protestants, as we have seen, was frequently repeated in his later writings.[75]

This "politicization" of the term "slavery" to include virtually all instances of persistent unjust oppression or even exploitation clearly differed from Bentham's earlier attempts to define and limit the application of the term. But at the same time it followed from his belief that subjection was characteristic of the human condition and persisted everywhere.[76] When he began to assert the importance of radical reform, he also asserted that certain conditions, analogous to slavery, could both be defined in these terms and then remedied. It was as if by calling these conditions those of servitude and slavery, Bentham was attempting to arouse interest in reform by showing how degrading numerous existing political and legal institutions were to the mass of the people. At the same time he seemed to have implicitly adopted the view, or, at least, the rhetoric attached to it, that there was a remedy for all slavery. If black plantation slavery or domestic slavery in North Africa was less easily abolished, Bentham seemed in the 1820s to have taken these forms on the agenda of reform by now attacking all forms of politically and legally established servitude.[77]

VI

The sheer scale of the problem of slavery throughout the world was enormous. In 1833 when 800,000 slaves were about to be liberated in the British colonies after they served periods of apprenticeship that would extend from 1834 for a further four years for nonagricultural and six years for agricultural slaves, there would still be 2.75 million slaves in the United States, 2.5 million in Brazil, 600,000 in the Spanish colonies, 30,000 in Danish and Swedish colonies, 25,000 in Texas, and nearly a million more in French, Dutch, and Portuguese colonies.[78] In addition, the human beings who were enslaved in North Africa and the Middle East, were Russian serfs, were employed in various conditions of servitude in India, China, Japan and other Far Eastern countries, or were sentenced as criminals to lifelong penal servitude must have numbered many millions more.

The hard-fought struggle to abolish the slave trade, which extended from 1787 to 1807, had very limited practical success, in that it did not lead to a decline in slavery, as was hoped, and, in addition, there was widespread evasion. The Anti-Slavery Society, founded in 1823, bore the full name of the Society for the Mitigation and Gradual Abolition of Slavery throughout the British Dominions, reflecting the fact that those who pressed hardest for the abolition of slavery expected only gradual progress toward their goal.[79] It is of some interest that the movement to abolish the slave trade and slavery followed fairly closely the development of radical politics generally in Britain, starting with growing enthusiasm for reform at and just prior to the French Revolution, retreat during the French wars and anti-Jacobin reaction, and determined progress during the 1820s, culminating in the Reform Bill of 1832 and the abolition of slavery in British colonies from 1833, with the promise of further reform in numerous fields in the future. And the names of prominent figures in the antislavery movement feature in numerous other reform movements from Greek independence, the liberation of the South American colonies, prison reform, law reform, and so forth. With respect to this period, there seems little point in attempting to distinguish between humanitarian and Benthamite impulses toward reform. In some recent scholarship "humanitarian" as opposed to "Benthamite" seems a code word for "religious," as opposed to a secular, calculating economics, but at the time there was little or no tension between Bentham and his friends on the one hand, and reforming Evangelicals, Methodists, Quakers, and others dedicated to the relief of suffering humanity on the other.[80] Many of the Church of England clergy simply followed the Tory line in politics, and if that line moved to embrace antislavery, so would the clergy change their stance.[81] According to Walvin, by 1830 most religious bodies, including the Church of England, Church of Ireland, and Roman Catholic Church, opposed slavery.[82] Furthermore, there seemed to have been a major shift in popular sentiment with regard to a belief in divinely ordained rights that opposed slavery.[83] These changes were reflected in the fact that opposition to slavery became almost a condition for standing as a parliamentary candidate at this time.[84]

Recent research on Atlantic slavery has tended to discredit the view (advanced in Eric Williams's *Capitalism and Slavery*) that slavery was already in decline economically prior to the movement for abolition. This view had tended to stress economic factors rather than "moral outrage" as the determining factor in the movement to abolish the slave trade. Seymour Drescher has recently reaffirmed the view he set forth in *Econocide*:

> Slavery's decline did not occur during the final quarter of the eighteenth century nor, *pace* Williams as a consequence of the American Revolution. Both the emergence of political abolitionism, in 1787-1792 and the abolition of the British slave trade in 1806-1807 occurred against a background of slave expansion, and at the peak of slavery's value to British imperial political economy.[85]

In other words, British slavery declined after and not before the movement to abolish it succeeded. It is worth quoting Drescher a second time to obtain his view of what turned opinion against slavery and the slave trade:

> The crucial change in attitudes towards the slave trade occurred neither because the West Indian slave system became economically redundant, nor because of the triumph of free market ideology. It occurred when certain non-commercial judgments on the slave trade gained ground and prevailed. This was not so much an intellectual revolution as a revolution in public and parliamentary opinion.[86]

What surely counted in this "revolution in public and parliamentary opinion" was the "intellectual revolution" that preceded it. That "intellectual revolution" in part concerned liberty and the utility of liberty to human happiness. The view (developed by Smith) that free labor was more productive and happier than slave labor was important to this intellectual revolution and equally important to the revolution in public and parliamentary opinion that took place in the 1820s.[87]

Bentham might easily stand with Wilberforce and Romilly as an opponent of slavery and the slave trade. Some recent scholarship on Bentham, as we have seen, takes him out of context in expecting more from him or mistakes his philosophical ambitions for an unwillingness to stand more publicly against the evil of slavery. Furthermore, there is no evidence that he emphasized security of property *over* abolition. Security was a complex idea and tended to preclude reform by force and violence. Bentham believed that "to reform the world by force, you might as well reform the moon, and the design is fit only for lunatics."[88] Bentham apparently adhered to this view throughout his life. It stood behind his strategy of gradual reform,

which included the abolition of slavery and other forms of injustice and oppression. I should call Bentham a *comprehensive* abolitionist, one who
might have foreseen that the bloody struggle in America could produce a
kind of abolition, but not one that would establish well being among the
newly liberated slaves. But his main object would have been, as it was in his
numerous writings, to show which forms of servitude were part of the human condition itself and which formed the basis of oppression and injustice. The remedy then remained with humanity, and Bentham attempted to
design the institutions and laws that would enable human beings to
progress toward happiness. Slavery and the slave trade, together with numerous other activities, would thus have to be abolished as part of this journey toward human happiness. In this journey the issue of rights versus utilitarianism remained important, but mainly as part of an account of truth
rather than one concerning human entitlements. If rights theory obscures
the basic truth about subordination and leads one to proclaim one's freedom where there is none and will not be any for the foreseeable future, its
relevance to human happiness will at best be consigned to a rhetorical
flourish and at worst to useless conflict and even war.[89]

NOTES

1. P. J. Kelly, *Utilitarianism and Distributive Justice, Jeremy Bentham and the
Civil Law* (Oxford: Clarendon Press, 1990), 213–14.

2. Kelly, *Utilitarianism and Distributive Justice*, 213.

3. Kelly, *Utilitarianism and Distributive Justice*, 213

4. Douglas G. Long, *Bentham on Liberty: Jeremy Bentham's Idea of Liberty in Relation to His Utilitarianism* (Toronto and Buffalo: University of Toronto Press, 1977),
194.

5. Long, *Bentham on Liberty*, 194.

6. Lea Campos Boralevi, *Bentham and the Oppressed* (Berlin and New York: Walter de Gruyter, 1984), 142–64.

7. Boralevi, *Bentham and the Oppressed*, 142–43, 146.

8. Boralevi, *Bentham and the Oppressed*, 152–53.

9. Boralevi, *Bentham and the Oppressed*, 147.

10. J. Bentham, "To the Printer of the *Public Advertiser*," June 6, 1789, 1–2, signed
"J. B." For confirmation of Bentham's authorship, see Bentham to George Wilson, 12
June 1789, *Correspondence of Jeremy Bentham, Volume 4, October 1788 to Decem-
ber 1793*, ed. A. Taylor Milne [*The Collected Works of Jeremy Bentham*—henceforth
CW] (London: The Athlone Press, 1981), 73.

11. See *The Parliamentary History of England, from the Earliest Period to the Year
1803*, volume xxviii (London: T.C. Hansard, 1816), 70–71.

12. *The Parliamentary History of England*, volume xxviii, 72–73.

13. Hugh Thomas, *The Slave Trade, The History of the Atlantic Slave Trade:
1440–1870* (London: Picador, 1997), 559.

14. Thomas Clarkson, *The History of the Rise, Progress, and Accomplishment of the Abolition of the African Slave-Trade by the British Parliament*, 2 vols. (London: Longman, Hurst, Rees, and Orme, 1808), i.8 (italics added). See, more recently, David Turley, *The Culture of English Antislavery, 1780–1860* (London and New York: Routledge, 1991), 7.

15. Clarkson's claim regarding Christianity has some basis, in that nine of the twelve members of the original committee to abolish the slave trade were Quakers, and this Quaker opposition to slavery and the slave trade might easily have been derived from the Quaker opposition to war, a position that has distinguished this sect from many other branches of Christianity. See Clarkson, *The History of the Rise, Progress, and Accomplishment of the Abolition of the African Slave-Trade by the British Parliament*, i.256ff. But see also Thomas Clarkson, *An Essay on the Doctrines and Practice of the Early Christians, as They Relate to War* (London: Society for the Promotion of Permanent and Universal Peace, Tract III, 1817).

16. See Maurice Cranston, *John Locke, A Biography* (Oxford: Oxford University Press, 1985), 115n; John Dunn, *The Political Thought of John Locke: An Historical Account of the Argument of the "Two Treatises of Government"* (Cambridge: Cambridge University Press, 1969), 108, 173–77, 211.

17. See Claudine Hunting, "The *Philosophes* and Black Slavery: 1748–1765," *Journal of the History of Ideas* 39 (1978): 405–18.

18. Montesquieu, *The Spirit of the Laws*, trans. Anne Cohler, Basia Miller, and Harold Stone [*Cambridge Texts in the History of Political Thought*] (Cambridge: Cambridge University Press, 1989), Books XV–XVII, 246–84.

19. Montesquieu, *The Spirit of the Laws*. Book XV, chapter 5, 250.

20. Montesquieu, *The Spirit of the Laws*, Book XV, chapter 9, 253.

21. Montesquieu, *The Spirit of the Laws*, Book XV, chapter 11, 254.

22. Montesquieu, *The Spirit of the Laws*, Book XV, chapter 6, 251.

23. Montesquieu, *The Spirit of the Laws*, Book XV, chapter 7, 251. See also chapter 8, 253.

24. Montesquieu, *The Spirit of the Laws*, Book XV, chapter 18, 261.

25. See Montesquieu, *The Spirit of the Laws*, Book XVI, 264–77.

26. Jean-Jacques Rousseau, *The Social Contract,* trans. M. Cranston (Harmondsworth: Penguin Books, 1968), I.4, 53–58.

27. Voltaire, *Candide and Related Texts*, trans. D. Wootton (Indianapolis: Hackett Publishing Company, 2000), chapter 19, 42–43. The hand had been amputated (according to current policy) when a finger became caught in the machinery of a sugar refinery, and the leg, for attempting to escape.

28. Adam Smith, *An Inquiry into the Nature and Causes of the Wealth of Nations*, 2 vols., eds. R. H. Campbell, A. S. Skinner, and W. B. Todd (Indianapolis: Liberty Classics, 1981), i.98–99. 387–89, ii.684.

29. See, for example, *Jeremy Bentham's Economic Writings*, 3 vols., ed. W. Stark (London: George Allen and Unwin, 1952–54), iii.77; *The Works of Jeremy Bentham*, 11 vols., ed. J. Bowring (Edinburgh: William Tait, 1838–43), i.345, 441. I am indebted to Boralevi, *Bentham and the Oppressed*, 148, 160–61, for these references and for those in note 28 above.

30. See Cheryl B. Welch, *Liberty and Utility, The French Idéologues and the Transformation of Liberalism* (New York: Columbia University Press, 1984), 23, 204n.

31. Clarkson, *The History of the Rise, Progress, and Accomplishment of the Abolition of the African Slave-Trade*, i.289.

32. See Patrick Medd, *Romilly, A Life of Sir Samuel Romilly, Lawyer and Reformer* (London: Collins, 1968), 153, 155ff.

33. See Thomas, *The Slave Trade*, 555. See also *The Parliamentary Debates from the Year 1803 to the Present Time* (London: T. C. Hansard, 1812), vol. 8, February 23, 1807, 977–79; Medd, *Romilly*, 165.

34. Boralevi, *Bentham and the Oppressed*, 156, 157.

35. Wilberforce's name enters Bentham's *Correspondence* first in relation to the Panopticon prison scheme, and Bentham was aware, at least from early 1791, of the fact that Wilberforce formed one important channel for his ideas and proposals to reach the attention of Pitt. See Bentham to Pitt, November 26, 1791, *Correspondence of Jeremy Bentham, Volume 4*, 343. Wilberforce was also a major supporter of the Panopticon project over many years. See Janet Semple, *Bentham's Prison: A Study of the Panopticon Penitentiary* (Oxford: Clarendon Press, 1993), as index. Furthermore, when Pitt turned to Wilberforce in 1796 for assistance in drafting a measure to deal with poor relief, Wilberforce turned to Bentham, and "was primarily responsible for stimulating Bentham to develop his thinking on poverty." J. Bentham, *Writings on the Poor Laws, Volume I*, ed. M. Quinn (*CW*) (Oxford: Clarendon Press, 2001), xiv–xv. Wilberforce would have known of Bentham's friendship with Romilly and may well have known of his letter to the *Public Advertiser* in 1789. There are some references to slavery and the slave trade in their correspondence. See Bentham to Wilberforce, September 1, 1796, *The Correspondence of Jeremy Bentham, Volume 5, January 1794 to December 1797*, ed. A. Taylor Milne (*CW*) (London: The Athlone Press, 1981), 253; Wilberforce to Bentham, April 2, 1798, *The Correspondence of Jeremy Bentham, Volume 6, January 1798 to December 1801*, ed. J.R. Dinwiddy (*CW*) (Oxford: Clarendon Press, 1984), 19; Bentham to Wilberforce, May 31, 1803, *The Correspondence of Jeremy Bentham, Volume 7, January 1802 to December 1808*, ed. J. R. Dinwiddy (*CW*) (Oxford: Clarendon Press, 1988), 232. Most probably, however, slavery was not a topic on which Bentham could assist Wilberforce, and Wilberforce did not seek assistance on it.

36. See *Correspondence of Jeremy Bentham, Volume 4*, 17n–18n.

37. *Memoirs of the Life of Sir Samuel Romilly, Written by Himself; with a Selection from His Correspondence, Edited by His Sons*, 3 vols., 2nd ed. (London: John Murray, 1840), ii.134.

38. See J. H. Burns, "Bentham and the French Revolution," *The Transactions of the Royal Historical Society*, 5th Series, xvi (1966), 95–114. See also the editorial introductions to J. Bentham, *Political Tactics*, ed. M. James, C. Blamires, and C. Pease-Watkin (*CW*) (Oxford: Clarendon Press, 1999) and J. Bentham, *Rights, Representation, and Reform, Nonsense upon Stilts and Other Writings on the French Revolution*, ed. P. Schofield, C. Pease-Watkin, and C. Blamires (*CW*) (Oxford: Clarendon Press, 2002).

39. *Memoirs of the Life of Sir Samuel Romilly*, i.348–49. See also Lawrence Jennings, *French Anti-Slavery, The Movement for the Abolition of Slavery in France, 1802–1848* (Cambridge: Cambridge University Press, 2000), 1–3. Unfortunately, Jennings fails to consider the Dumont-Romilly connection with early French antislavery.

40. *Memoirs of the Life of Sir Samuel Romilly*, i.368.

41. *Memoirs of the Life of Sir Samuel Romilly*, i.388.

42. See Clarkson, *The History of the Rise, Progress, and Accomplishment of the Abolition of the African Slave-Trade*, ii.122–23.

43. See Clarkson, *The History of the Rise, Progress, and Accomplishment of the Abolition of the African Slave-Trade*, ii.124, 141.

44. See Clarkson, *The History of the Rise, Progress, and Accomplishment of the Abolition of the African Slave-Trade*, ii.143ff.

45. Mirabeau, *Les Bières flottantes des négriers: Un discours non prononcé sur l'abolition de la traite des Noirs (novembre 1789-mars 1790*, ed. M. Dorigny (Saint-Etienne: L'Université de Saint Etienne, 1999), 8ff, 14.

46. See Clarkson, *The History of the Rise, Progress, and Accomplishment of the Abolition of the African Slave-Trade*, ii.517, 523.

47. See Bentham, *Rights, Representation, and Reform (CW)*, xl; see also Burns, 'Bentham and the French Revolution,' 95–114.

48. See Bentham, *Political Tactics (CW)* and *Rights, Representation, and Reform (CW)*.

49. Bentham, *Rights, Representation, and Reform (CW)*, xlii–xliii, xliv.

50. Bentham, *Rights, Representation, and Reform (CW)*, 310.

51. Bentham, *Rights, Representation, and Reform (CW)*, 291.

52. Bentham, *Rights, Representation, and Reform (CW)*, 202.

53. Bentham, *Rights, Representation, and Reform (CW)*, 322–24.

54. J. Bentham, *An Introduction to the Principles of Morals and Legislation*, ed. J. H. Burns and H. L. A. Hart, with a new introduction by F. Rosen (*CW*) (Oxford: Clarendon Press, 1996), 241.

55. See J. Bentham, *Traités de legislation civile et pénale*, 3 vols., ed. E. Dumont (Paris: Chez Bossange, Masson et Besson, 1802), ii.1–236; *Works*, ed. Bowring, i.297–364.

56. Bentham, *Works*, ed. Bowring, i.344.

57. Bentham, *Works*, ed. Bowring, i.344.

58. See Bentham, *Works*, ed. Bowring, i.344–47.

59. Boralevi, *Bentham and the Oppressed*, 150–51.

60. See Boralevi, *Bentham and the Oppressed*, 157–58.

61. See J. Bentham, *Deontology together with a Table of the Springs of Action and Article on Utilitarianism*, ed. A. Goldworth (*CW*) (Oxford: Clarendon Press, 1983), 314–16.

62. See F. Rosen, *Bentham, Byron and Greece: Constitutionalism, Nationalism, and Early Liberal Political Thought* (Oxford: Clarendon Press, 1992), 25–76; *Classical Utilitarianism from Hume to Mill* (London: Routledge, 2003).

63. J. Bentham, *Colonies, Commerce, and Constitutional Law: Rid Yourselves of Ultramaria and Other Writings on Spain and Spanish America*, ed. P. Schofield (*CW*) (Oxford: Clarendon Press, 1995), 128.

64. Bentham, *Colonies, Commerce, and Constitutional Law (CW)*, 129.

65. J. Bentham, *Securities against Misrule and Other Constitutional Writings for Tripoli and Greece (CW)* (Oxford: Clarendon Press, 1990), 134–35.

66. See Bentham, *An Introduction to the Principles of Morals and Legislation (CW)*, 191–4. This is not meant to suggest that Bentham ignored offences arising out of relationships between masters and servants (including slaves); see 239–43.

67. Bentham, *Securities against Misrule* (*CW*), 135.

68. See F. Rosen, *Jeremy Bentham and Representative Democracy: A Study of the Constitutional Code* (Oxford: Clarendon Press, 1983), 19–40.

69. In the manuscripts on "Scotch Reform," written in 1806–1807 at the time of the abolition of the slave trade, Bentham on several occasions conceived of the power of "Judge and Co." over the British people in terms of slavery. See, for example, Bentham Manuscripts, University College, xci. 34 (July 31, 1806), xciv. 307 (April 14, 1807?), xcii. 228 (June 6, 1807), xcii. 164 (June 7, 1807), and xciii. 246 (January 11, 1807), where he wrote: "Your Lordship is in the act of abolishing the slavery of the body by delivering Africans from the tyranny of their avowed despots and oppressors. Advance one step further, my Lord, and deliver Britons from the bondage of the mind imposed upon them by the unavowed and more degrading tyranny of their pretended friends, patrons and benefactors." At one point he referred to earlier writings by Jonathan Swift in a similar vein. See UC xci. 246 (January 28, 1808). I am indebted to Dr. Tony Draper of the Bentham Project for these references.

70. J. Bentham, *Constitutional Code, Volume I*, ed. F. Rosen and J. H. Burns (*CW*) (Oxford: Clarendon Press, 1983), 53–54.

71. Bentham, *Constitutional Code* (*CW*), 455.

72. J. Bentham, *Official Aptitude Maximized; Expense Minimized*, ed. P. Schofield (*CW*) (Oxford: Clarendon Press, 1993), 377.

73. J. Bentham, *First Principles Preparatory to Constitutional Code*, ed. P. Schofield (*CW*) (Oxford: Clarendon Press, 1989), 171.

74. Bentham, *Colonies, Commerce, and Constitutional Law* (*CW*), 264.

75. See, for example, *Deontology* (*CW*), 316.

76. See Bentham, *An Introduction to the Principles of Morals and Legislation* (*CW*), 11.

77. Boralevi, *Bentham and the Oppressed*, 153–54, confuses matters somewhat in suggesting that Bentham's later vehemence against slavery and the slave trade was due to the fact that these writings were mainly unpublished. She particularly examines a draft of Letter 16 for *Rid Yourselves of Ultramaria*, which is particularly outspoken. She could not have known (as the text had not then been edited as part of the *Collected Works*) that Bentham himself rejected this draft (UC clxxii. 331–34, 344–43, July 19–20, 1821) and wrote another nearly a year later (UC clxxii. 345–48, April 6, 1822), which he then revised a week later (UC viii. 131–34, April 12, 1822). It is possible that copies of the final version were sent to Bowring in Spain and elsewhere. See note at UC viii. 131, dated April 21, 1822, and *Colonies, Commerce, and Constitutional Law* (*CW*), lv–lvi. While the final version was not formally published until 1995 in the *Collected Works*, it was available for circulation. Nevertheless, there are considerable differences between the first and later versions. The early version ranges more widely over the evil of slave trading and slave owning, while the final version sticks more narrowly to comparisons between various countries, such as Spain, the United States, England, and France. Bentham had obviously selected a particular rhetorical focus to persuade the Spanish "to clear her morals and reputation from the taint of the Slave Trade and Slave-holding" (UC viii. 131, April 12, 1822), and he excluded material that might offend the Spanish. Boralevi is only partly correct in seeing Bentham's vehemence in his later writings as being due to some of them never having been published rather than, as I have argued, to his strengthening radicalism.

In the final version, which he did circulate, he referred to the slave trade, as we have seen, as "this foulest of all political and moral leprosies" (*Colonies, Commerce, and Constitutional Law* (*CW*), 128). I am indebted to Professor Philip Schofield for providing me with edited transcripts of the three versions of the text.

78. See Howard Temperley, *British Antislavery 1833–1870* (London: Longman, 1972), xi–xii.

79. Temperley, *British Antislavery*, 10.

80. See Samuel Clyde McCulloch, ed., *British Humanitarianism, Essays Honoring Frank J. Klingberg* (Philadelphia: The Church Historical Society, 1950), 12. Although Klingberg distinguished between an evangelical party and a reform party (including Bentham), he believed that both contributed to the antislavery movement (F. Klingberg, *The Anti-Slavery Movement in England* (New Haven: Yale University Press, 1926), 51–53, 130. See also Charles Blacton, "Convicts, Colonists and Progress in Australia, 1800–1850" in *British Humanitarian Essays*, 34–35; Ernest Marshall Howse, *Saints in Politics, The "Clapham Sect" and the Growth of Freedom* (London: George Allen and Unwin, 1971), 131, 135. There was no hostility toward religion in the Lansdowne circle, but Bentham himself on several occasions, raised questions in manuscripts about the connection between Christianity and slavery: "A religion which suffices not to restrain men from the constant practice of the most flagitious enormities, what can it be good for, what the value of it, what the use of it?" He continued in this vein: "Be it what it may with reference to the happiness of a future life—of that life in comparison of which the present is but as a grain of sand in the universe—in its effects on the happiness of the present life, would such a religion be any thing better than a nuisance? the prevalence of it any thing better than a public calamity? the support of it than a public grievance?" (UC clxxii. 335, July 19, 1821). Bentham took a particular interest in the case of Arthur Hodge, who was executed in Tortola in 1811 for causing his slave, Prosper, to be flogged to death for not paying 3d of 6d of a fine for negligence. Hodge had attended Oriel College, Oxford, as a "Gentleman Commoner" and was well instructed in the Church of England. From the evidence he seemed to have indulged in the maltreatment, if not the murder, of other slaves (including the use of torture—e.g., pouring boiling water down their throats), but he was much sustained by his religion at his trial, his final farewells with his family, and his execution. While Bentham could accept that religion might fail in the theological and moral instruction actually given, he wondered if there were problems with the instruction itself, particularly with regard to justice and the acceptance of human misery on earth. See BL Add. MSS 29,808, fos. 200–202 (September 4, 1811), fos. 58–59 (September 4, 1811), 29,807, fo. 47 (July 17, 1815), 29,809, fo. 421 (July 28, 1815), 29,809, fo. 253 (May 4, 1819). My thanks to Ms. Catherine Fuller for supplying me with copies of these transcripts from Bentham's religious writings in the British Library. The passage quoted from the UC manuscript was brought to my attention by Professor Schofield. See also *The Trial of Arthur Hodge, Esq.*, 2nd ed. (London: John Harding, 1811).

81. See F. Rosen, *Bentham, Byron, and Greece*, 175, 236, 239.

82. James Walvin, "The Public Campaign in England against Slavery, 1787–1834" in *The Abolition of the Atlantic Slave Trade, Origins and Effects in Europe, Africa, and the Americas*, ed. D. Eltis and J. Walvin (Madison: The University of Wisconsin Press, 1981), 75.

83. Walvin, "The Public Campaign in England against Slavery," 74.

84. Walvin, "The Public Campaign in England against Slavery," 71. On popular opinion and culture at this time, see J. R. Oldfield, *Popular Politics and British Anti-Slavery: The Mobilization of Public Opinion against the Slave Trade, 1787–1807* (Manchester: Manchester University Press, 1995).

85. Seymour Drescher, *From Slavery to Freedom: Comparative Studies in the Rise and Fall of Atlantic Slavery* (Basingstoke: Macmillan Press Ltd., 1999), 2–3. See Seymour Drescher, *Econocide: British Slavery in the Era of Abolition* (Pittsburgh: Pittsburgh University Press, 1977); Eric Williams, *Capitalism and Slavery* (Chapel Hill: University of North Carolina Press, 1944).

86. Drescher, *From Slavery to Freedom*, 15. See also Judith Jennings, *The Business of Abolishing the British Slave Trade, 1783–1807* (London: Frank Cass, 1997).

87. See Howard Temperley, "The Ideology of Anti-Slavery," in *The Abolition of the Atlantic Slave Trade*, ed. D. Eltis and J. Walvin, 28. See also D. Turley, "British Anti-slavery Reassessed," in *Rethinking the Age of Reform: Britain in 1780–1850*, ed. A. Burns and J. Innes (Cambridge: Cambridge University Press, 2003), 198–99.

88. See above, note 50. In *Constitutional Code* (*CW*), 142–43, Bentham's legislators declare their opposition to conquest and war (except for self-defense).

89. My thanks to Professor J. H. Burns for kindly reading a draft of this article and making numerous suggestions for its improvement. I am also grateful to Dr. Mark Philp for a helpful bibliographical suggestion and to the two editors of this volume for their kindness and patience.

3

Jeremy Bentham

Legislator of the World?

Jennifer Pitts

UTILITARIANS AND THE BRITISH EMPIRE

The pervasive influence of utilitarians in the nineteenth century on the justification and exercise of British imperial power in India has led many to conclude that utilitarianism was, from its inception, an imperialist theory.[1] Eric Stokes's classic work *The English Utilitarians and India* established the important role that Benthamites—from James and John Stuart Mill, to colonial administrators, to the professors at Haileybury College who trained them—played in the expansion of British rule in India throughout the nineteenth century. Stokes relates an anecdote about Lord William Bentinck, who in 1827 had just been appointed governor-general of India. As James Mill delightedly reported to Bentham, Bentinck had told him at a farewell dinner, "I am going to British India; but I shall not be Governor-General. It is you that will be Governor-General."[2] Indeed, reformers directly or indirectly influenced by Bentham, men who believed they were carrying out the Benthamite project, were powerful in Indian administration throughout the nineteenth century. Benthamites who felt they were too regularly thwarted in England by entrenched powers and the recalcitrant body of common law reveled in the opportunity that they believed despotic power provided for the establishment of a complete legal code (what Bentham liked to call a *pannomion*) and a rational bureaucracy.[3]

A closer look at Bentham's own views on empire, however, reveals significant differences between Bentham's ideas about European imperialism and those of his followers. Not only was Bentham an often vehement opponent of the Spanish, French, and British empires, in writings such as "Emancipate Your Colonies!" and "Rid Yourselves of Ultramaria," beginning in the 1790s and continuing into the 1820s, but he also largely resisted the judgmental stance later utilitarians took toward non-European cultures, as well as their civilizing aspirations. A study of his "emancipation" writings and his ideas about British India should serve as a corrective to a pervasive view that either utilitarianism or English liberalism, as such, were imperialist. To John Stuart Mill's claim that "despotism is a legitimate mode of government in dealing with barbarians, provided the end be their improvement, and the means justified by actually effecting that end,"[4] we have Bentham's likely response: "Reform the world by example, you act generously and wisely: reform the world by force, you might as well reform the moon, and the design is fit only for lunatics."[5]

Bentham's views on conquest, expansion, and colonial rule were not entirely consistent, as is to be expected given his remarkably long career, his voluminous and often unedited output, and his diverse audiences. A wide range of related considerations also caused his views on colonialism to vary, including his fitful pacifism, his periodically expressed hopes that emigration might aid Europe's poor, and the differences between settler colonies such as Latin America and colonies like British India that primarily involved the domination of a large indigenous population.[6] Still, it is important not to settle the ambiguities in Bentham's own writings by reading back onto him the views of his successors, as many interpreters have done.[7] If we attempt to read Bentham without attributing to him the arguments of later utilitarians and "Benthamites," what emerges is a thinker deeply skeptical about European colonial rule and much less presumptuous than he has widely been taken to be. This article revisits Bentham's work in an effort to recover the critical stance toward colonial rule afforded by his own political and moral views, often far more democratic and broad-minded than those of many later utilitarians. By calling attention to significant departures from Bentham's thought introduced by the later thinkers, the article also tries to reassess some of the sources of justification for colonial rule in Britain in the early nineteenth century, formative years in the development of the British empire, especially in India.

The concerns that Bentham brought to bear when considering colonial rule, in particular his belief that colonial rulers and administrators could never be trusted to rule well and his hostility to the notion of civilizing non-Europeans, stand in sharp contrast to the technocratic and cultural confidence of Bentham's successors. Several philosophical positions in particular stand out as introduced wholly by Bentham's followers and quite alien to his own theory: their narrow and hierarchical understanding of progress; their belief that British rule of "backward" peoples was both morally justified (even a moral duty) and good for the conquered nations; and their conviction that certain peoples were unfit for self-government. Bernard Williams has remarked about utilitarianism generally that "it is not surprising that one should be reminded of colonial administrators, running on a system of indirect rule."[8] While the comment seems apt enough at first glance, I shall argue that Bentham did not regard utilitarianism as legitimating the sort of dictatorial imperial rule that characterized the hopes of many of his successors: the imposition from above without concern for the opinions of the ruled or for their interests as they themselves understood them.

The curious evolution of utilitarian theory in Britain on the subject of empire can perhaps best be observed in the writings of Bentham and John Stuart Mill, the philosophically richest thinkers in the tradition; James Mill, who is also examined here, played a crucial intermediary role in the transformation of the utilitarian tradition. James Mill showed Bentham's influence in several articles he wrote to deny that colonies benefited the conquering country and to argue instead that sinister private interests foisted colonies on European nations.[9] Yet he also wrote the *History of British India*, a work, highly influential in colonial circles, which was nonetheless remarkable even for its time in its disparagement of Indians' intellectual and moral capacities. Mill concluded that Indians were utterly incapable of any participation in their government, which, he believed, should be a "simple form of arbitrary government" by Britain.[10] When recommending policies toward India, the elder Mill was driven far more by his ideas about Indians' mental and cultural deficiencies than by his doubts as a political economist about the colony's benefit to Great Britain.

John Stuart Mill, in so many arenas a great critic of his father, adopted many of James Mill's central claims about India and British government there: most importantly, that there was a sharp dichotomy between civilized and uncivilized nations, that Indians were barbarians incapable of self-government, and that British "despotism" was the most appropriate form of government for the country for the foreseeable future. Mill called his father "the historian who first threw the light of reason on Hindoo society" and had only praise for the *History of British India* in his *Autobiography*.[11] J. S. Mill's writings on India and empire, and his career in the East India Company, long ignored, have received considerable attention in recent years, although this scrutiny has not extended to Mill's intellectual debts to and departures from Bentham.[12]

As I have suggested, the selective reading of Bentham's views on colonies began with his own disciples, and they indeed bear considerable responsibility for the misrepresentation of Bentham that has become so widespread.[13] James Mill was most influential in this regard, for it was he who took the greatest interest in governing India and who attached the utilitarian name to his narrow-minded descriptions of Indian civilization and to his own projects for the country's domination and improvement.[14] Although there is little on record of Bentham's own judgments of James Mill's imperial projects, what we have is instructive. The following sentence is most often cited as proof of Bentham's desire to improve India by transforming its legal (and thereby its social) structure: "Mill will be the living executive—I shall be the dead legislative of British India."[15] The sentence is quoted by Stokes, Donald Winch, Uday Mehta, and many others to suggest that it expresses Bentham's fond hope of civilizing backward peoples. The rest of the original passage, however, which is never cited, shows that Bentham said it with his characteristic irony and with the odd relish with which he contemplated his own death and afterlife: "Twenty years after I am dead, I shall be despot, sitting in my chair with Dapple in my hand, and wearing one of the coats I wear now" (Dapple was the name Bentham gave his walking stick).[16] Bentham went on to suggest that Mill was wrong to believe that his project of legislating for India was his own as well, and that the intellectual and political distance between the men was far greater than Mill understood:

> His creed of politics results less from love for the many, than from hatred for the few. It is too much under the influence of selfish and dissocial affection. . . . His manner of speaking is oppressive and overbearing. He comes to me as if he wore a mask upon his face. His interests he deems to be closely connected with mine, as he has a prospect of introducing a better system of judicial procedure in British India. His book on British India abounds with bad English, which made it to me a disagreeable book. His account of the superstitions of the Hindoos made me melancholy.[17]

In the same paragraph, John Bowring, a member of the first generation of Bentham's disciples and his amanuensis and editor, quotes Bentham's view that Mill had "an abominable opinion" with respect to the inaptitude of women, and one "scarcely less abominable" that men should not hold office till they are forty years of age. On these issues, as on the capacity of non-Europeans for self-government, James Mill showed a considerably narrower mind than his mentor.

Even Bowring, who reported these differences between the men and knew at first hand Bentham's doubts about Mill's ideas and policies, believed that Mill's views on international politics represented a fair approximation of Bentham's own.[18] Bowring, like both Mills, praised the pacific implications of utilitarianism for politics among "civilized" nations but then abruptly and unthinkingly cut non-Europeans out of consideration. "The civilized part of the world is coming, day by day, nearer to just principles of international intercourse," Bowring wrote in his introduction to Bentham's works. "France affording a highway for our communication with our great oriental empire, and conveying through its government telegraph the earliest news of our operations in the east, is a symptom of progress which it would have afforded Bentham the liveliest gratification to witness."[19] The complacency of Bowring's phrase "our operations in the east," however, shared nothing with Bentham's own ambivalence toward imperial rule.

If John Stuart Mill overcame his father's prejudices about women's capacities, he remained uncritical about his father's view of the people of "backward" nations, adopting and even elaborating it himself.[20] Mill himself emphasized his distance from Bentham, but Mill's account of the evolution of utilitarianism must be read with a critical eye. For Mill claimed to humanize an austere doctrine that was insensitive to humanity's higher aspirations, to temper Bentham's theory with a respect for poetry and traditions.[21] He suggested that he had taken a narrow doctrine, one incapable of understanding most of the ways that people have interpreted and responded to the human condition, and broadened it, pluralized it.[22] In some senses, as I shall suggest, precisely the opposite is the case. Unfortunately for Bentham and for our understanding of the history of utilitarianism (and British liberalism more broadly), James and J. S. Mill's versions of the story of utilitarianism and empire have largely prevailed.

If we take seriously Bentham's many remarks on the dangers and immorality of imperial rule, we will be more skeptical than either Bentham's immediate successors or his more recent readers that Bentham would have celebrated the consolidation of the British Empire in India. We will be able to make better sense of the writings and historical events that led Elie Halévy to elide the distance between Bentham and later utilitarians and to suggest obliquely that those later utilitarians were merely continuing after his death an imperial project that Bentham had initiated:

> Bentham was the disciple of Adam Smith and up to the end of his life stood as an adversary of the colonial system: when he became a Radical, his economic objections were reinforced by political objections against a system which handed over the colonists to the mercy of functionaries sent out by the metropolis. Yet England was preserving a part of her colonial empire and founding new colonies. Were Bentham and his disciples going to demand that all the colonies should be abandoned? Colonisation is a fact before which their logic capitulated; and besides the logic of their system is double: in so far as their philosophy advocates the artificial and despotic identification of interests, might they not be tempted to consider the colonial empire as a vast field for experiments in philanthropy and reform? Bentham had always dreamed of making laws for India: now that James Mill occupied an important post in the India Company, might not his dream become a reality?[23]

This passage wrongly attributes to Bentham the notion that interests should be identified "despotically" rather than by people—any people—themselves; it also resorts to the weak and unexamined claim that the utilitarians' "logic" simply "capitulated" before the tempting prospect of a captive legislative laboratory.[24] In fact, however, Bentham did not capitulate in this way, and James Mill, for his part, never shared Smith or Bentham's moral objections to empire. With regard to colonies, there was no unitary utilitarian logic but rather a transformation of the tradition that reflected a broader shift in European thought on empire from the late eighteenth to the early nineteenth century, away from profound doubts about colonial aspirations and toward vehement and often self-righteous support for them.

BENTHAM'S CRITIQUE OF COLONIAL RULE

Bentham held that justice and prudence demanded the emancipation of colonial possessions. He believed that one of the greatest advantages that new countries such as the United States and, later, Greece (after its independence from the Ottoman empire) had over the European powers was their freedom from the burden of colonial possessions.[25] The early 1790s are often cited as the period of Bentham's turn away from enlightened despotism in favor of democracy and universal suffrage.[26] These were also the years during which Bentham first expressed his opposition to colonialism. In 1789, he wrote a series of open letters to the Comte de Mirabeau in an effort to influence the proceedings of France's newly assembled Estates General. One of these letters, arguing against French colonialism, was expanded and published in 1793 as the first of his pamphlets entitled "Emancipate Your Colonies!"[27] That pamphlet includes, in rapid-fire succession, most of Bentham's anticolonial arguments. He opened: "*Emancipate your Colonies.* Justice, consistency, policy, economy, honour, generosity, all demand it of you: all this you shall see. Conquer, you are still but running the race of vulgar ambition: emancipate, you strike out a new path to glory. Conquer, it is by your armies: emancipate, the conquest is your own, and made over yourselves. To give freedom at the expense of others, is but conquest in disguise: to rise superior to conquerors, the sacrifice must be your own" (RRR 291). Bentham revived these arguments in the early 1820s in an attempt to persuade the new liberal government in Spain to emancipate its colonies in the New World. Many of his arguments against colonial rule remained unchanged.[28]

Many of Bentham's arguments against colonies were, not surprisingly, based on calculations of interest. As he wrote in "Rid Yourselves of Ultramaria," written as a sort of open letter to the Spanish people ("Spaniards!"), "Will you sacrifice—will you sit and see your rulers sacrifice—every substantial interest to the fantastic interest that has its root in national pride?"[29] He believed that empires undermined the greatest happiness of the greatest number in both metropole and colony. He argued that they were financially unsound and inefficient; that they exacted a tax on the poor of the metropole for the benefit of the wealthy; that they encouraged unnecessary growth of the state's military apparatus but left the metropole vulnerable; and that they were fueled by illusory, misguided, and dangerous conceptions of honor and glory.

Bentham's interest-based or economic arguments against colonies were certainly typical of a strong strand of late-eighteenth-century suspicion of colonial rule, a strand that included figures such as Adam Smith.[30] Bentham believed, with Smith and others, that colonies drained national resources, bloated the military, and jeopardized the security of the metropole. He reminded metropolitan populations that colonial rule was not in their interest but in that of a cabal of their rulers: that they, too, were victims of colonialism. He contended that colonies could not be profitable without being oppressive and that the oppression necessary to extract a profit from a distant colony was both unjust and likely to provoke a costly and destructive war: "Over the inhabitants of the dependency in question, power cannot be exercised—from them such profit cannot be extracted, without manifest injury done to them, without manifest oppression exercised upon them. . . . [If] the maintenance of the power of the ruling people, or rather the rulers of the ruling people, is persevered in, here then is war, civil war."[31] Many of Bentham's anticolonial arguments draw little from utilitarian principles but appeal instead to equity, glory, and the psychology of power and corruption. "If the happiness of mankind is your object, and the declaration of rights your guide, you will set them free. . . . The sooner the better: it costs you but a word: and by that word you cover yourselves with the purest glory" (iv.418). It is this complex assortment of arguments that is wholly missing from James Mill's critique of colonies, which adopted the Benthamite economic position and ignored the rest of Bentham's views.

Unlike James and J. S. Mill, Bentham believed that colonial rulers could not know the subject population's interests better than the people themselves and therefore could not rule them better than they could rule themselves. Bentham had long been committed to the necessity of publicity and public opinion as a way of curbing corruption and misrule.[32] While the Mills made similar arguments regarding civilized nations, both believed that barbarous countries were incapable of benefiting not only from legislative assemblies but even from the exercise of public opinion more broadly understood. J. S. Mill argued that "the public of India afford no assistance in their own government. They are not ripe for doing so by means of representative government; they are not even in a condition to make effectual appeals to the people of this country" (CW 30:49); his solution was technocratic rule by East India Company civil servants. James Mill made clear that in addition to thinking Indians unable to exercise the power of public opinion, he believed them incapable even of perceiving and acting on their own interests.[33] Bentham had, that is, a respect unmatched by any of his successors for *everyone's* ability to know what was in their interest and consequently to govern themselves. Bentham's lack of interest in distinctions between civilized and barbarous peoples, which J. S. Mill criticized as a lack of historical understanding,[34] enabled him to make the same

argument for all colonial peoples, whether European settlers or native inhabitants: they knew their own interests far better than any distant metro-
politans, who were sure to be ignorant about their lives and uninterested
in their fate, and whose colonial policy would necessarily be dictated by
their own interests.

The opening pages of "Emancipate Your Colonies!" are written in a crisp,
direct style reminiscent of Tom Paine's, with a series of rhetorical questions
exposing the absurdities and hypocrisies of empire. "You choose your own
government: why are not other people to choose theirs? Do you seriously
mean to govern the world, and do you call that *liberty?*"[35] Speaking as an
honorary citizen of France, Bentham invoked the principles and icons of the
revolution and demonstrated the incoherence and injustice of conquest from
the republican perspective: "With fraternity in your lips, you declare war
against mankind" (RRR 308). "One common Bastille inclosed them and you.
You knock down the jailor, you let yourselves out, you keep them in, and
put yourselves into his place" (RRR 292). Bentham emphasized the inherent
problems of distance and made the case, to which he was to return in almost
all his writings on colonies, that Europeans could not possibly imagine the
lives, desires, and problems of subjects—whether of European descent or
not—thousands of miles away. "What care you, or what can you care, about
them? . . . What conception can you frame to yourselves of manners and
modes of life so different from your own? When will you ever see them? . . .
If they suffer, will their cries ever wound your ears? Will their wretchedness
ever meet your eyes?" (RRR 293). Indeed, Bentham often intertwined his arguments from interest with more abstract appeals to justice, nature, and humanity. "To yield to justice is what must happen to the mightiest and proud-
est nations," he wrote. "Sitting where you do, call it not courage to drive on
in the track of war and violence. There is nothing in such courage that is not
compatible with the basest cowardice" (RRR 307).[36]

Bentham never addressed such a critical pamphlet to the British government, and this fact, along with the essay "On the Influence of Time and Place
in Matters of Legislation," has led to the claim that Bentham was an enthusiastic supporter of British rule over India and was eager to see his own legislative reforms tested there.[37] Like Adam Smith, however, Bentham was
surely well aware of the futility of most appeals to a country to free its
colonies.[38] In the cases of France and Spain, conscious of the great respect
in which republicans in both countries held him, he appears to have nour-
ished hopes that he could actually persuade them to give up their colonies.[39]
He wrote to each at a time when a new liberal republican regime had just
come to power, and he seems to have believed that his rational and passionate arguments could help them make a clean break with their countries'
colonial pasts. He knew only too well of his limited influence in Britain, having failed, disastrously and famously, to persuade the British government to

institute his panopticon prison-workhouse in the 1790s. The absence of an "Emancipation" pamphlet to the British may well have been due to his sense that such a gesture would be useless. It was not a result of Bentham's enthusiasm about the benefits of British imperial rule, about which he wrote venomously in the course of his writings on France and Spain; indeed, he criticized the entire British political system that had fostered the empire.

Thus, we find Bentham's judgments of the British Empire, both moral and practical, scattered throughout his anticolonial writings. To the French, he wrote: "By emancipating your own colonies, you may emancipate ours: by setting the example, you may open our eyes and force us to follow it"; and "By emancipating our colonies you may thus purify our parliament: you may purify our constitution—you must not destroy it. Excuse us, we are a slow people, and a little obstinate" (RRR 310). It should be noted that unlike James Mill (who also argued for the emancipation of Spanish America), Bentham did not, in these arguments, tend to distinguish between settler colonies and colonies populated mostly by indigenous peoples: the arguments against empire were the same for all. For instance, he wrote to the Spanish,

> "Well" (say you) "and you with all your foreign dependencies all over the world, how do you in England manage?" Manage indeed? it would require volumes upon volumes to attempt giving your any thing like an explanation—in anything like detail. In a general point of view, a few words may serve. Uncertainty, inconsistency, complication, delay, vexation and expense, all factitious and enormous—denial of justice, oppression, extortion, corruptive influence, despotism. Enquire in East, West, South: to the North not, because no dependencies have we there. Enquire in Hindostan, in the West Indies, in South Africa, in Canada, in New Holland, in Mauritius, in Saint Helena, in the Seven Islands, over which, on pretence of protection, our rulers have extended their own yet rotten sceptre.[40]

Bentham lamented Britain's insatiable acquisition of colonies since her loss of America: colonies "pursued with that eagerness and that disastrous success, of which the bitter fruits continue to be forced down our throats in such sad abundance. Witness the last-gathered of them—the Ionian isles: and that English '*protection*,' the infamy of which, without any of the profit, vies so successfully with that of the primaeval Persian tyranny."[41] In short, Bentham viewed British colonialism with the same disapproval that he did French and Spanish, even if he described his opposition to it in less detail.[42]

Bentham did call on the British government to give up its colonies and its colonial ambitions in an essay that Bowring published as Bentham's "Plan for an Universal and Perpetual Peace."[43] There Bentham pursued the two classic eighteenth-century arguments against colonization: that it is unjust to the conquered and foolish from the perspective of the metropolitan population. The plan offered as its first proposition, "That it is not the interest of Great Britain to have any foreign dependencies whatsoever."[44] As Bentham wrote in "Panopticon versus New South Wales," his essay comparing his own prison design to the Australian penal colony, "My Lord—to confess the truth, I never could bring myself to see any real advantage derived by the mother country, from anything that ever bore the name of a *Colony*" (iv.206).[45]

The argument he made as well to the French and Spanish, that distance alone ensures that colonies cannot be well governed, takes on particular poignancy here with his reference to the cruelties exposed by the impeachment trial in the 1780s and 1790s of Warren Hastings, the former governor-general of Bengal: "Distant mischiefs make little impression on those on whom the remedying of them depends. A single murder committed in London makes more impression than if thousands of murders and other cruelties were committed in the East Indies. The situation of Hastings, only because he was present, excited compassion in those who heard all of the cruelties committed by him with indifference" (ii.547–48). This passage was one of several in which Bentham expressed his support for the prosecutors in the Hastings impeachment trial; he maintained this support well after the long trial had wearied the patience of even its most sympathetic early advocates.[46]

Even if James and John Stuart Mill questioned whether possession of colonies benefited the European colonizers, both insisted that colonial rule benefited its backward subjects. Bentham never adopted such ardor for despotic colonial rule, though his views about whether Indians—as well as American colonists—could benefit from British rule remain somewhat enigmatic and indeed contradictory. Several passages scattered throughout his work, that is, conflict rather starkly with his many strong claims about the damage and injustices colonial rule inflicted on the colonized. In the "Institute of Political Economy" of 1801-1804, Bentham claimed that both Egypt and America would have benefited from British government, because in addition to having a government of "universal and perpetual security," Britain's "moral conduct forms the natural standard in points exempt from regulation."[47] Egypt, subject to a religion "of which incurable barbarity and ignorance seem to be inseparable features," and the new American states, an "unvaried scene of sordid selfishness, of political altercation, of discomfort, of ignorance, of drunkenness," might have profited from the stability provided by new or continued British rule. Donald Winch has described the period of 1800-1804 as one in which "Bentham's Toryism seems to have reasserted itself," possibly in response to developments in France, and it is to this revived Toryism that he plausibly attributes the "patriotic sentiments that verge on jingoism" expressed in such passages.[48] Certainly they run counter to the sustained anticolonial arguments Bentham developed at some length in both earlier and later works, including his strong claims about the impossibility of governing well from a great distance and his persistent belief that colonial rule was in the hands of a small group of "sinister interests" rather than in the hands of beneficent and farsighted governors.[49]

Finally, Bentham's discussion of India in "Emancipate Your Colonies!" also expresses some doubts about Indians' capacity for self-government: "The power of Tippoo is no more. Would the tree of liberty grow there, if planted? Would the declaration of rights translate into Shanscrit? Would Bramin, Chetree, Bice, Sooder, and Hallachore meet on equal ground? If not, you may find some difficulty in giving them to themselves. . . . If it is determined they must have masters, you will then look out for the least bad ones that could take them."[50] He suggested that France sell its Indian possessions to the British East India Company, and he responded with sarcasm to the anticipated French accusation that he was a hireling of the Company, arguing that even if he were, the French should see that the exchange would be in their interest. In the end, though, it mattered little from France's perspective, he thought, who ruled India. "*How* you part with the poor people who are now your slaves, is after all a subordinate consideration: the essential thing is to get rid of them. . . . Whatever be their rights, they have no such right as that of forcing you to govern them to your own prejudice." We see, then, that Bentham was capable of suggesting that democratic self-government was unlikely to emerge in India in his day, although the suggestion was framed in terms of questions and through vague, impersonal phrases such as "if it be determined." The reference to the declaration of rights, something toward which Bentham was notoriously hostile, makes the passage all the more odd.[51]

In another of the few passages in which he directly addressed British rule over India, Bentham produced quite an ambiguous answer to the question of whether the subject populations would benefit from an end to colonial rule:

> On the question—by the metropolitan country shall this or that distant dependency be kept up?—there are two *sides*—two *interests*—that require consideration: that of the metropolis herself and that of the dependency. . . . On the question whether [the dominion of British India] would be for the advantage of *Brithibernia*, much might be said on both sides. On the question as applied to the nation of British India,—in the minds of those who have read the documents, and in particular the work of the so well-informed, intelligent, and incontestably well-intentioned Bishop Heber,—scarcely can there be a doubt. By the withdrawal of the English regiments from British India, in what respect or degree would Hindoos or Mahometans profit? Answer—in much the same as did the ancient *Britons* by the withdrawal of the *Roman* legions.[52]

Did the ancient Britons, by the withdrawal of the Roman armies, gain their liberty, or were they merely reduced to barbarism? Either view was certainly possible in Bentham's day, and he himself gives no indication here about which he meant; indeed, it is possible that he intended both answers at once. Despite the decisiveness of Bentham's language, the reference to Bishop Heber does not make the passage much more straightforward. Bishop Heber, Bishop of Calcutta in the 1820s and a religious and political moderate, certainly supported missionary efforts in India and probably believed, on the whole, that British rule benefited Indians, but he by no means considered Indians barbarous or hopeless. On the contrary, he had more respect than was usual among Britons of his day for Indians' intelligence and cultural achievements, and he "disagreed with the policy of excluding even upperclass Indians from participation in government."[53] When Bentham did support certain British policies in India, it was in preference to some other, far worse, British policy, rather than from a desire to perpetuate British colonial rule. Thus when he declared that he would have voted for Fox's East India Bill (the bill supported and largely drafted by Edmund Burke), Bentham outlined the appalling alternatives:

> Mr. Fox's E. India Bill I regarded as eminently good with reference to the natives, as bad rather than otherwise with reference to the *permanent* interests of our own island. It was good in as far as it took the people out of the hands of by far the worst constituted species of government conceivable, and that a secret and irresponsible one: the government of a fluctuating body of merchants . . . residing at the opposite end of the world. It was bad in as far as it concentrated a large body of influence and vested it in the hands of the Ministers. I should notwithstanding at that time have voted for the bill: by hopes from it in favour of the people of Hindostan being much stronger than my fears from it in favour of the people of Great Britain. I should have voted for it in preference to Mr. Pitt's. But I should not . . . now. The goodness of Mr. Pitt's measure has been proved by experience. A happy choice of persons at the outset put things into a good frame: in that frame, having once got into it, it seems reasonable to hope they will continue.[54]

Similarly, although the support Bentham gave to James Mill's proposed reforms for India was always grudging, he, for instance, preferred them to what he called "the abominable existing system" (x.590). The passages cited above are those in Bentham's oeuvre that I believe stand most starkly in tension with his critique of European colonies. In seeking to recover the sharply critical stance that characterized so much of his thought on empire and to resist reading into Bentham the views of later utilitarians, we must acknowledge as well the inconsistencies in his enormous body of writings. The fully articulated argument for the benefits of colonial rule for the conquered that we find in James and John Stuart Mill does not appear, nor did Bentham ever produce the sort of theory of progress they did to support that argument. He also, as we have seen, wrote powerfully against the cruelties, injustices, and presumptions of Europe's colonizers to a degree that followers such as the Mills did not.

BENTHAM'S LEGISLATIVE AMBITIONS AND THEIR LIMITS

It is clear that Bentham was deeply critical of European colonial rule on both moral and practical grounds and that he was not, as his successors were, an enthusiastic supporter of the British government in India. I have argued, as well, that the passage most commonly cited as evidence for Bentham's own appetite for colonial rule ("I shall be the dead legislative of British India") is not, when read in its entirety, the clear indication of his colonial aspirations most commentators claim it to be. Bentham's legislative ambitions, to be sure, were notorious, and titles such as "Idea of a Proposed All-Comprehensive Body of Law, with an Accompaniment of Reasons" (1827), and "Constitutional Code; for the Use of All Nations and All Governments Professing Liberal Opinions" (1830), have encouraged the idea that he believed himself capable of legislating for the world. It has been an easy step for his followers and later readers to assume that Bentham was particularly keen on legislating for India and keeping the colony under British rule in order to see his reforms through.

In addition to the "dead legislative" passage, two other pieces of writing form the rest of the evidence usually presented that Bentham supported the British empire as a vehicle for his aspiration to legislate for the world: a short passage in a letter to Henry Dundas, president of the East India Company's Board of Control; and the "Essay on the Influence of Time and Place in Matters of Legislation," which discusses the role of culture and climate in law and society by examining what steps would be necessary to make British laws suitable for application to Bengal. Eric Stokes's *English Utilitarians and India*, the source usually cited by later commentators, claims that "Bentham had always been eager to take a hand in framing the law system of India. In 1793 he had made an offer of his services, as a sort of Indian Solon, to Dundas."[55] In the letter Stokes cites, Bentham made no such grandiose claims; nor does the letter indicate that Bentham supported the empire because he believed India needed British, or indeed utilitarian, legislators. Instead, it merely observes that

> something in the way of legislation may be deemed wanting for Hindostan. Divested of all local prejudices, but not the less sensible of their force, and of the necessity of respecting them, I could with the same facility turn my hand to the concerns of that distant country, as to those of the parish in which I live.[56]

The passage instead suggests that Bentham believed that the British rulers of India (whatever he might have thought of the justice or prudence of their position) would need to legislate for their subjects and that he thought himself capable of writing appropriate legislation. For a fuller account of how Bentham thought one should go about applying laws that one had necessarily developed in one cultural and historical context to a quite different context, we must turn to the "Essay on the Influence of Time and Place in Matters of Legislation."[57]

Bentham seems to have intended the essay to form a part of the *Theory of Legislation*.[58] It opens with the presumed response of the larger work's reader to its author's seemingly limitless ambition to legislate for everywhere and all time. Bentham's apparent insensibility to cultural particulars, his arrogant confidence in his own ability to legislate for the world, is still considered one of his great failings, so this essay is of particular interest, for it directly addresses the question of how feasible it might be to legislate universally. The essay demonstrates Bentham's awareness of the problem, as well as the limits of his understanding. Characteristically, he posed the question in abstract, general terms:

> To give the question at once a universal form: What is the influence of the circumstances of place and time in matters of legislation? What are the coincidences, and what the diversities, which ought to subsist between the laws established in different countries and at different periods, supposing them in each instance the best that can be established? (i.171)

In order to illustrate his argument, Bentham adopted England as his "standard" and Bengal as the country to be studied in order to determine to what degree climate, custom, religion, present laws, and other factors would make it necessary to alter the "standard" legal code for its new application.

Why England and Bengal? The explicit reasons Bentham gave for his choices of theme and variation were not what we might expect from the standard portrait of the nineteenth-century British imperialist, for he did not claim to choose England because its laws were best, or Bengal because he, as a Briton, wanted to legislate for a backward India.[59] Rather, he chose England, he wrote, because he knew it best, and because he was partial, "if to any" country, to England. He chose Bengal because it (unlike Canada, for instance) provided a strong contrast to England in climate and manners but was a country that, given British rule, could be expected to have English laws imposed on it (whereas, he wrote, it would be difficult to imagine such an event occurring in Russia).[60] For the purposes of the essay—that is, for the purposes of this clearly artificial exercise of legislative translation—Bentham "indulged" himself in a "magnificent and presumptuous dream" that his country's laws were the best possible laws.[61] About actual English laws, however, Bentham remained as critical as ever: having developed piecemeal from their origins in a "barbarous age," they were often incoherent, unnecessarily complex, badly articulated, and likely to promote corruption. "The farther we penetrate into the recesses of English law (taking utility for our guide)," Bentham wrote, "the better shall we be convinced that . . . for the greater part of it, it is a piece of cobweb work, spun out of fantastic conceits and verbal analogies, rather than a mass of substantial justice cast in the mould of reason."[62]

Frustration with the absurdities and corruptions of the British legal system had driven Bentham from a legal career as a very young man.[63] In Bengal, he claimed in "Time and Place," these imperfections were compounded by the inappropriateness of British laws to Bengali society, by Britons' failure to see the problems with their laws, and by the incapacity of metropolitan laws to deal with colonial circumstances—especially the rampant greed and corruption that despotic rule encouraged. The imposition of a foreign legal system (especially such a mediocre one) inevitably led to resentment among the conquered people, and chauvinism prevented the British rulers from acknowledging its flaws. "When a body of very imperfect laws, such as are the best of those of which the groundwork has been laid in barbarous ages, is imported in the lump from one country into another, it will be found that opposite judgments will be entertained of it by the two nations: the one will be disposed to think a great deal better of it; the other, if possible, a great deal worse of it, than it deserves" (i.184). The laws were nefarious not only in their direct effects but also because they were sure to undermine any sense of trust or good will that managed to emerge on the part of Indians toward their British governors:

> What, then, must have been the sensations of the poor Hindoo, when forced to submit to all these wanton and ridiculous vexations? Unable to attribute to an European mind the folly adequate to the production of such a mass of nonsense and of gibberish, he must have found himself compelled to ascribe it to a less pardonable cause; to a deliberate plan for forcing him to deliver himself up, without reserve, into the hands of the European professional blood-suckers, carrying on the traffic of injustice under the cloak of law (i.187).

The imposition of British law on India was either foolish or wicked, probably both, Bentham suggested; under the circumstances, any effort to lessen Bengal's predicament represented an improvement. The restrained and indeed pessimistic tone of the essay, however, is far from that of the crusading legislator.

In addition, Bentham made no strong claims for the applicability of his analysis in this essay to the production of actual legislation. "Time and Place" is in large part a theoretical exercise and should not be taken as evidence of Bentham's own desire to become an "Indian Solon." Early in the essay, he offered a caveat. While he could glimpse "perfection" in the endeavor of translating a body of laws, it was clear that perfection was unattainable: in this case, it would require infinite detail in the description of the perfect English laws, of the "leading principles upon which the differences between those and the laws for Bengal appear to turn," and finally, of the way in which those principles would be put into practice to create laws for Bengal.

> According to this plan, were it rigorously pursued, a complete code of laws for England, accompanied with a collection of all the laws for Bengal which would require to be different from those which are for England, would form a part only of the matter belonging to the present head. The impracticability of this plan is such, as need not be insisted upon (i.172).

Bentham's more limited goal in this essay, then, would be to sketch some of the considerations a legislator would have to take into account when attempting such a task. It should be noted, then, that while Bentham's aspirations may well have lived up to his reputation for grandiosity, he was far more aware than the "Benthamites" of the East India Company that such aspirations were unfulfillable and that in actual practice a legislator would have to be infinitely more modest. The essay, to be sure, contains flights of optimism as well, as in the following passage:

> Legislators who, having freed themselves from the shackles of authority, have learnt to soar above the mists of prejudice, know as well how to make laws for one country as for another: all they need is to be possessed fully of the facts: to be informed of the local situation, the climate, the bodily constitution, the manners, the legal customs, the religion, of those with whom they have to deal. These are the data they require: possessed of these data, all places are alike (i.180-81).

Here it is worth noting the distinction between the legislator and the governor or administrator, for Bentham appears to propose a system that, after it being established by an all-knowing legislator who has risen above prejudice, would then be run by the people of India.[64] Bentham, indeed, never tried to claim, as James and John Stuart Mill did, that Indians were barbarous or incapable, and indeed he criticized the easy move made by many Europeans of assuming, when they observed bad laws, that the people they were designed for must be inferior. When you encounter ridiculous or destructive laws, he observed sarcastically, "What is to be done? There is but one thing; which is, to take the blame off the shoulders of the legislator, and lay it upon the people. Say they were stupid, stubborn, prejudiced, intractable: this will put you at your ease" (i.190). Where James Mill wrote with unrelenting scorn not only about Indian legal forms but about the Indian notables and jurists who had carried out justice under the old system, Bentham believed that the English had wantonly displaced systems, practices, and agents that, even if they would benefit from reforms, were far from wholly iniquitous. "The most

remarkable circumstance connected with these absurdities in English procedure is, that the judges are aware of the evils, and every now and then act
upon a different system; but where the English judge acts rightly, once in a
hundred times, the Cawzee and the Bramin were in the habit of acting rightly
every day" (i.187).

Bentham admired the Bengali reformer Rammohun Roy and maintained a
sporadic correspondence with him. In a late letter to Roy, Bentham sounds
almost sanguine about British reforms and even about James Mill (x.590-91).
What is particularly notable in this letter, however, is the restricted scope of
the reforms he envisioned: reform of the judicial structure (including the inclusion of more Indians throughout the judicial ranks) and the introduction
of the panopticon. Even in this, his most enthusiastic statement about what
the British might do in India, Bentham made no grand claims about civilizing India but instead proposed reforms just as he did for England, Spain,
France, Latin America, Greece, and Tripoli.

Bentham also developed a suggestion for jury trials in India, in his *Principles of Judicial Procedure*. This quite rare instance in his work of a specific
reform for British India (and even this one is offered in passing, as an example, rather than as an actual proposal) illustrates the contrast between his understanding of education and development and those of James and John Stuart Mill.[65] Although Bentham believed that the level of education among the
general Indian population was too low to enable the proper function of juries selected from the whole population, he made no claims that Indian society as such was so rude or barbarous as to prevent the possibility of juries
altogether. Bentham's views about the franchise appear to follow a similar
logic. His constitutional code for Greece includes a justification for the denial of voting rights to Muslims there, but this passage demonstrates that
Bentham believed that a community should be denied voting rights only in
the most extreme circumstances and for the shortest possible time. It seems
clear that he did not approve of the exclusion of any community from political participation on the grounds of immaturity or incapacity for self-
government. He wrote,

> By self-preservation—an altogether unopposable law—by that and nothing
> else, for neither can any thing else be requisite, are men of this class excluded
> from the faculty of giving any degree of efficiency to their will to the purpose in
> question [i.e., from voting]. The character in which they stand subjected to the
> exclusion is that of enemies: natural and, for a time, unhappily irreconcileable
> enemies. In their case so long as the danger from admission continues, so long
> must the exclusion be continued. So long must it be, but not a moment longer
> ought to be.[66]

Although the judgment about the danger Muslim voters would have posed
to the state may be contested, the passage shows how high Bentham placed

the bar for the denial of suffrage to communities within a state. It seems clear that he did not approve of the exclusion of any community from political participation on the grounds of immaturity or incapacity for self-government.

In taking these positions, Bentham bore out the argument he made in the "Time" section of the essay on "Time and Place" against the common view that the best laws for "civilized" ages must be different from the best laws for "rude" ages.[67] Importantly, in discussing these different "ages" of society, Bentham always compared particular societies with their own pasts, European with the European past and Islamic society with the age of Mohammed, rather than positing, as both Mills did, that India or Asia generally represented the "rude" age of humanity. Systematic cultural differences between rude and civilized ages might be observed, he noted; for instance, in a rude age people might on the whole be less accustomed to cooperating spontaneously with the laws. "The differences, however, that may be occasioned by these circumstances, can at the utmost be but very slight" (i.190).

Thus his jury proposal shows Bentham discussing India not as a characteristically "barbarous" society but rather simply as one in which there was not a large pool of people educated enough to serve usefully on juries. The "general complexion of the public mind," Bentham wrote, was too uninformed to make feasible a regular supply of competent jurors from the general population. His resourceful proposal for a limited system of Indian juries was designed on the one hand as a check, in the form of publicity and public opinion, on the judges, and on the other hand as a form of civic education, both for the relatively small number of elected jurors and for the larger public as spectators. Juries would be elected for trials of particular importance: they would hear the entire trial and deliver a public verdict. Although the judge would not be bound to comply with their verdict, "in the event of non-compliance on the part of the judge—the effect of the verdict would be, that of an appeal from his decision to the tribunal of public opinion" (ii.137). Where the population was mixed, the juries would be composed of both Muslims and Hindus; representatives of each community would be elected by members of the other to encourage impartiality and suppress corruption. Unanimity would not be required, as that would encourage bribery of poor jurors by those defendants who could afford it. The plan sought to restrain corruption on the part of the governors and to educate the public; it accommodated communal differences while at the same time attempting to use public institutions to mitigate, over time, their harmful effects. In formulating a reform plan tailored to Indian society, Bentham resisted suggesting that that society or its members were in particular need of improvement. For reasons such as these, Bentham's proposal for jury reform in India should not be confused with the "improvements" proposed by his successors, which rested precisely on claims about the peculiar backwardness or incapacity of Indians.

Although "Time and Place" indicates that Bentham was far more aware of the problems with attempting to legislate for all people than his detractors suggest, Bentham's method—his assumption that the way to go about legislating is to produce general code and then tailor them to circumstances—remained problematic, or at the very least, easily subject to abuse. This method became particularly dangerous when, in the hands of Bentham's disciples, the general code was enforced from outside and from above, and when Bentham's followers abandoned his convictions that people knew their own interests best, that non-European notables and officials were capable of governing well, and that all people were capable of using public opinion to curb abuses by their governors. Of all Bentham's followers, James Mill offered the most thorough account of Indian society and the British empire, and, until his son's, the most fully developed theory of social development, in his *History of British India*. The views that he expressed there influenced not only his own policy making as an influential agent of the East India Company but also the opinions and policies of a generation of civil servants, including such powerful figures as Governor-General Bentinck, and theorists, John Stuart Mill foremost among them. If we are to understand how Bentham's views were transformed to become the foundation of one of the most self-confident and interventionist branches of British imperial practice, then, we must turn to the thought of James Mill.

THE MILLS AND THEIR LEGACY

James Mill occupies a peculiar place in the history of utilitarian arguments about empire, a position whose oddities and potential contradictions have not fully been explored in the literature on the subject. For many, Mill represents the classic instance of the utilitarian imperialist: as a highly placed member of the East India Company's executive government from 1819 until shortly before his death in 1838, Mill was, as has often been observed, well placed to institute utilitarian reforms in judicial and land-use policy, among other areas.[68] Mill's *History of British India* (1817), wholly dismissive of Indian society as barbaric and of the Indian population as incapable of participating in their own governance, guided not only his own views about what was desirable and possible for the British to do in India but also those of a generation of policy makers, including his son. The intolerance and crude inadequacy of James Mill's accounts of Indian society, Sanskrit, Hinduism, and indeed all aspects of Indian civilization have been well documented and need not be labored here.[69] The peculiarity of Mill's position is most evident in the combination that he managed to sustain of strident criticism of colonies from the colonizers' perspective, primarily on classic political economy grounds, and his disdain for non-European societies and his conviction that India, in particular, should be governed by a British despotism, with no participation by Indians themselves. Most of his writings of both sorts appeared between about 1809 and 1823, so that these two strands of thought coexisted, with little apparent discomfort to Mill. Mill's economic critique of colonies resembled Bentham's, although he never expressed any of the moral concerns present in Bentham's work and instead focused purely on the question of whether colonies provided any financial benefit to the ruling country.[70]

James Mill never doubted that the rule of India was a drain on British resources, but he believed that the British had a duty to impose a civilizing government on the unfortunate natives. In addition to believing that utility could be adopted straightforwardly as a standard of judgment for any society, Mill claimed that Britain ranked highest among all nations and that its laws, even if flawed, ought to be imposed on backward nations in anticipation of improvements in Britain.

> If we wish for the prolongation of an English government in India, which we do most sincerely, it is for the sake of the natives, not of England. India has never been anything but a burden; and any thing but a burden, we are afraid, it cannot be rendered. But this English government in India, with all its vices, is a blessing of unspeakable magnitude to the population of Hindustan. Even the utmost abuse of European power, is better, we are persuaded, than the most temperate exercise of Oriental despotism.[71]

James Mill saw himself at once as a utilitarian and as an heir to the philosophical historians of the Scottish Enlightenment. Mill adopted a notion of the standard of utility from Bentham and an idea of progressive social development from Scottish thinkers such as Smith and Ferguson, and thereby produced a problematic fusion: an index of progress in which utility is the sole standard against which any nation can be measured. As he wrote in the *History*, "exactly in proportion as Utility is the object of every pursuit may we regard a nation as civilized. Exactly in proportion as its ingenuity is wasted on contemptible or mischievous objects . . . the nation may safely be denominated barbarous."[72] This was a notion that did justice to neither tradition (not to mention the nations deemed barbarous). In addition to abandoning Bentham's moral objections to colonial rule, Mill transformed what was, in Smith and Ferguson, a broad-minded description of social development into a "scale of excellence or defect."[73] In developing a theory of progress that culminated in the civilized "Utilitarian" nation, James Mill disavowed, perhaps even unwittingly, Bentham's own objections to colonial rule.

Although John Stuart Mill's views on social development and national character were much more thoroughly theorized than those of his father, he shared to a surprising extent his father's judgments about Indian society, about the proper relationship between India and its British rulers, and about the usefulness of making a dichotomous distinction between civilized and barbarous peoples. In the 1859 essay "A Few Words on Non-Intervention," for instance, Mill defended his notion that different standards of international relations should apply to civilized and barbarous peoples, with the claim that "barbarians will not reciprocate. They cannot be depended on for observing any rules. Their minds are not capable of so great an effort." Both the dichotomy and the casual claim about the inferior "minds" of non-Europeans (for it seems that only European nations fit Mill's criteria for civilized nations, in contrast to earlier Europeans ideas about the advanced civilizations of India and China) can be traced to James Mill's writings on India.[74]

J. S. Mill's departure from Bentham's views on the question of colonization went well beyond his adoption of his father's simplistic view of India, however. It was the younger Mill's effort to introduce into utilitarian thought a consideration of "character," both individual and national, and his belief in progress, which he saw as an essential element of liberty, that mark some of his greatest philosophical departures from Bentham. These theoretical developments had significant implications for the way Mill drew on utilitarian concerns when writing about empire. Although Mill is often credited with exposing the narrowness of Bentham's vision, their writings on India and colonization demonstrate Bentham's greater flexibility on questions of social organization: his far greater willingness, for instance, to attribute value to non-British institutions and to respect the ability for and right to self-government on the part of non-Europeans, a difference between the thinkers that I discuss at greater length below.

Mill's efforts to dissociate his philosophy from what he saw as the crudeness of Bentham's understanding of human nature were so successful that his own critical portrayal of Benthamite utilitarianism has survived as probably the dominant characterization of Bentham's thought. Mill's portrait of Bentham has done a great disservice to the ironic and passionate thinker who emerges from writings from throughout his life, and who, as we have seen, appealed to people's sense of justice, reciprocity, and glory as well as to their pleasures and pains. Mill instead memorably depicted a man of great reforming ambition but stunted emotional capacity and intellectual scope. "Remarks on Bentham's Philosophy" (1833), published shortly after Bentham's death, is less judicious than the better-known "Bentham" (1838), but they share a common theme: Bentham's lack of understanding of the importance of human nature and character in both morals and politics.[75] His charge was that Bentham's utilitarianism considered only an action's immediate consequences, whereas a philosopher of ethics must also consider its effects on the development of the actor's character. Mill offered a caricature of Bentham as a bachelor whose philosophy suffered from his emotional isolation from others and his personal unfamiliarity with the full human experience. "In many of the most natural and strongest feelings of

human nature he had no sympathy," Mill wrote; "from many of its graver
experiences he was altogether cut off; and the faculty by which one mind
understands a mind different from itself, and throws itself into the feelings
of that other mind, was denied him by his deficiency of Imagination."[76] Mill
argued that this failing in Bentham's thought meant that while he might
have excelled as a legislator, he was not a great moral philosopher or "an-
alyst of human nature."[77]

The later essay on Bentham expanded these themes with a discussion of
"national character," which Mill treated, straightforwardly and problemati-
cally, as something essentially like individual character: the same phenomenon at a "higher generalization" (CW x.99). Having dismissed Bentham's
"theory of life" as useless to the practical reasoning of individuals, Mill went
on to argue that Bentham's failure to understand character also strictly limited the use of Bentham's philosophy to society. "A philosophy of laws and
institutions, not founded on a philosophy of national character, is an absurdity. But what could Bentham's opinion be worth on national character?
How could he, whose mind contained so few and so poor types of individual character, rise to that higher generalization?" (CW x.99). Mill regarded his
attention to the formation of individual and national character as perhaps the
greatest advance that his own philosophy made over Bentham's. He hoped
to develop a science of individual and national character, which he called
ethology and described in outline in a chapter of the *System of Logic*.[78] While
he never developed that chapter into the treatise that he hoped might launch
such a field of study, we find, scattered throughout his works, observations
on national character that would have contributed to the new science.[79] The
thought that an understanding of how both individual and national character develop was essential to moral and political theory underlay much of his
work. But Mill tended to regard national character as simply a question of
progress and decline: "forming" this character meant either "carrying forward
the members of the community toward perfection, or preserving them from
degeneracy" (CW x.9). Mill did resist racial or biological determinism, and he
emphasized that national characters were mutable over time, even in unex-
pected directions. Still, he tended to describe these characters through a series of dichotomies—advanced-backward, active-passive, industrious-sensu-
ous, sober-excitable—and to assign the first terms above all to the English
and Germans and the latter terms to the Irish, French, Southern Europeans,
and "Orientals" (more and more so as one moved south and east).[80] Mill's
notion of national character, despite his insistence on its importance and his
sophisticated theoretical framework, was fairly thin: it had none of the connotations of complex specificity, of a unique constellation of institutions,
practices, and beliefs, that we find, for instance, in Burke or Herder.[81] For all
Mill's insistence, then, on the parallel between individual and national character, it would be a mistake to assume that by national characters he had in

mind anything analogous to the riot of eccentricity and individual singularity that he envisioned for individuals within civilized society.

Mill's rather impoverished understanding of national character undercuts his own criticism of Bentham's narrowness.[82] Indeed, Mill went on to argue that the "imperfections of [Bentham's] theory of human nature" prevented him not so much from appreciating human diversity as from ranging nations appropriately along a scale of progress.

> For, taking, as we have seen, next to no account of national character and the causes which form and maintain it, he was precluded from considering, except to a very limited extent, the laws of a country as an instrument of national culture: one of their most important aspects, and in which they must of course vary according to the degree and kind of culture already attained; as a tutor gives his pupil different lessons according to the progress already made in his education (CW x.105).

Although Mill regularly cautioned that nations and national characters must be understood as diverse, as formed by "time, place, and circumstance," he nonetheless tended at just these moments to reduce diversity among societies to variation along a single axis of progress.[83] Mill's perfectionism, his belief in self-development as a preeminent moral duty and his conviction that societies, like individuals, must continue to "improve" or else stagnate or decline supported a view of social progress that in many of its details restated and affirmed the much less complex ideas of his father. The differences between Bentham's "Time and Place" essay and Mill's commentary on it are therefore instructive. Mill takes national differences to signify degrees of advancement in a rigid hierarchy of progress; also, like his father, he characterizes members of "backward" societies as children. Such an approach is quite alien to that of Bentham, who accepted a great number of cultural differences as simply variety and never presumed to rank nations as inferior or superior in "character," however much he castigated despotic governments.

The disagreements between Mill and Bentham on the question of character go an important part of the way toward explaining their very different judgments of colonial rule.[84] Mill's tendency to regard Bentham as devoid of imagination about the possibilities of human endeavor led him to criticize as lack of discrimination a quality in Bentham that might better be considered liberality or tolerant agnosticism on questions he considered morally indifferent. For Bentham, nothing was at stake, morally speaking, in a great number of questions of taste or aesthetics, and he considered it particularly egregious to base legislation or public policy on judgments of taste. Mill, objecting to this ecumenism, wrote:

> There were certain phrases which, being expressive of what he considered to be
> . . . groundless liking or aversion, he could not bear to hear pronounced in his
> presence. Among these phrases were those of good and bad taste. He thought

it an insolent piece of dogmatism in one person to praise or condemn another
in a matter of taste: as if men's likings and dislikings, on things in themselves indifferent, were not full of the most important inferences as to every point of their
character: as if a person's tastes did not show him to be wise or a fool, cultivated
or ignorant, gentle or rough, sensitive or callous, generous or sordid, benevolent or selfish, conscientious or depraved.[85]

Bentham refused such inferences, and this difference also informed their respective attitudes toward colonial rule: in leaving people to determine their
desires and interests for themselves, Bentham took a position fundamentally
less judgmental and more respectful of difference than did Mill.

Mill, although he declared the three realms of morals, aesthetics, and sympathy to be separate, reflected in his own work his father's tendency to take
"aesthetic" evidence for backwardness (coarse pottery, on James Mill's view,
indicating moral immaturity and an incapacity for self-government) and to
see all realms of human endeavor as tending to progress simultaneously.[86]
The element of paternalism in Mill's views on cultural difference and the absence of such a posture in Bentham's writing are analogous to their different
positions on the role of the people in representative democracy. Mill was
concerned to bring about a "readiness" for representative government in the
bulk of the population; he regarded the people as in a state of tutelage and
saw it as the task of governing elites and the educated to develop their capacity for participation. Bentham, in contrast, believed that representative
democracy was most vulnerable to the corruption and self-interest of the ruling elites; he believed that people, as they are, are quite capable of participation under a system of good laws.[87]

In "Bentham" and his twin essay on Coleridge, Mill constructed an appealing and vivid dichotomy between two seminal minds, each of which,
however, had apprehended only a half truth.[88] Mill saw his own philosophical project as a synthesis of these half truths and was confident that
such a synthesis was possible, even if he never fully carried out the reconciliation. He seems untroubled by any apprehensions that there might
be incompatible truths, or that values or ideas might be lost in the yoking
together of Bentham's critical spirit and Coleridge's reverential one.[89]
Mill's confidence that he could reconcile all these truths is, in a sense, a
microcosm of his certainty that whole cultures could be deliberately engineered: his insistence that the best achievements of one society could be
injected, through legislation and education, into another less fortunate
one, and what is more, without any sacrifice of legitimate values or worth-
while ways of life.

Bentham, for all his aspirations to see legal systems reformed around the
world, did not embrace British colonial rule, as many of his self-designated
followers did, as a convenient means of imposing his schemes on power-

less or incompetent subjects. Although Bentham's views on the justice and prudence of colonial rule do not form a consistent whole, he was far more critical of European powers and more suspicious of their colonizing aspirations than either his immediate successors or recent scholarship would have us believe. In this essay I have sought to call attention to Bentham's lively skepticism about colonial rule: his sensitivity to the chauvinism and presumptuousness of European colonial rulers, his unwillingness to class peoples along a spectrum of development that would legitimate the despotic rule of the civilized over the backward. Once Bentham is understood in this light, our picture of his successors shifts as well: James Mill, who attempted an unhappy synthesis of conjectural history and utilitarianism, takes on a new importance, for he both foreshadowed and influenced political developments that were to become prominent in the East India Company and intellectual developments among the colonialist vanguard. And, finally, John Stuart Mill's philosophy begins to seem less a theoretical refinement of what had been an unsubtle theory out of touch with human experience, as he portrayed it. His analysis of "character," which he took to be one of his key contributions to utilitarian thought, appears instead to sap some of the lively ecumenism from Bentham's utilitarianism and put in its place a sociologically thin and politically destructive account of social progress and of the rights and duties that accompanied European civilization.

NOTES

1. Scholars that have portrayed utilitarianism as an inherently imperialist doctrine and attributed to Bentham the views on empire expressed by his self-declared disciples include Halévy, *Growth of Philosophic Radicalism*, trans. Mary Morris (Boston: Beacon Press, 1955); Stokes, *English Utilitarians and India* (Oxford: Clarendon Press, 1959); Iyer, *Utilitarianism and All That* (London: Concord Grove Press, 1983 [1960]); and Uday Mehta, *Liberalism and Empire* (Chicago: University of Chicago Press, 1999). For a recent corrective to this argument, see Allison Dube, "The Tree of Utility in India: Panacea or Weed?" in *J. S. Mill's Encounter with India*, ed. Martin I. Moir, Douglas M. Peers, and Lynn Zastoupil (Toronto: University of Toronto Press, 1999), 53–71. William Thomas has written that "[James] Mill is very much Bentham's pupil in much of what he says about Indian government," but he demonstrates as well the elder Mill's departures from Bentham, and some of the other sources of influence on Mill's interpretation of India, especially "puritanism" and Christian missionary testimony; Thomas, *Philosophic Radicals*, 101 and 96–119.

2. Stokes, *English Utilitarians*, 51; from *The Works of Jeremy Bentham*, ed. John Bowring (London, 1843) x.577. This edition is hereinafter cited in the text by volume and page number.

3. The influence of utilitarian reformers in the transformation of Victorian England has been much debated: while scholarship of the 1950s and 1960s tended to downplay

utilitarian influence, more recent scholarship suggests that utilitarian ideas affected reform both directly, through Bentham's followers in administration, and indirectly, through reformers who were quite unaware of the Benthamite origins of the reforms they sought; see Conway, "Bentham and the Nineteenth-Century Revolution in Government," in *Victorian Liberalism*, ed. Richard Bellamy (New York: Routledge, 1990).

4. *On Liberty* (1859), in *John Stuart Mill, Collected Works*, ed. J. M. Robson and R. F. McRae (Toronto: University of Toronto Press, 1974), XVIII.224 (hereafter cited as CW.)

5. Bowring iv.416. The moon was Bentham's usual analogy for distant dependencies. In a passage typical of Bentham's quirky and biting wit on the subject of colonies, he wrote of the Spanish imperialists: "Spain is *one*! such will be their *arithmetic*. It has its *Peninsular* part and its *Ultramarian* part! such will be their *geography*. As well might it be said—Spain and the Moon are *one*! it has its *earthly* part: it has its *lunar* part. Such, it is but too true, is the language of your *Constitutional Code*. But, a body of human law, how well soever arranged in other respects, does not suffice for converting *impossibilities* into *facts*"; Bentham, "Rid Yourselves of Ultramaria," in *Colonies, Commerce, and Constitutional Law*, ed. Philip Schofield (Oxford: Clarendon Press, 1995), 52 (hereinafter referred to as *Ultramaria*).

6. Stephen Conway has discussed Bentham's ambivalent pacifism in "Bentham on Peace and War," *Utilitas* 1 (1989), 82–201; and "The Nineteenth-Century British Peace Movement," *Utilitas* 2 (1990), 221–43. Some of Bentham's economic objections to settler colonies were overcome at the very end of his life, when he was persuaded by the arguments of Edward Gibbon Wakefield for "systematic colonization" of Australia: see Semmel, "The Philosophic Radicals and Colonialism," 518–19. But Semmel, by discussing the "Benthamite Radicals" as a group, too readily assimilates Bentham's views and doubts about colonialism to the more consistently enthusiastic views of his followers. It is also important to note the great extent to which Bentham left the writing of his later works to his disciples; see Robson, "John Stuart Mill and Jeremy Bentham," in *Essays in English Literature from the Renaissance to the Victorian Age*, ed. Millar MacLure and F. W. Watt (Toronto: University of Toronto Press, 1964), 245–68 at 257.

7. Commentators often speak of a utilitarian "logic" (Halévy, *Philosophic Radicalism*, 510), or of the "utilitarian mind" (Winch, *Classical Political Economy*, 167) on the subject of colonies.

8. In Smart and Williams, *Utilitarianism: For and against* (Cambridge: Cambridge University Press, 1973), 138.

9. These anti-imperialist arguments are presented most thoroughly in "Colony," written in the late 1810s as a supplement to the fifth edition of the *Encyclopedia Britannica* (1823), the views on India most succinctly in "Affairs of India," *Edinburgh Review* XVI, April 1810, 128–57, but also, of course, in the *History of British India*.

10. "A simple form of arbitrary government, tempered by European honour and European intelligence, is the only form which is now fit for Hindustan ("Affairs of India," 156). Even Alexander Bain, whose biography of James Mill is on the whole deaf to criticism of Mill and often verges on hagiography, wrote of the *History* that "the analysis of the Hindoo institutions is methodical and exhaustive, and is accompanied with a severe criticism of their merits and their rank in the scale of development. . . . Being written while the public was prepossessed by an excessive admiration for Hin-

doo institutions and literature, due to Sir W. Jones and others, the review was too disparaging—the bow bent too far in the opposite direction"; Bain, *James Mill* (London: Longman, Green, and Co., 1882), 176–77.

11. "The Positive Philosophy of Auguste Comte" (1865), in Mill, CW X.320; also see Mill's *Autobiography*, CW I.27–29.

12. Stokes's *English Utilitarians* was one of the few works to deal in any depth with the question of Mill's views on empire until the 1990s. Some of the best recent works include Zastoupil, *Mill and India*; Moir, Peers and Zastoupil, eds, *J. S. Mill's Encounter with India*; Mehta, *Liberalism and Empire*; and Lloyd "Mill and the East India Company." While some of Mill's most important texts on India were published in 1990 in CW XXX, Mill's many dispatches for the East India Company, housed in the British Library's Oriental and India Office Collection, are unlikely to be published; see Robson, "Civilization and Culture as Moral Concepts," 369n27. Only Fred Rosen's brief but suggestive article "Eric Stokes, British Utilitarianism, and India" begins to address these connections, in J. S. *Mill's Encounter with India*, 18–33.

13. An important exception is Eileen Sullivan, who draws a contrast between J. S. Mill's justification of empire and "a liberal tradition which was primarily anti-imperialist," including Smith, Bentham, and James Mill; Sullivan, "Liberalism and Imperialism," *Journal of the History of Ideas* 44, no. 4 (1983): 599–617 at 599. Although Sullivan notes that James Mill argued for "arbitrary government" by Britain over India, she concludes rather abruptly that he, like Bentham, was fundamentally an anti-imperialist.

14. Halévy's *Philosophic Radicalism*, which itself heavily influenced Stokes's reading of the utilitarian tradition, is also partly to blame for conflating Bentham's thought with that of James Mill. Fred Rosen has discussed this problem, claiming that "Halévy uses their association to suggest that they created a sect isolated from both the Whig tradition and from other more libertarian, radical movements. This conflation of the two fails to appreciate the fact that Bentham, if not Mill, addressed a wide and varied audience on a number of different levels . . . [and] tends to minimize the creative side of Bentham's thought, which is not as strong in Mill"; Rosen, "Elie Halévy and Bentham's Authoritarian Liberalism," in *Jeremy Bentham: Critical Assessments*, ed. Bhikhu Parekh (London: Routledge, 1993), 923.

15. We should note that it was the notoriously unreliable Bowring who attributed these words to Bentham (x.450; Stokes and others cite the wrong page). The sentence is repeated or paraphrased in almost every treatment of the subject. Even Sullivan, in a nuanced account that is almost alone in drawing attention to the contrast between Bentham's views on empire and those of J. S. Mill, claims that Bentham "was primarily interested in reforming the Indian legal system though he left most of the specific discussion to James Mill. Bentham came to believe that through James Mill he would be the dead legislator of India" (604).

16. The image Bentham describes here strikingly resembles the Auto-Icon, Bentham's preserved body that still sits at the University College London, as well as the instructions Bentham gave in an addendum to his will for the construction of the Auto-Icon. I am grateful to Richard Tuck for making the connection with the Auto-Icon and to Fred Rosen for confirming Dapple's identity.

17. Bowring x.450. The last sentence is suggestive, though Bentham unfortunately says no more on the subject. Some of Bentham's other treatments of the beliefs of Indians of various religions suggest a more respectful attitude than Mill's, as I discuss

below. It should, perhaps, be noted that John Stuart Mill was so outraged by Bowring's inclusion of these remarks in his "Memoirs of Bentham" that he wrote a long letter to the *Edinburgh Review*, which had quoted these words in a review of the "Memoirs." Mill called the passage "idle word[s spoken] . . . under some passing impression or momentary irritation." CW i.536. It is also worth noting the similarity of Bentham's judgment of James Mill to an observation Burke made in the *Reflections* on the unsuitability of dogmatic critics for political reform: "It is undoubtedly true, though it may seem paradoxical; but in general, those who are habitually employed in finding and displaying faults are unqualified for the work of reformation, because their minds are not only unfurnished with patterns of the fair and good, but by habit they come to take no delight in the contemplation of those things. By hunting vices too much, they come to love men too little"; *The Writings and Speeches of Edmund Burke*, vol. 8, Paul Langford (Oxford: Oxford University Press, 1981–2000), 8.

18. In his "Introduction to the study of Bentham's works," Bowring wrote, "From observations here and there scattered through [Bentham's] works, his opinions on the subject might be gathered; but it was almost solely in the great article by Mr. Mill on the "Law of Nations" in the Encyclopedia Britannica, that the public could find a distinct account of the utilitarian theory of International law" (i.75).

19. i.75. J. S. Mill, as I argue below, similarly drew an almost impermeable boundary between the civilized and the uncivilized worlds, though he theorized the distinction more carefully than Bowring did.

20. In the *Essay on Government*, James Mill wrote that women justly may be denied suffrage, as "the interest of almost all of [them] is involved either in that of their fathers or in that of their husbands"; J. S. Mill later wrote that this paragraph was "the worst . . . he ever wrote." See James Mill, *Political writings*, xxii and 27.

21. On Bentham's narrowness, it is worth calling attention to the popular misconception about Bentham's supposed philistinism, initiated by J. S. Mill's remark that Bentham found "pushpin and poetry" equally valuable. As Ross Harrison has explained, Bentham was discussing political and legal structures rather than personal ethics. Bentham's point was that if the people of a state value something, their pleasure in it should be taken into account by the governing authorities. Harrison notes that while this latter point is still a matter of debate, "it is nothing like as contentious as the suggestion that it is an appropriate system of personal values"; Harrison, *Bentham* (London: Routledge and Kegan Paul, 1983), 5. Bentham did not mean, or believe, that intellectual or artistic cultivation is nonsensical or pointless.

22. Anderson, "Mill on Bentham," adopts Mill's assessment of Bentham's limitations. Uday Mehta echoes Mill's view that Bentham's utilitarianism was more "mechanical and authoritarian" than Mill's own (*Liberalism and Empire*, 101); while this may be a fair description of their respective theories about European government and society, it misrepresents, I think, their views about non-Europeans.

23. *Philosophic Radicalism*, 510. After quoting the "dead legislative" passage, Halévy writes, "Twenty-eight years after his death the Indian penal code came into force; it had been drawn up by Macaulay under the influence of Bentham's and James Mill's ideas, so that Bentham, who had failed to give a legal code to England, did actually become the posthumous legislator of the vastest of her possessions."

24. Fred Rosen has argued compellingly that Bentham was a more committed democrat than either Mill; Rosen, "Halévy and Bentham's Authoritarian Liberalism,"

Bentham and Representative Democracy (Oxford: Clarendon Press, 1983), and *Bentham, Byron, and Greece* (Oxford: Clarendon Press, 1992); also see Crimmins, "Bentham's Political Radicalism Reexamined," asserting that Bentham's "democratic convictions" long preceded his encounter with James Mill; *Journal of the History of Ideas* 55, no. 2 (1994), 259–81 at 262. For an influential statement of the contrary view, see Douglas Long, who argues that Bentham regarded liberty as merely instrumental to security and that "attempts by recent commentators [such as Mary Mack] to show that Bentham was fundamentally a 'democrat' or a 'liberal' seem to miss the point"; Long, *Bentham on Liberty: Jeremy Bentham's Idea of Liberty in Relation to His Utilitarianism* (Toronto: University of Toronto Press, 1977), 206–8.

25. In a letter addressed to Greek legislators, Bentham wrote, "You stand clear from the temptation afforded by distant dependencies: you stand exempt from the danger of splitting upon that rock. . . . In this respect, you have the advantage over Spain, Portugal, England, France, and the Netherlands." In Bentham, *Securities against Misrule and Other Constitutional Writings for Tripoli and Greece (The Collected Works of Jeremy Bentham)*, ed. Philip Schofield (Oxford: Clarendon Press, 1990), 195.

26. See, for instance, Mack, *Jeremy Bentham: An Odyssey of Ideas 1748–1792* (London: Heinemann, 1963), 412–13; and Ross Harrison, *Bentham*, 8–9.

27. On the letters to Mirabeau, see Mack, *Odyssey of Ideas*, 417–19; for the pamphlet, see iv.408–18, and *Rights, Representation, and Reform (The Collected Works of Jeremy Bentham)*, ed. Philip Schofield, Catherine Pease-Watkin, and Cyprian Blamires (Oxford: Clarendon Press, 2002): 289–315 (hereafter RRR).

28. Donald Winch has argued that Bentham's anticolonialism was simply an "early," largely superseded, phase of his career. Winch, following the general lines of Stokes's argument, regards Bentham's thought as an integral episode in a tradition of "classical liberal imperialism" stretching from the eighteenth century through J. S. Mill; *Classical Political Economy and Colonies*. While Winch rightly characterizes the "story" of Bentham's views on colonization as one of "recurring ambivalence," he uses a selection of passages to argue that Bentham tended to support both settler colonies and rule over territories such as India. His conclusion that such a tradition encompassed thinkers with such diverse views on empire as Adam Smith, Bentham, and the Mills leads to mischaracterizations, particularly of Smith and Bentham. In a more recent article Winch insists on Bentham's "dream of being 'the dead legislative hand of British India,'" and he regards the "imperialism . . . of Bentham and his colonial reforming followers" as a continuous movement: see Winch, "Bentham on Colonies and Empire," *Utilitas* 9, no. 1 (1997), 153–54.

29. Bentham, "Ultramaria," 92. "Rid Yourselves of Ultramaria," Bentham's "most sustained piece" on the emancipation of Spanish America, remained in manuscript, although Bentham published a number of other essays on Spanish affairs in the 1820s, after the restoration of the liberal constitution and the reinstatement of the Cortes. Bentham did most of the writing of "Ultramaria" in 1821. See Schofield's introduction (xv and xliv).

30. In "Liberalism and Imperialism," Eileen Sullivan makes a good case for the similarities between Smith's and Bentham's arguments. Other late eighteenth-century thinkers critical of European colonial conquest and rule, for diverse but overlapping reasons, included Burke, Diderot, and Kant. See Sankar Muthu, *Enlightenment against Empire* (Princeton: Princeton University Press, 2003).

31. In "Constitutional Code," Book I chapter 6 ("financial law"), ix.33.

32. See Rosen, "Halévy and Bentham's Authoritarian Liberalism," 928, who argues that Bentham's "emphasis on publicity and public opinion predated his democratic theory but nonetheless played an important role in it."

33. With "a barbarous, or semicivilized government, its view of its true interests is so feeble and indistinct," James Mill wrote, that it acted mostly from ungoverned passion and was completely unreliable. He thought the same was true for the individual members of such societies. "Affairs of India," 147.

34. J. S. Mill often criticized Bentham as an unhistorical thinker: see CW x.325 (where he refers to "philosophers who, like Bentham, theorize on politics without any historical basis at all"); and his (incorrect) argument in "Bentham" that Bentham believed the same legislation was appropriate for every society: "He places before himself man in society without a government, and, considering what sort of government it would be advisable to construct, finds that the most expedient would be a representative democracy. Whatever may be the value of this conclusion, the mode in which it is arrived at appears to me to be fallacious; for it assumes that mankind are alike in all times and all places, that they have the same wants and are exposed to the same evils, and that if the same institutions do not suit them, it is only because in the more backward stages of improvement they have not wisdom to see what institutions are most for their good" (443).

35. The writings on empire are some of Bentham's rhetorically most powerful works; neither James nor John Stuart Mill (undoubtedly a far greater writer than his dry, didactic father) could match Bentham's sardonic humor, which appears in abundance in works such as "Emancipate Your Colonies!" Bentham himself did not think well of James Mill's style, claiming that the *History of British India* "abounds with bad English, making it to me a disagreeable book"; toward the end of his life, he wrote to Rammohun Roy that Mill's *History* contained some useful practical information, "though as to style, I wish I could, with truth and sincerity, pronounce it equal to yours" (x.590).

36. The security, political, and economic interests of the metropole all militated against empire. Bentham envisioned the National Assembly responding to his arguments, "Oh, but they are a great part of our power." He responded, "Say rather, the whole of your weakness. In your own natural body, you are impregnable; in those unnatural excrescences, you are vulnerable" (iv.414).

37. In 1838, after Bentham's death, his 1793 essay to France was published in London by an anonymous supporter, who titled it "Canada. Emancipate Your Colonies!" and attached a preface, signed "Philo-Bentham," applying his arguments to the British Empire.

38. For Smith's argument, see *An Inquiry into the Nature and Causes of the Wealth of Nations*, ed. R. H. Campbell, A. S. Skinner, and W. B. Todd, 2 vols. (Indianapolis: Liberty Press, 1976), 616: "To propose that Great Britain should voluntarily give up all authority over her colonies . . . would be to propose such a measure as never was, and never will be adopted, by any nation in the world."

39. William Hazlitt quipped that Bentham's influence increased in proportion to the distance from his house in Westminster; Hazlitt, *The Spirit of the Age* (London: Henry Colburn, 1825), 3–4.

40. From "Emancipation Spanish. From Philo-Hispanus to the people of Spain," in *Colonies, Commerce, and Constitutional Law*, 153.

41. "Ultramaria," 137.

42. Lea Campos Boralevi argues that Bentham held different views about existing colonies, which he saw as a complex problem involving the oppression of colonial inhabitants, and about the prospect of future colonization, which he regarded as primarily an economic problem, and favored as a way to release excess of capital or labor to the benefit of the colonizing nation; Boralevi, *Bentham and the Oppressed*, 127. While Boralevi is right to point to Bentham's sporadic enthusiasm for colonization as a release of labor and capital, she fails to note the many reasons he offers against new plans of colonization, as in the passage just quoted.

43. This piece was "Essay IV" of his *Principles of International Law*, and it demonstrates how wrong Bowring was to suggest that James Mill's writings on international law offered a fair approximation of Bentham's own views (see i.75). Recent editors and other scholars have pointed out difficulties with the text as it appears in the Bowring edition: see Hoogensen, "Bentham's International Manuscripts versus the Published 'Works.'" Hoogensen argues that the "Plan" was a "compilation of at least three essays" found among Bentham's manuscripts—*Pacification and Emancipation, Colonies and Navy*, and *Cabinet No Secresy*—which were "dismembered, reconfigured, and arbitrarily 'sewn' together"; Gunhild Hoogensen, "Bentham's International Manuscripts versus the Published 'Works,'" *Journal of Bentham Studies* 4 (2001), 3–4.

44. Bowring, ii.546. "The following, then, are the final measures which ought to be pursued:—1. Give up all the colonies. 2. Found no new colonies" (ii.548).

45. Boralevi emphasizes that his general opposition to colonial rule stemmed far more from its negative consequences for the colonizing country than from a concern about the oppression of the colonized. While Boralevi's treatment of this topic is one of the most sensitive in the literature, she nonetheless assimilates his view of Indians to those of the Mills and Bentham's other followers in the colonial administration. While his writings undoubtedly include scattered doubts about the readiness of Indians for democracy (such as the passage quoted above), Bentham's posture of respect for such colonized non-Europeans, such as his insistence on Indian participation in juries, and his failure or refusal to develop a theory of progress justifying colonization, mark him as crucially different from his followers.

46. On the public reception of the Hastings trial, see P. J. Marshall, *The Impeachment of Warren Hastings* (Oxford: Oxford University Press, 1965) and Carnall and Nicholson, eds., *Impeachment of Warren Hastings* (Edinburgh: Edinburgh University Press, 1989).

47. These passages all appear in a section of the essay entitled "Non-Agenda: Non-faciendum the Fourth: Encreasing the Quantity of Land, viz. by Colonization," which presents a series of arguments against colonization, as detrimental to the interests of the colonizing country, followed by several paragraphs arguing that colonial settlers would do best to remain under the rule of Britain because of its sound moral conduct, its system of education, and its security.

48. Winch, *Classical Political Economy*, 34.

49. In "Rid yourselves of Ultramaria" Bentham identified twenty-nine classes of people with sinister, particular interests in colonial dominion ("Ultramaria," 38–39).

50. "Emancipate your colonies!" iv.417. Bice referred to Vaishya (a trading caste), Sooder to Sudra (an agricultural caste); see *Writings and Speeches of Edmund Burke*, ed. Paul Langford, (Oxford: Oxford University Press, 1991), VII.266.

51. A puzzling postscript was attached to this essay in 1829; it reads, "As a citizen of Great Britain and Ireland, he is thereby confirmed in the same opinions, and accordingly in the same wishes. But, as a citizen of the British Empire, including the sixty millions already under its government in British India, and the forty millions likely to be under its government in the vicinity of British India . . . his opinions and consequent wishes are the reverse" (iv.418).

52. "Official aptitude maximized—expense minimized"; Bowring v.268–9. By Brithibernia, a typical neologism, Bentham simply meant the British and Irish understood together as a nation.

53. See Laird, "Introduction," in *Bishop Heber in Northern India: Selections from Heber's Journal*, ed. M. A. Laird (London: Cambridge University Press, 1971), 32.

54. 1790; quoted by Mack, *Odyssey of Ideas*, 396–97, citing University College Collection Box 126, p. 7.

55. Stokes, *English Utilitarians*, 51. Leslie Stephen had earlier claimed likewise that "Bentham was as ready to legislate for Hindoostan as well as for his own parish"; *English Utilitarians*, 300.

56. Bentham to Henry Dundas, 20 May 1793; in *Correspondence of Jeremy Bentham* iv.430. Dundas was president of the Board of Control, the chief governing body in the East India Company, at this time (editor's note).

57. Uday Mehta writes that Bentham, like other British liberals, wrote "copious[ly]" on the British empire in India; this essay, however, is a rare example (perhaps the only one) of an extended discussion of India by Bentham (*Liberalism and Empire*, 4). Occasional examples from Indian law come up in the course of Bentham's work, and many of these are discussed here.

58. First published, along with the rest of the *Theory of Legislation*, in *Traités de législation civile et pénale*, edited by Etienne Dumont (1802), the essay appears in Bowring i.169–94.

59. Whereas later, less theoretically minded utilitarians often simply assumed the excellence of British laws and legal structure, Bentham himself was generally careful to distinguish the ideal legal codes that he composed from scratch and what he knew to be the very imperfect British system, marred as it was by its uncritical dependence on custom and precedence.

60. "I take England, then, for a standard; and referring everything to this standard, I inquire, What are the deviations which it would be requisite to make from this standard, in giving to another country such a tincture as any other country may receive without prejudice, from English laws? I take my own country for the standard, partly because to that country, if to any, I owe a preference; but chiefly because it is that, with the circumstances of which I have the best opportunity to be informed" (i.171).

61. i.171. Allison Dube notes that this line introduces the "satirical dimension" of the entire essay; "The Tree of Utility in India: *Panacea* or Weed?" 35. Dube argues convincingly that the essay demonstrates that it is a mistake to identify Bentham, as Stokes and his followers have done, as one of the utilitarian "crusading men of system," given Bentham's "humility," his understanding of the great limits on what a legislator can hope to achieve. I disagree, however, with Dube's claim that "most of what has passed for utilitarian thought on India . . . is not utilitarian at all, though parts of it may be awarded the consolation title of liberal" (40–41), for their understandings of utility as the highest goal of public policy, and in particular their (rather different) ef-

forts to marry utility with theories of progress, deeply informed the imperial policies of both James and John Stuart Mill.

62. i.186. Bentham condemned English laws as much for the absurdities apparent in their refined form as for those left over from a barbarous age. After describing the interminable, labyrinthine process involved in an English lawsuit, he concluded, "And who would think it? This mass of absurdity is the work of modern refinement, not of ancient barbarism. . . . Why, then, were these simple and pure forms abandoned? Why were they not re-established, when new tribunals were instituted in another country, instead of transferring this system of possible equity and certain misery to Bengal?" (i.188).

63. Lafleur, "Jeremy Bentham and the *Principles*," vii.

64. His successors, in contrast, saw a much more prominent role for such "impartial" governors—notably John Stuart Mill in his depiction of the perfectly trained and knowledgeable technocrats who would govern India and whose ranks would only very slowly be opened to Indians themselves. Bentham was much less confident than John Stuart or even James Mill that Company civil servants could indeed preserve impartiality and resist corruption or the pursuit of their own private interests.

65. "Jury-trial," in *Principles of Judicial Procedure* (ii.137–38). For the contrast with James Mill, see Mill's *Encyclopaedia Britannica* article on education; *Political Writings*, 139–94.

66. In *Securities against Misrule*, 263.

67. See "Time and Place," i.190–91.

68. Stokes, *English Utilitarians*, 48. James Mill entered the company as assistant examiner of correspondence and in 1830 was promoted to the position of chief examiner, a post John Stuart Mill took up in 1856. I discuss James Mill's views further in *A Turn to Empire* (Princeton University Press, 2005).

69. See, for some thorough accounts, Javed Majeed, *Ungoverned Imaginings*; Makdisi *Romantic Imperialism*; and Thomas, *Philosophic Radicals*, 98–119, which astutely points out the "puritanism" of Mill's interpretation of India, as well as his reliance on missionary sources for "detailed accounts the grosser customs of a people he had placed so low in his scale of civilization" (108). Uday Mehta has aptly noted that "Mill's views regarding India, its past and its present" were "pathetically foolish in their lack of nuance"; *Liberalism and Empire*, 90. J. H. Burns offers a concise and often searing critique of James Mill's method and judgments; he concludes that "the almost blood-curdling arrogance of Mill's cultural chauvinism" is unredeemed by either felicity of language or "any clearly articulated method"; Burns, "The Light of Reason," 18.

70. See the article "Colony," published in 1823 as a supplement to the *Encyclopedia Britannica*.

71. Review of *Voyage aux Indes Orientales*, by le P. Paulin de S. Barthélemy, missionary, *Edinburgh Review* XV (January 1810), 371.

72. *The History of British India* (London: Baldwin, Cradock, and Joy, 1820) ii.134.

73. *The History of British India*, ed. H. H. Wilson (London: James Madden, 1858); reprint New York: Chelsea House, 1968, i.155. James Mill saw the *History of British India* as a work in the tradition of (and as an improvement over) the histories of Ferguson, Smith, and especially his mentor John Millar, author of *Observations Concerning the Distinction of Ranks in Society* (1773). Scholars too often assimilate his

work into that tradition without considering the quite radical departure he made from their relatively nonjudgmental and multidimensional accounts of social development (see Duncan Forbes, "James Mill and India," *Cambridge Journal* V, October 1951, 19–33, and, citing Forbes, Winch, *Classical Political Economy*, 162). For a corrective to this view, see Knud Haakonssen, "James Mill and Scottish Moral Philosophy." *Political Studies* 33 (1985), 628–36.

74. CW xxi.118. Compare James Mill's argument in "Affairs of India": "On a barbarous, or semi-civilized government, its view of its true interests is so feeble and indistinct, and its caprices and passions are so numerous and violent, that you can never count for a day. From its hatred of all restraint, and its love of depredation, it is naturally and essentially at war with all around it. The government of India, therefore, is not to be preserved with less than a perpetual war expenditure" (147–48).

75. Mill's discussion of Bentham in the *Autobiography* is considerably more generous than either of the early essays; there, Mill claimed that while he still agreed with his earlier judgments, he worried that they had helped to discredit Bentham's philosophy before it had "done its work" and therefore that these articles had hindered rather than contributed to "improvement" (CW i.227). He probably began writing the *Autobiography* in the early 1850s; it was first published in 1873, shortly after his death (i. xxii ff. and 3).

76. "Bentham," CW x.91.

77. "Remarks," x.163–70 at 167.

78. Book VI, Chapter V: "Of Ethology, or the Science of the Formation of Character" (CW viii.860–74). Here Mill calls ethology "the science which corresponds to the art of education; in the widest sense of the term, including the formation of national or collective character as well as individual" (CW viii.869).

79. The best treatment of Mill's ethology is Janice Carlisle's *John Stuart Mill and the Writing of Character*. See also *That Noble Science of Politics*, Stephan Collini, Donald Winch, and John Burrow (Cambridge: Cambridge University Press, 1983), 150, and John M. Robson, "Civilization and Culture as Moral Concepts." In "The Formation of Character: Mill's Ethology Reconsidered," *Polity* (Fall 2000), Terence Ball makes the compelling case that although Mill did not produce his promised treatise on ethology, some of his most influential works can be read as ethological case studies.

80. For a thoughtful analysis of this point and Mill's ambiguities on the subject of race, see Georgios Varouxakis, "John Stuart Mill on Race," *Utilitas* 10, no. 1 (March 1998), 17–32. Varouxakis cites many of the key passages on national character, including a passage on Oriental fatalism from *Considerations on Representative Government* (CW xix.406) and comparisons of the pleasure-loving Irish with the industrious English from *Principles of Political Economy* (CW ii.319) and Mill's essay on Michelet (CW xx.235). Also see Varouxakis, *Mill on Nationality* (London: Routledge, 2002).

81. L. S. Feuer discusses Mill's theoretical approach to the study of character in "John Stuart Mill as a Sociologist: The Unwritten Ethology," in *James and John Stuart Mill: Papers of the Centenary Conference*, eds. John M. Robson and Michael Laine (Toronto: University of Toronto, 1976), 86–110. Feuer cites James Mill's *History of British India* "as a model [for JSM] of what a science of ethology could do" and presents the elder Mill's methods and judgments quite uncritically. He concludes rather too optimistically that J. S. Mill "is the only sociologist of the nineteenth century whose pages are not discolored with the acid of bias" (110).

82. J. H. Burns sums up well the faults of Mill's ethology: "The price of gaining the whole world of sociological laws may be too high if it costs the historian his saving grasp of the concrete and the specific. The question must in the end be bluntly asked, whether the kind of history to which these concepts lead is either possible or useful" ("The Light of Reason," in *James and John Stuart Mill: Papers of the Centenary Conference*, ed. J. M. Robson and M. Laine. Toronto: University of Toronto Press, 1976), 20.

83. See *Autobiography*, CW I.77, where, after claiming that he had "ceased to consider representative democracy as an absolute principle, and regarded it as a question of time, place, and circumstance," Mill went on to say that he now sought to understand "what great improvement in life and culture stands next in order for the people concerned, as the condition of their further progress."

84. It should be noted, however, that some of Bentham's writings on empire show that he was more interested in the effects of policy on the character of a nation's inhabitants than Mill admitted. Bentham argued, for instance, that imperial rule was contrary to the interests of the ruling country not simply for economic or military reasons, but because it was corrupting.

85. "Bentham," CW x.113.

86. See James Mill's "Review of M. de Guignes," *Edinburgh Review* (July 1809), 424–25.

87. See Rosen, *Jeremy Bentham and Representative Democracy*, for the best discussion of this difference in Bentham and Mill's views of popular participation; see especially chapter 10.

88. In the imperious tone characteristic of these essays, Mill wrote, "Do we then consider Bentham's political speculations useless? Far from it. We consider them only one-sided" (CW X.109); Mill applied the phrase "half-truth" to Bentham's thought in "Remarks on Bentham's Philosophy," CW X.18).

89. See Pratap Mehta, "Liberalism, Nation, and Empire: The Case of J. S. Mill," 3–4, paper presented at the American Political Science Association, San Francisco, 1996, for a subtle articulation of this idea.

4

James Mill's
The History of British India

The Question of Utilitarianism and Empire

Javed Majeed

James Mill's *The History of British India*, published in 1817, has been described as transforming utilitarianism into a militant faith.[1] In his edition of
Mill's *History*, the famous orientalist Horace Hyman Wilson,[2] argued that Mill
had "entered the lists" against Sir William Jones's "amiable enthusiasm" for
Indian civilization.[3] Wilson's claim has some cogency, but as we shall see,
Mill's critique of Indian civilization and its representations by British orientalists was part of a larger critique of the conservatism of British institutions
in Britain itself. Nonetheless, Wilson's edition of Mill's *History* characterizes
the complexity of the debates about India in British intellectual circles in the
first half of the nineteenth century, as different figures defined themselves
against each other, and in doing so developed and reformulated their own
traditions of thought. Wilson's edition was composed of three strands,
Jones's orientalism as formulated and critiqued by Mill's philosophic radicalism (itself articulated in part against Jones), which in turn was countered by
Wilson's voluminous notes and his addition of three volumes to Mill's *History*. In many ways, as an editor of Mill's History, Wilson not only defended
Jones but also elaborated and developed his own position as an advocate of
an orientalist policy in India in general.

Thus, Wilson's edition reflects the way in which different strands of
thought in British intellectual circles engaged with each other as they grap-
pled with the host of political and philosophical problems which were implicit in the growth of British power in India. In part, these problems reflected the changing character of the British Empire itself, which from the
late eighteenth century onward no longer consisted of communities of
British origin only. It now included numerous groups who were not British
in origin and who were incorporated into the empire by conquest and ruled

without representation.[4] This presented two key problems: the first was the extent to which a system of laws derived from another society might be applicable to very different societies, and the second was the question of the relationship between government overseas and government at home. It was anxiety about this relationship that lay at the heart of Edmund Burke's vociferous critique of the East India Company's policies in India and the impeachment of Warren Hastings. In some ways, Burke's discourse on the nature of cultural identity and its relationship to historical processes in his *Reflections on the Revolution in France* (1790) was a development of his earlier reflections upon the role of the British in India, reflections which were framed by an emerging argument about the importance of fashioning an administration which was based upon the protection of "the original Laws and rights of the Natives."[5]

There was some continuity between Burke's position and the position of Sir William Jones, and in fact in the early 1780s Burke had been in frequent conference with Jones on the question of Indian legislation.[6] Burke's position presupposed that the British would first have to identify what the "original Laws" of the "natives" were before they could set about administering them. This was a central theme of Jones's own work. He identified his most important project to be the compilation of a digest of "Hindu" law, based on the Sanskrit text, the *Manavadharmasastra*.[7] Indeed, the main reason Jones learned Sanskrit was to compose a reliable digest of Indian laws in order to control the legal authority of the sacerdotal classes of Bengal.[8] But more than simply identifying the "original laws" of the "natives," Jones's project constituted the actual recovery and codification of those laws as part of a more general rhetoric of reconstituting an ancient Indian polity.[9] This also reflected Jones's agreement with the general thrust of British legal policy in India at the time, as expressed by an act of Parliament in 1781, which recognised the customs and usages of "Hindus" and "Muslims" in inheritance and contract. It was also part of a more general project, that of recovering a historical narrative of the ancient Indian past as a whole.[10]

Although there had been a strand of political radicalism in Jones's work before he arrived in India,[11] I have argued elsewhere that his views became part of the revitalized conservatism of British institutions both at home and abroad, which emerged in response to the Jacobin threat of the French revolution.[12] This revitalized conservatism also played a role in British institutions abroad, for example, in the establishment of Fort William College in 1800. In part, the creation of the college was motivated by the need to counteract the spread of French revolutionary ideas in India, a fear reinforced by the military successes of the French in the Middle East in 1799.[13] However, although Jones's complex views had acquired a coherence in the context of revitalized conservatism, it was James Mill who in his 1817 *History* first clearly defined Jones's views as conservative. In doing so, he was to grapple with the problems that were implicit in Jones's own work. In general terms, these problems might be defined as the questions of whether it is possible to arrive at an idiom in which different societies and their cultures might be compared and contrasted; whether it is possible to find a language which secures a consistency (and resolves the tensions) between one's political views on Britain and on India; and the question of the precise role of the practices of the past in the defining and advocating practices for the present day. At the heart of both Jones's work and Mill's attempt to articulate utilitarianism is this grappling with the general problems of what might be called comparativism, which by its very nature is unstable and provisional.

The general shape of Mill's project in the *History* as he defined it against Jones's work is clear enough.[14] Mill's views on education and psychology were central here. As an adherent of Hartley's associationist psychology, which claimed that the organizing principle of the human mind was the association of ideas, Mill argued that since the human mind was a tabula rasa at birth, education was capable of moulding it by inculcating the ideas best calculated to further individual and general happiness.[15] By analogy, his *History* argued that India might be treated as a tabula rasa which could be molded according to utilitarian dictates. This involved refusing the cogency of Jones's argument that a historical narrative could be recovered from Indian mythological and legendary material, and Mill also ignored significant advances since Jones's time in the empirical study of the past, for example, numismatics.[16] But this disregard for the past was also rooted in the work of Jeremy Bentham, who had argued in his *Introduction to the Principles of Morals and Legislation* (1789) that the legislator should be concerned with censorial jurisprudence, or defining what the law ought to be, rather than expository jurisprudence, or describing what the law is.[17] In *Of Laws in General*, Bentham envisaged the establishment of a school to teach the "art of legislation for empires" which would create a "universal harmony of the laws."[18] The central importance of censorial and universal jurisprudence in Bentham's conception of the legislative task was in opposition to the notion of law and legislation that underlay the common law tradition, upon which the legal administration of British India also rested.[19] Mill's disregard for the past in assessing societies and their cultures and institutions was in keeping with what Bentham criticized as the "superstitious respect for antiquity"[20] in common law theory and its embodiment of what he colourfully called the "relentless tyranny of the dead."[21] It was the English common law tradition, as defined by Edmund Burke in terms of a political ideology, which Bentham attacked as the creed of the British ruling elite.[22] For both Bentham and Mill, arguments from precedence had to be treated with caution where the critique and reform of institutions were concerned. In his *History*, Mill made clear the criteria he used to assess cultures: "Exactly in proportion as Utility is the object of every pursuit, may we regard a nation as civilized."[23]

The formulation of this scale was based on the Benthamite notion of the universal legislator, who compared and contrasted legal traditions through the principle of utility. It was also on this basis that Mill argued the legal systems of both Britain and India could be critiqued, and the different codes of law in India replaced by a single, comprehensive code, formulated in a similar manner. It was on these grounds that Mill argued that cultures and societies could be understood more comprehensively from a distance, when the sympathies of the commentator were not engaged in the detail of minute observations.[24]

However, it is also clear that there were gaps and tensions in Mill's project as a whole. In part, this is reflected in the fact that Mill makes no attempt to draw any conclusion at the end of his *History*. Instead, the last two sentences read: "With regard to subsequent events, the official papers, and other sources of information, are not sufficiently at command. Here, therefore, it is necessary that, for the present, this *History* should come to a close."[25] In a sense, this reflects the open-ended nature of the *History*, as an ongoing narrative and project, which enables Wilson to incorporate it into his own edition of the *History* as part of a reformulation of an orientalist position. This open-ended nature of the text therefore reflects not just the tensions in Mill's project which work against any confident closure of the text but also the way in which utilitarianism itself as a body of thought became just one set of ideas among many which influenced British policy in India over the course of the nineteenth century.[26] Perhaps the clearest indication of this is the way in which John Stuart Mill redefined his own intellectual heritage by working toward reconciling the opposing intellectual traditions of utilitarianism and romanticism.[27] In some ways, the younger Mill's narrative of his own intellectual trajectory reflected the complex ways in which different and competing sets of ideas were brought to bear on British policy in India during the nineteenth century as a whole.[28] But the inconclusive nature of the *History* also reflects how the elder Mill was reliant both on the translations of the very orientalists (such as Jones) whom he criticized, and on the documents produced by those in India itself, against whom he defined his own notion of philosophic historiography.

Furthermore, the tensions in James Mill's project stem from his ambivalent stance on empire. On the one hand, Mill took an economic view of imperialism in India and argued that the expense of government, administration, and wars meant that Britain had not derived any economic benefits from India. In his economic writings, he denied the importance of colonies as markets and stressed that they did not yield any economic benefits. He also argued that colonies served as a source of power and patronage for the ruling elite and were used to perpetuate their position.[29] But Mill's *History* was divided between this negative view of contemporary imperialism and the possibilities that empire opened up as the testing ground for new bodies of thought which had emerged in the metropolis and which had as their aim the critique and reform of the establishment in Britain itself.

There is also a deeper contradiction at work in Mill's philosophy. In his associationist psychology Mill argued that the human mind was passive, and yet he also believed that society could be molded and shaped according to principles arrived at systematically.[30] He needed both these views, of the mind as passive and capable of being formed through careful education, and of the mind as actively molding its environment and culture, for his case against the British in India to stand up. He also needed both these views for his own view of history as progress to work. Ultimately it was conservative figures such as the poet Robert Southey, embracing aspects of Kantian epistemology, who were able to make significant use of the notion of history as progress as part of their defence against radical attacks on the status quo.[31] For those who adopted something akin to Kantian epistemology, there was less of a tension between the assumption of history as a narrative of progress and their concept of mind than there was in Mill's thinking.

In fact, if there was a unifying strand to Mill's *History* it was a distrust of the concept of the imagination, which, he argued, was implicit in Jones's writings on India, and later in Kantian epistemology in general. A particular set of aesthetic and linguistic beliefs were central to Mill's attempted critique of Jones and British policy in India. In general, these beliefs indicated how important aesthetic concepts were for political creeds in the early nineteenth century and how they were related to ways of defending societies and envisaging new political orders.

Both Bentham and James Mill were influenced by the work of Horne Tooke, whose *Diversions of Purley* had argued that all words could be traced through etymology to the names of sensible objects. For Mill, this meant that language could be analyzed in terms of associationist psychology, with reference to sensation.[32] The ascendancy of Horne Tooke's views, in part due to the adoption of his work by the utilitarians in England, meant that the study of language remained philosophical rather than historical or philological for much longer than on the continent, where the new philology, pioneered by Jones, developed into a historical discipline.[33]

Mill's adoption of Tooke was therefore in opposition to Jones's notion of language, but Mill was also to define himself against what he saw as Jones's aesthetic views, and in particular his notion of the imagination. In 1772 Jones had argued in two essays for a rejuvenation of European literature through translations of Oriental texts, and alongside this, for a view of art and the imagination that was anti-mimetic in its implications.[34] James Mill, on the other hand, followed Hartley, who in his *Observations on Man* placed the imagination low in the hierarchy of mental activities.[35] What is interesting in Mill's *History* is how his characterization of the imagination as a faculty dictated by ingenuity and desire, and so leading to the distortion of reality,

keeps coming to the fore.[36] He goes so far as to argue that it is the sub-
servience to this faculty that accounted for English credulity regarding the
wealth of India. According to Mill, a number of British figures, from Robert
Clive to Sir William Jones, were responsible for the myth of India as "over-
flowing with riches."[37] In Mill's writings, there was also often a slippage between economic and cultural riches. Thus, Mill denigrated Indian historical
records and literature as typical of the early stages of society in which poetry
was held in such esteem. [38] In this, his views were similar to those of his colleague at the East India Company, Thomas Love Peacock, whose influential
essay on "The Four Ages of Poetry" in 1820 was also to argue that poetry
played a less important role in advanced than in primitive society.[39] Thus, the
scale of utility on which Mill based his assessment of cultures in the *History*
was formulated partly on his distrust of a particular construct of the imagination. It is for this reason, too, that Mill argued the philosophic historian
ought to carefully control his imagination in order to make accurate judgments by weighing facts.[40]

Whereas one of Bentham's targets for attack was what he called the
"pestiliential breath of fiction" in common law,[41] Mill's *History* delineates
what he sees as the fiction of the economic and cultural riches of India,
which he argued was rooted in a relationship between the workings of the
imagination and desire. It is clear in some of Mill's letters to Francis Place
that by the time of the publication of the *History* in 1817, Mill was conversant with Kantian epistemology.[42] 1817 was also the year of the publication
of Coleridge's *Biographia Literaria*, which represented Coleridge's final
break from the radicalism of his youth. The *Biographia* rejected Hartlean associationist psychology in order to argue for a theory of the imagination
which was based on Schelling's modification of Kant. In this argument, Coleridge uses a distinctive notion of the imagination (the "secondary" imagination) to defend the established church.[43] This argument was to be developed later in *On the Constitution of the Church and State* of 1830. This was
anti-utilitarian in its approach to institutions and tried to redefine and salvage the cultural authority of the establishment in the wake of the Catholic
Emancipation of 1829. Thus, the publication of Mill's *Analysis of the Phenomena of the Human Mind* in 1828, as a restatement of Hartley's psychology with its distinctive criticisms of the imagination, was part of a debate between different notions of the imagination and of the relationship between
aesthetics and the language of political institutions at the time. In fact, both
James Mill and Coleridge were trying to formulate a new idiom for the middle classes. Mill's 1817 "Essay on Government" was interpreted at the time
as the manifesto of the philosophic radicals and as an attempt to prepare the
middle classes for leadership in a reformed political system.[44] Earlier, in 1812,
Mill had vehemently criticized the very notion of an established church,
whereas Coleridge attempted to transform the idiom of the ancien regime to

fit new political realities, partly by appropriating a Kantian language to defend the idea of an established church.

In part, then, Mill's formulation of a language of utilitarianism in his *History* has to be approached against the background of the aesthetic attitudes that underpinned the revitalized conservatism of the British establishment both at home and abroad. His formulations also need to be seen as delineating the aesthetic attitudes that he saw as implicitly structuring Jones's own position. Even as late as 1828, in his *Analysis of the Phenomena of the Human Mind*, Mill analyzed the categories of the beautiful and the sublime in terms of the association of ideas.[45] He did not engage with Kant's notion of the sublime, which had influenced both Coleridge and Wordsworth.[46] That this might not be accidental is clear in the increasing role the sublime as a concept was playing in the European reevaluation of Indian art in the early nineteenth century.[47] But there may have been another reason for Mill's distrust of the politics of the imagination. This stemmed from the way in which such notions of the imagination could play a role in redefining cultural and national identities. On the whole, Mill's *History* paid little attention to cultural, religious, and linguistic differences. It embodied a version of what Ernest Gellner called "world-levelling, unificatory epistemologies."[48] To a certain extent, this aspect of the *History* was in keeping with the greatest happiness principle, which was universalistic in character,[49] but Mill lacked Bentham's attention to the importance of circumstances influencing sensibility as data that the legislator should take into account.[50] However, in the late eighteenth and early nineteenth centuries, there was a major trend in defining cultural identities with reference to newly discovered historical and mythological material. In general terms, Jones's work in India and his argument that a historical narrative could be recovered from ancient mythological and legendary material was part of this trend. Furthermore, his own original and revised plan for a projected epic, *Britain Discovered*, reflects the role that this positive reevaluation of mythology played in the definition of group identities.[51] The new value placed on myth also influenced Coleridge, one of whose lifelong preoccupations was to write a mythological epic which would be a unifying symbol for the community in the process of self-construction. In this, Coleridge was also influenced by the impact of German biblical criticism which sought to reevaluate myth not as mere fable or unworthy fiction but as an important part of the process by which communities were imagined and through which they constituted their own sense of the past.[52] As such, this positive reevaluation of myth, and its implicit valorization of the imagination, stood in opposition to Mill's view of the stringent discipline of a philosophic historiography, rooted in the careful scrutiny of written documents. Coleridge on the other hand, explicitly equated the predominance of what he called "mechanic philosophy" (under which he would have included utilitarianism) with the decay of the sense of being a historical community.[53] Thus at stake in the debate between Mill's version of utilitarianism and some strands of romanticism were also different notions of what constituted historical narrative itself as well as the role played by the imagination in defining identities on the basis of these narratives.

However, there was another dimension to the reevaluation of myth in this period. Jones's work on comparative mythology in the *Asiatick Researches*, the periodical established by the Asiatic Society of Bengal, also fed into a tradition of comparativism established by such writers as Volney, Dupuis, Sir William Drummond, Erasmus Darwin, and Richard Payne Knight, all of whom drew parallels between Christianity and non-Christian mythologies in order to refute the former's claims to a unique revelation. This tradition of "infidel radicalism" displayed a marked interest in fertility rites and cults, with a corresponding celebration of sexuality, in opposition to what were seen as the ascetic tendencies of contemporary Christian mores.[54] Although Sir William Jones was anxious to safeguard the Mosaic chronology of the Bible from the implications of his own research,[55] his own hymns to Hindu deities were characterized by images of fertility, and in another of his poems, *The Enchanted Fruit or, the Hindu Wife: An Antediluvian Tale*, there is an explicit association between a liberating sexuality and matriarchy.[56] The reevaluation of myth in Jones's work and his own literary pieces celebrated a mythological and religious system, which according to Mill was characterized by "images of sensual pleasure."[57] In his *History*, the imagination as a faculty is often depicted in terms of a threatening eros. Mill saw the celebration of sexuality through non-Christian myths not only as part of this eros but also as a positive comment on certain forms of religious experience. Mill's formulation of utilitarianism was avowedly secular, and Mill himself was an atheist.[58] Any valorization of religious experience was thus anathema to Mill's militant secularism.

Alongside the tradition of infidel radicalism, Mill was also reacting against the libertine tradition of radicalism. This tradition consisted of hostility to religious authority and a belief in hedonism that celebrated sexuality. Its literature was often anti-establishment. John Wilkes's *Essay on Woman* was part of this tradition, which reached its height during the Queen Caroline affair of 1820–1821.[59] Mill was clearly sensitive to the growing influence of evangelicalism on the moral tone of the age.[60] As such, he was anxious to present political radicalism as respectable as possible. This could only be achieved if it distanced itself from the libertine tradition. In part, the increasing importance of Mill's brand of utilitarianism had a lot to do with the absorption of the ethic of respectability in some radical circles in the 1820s and 1830s. Mill also distanced himself from Bentham's hedonism and defined utility in terms of usefulness, as opposed to Bentham, who defined it in terms of pleasure.[61]

It is clear, then, that aesthetic categories played an important part in Mill's formulation of utilitarianism, much of which was defined against what Mill saw as the collusion between aesthetic philosophies and politics in the revitalized conservatism of British institutions at home and abroad. Nonetheless, despite the harsh strictures in the *History* about the "Muslim" and "Hindu" cultures of India, it is also important to draw attention to fragments of another discourse in Mill's project which may have an important resonance in contemporary South Asia. As postcolonial critics we need to consider how colonial texts in the past have constructed groups in South Asia and how those groups have internalized such constructions in their own self-definitions.[62] But we also need to be able to selectively appropriate these texts and their questions so that our current political practices can be informed by any perspectives whose potential might otherwise be ignored in these texts. In the case of Mill, we have seen how the *History* is riddled with contradictions and tensions, and also how it was both incomplete and appropriated by Wilson for his own purposes. It is clear that there is much that is repugnant in Mill's *History*; this includes not just his denigration of "Hindu" and "Muslim" cultures, which extends to his divisive tactic of dividing Indian history itself into "Hindu," "Muslim" and "British" periods[63] but also his puritanical attitude to sexuality. Nonetheless, the questions Mill raises about the relationship of the past to current political practices, and in particular the possibility of opening up a space for self-definition which is rooted in a provocative disrespect of the ways in which the past has been constructed, might be revisited again. This is especially so given the centrality of communalism in South Asia and the growth of "Muslim" and "Hindu" militancies which rely on the invocation of ready-made pasts and ready-made origins, and which have partly emerged from the labors of European orientalists in interaction with a variety South Asian thinkers, authors, and polemicists themselves.[64] Furthermore, Mill was equally harsh about British society at the time; it is clear that his *History* was a matrix in which a critique of British society itself was shaped. It was because Mill saw empire as buttressing powerful groups at home that his *History* was a critique of the legal, political, and religious institutions in Britain and of their influence on British rule in India. It is for this reason that the *History* contains extensive Benthamite criticisms of the English legal system.[65] It was against the background of India that the ideology of the British establishment was clearly marked out. This also gave Mill the distance necessary to fashion the tools and principles to critique this ideology. Hence Mill contemplated writing a critical history of the English legal system after completing his *History*;[66] such a history would be a logical development of his *History of British India*. Thus, there was a self-critical and self-reflexive aspect to Mill's *History* which reflected an attempt to formulate an idiom in which societies might be not just compared and contrasted but also criticized. Both Bentham and Mill made it clear that any critique of another society necessarily involved a critique of one's own society.[67] Mill's *History* articulated an opportunity to reform social and legal practices in India but also to reform practices in Britain itself. In so doing, they also tried to formulate an idiom that was secular; however imperfect this secularism was, it nonetheless suggested some ways at the time in which the question of the relationship between the past and the present might be negotiated in an attempt to redefine politicized cultural identities.

NOTES

An earlier version of this paper was published as "James Mill's *The History of British India*: a re-evaluation," in *J. S. Mill's encounter with India*, ed. Martin I. Moir, Douglas M. Peers, and Lynn Zastoupil (Toronto: University of Toronto Press, 1999), 53–71. I have also drawn on my *Ungoverned Imaginings: James Mill's* The History of British India and Orientalism (Oxford: Clarendon Press, 1992).

1. Duncan Forbes, "James Mill and India," *Cambridge Journal* 5 (1951–52): 31.

2. Wilson's edition of Mill's *History* was first published in 1840. Wilson was renowned for his defense of the so-called orientalist educational policy against the anglicist measures of the Bentinck government, for which see Martin Moir and Lynn Zastoupil, *The Great Indian Education Debate: Documents Relating to the Orientalist-Anglicist Controversy 1781–1843* (Richmond: Curzon Press, 1999), especially 205–24. Wilson was also the first professor of Sanskrit at Oxford; he took up his chair in 1833.

3. James Mill, *The History of British India* (1817, 3 vols.), ed. with notes and continuation by H. H. Wilson, 10 vols. (London: James Madden, Piper, Stephenson, and Spence, 1858) 1: xii. All subsequent references to Mill's *History* are to this edition.

4. P. J. Marshall, "Empire and Authority in the Later Eighteenth Century," *Journal of Imperial and Commonwealth History* 15 (January 1987), 115.

5. *The Writings and Speeches of Edmund Burke: India: Madras and Bengal 1774–1785*, ed. P. J. Marshall (Oxford: Clarendon Press, 1981), 178. See also Javed Majeed, *Ungoverned Imaginings*, 8–9.

6. Garland Cannon, "Sir William Jones and Edmund Burke," *Modern Philology* 54 (1956–1957), 174.

7. Sir William Jones, "To the second Earl Spencer," October 19, 1791, in *The Letters of Sir William Jones*, ed. Garland Cannon, 2 vols. (Oxford: Clarendon Press, 1970), 2: 898–99.

8. This can be gathered from the position Jones himself expressed in some of his letters. See Sir William Jones, "To Sir John Macpherson," May 6, 1786, and "To the Second Earl Spencer," October 19, 1791, *Letters of Sir William Jones*, ed. Cannon, 2: 699, 898–99.

9. For a more detailed analysis of Jones' legal position, see Majeed, *Ungoverned Imaginings*, 16–28. For an important discussion of the British codification of "Hindu" law in particular, see J. D. M. Derrett, *Religion, Law, and the State in India* (London: Faber and Faber, 1968), chap. 8.

10. For which, see Majeed, *Ungoverned Imaginings*, 31–40. I have put the terms "Hindu" and "Muslim" in quotation marks in an attempt to distance my use of them from the way in which they are now used as self-evident and ahistorical categories, supposedly relating to two homogenous and opposed communities.

11. For a discussion of these views, see S. N. Mukherjee, *Sir William Jones: A Study in Eighteenth Century Attitudes to India* (Cambridge: Cambridge University Press, 1968), chap. 4.

12. C. A. Bayly, *Imperial Meridian: The British Empire and the World 1780–1830* (London: Longman, 1989), makes a detailed case for the relationship between the rise of Britain as a global power and the growth of a revitalised conservatism in Britain, as a reaction against the threat of the French Revolution. For the ways in which Jones's views came to be part of this conservatism, and the whole problematic of "liberal imperialism," see Majeed, *Ungoverned Imaginings*, 40–46.

13. David Kopf, *British Orientalism and the Bengal Renaissance: The Dynamics of Indian Modernizaton 1773–1835* (Berkeley: University of California Press, 1969), 46–47.

14. In what follows, I draw upon Majeed, *Ungoverned Imaginings*, chapters 4 and 5.

15. Mill's *Analysis of the Phenomena of the Human Mind* of 1828 was a restatement of Hartleian psychology. In his 1869 edition of this text, John Stuart Mill described his father as the "reviver and second founder of Associationist Psychology." See James Mill, *Analysis of the Phenomena of the Human Mind*, ed. John Stuart Mill, 2 vols. (London: Longmans, Green, Reader, and Dyer, 1869), 1: xi.

16. For an account of these advances, see O. P. Kejariwal, *The Asiatic Society of Bengal and the Discovery of India's Past 1784–1838* (Delhi: Oxford University Press, 1988), 57, 158.

17. Jeremy Bentham, "An Introduction to the Principles of Morals and Legislation" (1789) in *The Collected Works of Jeremy Bentham*, ed. J. H. Burns and H. L. A. Hart (London: Athlone Press, 1970), 274.

18. Jeremy Bentham, *Of Laws in General*, in *Works*, ed. Hart, 242–44.

19. Mukherjee, *Jones*, 59–60, 126. For Jones's views on common law, see Jones, "To Thomas Yeates," June 7, 1787, *Letters* 1: 553.

20. Gerald J. Postema, *Bentham and the Common Law Tradition* (1986; Oxford: Clarendon Press, 1989), 279.

21. University College London, Bentham MS., "Parliamentary Reform" 1794–95, box 44, folio 5.

22. Postema, *Bentham and the Common Law Tradition*, 311.

23. Mill, *History*, 2: 105.

24. Mill, *History*, 1: viii–xxiii.

25. Mill, *History*, 6: 479.

26. Majeed, *Ungoverned Imaginings*, 192–94.

27. This attempt at reconciliation and synthesis is clear in the intellectual trajectory John Stuart Mill defines for himself in his *Autobiography*, for which see volume 1 of *Collected Works of John Stuart Mill*, ed. J. M. Robson and Jack Stallinger (Toronto: University of Toronto Press, 1981).

28. For which, see Lynn Zastoupil, *John Stuart Mill and India* (Stanford: Stanford University Press, 1994).

29. These arguments are to be found in James Mill, *Commerce Defended* (1807) and *Elements of Political Economy* (1821) in *James Mill: Selected Economic Writings*,

ed. Donald Winch (Edinburgh: Oliver and Boyd, 1966), 87–158 and 210–364. See also *James Mill, 'The Article Colony,"* reprinted from the *Supplement to the Encyclopaedia Britannica* (London: J. Innes, c. 1820).

30. W. H. Burston, *James Mill on Philosophy and Education* (London: Athlone Press, 1973) 187.

31. Majeed, *Ungoverned Imaginings*, chap. 2.

32. Hans Aarsleff, *The Study of Language in England 1760–1860* (Minneapolis: University of Minnesota Press, 1983), 71–74, 93–95. For Mill's positive comments on Tooke, see his "Horne Tooke's Diversions of Purley," *Literary Journal of Domestic and Foreign Literature* 1 (1806), 1–16.

33. Aarsleff, *Study of Language*, 96.

34. These two essays were "On the Poetry of the Eastern Nations" and "On the Arts Commonly Called Imitative." Both appeared in his *Poems, Consisting Chiefly of the Translations from the Asiatick Languages* (1772) in *The Works of Sir William Jones*, ed. A. M. Jones, 6 vols. (London: G. G. and J. Robinson, 1799) 4: 397–561.

35. David Hartley, *Observations on Man, His Frame, His Duty and His Expectations*, 2 vols. (London: James Leake and Wm. Frederick, 1749), 1: 431.

36. Mill, *History*, 1: 239.

37. Mill, *History*, 2: 84, 3: 307, 213. See also Mill's comments on Jones's "susceptible imagination" in "Voyage aux Indes Orientale," *Edinburgh Review* 15 (1980), 369.

38. Mill, *History*, 1: 112, 115–16, 2: 63.

39. *The Works of T. L. Peacock*, ed. Henry Cole (London: Richard Bentley and sons, 1875), 3: 324–38.

40. Mill, *History*, 1: xvii.

41. Cited by Ross Harrsion, *Bentham* (London: Routledge, 1983), 24.

42. British Library, Mill to Place, October 2, 1816, Add. MS. 35 152, f. 217; Mill to Place, October 8, 1816, Add. MS. 35 152, f. 127, Francis Place papers. See also James Mill, "Essay on Education," in *James Mill on Education*, ed. W. H. Burston (Cambridge: Cambridge University Press, 1969), 66.

43. S. T. Coleridge, *Biographia Literaria or Biographical Sketches of My Literary Life and Opinions* (1817; London: J. M. Dent, 1975), ed. George Watson, 167.

44. James Mill, *Essay on Government, Jurisprudence, Liberty of the Press, and Law of Nations. Written for the supplement to the Encyclopaedia Britannica* (London: J. Innes, c. 1825), 3– 32.

45. James Mill, *Analysis of the Phenomena of the Human Mind*, 2: 230–37.

46. Mary Warnock, *Imagination* (London: Faber and Faber, 1976), parts 1–3.

47. Partha Mitter, *Much Maligned Monsters: History of European Reactions to Indian Art* (Oxford: Clarendon Press, 1977), 119–22.

48. Ernest Gellner, *Relativism and the Social Sciences* (Cambridge: Cambridge University Press, 1985), 76.

49. Frederick Rosen, *Jeremy Bentham and Representative Democracy: A Study of the Constitutional Code* (Oxford: Clarendon Press, 1983), 205–6.

50. Jeremy Bentham, *Principles of Morals and Legislation*, 51–72, and "Essay on the Influence of Time and Place in Matters of Legislation," in *The Works of Jeremy Bentham*, ed. John Bowring (Edinburgh: William Tait, 1843), 1: 173.

51. *Memoirs of the Life, Writings, and Correspondence of Sir William Jones*, ed. Lord Teignmouth (London: J. Brettell, 1804), 475–89.

52. E. S. Shaffer, *Kubla Khan and the Fall of Jerusalem: The Mythological School in Biblical Criticism and Secular Literature 1770–1880* (Cambridge: Cambridge University Press, 1975), chap. 1–4.

53. S. T. Coleridge, "To Lord Liverpool," July 28, 1817, *Collected Letters of Samuel Taylor Coleridge*, ed. E. L. Griggs, 6 vols. (Oxford: Clarendon Press, 1959), 4: 761.

54. Marilyn Butler, *Romantics, Rebels and Reactionaries: English Literature and its background 1760–1830* (Oxford: Oxford University Press, 1981), 78, 130.

55. I discuss this conflict in Jones's work in Majeed, *Ungoverned Imaginings*, 34–35.

56. Jones's hymns are to be found in *Works*, ed. A. M. Jones, volume 6. "The Enchanted Fruit" is also in 6: 181.

57. Mill, *History*, 1: 294.

58. Alexander Bain, *James Mill: A Biography* (London: Longmans, Green, and Co., 1882) claims that Mill became an atheist in 1808. But for an examination of the complexities of Mill's rejection of his Presbyterian faith, see Majeed, *Ungoverned Imaginings*, 79–81.

59. Ian McCalman, "Unrespectable Radicalism: Radicalism, Infidels and Pornography in Early Nineteenth Century London," *Past and Present* 104 (1984), 84, 99.

60. Boyd Hilton, *The Age of Atonement: The Influence of Evangelicalism on Social and Economic Thought 1795–1865* (Oxford: Clarendon Press, 1988) 219.

61. Harrison, *Bentham*, 170. For a recent and excellent discussion of hedonism and utilitarianism, see Fred Feldman, *Utilitarianism, Hedonism, and Desert: Essays in Moral Philosophy* (Cambridge: Cambridge University Press, 1997).

62. *The Concept of Race in South Asia*, ed. Peter Robb (Delhi: Oxford University Press, 1995), deals with this question.

63. This division is evident in volumes 1–2 of Mill's *History*.

64. There are a number of scholarly works which deal with the relationship between the texts produced by European orientalist scholars and their interaction with South Asian textual traditions themselves, especially in the context of how Indian thinkers and writers began to refashion their own self-perceptions through this interaction. C. A. Bayly, *Empire and Information. Intelligence Gathering and Social Communication in India c. 1780–1870* (Cambridge: Cambridge University Press, 1996), V. Dalmia, *The Nationalization of Hindu Tradition: Bharatendu Harischandra and Nineteenth Century Benaras* (Delhi: Oxford University Press, 1997), and Tejaswini Niranjana, *Siting Translation. History, Post-Structuralism, and the Colonial Context* (Berkeley: University of California Press, 1992), all explore this issue from different perspectives. See also my "Nature, Hyperbole, and the Colonial State: Some Muslim Appropriations of European Modernity in Late Nineteenth Century Urdu Literature," in *Islam and Modernity*, ed. John Cooper, Ronald Nettler, and Mohamed Mahmoud (London: I. B. Tauris, 1998), 10–37. For a recent and excellent thesis which explores this area see Michael S. Dodson, "Orientalism, Sanskrit Scholarship, and Education in Colonial North India c. 1775–1875," Cambridge doctoral dissertation, 2003.

65. Mill, *History*, 3: 352; 4: 220, 242; 5: 205, 210, 355, 425.

66. British Library, Mill to Napier, August 5, 1818, Add. MS. 34612, ff. 212–13, Macvey Napier papers.

67. For example, see Bentham, *Principles of Morals and Legislation*, 184, 274, and "Essay on the Influence of Time and Place in matters of Legislation," 184–85.

5

Mill on Happiness

The Enduring Value of a Complex Critique

Martha C. Nussbaum

Who is the happy Warrior? Who is he
That every man in arms should wish to be?

> Wordsworth, *Character of the Happy Warrior*

Man does not strive after happiness; only the Englishman does that.

> Nietzsche, *Maxims and Arrows*

A

Few feminists would doubt that John Stuart Mill has made a contribution to the critique of sexual hierarchy that is of enduring value, and of value to feminists across lines of nation and race. Translated into many languages and influential, sometimes, more in distant places than in its own nation of origin, *The Subjection of Women*, first published in 1869, sounded a clarion call to both women and men, showing with convincing arguments that the male domination of women in the family was inconsistent with liberalism's noble aspiration to dismantle feudal and monarchical hierarchies of power. The idea that the marital family is a school of unearned privilege, unjustified hierarchy, and, often, of violence was not in principle difficult to discover. All that it required was a look at reality. But, as Mill said, few people whose daily lives are implicated in a pattern of injustice are willing to look at the reality of that injustice. So he predicted, correctly, that his work would have a difficult time gaining a hearing.

For all the neglect of the work by most of Mill's British readers and, until recently, by most of his philosophical commentators, it did find an audience. Chinese feminist scholars have told me that it was highly influential in the founding of the women's movement in China. It is widely known in South Asia as well. The radical feminist Catharine MacKinnon, who has little time for any other male philosopher, analyzes it with sympathy. And in general, we women in philosophy, around the world, feel that among the philosophers of the past Mill alone, or at least Mill supremely, is our friend, a partner not only in uncovering and criticizing hierarchies of sex and gender but a sensitive thinker about hierarchy more generally, whose thoughts are also applicable to hierarchies of class and race.

Mill's life itself gives much evidence of true friendship with women: consider that as a young man Mill went to jail for distributing contraceptive literature; consider that as a member of Parliament he seriously advocated female suffrage, well before such proposals were likely to gain a following; consider his relationship with Harriet Taylor, in which the idea of equality and mutual respect became more than a theoretical fancy. But it is above all the work that we feminists value. *Subjection* is far from a perfect feminist work: in particular, it fails sufficiently to criticize the domestic division of labor as an obstacle to women's full equality. But Mill, unlike most liberals, was willing to think the idea of equality and non-hierarchy straight into the bosom of the "private sphere," to demolish the idea that this sphere should be immune from legal regulation, and to address the subtle psychological obstacles that power creates against true equality. All this makes his thought much more useful than that of most other liberals not only for feminist thought but also for other projects of critique that tackle entrenched hierarchies of power.

The feminist achievements of *Subjection*, however, have been narrated before. In this essay, then, I want to attempt something both more controversial and, I believe, more fundamental: to defend Mill's conception of happiness as a rich resource for feminist thinking and for progressive thinking generally, including thinking about ethnicity and race. Since it is very difficult to figure out what Mill's conception of happiness is, indebted as it is to the very different conceptions of Aristotle and Bentham, I must spend time interpreting it. I shall then propose a theory about why Mill is unable fully to endorse Aristotle's activity-centered conception. I shall then suggest that Mill's idea is indeed one that we need, if we are to think well about the role of happiness in the formation of basic political principles for a just society.

B

Powerful philosophical conceptions conceal, even while they reveal. By shining a powerful light on some genuinely important aspects of human life,

British utilitarianism concealed others. Its concern with counting each and every person obscured, for a time, the fact that some issues of justice cannot be well handled through mere aggregation of the interests of all. Its radical and admirable concern with suffering, with bringing all sentient beings from pain to a state of well-being and satisfaction, obscured, for a time, the fact that satisfaction might not be all there was to the human good, or even all there was to happiness. Other things might also be involved, such as activity, loving, fullness of commitment.

Indeed, so powerful was the obscuring power of Bentham's insight that a question that Wordsworth takes to be altogether askable, and which, indeed, he spends eighty-five lines answering—the question of what happiness really is—soon looks to philosophers under Bentham's influence like a question whose answer is so obvious that it cannot be asked in earnest. Thus Henry Prichard, albeit a foe of utilitarianism, was so influenced in his thinking about happiness by Bentham's conception that he simply assumed that any philosopher who talks about happiness must be identifying it with pleasure or satisfaction. When Aristotle asks what happiness is, Prichard argued, he cannot really be asking the question he appears to be asking, since the answer to that question is obvious: happiness is contentment or satisfaction. Instead of asking what happiness consists in, then, he must really be asking about the instrumental means to the production of happiness.[1] Nietzsche, similarly, understands happiness to be (uncontroversially) a state of pleasure and contentment, and expresses his scorn for Englishmen who pursue that goal rather than richer goals involving suffering for a noble end, continued striving, activities that put contentment at risk, and so forth. Unaware of the richer English tradition about happiness represented in Wordsworth's poem, he simply took English "happiness" to be what Bentham said it was. So, much later, did Finnish sociologist Erik Allardt, when he wrote an attack on the idea that happiness was the end of social planning, entitling his book *Having, Loving, Being*—active things that he took to be more important than satisfaction, which Finns, heir of Nordic romanticism, typically think quite unimportant.[2] Like Nietzsche, he understood the "happiness" of the social scientists to be a state of pleasure or satisfaction. (He is correct about the social scientists, if not about "happiness.")

There is, however, an older and longer tradition of thinking about happiness, the tradition represented in Wordsworth's poem. It derives from ancient Greek thought about *eudaimonia* and its parts and is inherited via the standard English translation of *eudaimonia* as "happiness." According to this tradition, represented most fully in Aristotle's *Nicomachean Ethics*, what we all can agree about is that happiness is something like flourishing human living, a kind of living that is active, inclusive of all that has intrinsic value, and complete, meaning lacking in nothing that would make it richer or better. Everything else about happiness is disputed, says Aristotle, but he then goes on to argue for a conception of happiness that identifies it with a specific plurality of valuable activities, including activity in accordance with excellences[3] (valuable traits) of many sorts, including ethical, intellectual, and political excellences, and activities involved in love and friendship. Pleasure is not identical with happiness, but it usually (*not* always) accompanies the unimpeded performance of the activities that constitute happiness.

Something like this is the idea that Wordsworth is relying on when he asks, in each of the many areas of life, what the character and demeanor of the "happy Warrior" would be, and answers that question. As J. L. Austin memorably wrote in a devastating critique of Prichard on Aristotle, "I do not think Wordsworth meant: . . .'This is the warrior who feels *pleased.*' Indeed, he is 'Doomed to go in company with Pain/And fear and bloodshed, miserable train.'"

As Austin saw, the important thing about the happy Warrior is that he has traits that make him capable of performing all of life's many activities in an exemplary way, and he acts in accordance with those traits. He is moderate, kind, courageous, loving, a good friend, concerned for the community, honest,[4] not excessively attached to honor or worldly ambition, a lover of reason, an equal lover of home and family. His life is happy because it is full and rich, even though it sometimes may involve pain and loss.

Mill knew both of these conceptions of happiness and was torn between them. Philosophically he declared himself a utilitarian; despite his many criticisms of Bentham, he never stopped representing himself as a defender of Bentham's general line. He was also, however, a lover of the Greeks and a lover of Wordsworth, the poet whom he credits with curing his depression. The Aristotelian/Wordsworthian conception of happiness makes numerous appearances in his thought. Mill seems never to have fully realized the extent of the tension between the two conceptions; thus he never describes the conflict between them or argues for the importance of the pieces he appropriates from each one. The unkind way of characterizing the result is that Mill is deeply confused and has no coherent conception of happiness. The kinder and, I believe, more accurate way is that, despite Mill's unfortunate lack of clarity about how he is combining the two conceptions, he really does have a more or less coherent idea of how to combine them, giving richness of life and complexity of activity a place they do not have in Bentham, but giving pleasure and the absence of pain and depression a role that Aristotle never sufficiently maps out—in part because depression is a category that Aristotle never recognizes, as Mill, by dint of unfortunate experience, does. The result is the basis, at least, for a conception of happiness that is richer than either of its two sources, more capable of doing justice to all the elements that thoughtful people have associated with that elusive idea.

C

Bentham had a way of making life simpler than it is. He asserts that the only thing good in itself is pleasure and that the only thing bad in itself is pain. From the claim that these two "masters" have a very powerful influence on human conduct, he passes without argument to the normative claim that they are the proper goals of conduct. And he also equates pleasure with happiness (sometimes with enjoyment of happiness), pain with unhappiness. The principle of utility is "that principle which approves or disapproves of every action whatsoever, according to the tendency which it appears to have to augment or diminish the happiness of the party whose interest is in question: or, what is the same thing in other words, to promote or to oppose that happiness." Utility, in turn, is defined in a manner that shows Bentham's characteristic disregard of distinctions that have mattered greatly to philosophers, both before and since:

> By utility is meant that property in any object, whereby it tends to produce benefit, advantage, pleasure, good, or happiness, (all this in the present case comes to the same thing) or (what comes again to the same thing) to prevent the happening of mischief, pain, evil, or unhappiness to the party whose interest is considered.

Ignoring or flouting the long Western philosophical tradition that had debated whether happiness could be identified with pleasure—a tradition in which the negative answer greatly predominated, the positive answer being given only by Epicureans—Bentham simply declares what he takes to be the case and goes on from there. Nothing else is good but pleasure; pleasure and good are the same thing.

As for pleasure, an equally long philosophical tradition before Bentham had debated how we should understand its nature. Is it a single, unitary thing, or many things? Is it a feeling, or is it a way of being active, or, perhaps, activity itself? We speak of pleasure as a type of experience, but we also refer to activities as "my pleasures," saying things like, "My greatest pleasures are listening to Mahler and eating steak." Such ways of talking raise two questions: Is pleasure a sensation at all, if such very different experiences count as pleasures? And is it single? Could there be any one thing that both listening to Mahler's Tenth and eating a steak have in common?

Plato, Aristotle, and a whole line of subsequent philosophers subtly discussed these questions. Bentham simply ignores them. As Mill writes in his great essay "On Bentham," "Bentham failed in deriving light from other minds." For him, pleasure is a single homogeneous sensation, containing no qualitative differences. The only variations in pleasure are quantitative. They can vary in intensity, duration, certainty or uncertainty, propinquity or remoteness, and, finally, in causal properties (tendency to produce more pleasure, etc.). The apparent fact that pleasures differ in quality, that the pleasure of steak-eating is quite different from the pleasure of listening to Mahler's Tenth, bothered Bentham not at all; he does not discuss such examples. Perhaps the reason for this problem is that Bentham's deepest concern is with pain and suffering, and it is somewhat more plausible to think of pain as a unitary sensation varying only in intensity and duration. As Mill says, this is "the empiricism of one who has had little experience"—either external, he adds, or internal, through the imagination.

Nor was Bentham worried about interpersonal comparisons, a problem on which economists in the utilitarian tradition have spent great labor. For Bentham there was no such problem: when we move from one person to many people, we just add a new dimension of quantity. Right action is ultimately defined as that which produces the greatest pleasure for the greatest number. Moreover, Bentham sees no problem in extending the comparison class to the entire world of sentient animals. One of the most attractive aspects of his thought is its great compassion for the suffering of animals, which he took to be unproblematically comparable to human suffering.[5]

Another problem that has troubled economists in the Benthamite tradition is that of evil pleasures. If people get pleasure from inflicting harm on others, as so often they do, should that count as a pleasure that makes society better? Most economists who follow Bentham have tried to do some line drawing here, in order to leave the most sadistic and malicious pleasures out of the social choice function. In so doing, they complicate the system in a way that Bentham would not have approved, introducing an ethical value that is not itself reducible to pleasure or pain.

Activity plays no special role in Bentham's system. The goal of right action is to maximize pleasure, understood as a sensation. That is the only good thing there is in the world. So, in effect, people and animals are understood as large containers of sensations of pleasure or satisfaction. Their capacity for agency is of interest only in the sense that it makes them capable of choosing actions that produce utility. But in terms of the end result, agency really does not matter. A person who gets pleasure by being hooked up to an experience machine (a famous example of the late Robert Nozick) is just as well off as the person who gets pleasure by loving and eating and listening. Even when we are thinking about nonhuman animals, this is a very reduced picture of what is valuable in life; where human beings are concerned, it evidently leaves out more or less everything.

What is attractive about Bentham's program is its focus on urgent needs of sentient beings for relief from suffering and its determination to take all suffering of all sentient beings into account. But Bentham cannot be said to have developed anything like a convincing account of pleasure and pain, of happiness, or of social utility. Because of his attachment to a strident simplicity, the view remains a sketch crying out for adequate philosophical development.

D

Unlike Bentham, Aristotle sees that the question about happiness is a very difficult question. He is aware of many different answers people have given to that question. Some identify happiness with pleasure, some with honor, some with the life of virtue, some with the life of reflection or thought. But progress can be made, he suggests, if we pin down some key areas of agreement. In Book I of the *Nicomachean Ethics*, he sets about that task. He argues that there is general agreement about several formal characteristics of happiness. It must be *most final*, that is, inclusive of all that has intrinsic value. It must be *self-sufficient*, by which he means that there is nothing that can be added to it that would increase its value. (He immediately makes clear that self-sufficiency does not imply solitariness: the sort of self-sufficiency he is after is one that includes relationships with family, friends, and fellow citizens.) It must be *active*, since we all agree that happiness is equivalent to "living well and doing well." Moreover, we think that a person who is inactive all through life ("asleep" he says, but we could think of a coma) is not in the least happy but indeed quite miserable, even if he feels no pain and is in a very good ethical state. It must be *generally available*, to anyone who makes the right sort of effort, since we don't want to define happiness as something only a few can enjoy. And it must be relatively *stable*, not something that can be removed by any chance misfortune.

Aristotle concludes this (allegedly uncontroversial) part of his argument by arguing that there is a further deep agreement: happiness is made up of activity in accordance with excellence, either one excellence, or, if there are more than one, then the greatest and most complete. Scholars argue a lot about the precise understanding of this passage, but let me simply assert. At this point in his argument, Aristotle cannot be importing any precise or controversial content into the conception, and he explicitly says that he is not doing so. So he must mean, whatever the excellent activities of a human life are, happiness involves all of these in some suitable combination. He also makes it clear that the overall product is more than the mere aggregation of its parts: the way all the activities fit together to make up a whole life is itself an element in the value of the life.

In the remainder of the work, Aristotle moves through the areas of human life in which we characteristically act and make choices, trying to identify the excellent way of acting in each of these areas. He seems to think that there is relatively little controversy about the fact that courage, moderation, justice, etc., are worth pursuing: where the controversy occurs is in the more precise specification of what each of these is. Presumably the reason for this is that he conceives of these spheres of life as spheres in which we all have to make some choice or another: we have to have some way of facing the risk of death, some way of coping with our bodily appetites, etc. So there is no question of omitting that element altogether; one either does it well or does it badly, and the question is, what is it to do it well? Only with friendship and love does he face an imaginary opponent who urges the utter omission of these relationships as intrinsically valuable areas of human activity. But he brusquely dismisses that position by saying that nobody would want to live without friendship, even if he had all the other goods.

Where in all of this is pleasure? Early in the work, Aristotle dismisses the claim that pleasure is identical with happiness, saying that living for pleasure only would be "to choose the life of dumb grazing animals." Later he advances some further arguments against the identification. First of all, there is an issue about pleasure: it is by no means easy to say what it is. Aristotle himself offers two very different conceptions of pleasure, one in Book VII and one in Book X. The first identifies pleasure with unimpeded activity (not so odd if we remember that we speak of "my pleasures" and "enjoyments"). The second, and probably better, account holds that pleasure is something that comes along with, supervenes on, activity, "like the bloom on the cheek of youth." In other words, it is so closely linked to the relevant activities that it cannot be pursued on its own, any more than bloom can be cultivated by cosmetics. One gets it by doing the relevant activity in a certain way, apparently a way that is not impeded, or is complete. It is a kind of awareness of one's own activity. In any case, pleasure is not a single thing, varying only in intensity and duration (a position that Plato already knew and criticized). It contains qualitative differences, related to the differences of the activities to which it attaches.

But whatever one says about pleasure, one should still not say that it is identical with happiness. First of all, even if pleasure were single and homogeneous, happiness clearly is not: it is constituted by activities of many different sorts, which cannot be rendered commensurable on any quantitative scale.

Second, pleasure is just not the right thing to pitch on as a normative account of the good life for a human being. Some pleasures are bad, namely those that are closely associated with bad activities. Evil people take pleasure in their evil behavior. But happiness is a normative notion, meaning "the human good life," or "a flourishing life for a human being," so we cannot include evil pleasures in it.

Another problem, and a revealing one for Mill, is that some valuable activities are not accompanied by pleasure. Aristotle's example is Wordsworthian (perhaps the source for Wordsworth's poem): the courageous warrior who faces death in battle for the sake of a noble end. It is absurd to say that this person is pleased at the prospect of death, says Aristotle. Indeed, the better his life is, the more he thinks he has to lose, and the more pain he is likely to feel at the prospect of death. Nonetheless, he is acting in accordance with excellence, and is aware of that, and so he is still happy. This just goes to show, says Aristotle, that pleasure does not always go along with the activities that constitute happiness, only most of the time.

The courageous Warrior is still happy because he is living the sort of life he chooses, and it is a good one. There are other people whose circumstances deprive them of happiness, according to Aristotle. But they do so by blocking activity. For example, if one is imprisoned and tortured, one is no longer happy—because all one's activities are terribly "impeded." If one encounters "the luck of Priam," here too one can be "dislodged from happiness"—because friends, children, political activity, and indeed the entire sphere in which he lived and acted is suddenly snatched away by defeat and capture. So Aristotle does allow that certain sorts of misery are incompatible with happiness: but his question is not, "How does the person feel?" It is, instead, "What is the person able to do?" And he judges that in a wide variety of circumstances a good person will be able to use life's materials resourcefully and well, so as to continue being happy in a wide range of (somewhat reduced) circumstances.

E

Mill's *Utilitarianism* is organized as an extended defense of Bentham's program against the most common objections that had been raised against it. Mill defends both the idea that pleasure is identical with happiness and the idea that right action consists in producing the greatest happiness for the greatest number. Along the way, however, without open defection from the Benthamite camp, he introduces a number of crucial modifications. First of all, he admits that Bentham's theory has given no clear answer to the question of what pleasure is: "To give a clear view of the moral standard set up by the theory, much more requires to be said; in particular, what things it includes in the ideas of pain and pleasure; and to what extent this is left an open question."

One thing that Mill does shortly make very clear, however, is that, for him, "neither pains nor pleasures are homogeneous." There are differences "*in kind*, apart from the question of intensity," that are evident to any competent judge. We cannot avoid recognizing qualitative differences, particularly between "higher" and "lower" pleasures. How, then, to judge between them? Like Plato in *Republic* Book IX, Mill refers the choice to a competent judge who has experienced both alternatives.

This famous passage shows Mill thinking of pleasures as very like activities, or, with Aristotle, as experiences so closely linked to activities that they cannot be pursued apart from them. In a later text, he counts music, virtue, and health as major pleasures. Elsewhere he shows that he has not left sensation utterly out of account: he refers to "which of two modes of existence is the most grateful to the feelings." Clearly, however, the unity of the Benthamite calculus has been thrown out, to be replaced by an idea of competent judgment as to what "manner of existence" is most "worth having." And this talk of a "manner of existence which employs their higher faculties" suggests that, with Aristotle, he is thinking of this judge as planning for a whole life.

When Mill describes the way in which his judge makes choices, things get still more complicated. The reason an experienced judge will not choose the lower pleasures is "a sense of dignity, which all human beings possess in one form or other . . . and which is so essential a part of the happiness of those in whom it is strong, that nothing which conflicts with it could be, otherwise than momentarily, an object of desire to them." So a sense of dignity is a *part* of what happiness is for many people: it acts as a gatekeeper, preventing the choice of a life devoted to mere sensation. This judge will clearly reject Nozick's experience machine. Moreover, Mill continues, if anyone supposes that this sense of dignity will cause people to sacrifice some of their happiness, they are just confused: they "confound two very different ideas, of happiness, and content." One more of Bentham's equivalences has now been denied.

Summarizing his discussion, referring to the ancient philosophers he has been following, Mill writes, "The happiness which they meant was not a life of rapture; but moments of such, in an existence made up of few and transitory pains, many and varied pleasures, with a decided predominance of the active over the passive." At this point, Mill would appear to have jettisoned the identification of happiness with pleasure: for happiness is now "made up of" pleasures, and some pains, and activity; its "parts" include virtue and the all-important sense of dignity. Even though pleasure itself is complex and heterogeneous, standing in a close relation to activity, happiness is more complex still, including some pain, and extending to embrace the complexities of an extended "mode of existence." Happiness is, then, a full and active life, in Aristotle's manner.

And yet the emphasis on pleasure persists throughout the work; Mill cannot utterly leave it aside. And in one crucial passage, he shows us that his attitude toward pained virtue is subtly different from that of Aristotle, and of Wordsworth. Imagining a virtuous man in the present "imperfect state of the world's arrangements," he concludes that this man must sacrifice his own happiness, if he wishes to promote the happiness of others. Mill does not tell us enough about this man. If his sacrifice is very great, so that his life is deprived of activity, Mill's position may still be Aristotelian: for Aristotle, we recall, judges that Priam is "dislodged from happiness" by his many and great misfortunes. But if this man is more like the happy Warrior, enduring pain for the sake of a noble cause, then Mill is not Aristotle. Even though this man is living well and acting well according to his plan, the very fact of the adversity he faces (apparently political adversity, anxiety, and various types of pain) deprives him of happiness, according to Mill, although Aristotle and Wordsworth judge that such a person is happy.

F

Mill, then, appears to stop short of Aristotle and Wordsworth. People's emotional states and states of pleasurable and nonpainful awareness remain crucial elements in happiness, even though pleasure is seen to be elusive and complex, and even though happiness itself consists at least partly in valuable activities. We might put this point by saying that Mill sets the bar of fortune higher than Aristotle does. Aristotle thinks that fortune dislodges a person from happiness only when it impedes activity so severely that a person cannot execute his chosen plan of life at all. The pained Warrior is still happy because he can still live in his own chosen way, and that is a good way. For Mill, the presence of a great deal of pain seems significant beyond its potential for inhibiting activity. A life full of ethical and intellectual excellences and activity according to those excellences does not suffice for happiness, if pleasure (however we think about pleasure) is insufficiently present and if too much pain is present.

Why did Mill think this? Well, as he tells us, he had experienced such a life—not in a moment of courageous risk taking, but during a long period of depression. This life was the result of an upbringing that emphasized excellent activity to the exclusion of emotional satisfactions, including feelings of contentment, pleasure, and comfort.

Mill, as he famously records, and as much other evidence demonstrates, was brought up by his father to be hyper-competent and to share his father's shame at powerful emotions. Nor did he receive elsewhere any successful or stable care for the emotional parts of his personality. Mill's mother was evidently a woman of no marked intellectual interests or accomplishments, and she soon became exhausted by bearing so many children. Her son experienced this as a lack of warmth. In a passage from an early draft of the *Autobiography* (deleted prior to publication at the urging of his wife Harriet) Mill speaks of her with remarkable harshness:

> That rarity in England, a really warm-hearted mother, would in the first place
> have made my father a totally different being, and in the second would have

made his children grow up loving and being loved. But my mother, with the very best of intentions, only knew how to pass her life in drudging for them. Whatever she could do for them she did, and they liked her, because she was kind to them, but to make herself loved, looked up to, or even obeyed, required qualities which she unfortunately did not possess. I thus grew up in the absence of love and in the presence of fear; and many and indelible are the effects of this bringing up in the stunting of my moral growth.

In his early twenties, Mill encountered a crisis of depression. He remained active and carried out his plans, but he was aware of a deep inner void. He tried to relieve his melancholy through dedication to the general social welfare, but the blackness did not abate. The crucial turning point is a very mysterious incident that has been much discussed:

> I was reading, accidentally, Marmontel's *Memoirs*, and came to the passage which relates his father's death, the distressed position of the family, and the sudden inspiration by which he, then a mere boy, felt and made them feel that he would be everything to them—would supply the place of all that they had lost. A vivid conception of the scene and its feelings came over me, and I was moved to tears. From this moment my burthen grew lighter. The oppression of the thought that all feeling was dead within me, was gone. I was no longer hopeless: I was not a stock or a stone.

The crisis gradually lifts, and Mill finds great sustenance in Wordsworth's poetry. He returns to society. Several years later, after several unproductive infatuations with women of artistic and poetic tastes, he meets Harriet Taylor at a dinner party.

The Marmontel episode has typically been analyzed in terms of an alleged death wish by Mill toward his father. The assumption of such interpreters is that Mill is identifying himself with Marmontel and expressing the desire to care for his family, displacing the father he feared. No doubt this is not altogether misguided, for hostility toward his father is a palpable emotion in the narrative, if counterbalanced by a great deal of love and admiration. The problem with this account, however, is that Mill does not seem particularly keen on caring for others, either before or after this episode. Indeed, he tells us that he tried to lift his depression by active concern with the well-being of others but that this effort did no good. Instead, the focus of his search is all on finding care for himself, and in particular for the emotions and subjective feelings that his father's education had treated as shameful. It seems to me much more likely that Mill above all identified with the orphaned family, who were now going to receive the care that they needed. He imagines someone saying to him, your needs, your feelings of pain, deadness, and loneliness, will be recognized and fulfilled, you will have the care that you need. Your distress will be seen with love, and you will find someone who will be everything to you.

If we now examine the original Marmontel passage, as interpreters of the *Autobiography* usually do not bother to do, it strongly confirms this reading. Marmontel makes it clear that his consolation of his family was accomplished through the aid of a difficult control over his own emotions, as he delivered the speech "without a single tear." But at his words of comfort, streams of tears are suddenly released *in his mother and younger siblings*: tears no longer of bitter mourning, he says, but of relief at receiving comfort.[6] So Mill is clearly in the emotional position not of the self-contained son but of the weeping mother and children, as they are relieved to find a comfort that assuages sorrow.

In part, as the *Autobiography* makes clear, Mill's wish for care is fulfilled by a new relation to himself: he becomes able to accept, care for, nourish, and value the previously hidden aspects of himself. In part, too, he shortly discovers in Harriet Taylor—as her letters show, an extremely emotional person and very skilled at circumnavigating John's intellectual defenses—the person who would care for him as his mother (he felt) did not. And his strong statements of preference for French over British culture also show how much he prized freedom of emotional expression, which seemed to release his own imprisoned emotions. (Perhaps another aspect of the Marmontel episode is the language in which the releasing text was written.)

To relate the *Autobiography* to the complexities of Mill's relation to Bentham and Aristotle is conjectural. But it is the sort of conjecture that makes sense, and, moreover, the sort that Mill invites. For Mill, then, we may suppose, the Aristotelian conception of happiness is too cold. It places too much weight on correct activity, not enough on the receptive and childlike parts of the personality. One might act correctly and yet feel like "a stock or a stone." Here the childlike nature of Bentham's approach to life, which Mill often stresses, proves valuable: for Bentham understood how powerful pain and pleasure are for children and the child in us. Bentham did not value the emotional elements of the personality in the right way. He simplified them too, lacking all understanding of poetry (as Mill insists) and of love (as we might add). But perhaps it was the very childlike character of Bentham, the man who loved the pleasures of small creatures, who allowed the mice in his study to sit on his lap, that made him able to see something Aristotle did not see, the need that we all have to be held and comforted, the need to escape a terrible loneliness and deadness.

Mill's *Utilitarianism* is not a fully developed work. It frustrates philosophers who look for a tidy resolution to the many tensions it introduces into the utilitarian system. But it has proven compelling over the ages because it contains a subtle awareness of human complexity that few philosophical works can rival. Here as in his surprising writings on women, Mill stands out, an adult among the children, an empiricist *with* experience, a man who painfully attained the kind of self-knowledge that his great teacher lacked, and who turned that into philosophy.

G

How is Mill's conception of happiness relevant to his critique of male power, and how does that conception strengthen the critique, making it an even richer resource than it already is for contemporary feminist and, more generally, anti-hierarchical thinking?

First of all, Mill's intelligent critique of Benthamism gives us strong reasons to reject the most common economic models of welfare, which are Benthamist in spirit. Such models, ubiquitous in development and public policy, profoundly influence public thinking about gender and race around the world. *Subjection* itself makes the connection between the critique of Benthamism and the rejection of preference-based welfarism. Mill argues that women's sentiments are not a reliable guide to political principles, because male power has corrupted those very sentiments. More generally, background conditions of injustice produce adaptive sentiments and preferences, as people learn to acquiesce in the lower lot in life that hierarchical society has decreed for them. The phenomenon that progressive social scientists such as Jon Elster and Amartya Sen have christened that of "adaptive preferences" was well known to Mill, indeed implicit in his critique of Benthamism, and he applies it with fascinating effect to the case of women's subordination, using, like Elster, a judicious analogy with feudalism. What he newly does is to bring out the similarity between the adaptive preferences of lord and vassals and the adaptive preferences of men and women. Just as lords get used to being superior and vassals to being inferior, so too is it with women and men—with one salient difference. This is, that lords maintained their power by physical force. Men often do so, but they also want something more:

> Men do not want solely the obedience of women, they want their sentiments. All men, except the most brutish, desire to have, in the woman most nearly connected with them, not a forced slave but a willing one, not a slave merely, but a favourite. They have therefore put everything in practice to enslave their minds. The masters of all other slaves rely, for maintaining obedience, on fear. . . . The masters of women wanted more than simple obedience, and they turned the whole force of education to effect their purpose. All women are brought up from the very earliest years in the belief that their ideal of character is the very opposite to that of men; not self-will, and government by self-control, but submission, and yielding to the control of others.

Mill argues, further, that these ideals shape not only moral sentiments but also sexuality itself: for men come to eroticize submissiveness, and women to believe submissiveness erotically essential. (With Andrea Dworkin, he could have added that women, in turn, frequently learn to eroticize power and domination.)[7] Such a critique of desire is thought by many feminists to entail a rejection of liberalism; but these critics are thinking of the liberalism of economic libertarianism, not of Mill's deeper and subtler account.

How does Mill, a utilitarian, criticize adaptive preferences? Clearly, with a normative theory of liberty, equality, and opportunities for functioning. He makes some instrumental arguments about the social good that will be done by a more thorough use of women's talents, but the central advantage to which he points is "the advantage of having the most universal and pervading of all human relations regulated by justice instead of injustice." The justice for women of which he speaks has an Aristotelian flavor: for it consists in having a wide range of opportunities for functioning, not being cut off like a plant in a hothouse. Pleasure and satisfaction are not the proper goals of political planning; the realization of a wide range of human opportunities is.

Thus Mill's conception of the job of politics, where women are concerned, is both richer and more critical than contemporary economic conceptions. Welfare is not to be understood as mere satisfaction but rather as the just and equal creation of a range of what I might not too tendentiously call (using my own term) "central human capabilities." People are to be free to choose which lives to live and what functions to actualize, but the just society is one that creates material and institutional conditions on which all are genuinely capable of those functions, on a basis of real equality. I have argued in my own work on the "capabilities approach" that this type of conception is much more fruitful for political critique than are the simpler utilitarian conceptions, which simply validate, all too often, an unjust status quo.[8]

The Aristotelian side of Mill does important political work. At the same time, however, Mill keeps the importance of desire in balance with the Aristotelian goal. Unlike some contemporary theorists in the Kantian tradition who denigrate desire and refuse to give pleasure and satisfaction any role in the construction of political principles,[9] Mill thinks it highly relevant that the values he defends as basic to politics are in some sense rooted in human desire. Thus he argues, for example, that people who have tried both liberty and its lack will prefer liberty, that justice is a prominent object of human striving. He supports his proposals in *On Liberty* with reference to a quite Aristotelian account of the human powers and their flourishing, referring to "a Greek ideal of self-development" and calling human nature "a tree, which requires to grow and develop itself on all sides." In a manner closely related to my own argument, he speaks of liberty as a development of basic human mental powers, which, like physical powers, are developed only by being used; in a society without liberty, "human capacities are withered and starved." But he also links this Aristotelian notion of self-development with a notion of experienced desire, saying that liberty is good in part because it satisfied certain "permanent interests" of human beings and, further, permits individuals to satisfy more of their other interests (given differences of taste that need liberty for their expression). As in his more general discussion of happiness, so too in political matters: Mill regards it as more than a contingent matter that the constituent parts of flourishing are in fact powerfully and deeply desired. His view thus finds a complex and subtle middle ground between the Kantian dismissal of desire and the welfarist validation of all subjective preferences. And this seems right: for, as Mill's own experience shows, it would hardly be plausible to say that such important human goods as health, love, and political inclusion are good altogether independently of their relationship to human desire and choice. The welfarist project fails, in its simplest form, but it gets something important right.

In *Subjection* as well, as I have suggested, we find the delicate balance between Aristotelianism and Benthamism. Mill shows with daring and clarity how thoroughly the preferences and desires of women have been deformed by male power. So mere satisfaction of desire could not be the main criterion of justice, and Mill is perfectly aware that the changes he is proposing will cause pain—first of all to men, who will have to give up their unjust privileges, but also, possibly, to existing women, who were formed to please and who will now be asked to live in a world that allows women other choices about how to live. Thus the first and most central advantage of the proposed changes in women's political status is justice, defined independently of desire and satisfaction. On the other hand, Mill is also eager to point out that experiences of emotional satisfaction are opened up by these changes. For both men and women, the possibility for women to develop their talents will offer possibilities of intimacy and understanding that are now for the most part absent, when women are prevented from taking part in intellectual and political concerns. In a paragraph in which one can sense the memory of happiness, he writes:

> What marriage may be in the case of two persons of cultivated faculties, identical in opinions and purposes, between whom there exists that best kind of equality, similarity of powers and capacities with reciprocal superiority in them—so that each can enjoy the luxury of looking up to the other, and can have alternately the pleasure of leading and of being led in the path of development—I will not attempt to describe. To those who can conceive it, there is no need; to those who cannot, it would appear the dream of an enthusiast. But I maintain, with the profoundest conviction, that this, and this only, is the ideal of marriage. . . . The moral regeneration of mankind will only really commence, when the most fundamental of the social relations is placed under the rule of equal justice, and when human beings learn to cultivate their strongest sympathy with an equal in rights and in cultivation.

In this paragraph, written several years after Harriet's death in 1858, we sense the importance of pleasure and satisfaction, along with that of justice. Justice should lead us to cultivate our sympathies so that they accord with equality, but it is also true that this cultivation opens up the possibility of a deeper emotional satisfaction than any we might otherwise know.

The importance of this emotional satisfaction is to Mill so great that in one area it gets the better of rational argument. In "The Utility of Religion," written (as Harriet's daughter Helen Taylor informs us in her introduction) some time between 1850 and 1858, the brief era of Mill's happy marriage to Harriet—all too soon marred by her tuberculosis and the advent of death—Mill advances numerous arguments against the human value of theistic religion. He argues that even the consolation of a belief in the afterlife will not be necessary as humanity progresses. But then he admits an exception:

> Nor can I perceive that the skeptic loses by his skepticism any real and valuable consolation except one; the hope of reunion with those dear to him who have ended their earthly life before him. That loss, indeed, is neither to be denied nor extenuated. In many cases it is beyond the reach of comparison or estimate; and will always suffice to keep alive, in the more sensitive natures, the imaginative hope of a futurity which, if there is nothing to prove, there is as little in our knowledge and experience to contradict.

It is because Mill is capable of bringing love, in this way, into philosophy, complicating it, sometimes even undermining it, that he will remain a vital resource for all who care about the future of women and men, and of the justice that may possibly exist between them.

NOTES

1. H. A. Prichard, "The Meaning of *Agathon* in the *Ethics* of Aristotle," *Philosophy* 10 (1935), 27–39, famously discussed and criticized in J. L. Austin, "*Agathon* and *Eudaimonia* in the *Ethics* of Aristotle," in Austin, *Philosophical Papers*, ed. J. O. Urmson and G. J. Warnock (Oxford and New York: Oxford University Press, 1979), 1–31. My account of Prichard follows Austin's, including his (fair) account of Prichard's implicit premises.

2. Erik Allardt, *Att ha, alska, att vara: Om valfard I Norden* (*Having, Loving, Being: On Welfare in the Nordic Countries* (Borgholm: Argos, 1975). A brief summary of some of the argument in English can be found in Allardt, "Having, Loving, Being: An Alternative to the Swedish Model of Welfare Research," in *The Quality of Life*, ed. M. Nussbaum and A. Sen (Oxford: Clarendon Press, 1993), 88–94. (The original language of the book is Swedish because Allardt is a Swedish-speaking Finn.)

3. I thus render Greek *arête*, usually translated "virtue." *Arête* need not be ethical; indeed it need not even be a trait of a person. It is a trait of anything, whatever that thing is, that makes it good at doing what that sort of thing characteristically does. Thus Plato can speak of the *arête* of a pruning knife.

4. Here we see the one major departure from Aristotle that apparently seemed to Wordsworth required by British morality. Aristotle does not make much of honesty. In other respects, Wordsworth is remarkably close to Aristotle, whether he knew it or not.

5. He denied that animals suffered at the very thought of death, and thus he argued that the painless killing of an animal is sometimes permitted.

6. Jean François Marmontel, *Mémoires* (Paris: Mercure de France, 1999), 63: "'Ma mère, mes frères, mes soeurs, nous éprouvons, leur dis-je, la plus grande des afflictions; ne nous y laissons point abattre. Mes enfants, vous perdez un père; vous en retrouvez un; je vous en servirai; je le suis, je veux l'être; j'en embrasse tous les devoirs; et vous n'êtes plus orphelins.' À ces mots, des ruisseaux de larmes, mais de larmes bien moins amères, coulèrent de leurs yeux. 'Ah!' s'écria ma mère, en me pressant contre son coeur, mon fils! 'mon cher enfant! que je t'ai bien connu!'"

7. See my "Rage and Reason," *The New Republic,* August 11 and 18, 1997, 36–42, and chapter 9 in *Sex and Social Justice* (New York: Oxford University Press, 1999).

8. See Nussbaum, *Women and Human Development* (Cambridge and New York: Cambridge University Press, 2000), chap. 2.

9. See my discussion of Thomas Scanlon in *Women and Human Development,* chapter 2.

6

Liberalism's Limits

Carlyle and Mill on "The Negro Question"

David Theo Goldberg

A

In 1849 *Fraser's Magazine*, the popular London literary periodical, published an anonymous attack on the nature of black people under the title, "Occasional Discourse on the Negro Question." The vicious essay turned out to be written by Thomas Carlyle. Outraged by the incivility of its language, if not distressed by the intransigence of the sentiment it expressed, literate liberals in Britain and the northern states in the American union openly objected to the attack. Chief among the responses was a particularly impassioned essay published, again anonymously, in the following issue of *Fraser's* under the title, "The Negro Question." This time the author was England's leading public intellectual of the day, John Stuart Mill. Four years later, fueled no doubt by his increasingly acrimonious feud with his former mate Mill, Carlyle published in pamphlet form a revised and expanded version of the attack under the more pointed title, "Occasional Discourse on the Nigger Question." And there the matter was left to stand until 1971, when the two essays were first brought together with an introductory commentary by the editor Eugene August.[1]

It is curious that from their initial appearance to August's edition, and indeed since, no commentary exists on this exchange that offers a particularly revealing window to the excesses and limits of nineteenth-century racial discourse.[2] This semi-autonomous exchange, almost too sensitive to touch in their own names, exemplifies the parameters of Victorian racially conceived sentiment, explicitly racist in one direction, seemingly egalitarian in the other, as August hopefully has it. Indeed, while it exemplifies colonial racial configuation and racist derogation—colonialism's vicious recourse to neoscientific racism, on one hand, and liberalism's polite racism, on the other—the ex-change reveals at once the long reach of colonial discourse to elements of contemporary postcolonial racist expression. Carlyle on race was to mid-nineteenth-century Britain what Dinesh D'Souza is to late twentieth-century America, offering a totalizing rationalization of the sorry state of black folk in the most extreme, and thus eye-catching terms. By contrast, Mill's singular contribution to "The Negro Question"—just as his "On the Subjection of Women" was his seminal and remarkable contribution to "The Woman Ques-tion"—nevertheless marks the implicit limits to racially conceived egalitari-anism for liberal Victorianism. This suggests at once the challenge facing lib-eralism on the question of race more generally.

The sociohistorical background to the exchange concerned the fading prospects and conditions of the British plantation owners in the West Indies, though the questions of race addressed have to be understood in terms of the colonial condition more broadly. Emancipation of slaves in the British Empire in 1833 curtailed the supply of desperately cheap labor and cut into the artifi-cial profit margins enjoyed by the West Indies sugar planters. In 1846 the British parliament ended plantation subsidies, thus forcing plantation owners in the is-lands, those increasingly disaffected white British subjects, to compete unpro-tected on the world market. Carlyle's voice was that of the disenchanted colo-nial "aristocracy" abroad and (more ambiguously) of the distressed English working classes and Irish peasants closer to hand, combined under the racially promoted configuration of whiteness; Mill's by contrast was that of "enlight-ened" Victorian abolitionism. Here, then, are to be found the two prevailing pil-lars of nineteenth-century racial theory. Carlyle represented the bald claim to "the Negro's" inherent inferiority articulated by racist science of the day; Mill on the other hand was the principal spokesman for the European's historically de-veloped superiority, though (as Afrocentrists like Molefi Asante and their crit-ics like Mary Lefkowitz both should note) he temperately acknowledged the influence of ancient Egyptians on the Hellenic Greeks.

B

Carlyle's Negrophobia is interesting intellectually only because its vituper-ative language directed at black people was an expression of more than just bald prejudice, though it was clearly that. Thus, his objectionable lan-guage (revealing of equally objectionable presumptions) regarding people of African descent was expressed against the background of, if not prompted by, a critique of the conditions of the working classes in Britain. Carlyle's Negrophobia accordingly was tied up with a critique of *laissez faire* capitalist political economy prevailing at the time. The failure of the potato crop due to extended drought had devastated Irish peasants, and the mid-century recession had caused massive unemployment among the English working classes, represented in Carlyle's discourse in the forlorn figure of the "Distressed Needlewoman." Carlyle contrasted these desperately sad figures with the stereotype of the lazy, "sho 'good eatin'" Negro.[3] Carlyle assumed that the capitalism of his day somehow causally tied the alienation of working people in England and Ireland to the emancipation of shiftless and workless Negroes in the colonies. He thus predicated in this essay what might otherwise be deemed an insightful reading of unregulated capitalism that he had developed, for example, in *Past and Present* (1843), on a set of deeply racist premises. In the spirit of the early Marx, Carlyle criticized *laissez faire* capitalism for reducing *human* relationships (the paradigm for which he assumes to be between whites) to the "cash contract"[4] between employer and employee. Capitalist "Lords of Rackrent" (or landlords) lost all interest in the impoverished Irish peasant or English seamstress once the latter were unable to afford the rent. The latter's freedom, under *laissez faire* liberal capitalism, was reduced to the liberty to die by starvation. Carlyle accordingly predicted that the importation of English workers into the West Indies in response to planters' demands for workers who would work would render the Negro inhabitants as free to starve as their British counterparts.

Carlyle attributed the underlying cause of this general condition to the demise of paternalistic control by the British, superior on all counts, over the inherently inferior natives of the islands. Those in a situation of superiority had a paternalist obligation to effect the well-being of the inferior for whom the former were responsible. Carlyle insisted that the feudal serf was (materially) better placed than the Irish peasant, English needleworker, or "Negro" of his day. He concludes that "the Negro Question" was to be answered by turning "Negroes" into a relationship of loyal serfdom to the benevolent feudal-like lordship of their white masters. White men, wisest by birth (right), were destined by nature and God to rule, Negroes to serve; whites ought to try and convince Negroes to assume their God-given role as servants, failing which masters would be obliged to turn to "the beneficent whip."

Likely unaware first hand of any black people, Carlyle's "Nigger" of the "Nigger Questions" was the stereotypical figure of "Quashee," a polygenic form of black lowlife—lazy, laughing, rhythmic, musical, dance loving, language defective (p. 12). "Horse-jawed and beautifully muzzled" (p. 4), "Quashee" was the Carlylean equivalent of "Sambo," etymologically linked to squash and so to pumpkin—Carlyle's mean metaphor for any juicy tropical fruit like watermelon, cantaloupes, mango, or papaya—and drinking rum. Yet Carlyle insisted on finding "the Negro," "alone of wild-men," kind, affectionate, even lovable, and pointedly not the object of his "hate" (p. 12). The abundance of tropical fruit in Carlyle's view reduced the need on the part of West Indian natives to work. Carlyle's solution was to compel "the Negro" in the Islands to work by restricting to the laborless the right to own fruit-producing land or to enjoy its abundant products (p. 9).

In order to sustain this degraded image of the inherently inferior "Nigger," Carlyle (like his counterpart D'Souza a century and half later) was driven to reduce the debilitating effects of slavery's experience for people of African descent. Carlyle accordingly insisted that the debilitations of slavery were "much exaggerated" (p. 13). Slavery, and so mastery too, were considered "natural" conditions; slaves, as Aristotle once put it, are slaves by nature. Blacks are born to be servants (Carlyle's euphemistic bow to the abolitionists, p. 22) of whites, who "are born wiser . . . and lords" over them (p. 32). Indeed, Carlyle insisted that there is a slavery far worse than that of "Negroes" in the colonies, "the one, intolerable sort of slavery" (as though enslavement of black people is not): this, he remarked without a hint of irony, is the "slavery" throughout Europe of "the strong to the weak; of the great and noble-minded to be the small and mean! The slavery of Wisdom to Folly" (p. 14). Thus Carlyle diminished the horrible experience and effects of *real* slavery historically by reducing them to less than the "platonic" manifestations of a metaphorical servitude of the strong and wise to the weak and ignorant. Of course, it says little for the strength and wisdom of the European wealthy and wise that they should be so constrained by the weak and witless, a point to which Carlyle in all his critical power seems oblivious.

Carlyle emphasized that it was Europeans who developed the colonies from their supposed prehistory of "pestilence . . . and putrefaction, savagery . . . and swamp-malaria" (p. 28) through their creativity, ingenuity, and productivity; that it was the English (or "Saxon British," p. 27) who supposedly made the West Indies flourish and without whom the islands would reduce to "Black Irelands" (p. 33) or "Haiti" with "black Peter exterminating black Paul" (p. 29). Yet Carlyle repeatedly contrasted the conditions of "Negroes," those "Demarara Niggers," with the conditions of English laborers, white working women, and Irish peasants. Fat from the abundance of land, the consumption of fruit, and lack of labor, the character of the Negro was measured against, if not silently considered the cause of, working peoples' plight in the mother country and the colonies. Carlyle's discourse nevertheless reveals beneath the racially conceived overlay of this contrast a class-induced ambivalence. Thus he identified also the Distressed Needlewomen, Irish peasants, and English working classes through a nineteenth-century version of the discourse of an underclass (or lumpen) poverty of culture with "the Nigger" of the West Indies (pp. 20–21). Most of the 300,000 Distressed Needlewomen, he objected, were really "Mutinous Servingmaids" unable "to sew a stitch" and defying their inherent need for a master: "Without a master in certain cases, you become a Distressed Needlewoman, and cannot so much as live" (p. 21). Indeed, Carlyle further reduced this equation of posing seamstress and free "nigger" to the infantilized condition of babies and the animalized conditions of dogs and horses (pp. 23, 12), all of whom needed accordingly to be cared for, looked after, mastered by "philanthropic Anglo-Saxon men and women" (p. 23). Equal in quantity to an entire English county, black West Indians "in *worth* (in quantity of intellect, faculty, docility, energy, and available human valor and value)" amounted to a single street of London's working-class East End.

In Carlyle's view, the working classes and particularly Negroes were born to serve, to have masters. With little wit of their own, they would flourish only in servitude, in being told what to do and looked after. Carlyle concluded from this claim of inherent servility that the "Black gentleman" be hired "not by the month, but by a very much longer term. That he be 'hired for life.'" That, in other words, he be the slave he was to "Whites . . . born more wiser than [he]" (pp. 21-22, 33, 34-35). Ironically, and against the naturalist grain, such lifelong servitude was to be enforced through might and fright (pp. 26-27, 29, 31), for if "the Saxon British" failed to assert their dominance, some other colonial power would (p. 35). The colonial imperative was as much about relations of power, domination, and "the education of desire"[5] internal to Europe as it was straightforwardly about imposing European will upon its Other.

C

It was Carlyle's call to reinstitute slavery to which Mill principally objected in his response. This perhaps is predictable, given Mill's longstanding and well-known commitment to abolition. Mill's critical concern with Carlyle's racist sentiment was only secondary and much more understated. Moreover, not only did Mill not object to colonial domination, he insisted upon it, albeit in "benevolent" form. After all, Mill worked for the better part of his working life administering colonialism. Thus Mill opened his letter to the editor of *Fraser's* by emphasizing that abolition was "best and greatest achievement yet performed by mankind" in "the history of human improvement" (pp. 38-39). Slavery was wrong for Mill on utilitarian ground in that it produced much more pain than would liberty and equal opportunity, and it is for this reason that Mill considered slavery inherently inhumane (pp. 48-49), a view derided by Carlyle under the mocking title of the "Universal Abolition of Pain Association" (p. 2). In contrast to Carlyle's critique of *laissez faire* principles by insisting that all people, black and white, enjoy equal opportunity: "[Carlyle] . . . will make them work *for* certain whites, those whites *not* working at all . . . Does he mean that all

persons ought to earn their living? But some earn their living by doing
nothing, and some by doing mischief . . ." (pp. 42-43). Mill continued:

> Let the whole produce belong to those who do the work which produces it. We
> would not have *black* labourers [in the West Indies] compelled to grow spices
> which they do not want, and *white* proprietors who do not work at all ex-
> changing the spices for houses in Belgrave Square [an expensive neighborhood
> in London]. . . . Let them have exactly the same share in what they produce that
> they have in the work. If they do not like this, let them remain as they are, so
> long as they . . . make the best of supply and demand" (pp. 44-45, my em-
> phases).

Mill's quiet qualification of class by race—black laborers, white propri-
etors—was tied to his denial that every difference among human beings is
inherent, a "vulgar error" he rightly imputed to Carlyle (p. 46). In objecting
to Carlyle's racist hierarchical naturalism, however, Mill inscribed in its place,
and in the name of *laissez faire* and equal opportunity, an imputation of the
historical inferiority of blacks. Mill implied that this assumption of inferiority,
because historically produced and contingent, was not always the case
(Egyptians influenced Greeks) and might one day be overcome. Yet Mill's
superficial bow to what has become an Afro-centric cornerstone barely hid
beneath the surface the polite racism of his Euro-centric history. Contingent
racism is still a form of racism—not so usual, not so bald, not so vituperative,
and polite perhaps, but condescending nevertheless even as it is committed
to equal opportunity. Equal opportunity among those with the unfair, historically produced inequities of the colonical condition will simply repro-
duce those inequities, if not expand them.

   The very title of his response to Carlyle—"The Negro Question"—indicates Mill's presumption that (to use Du Bois's terms) blacks are a problem,
rather than that people of African descent in the New World faced problems—least of all that those problems were imposed by their masters—and
that such problems might best be resolved through the utility calculus. This
interpretation is borne out by placing Mill's response to Carlyle in the context of Mill's views on development, modernization, and race. These views
he developed most fully in terms of India and his experience in the English
East Indies Company but which he generalized to Africa and the West Indies
also. So to confirm that these premises indeed underpin Mill's liberal egali-
tarianism, it is necessary to turn to his views on the colonies.

   Mill worked as an examiner for the English East Indies Company from
1823 until 1856 and then, like his father, as chief examiner until his retire-
ment to politics in 1858. Thus he was central in, and ultimately responsible
for, all bureaucratic correspondence between the British government and its
colonial representation in India. (Mill was involved in writing 1,700 official
letters to India over this period.) It was in the context of India (and the Asi-

atic countries more generally), then, that he worked out his views on colonial intervention in those "underdeveloped" countries that he considered stagnant and inhibiting of progress, and he generalized from this context to other areas.

In *The Principles of Political Economy*, Mill wrote that "Colonization—is the best affair of business, in which the capital of an old and wealthy country can engage."[6] It would do so in order to establish:

[F]irst, a better government: more complete security of property; moderate taxes, and freedom from arbitrary exaction under the name of taxes; a more permanent and more advantageous tenure of land, securing to the cultivator as far as possible the undivided benefits of industry, skill, and economy he may exert. Secondly, improvement of the public intelligence: the decay of usages or superstitions which interfere with the effective employment of industry; and the growth of mental activity, making the people alive to new objects of desire. Thirdly, the introduction of foreign arts, which raise the returns derivable from additional capital, to a rate corresponding to the low strength of the desire of accumulation: and the importation of foreign capital, which renders the increase of production no longer exclusively dependent on the thrift or providence of the inhabitants themselves, while it places before them a stimulating example, and by instilling new ideas and breaking the chains of habit, if not by improving the actual condition of the population, tends to create in them new wants, increased ambition, and greater thoughts for the future.[7]

Mill picks out for application of these principles India, Russia, Turkey, Spain, and Ireland. The West Indies and African countries were not recognized as having the capacity for self-development at all.[8]

The difference between a developed and undeveloped country, between those more or less civilized, was defined by Mill in terms of the country's capacity to enable and promote representative self-government and individual self-development. In short, in terms of its capacity for autonomy and good government. "Good government" would enable a society, as Mill once said of himself, "to effect the greatest amount of good compatible with . . . opportunities"[9] with a view to maximizing well-being and happiness. Mill attributed the success of such promotion fundamentally to economic development which apparently would enable opportunities. Civilized countries like Britain limited government intervention in individuals' lives; those less civilized he thought should be ruled by those more so with the view to promoting their capacity for self-development. Liberal individualization was consonant with economic, political, and cultural modernization. This would require greater restriction in the ruled country on people's freedoms and so more government regulation. Progress was considered a function of education and enlightened institutions but also for people of "similar civilization to the ruling country," of Britain's "own blood and language." The latter—Mill mentioned Australia and Canada—were "capable of, and ripe for, representative government." India, by contrast, was far from it, for India had stagnated for many centuries under the sway of Oriental despotism.[10] In India's case, and even more perpetually in the case of the West Indies and African colonies, "benevolent despotism"—a paternalistic "government of guidance" imposed by more advanced Europeans—was the rational order of the day.[11]

Thus, for Mill, the justification of colonization was to be measured according to its aid in the progress of the colonized, its education of superstitious colonial subjects in the virtues of reason, and the generation of new markets for capital accumulation through the fashioning of desires. The purpose of education was to inform: both to provide the informational basis to make rational decisions and to structure the values framing practical reason in ways conducive to the colonial ends Mill deemed desirable. Mill considered progress to consist in being socialized in the values of liberal modernity, that is, in the sort of social, political, economic, cultural, and legal commitments best represented by the British example. As a colonized country exemplified such progress, the colonizing country progressively would give way to the colonized's self-governance. So Mill's "benevolent despotism" amounts to a colonialism with a human face. The world was to be directed by the most developed and capable nations whose self-interests nevertheless would be mitigated and mediated by the force of utilitarian reason.

Mill was blind to the internal tensions in his indices of progress. The ideal conditions for the generation of new markets and the fashioning of new desires for the sake of capital accumulation are likely inconsistent with genuine self-determination, autonomy, and self-governance. Colonization is straightforwardly consistent with developing new markets and desires—it is after all a central part of the historical *raison d'être* colonialism—in a way in which it is historically, if not conceptually, at odds with self-determination. Mill thought different socioeconomic imperatives face the "advanced," and "backward" nations: improved distribution of goods (not wealth) for the "advanced," better conditions of production for the "backward" countries.[12] So before worrying about distribution of goods among the people of the "backward countries," improving production was paramount, and in any case (re)distribution of wealth was never an issue.

Mill's "benevolent despotism," relatively benign and masked by humane application perhaps, nevertheless sought "to make provision in the constitution of the government itself, for compelling those who have the governing power to listen to and take into consideration the opinions of persons who, from their position and their previous life, have made a study of Indian subjects, and acquired experience in them.[13] Thus Mill recognized the relation between knowledge and power, specialized information and administration, as the underlying imperative of colonial governments. Knowledge of the Native was instrumental to establishing the condition for developing the colonies in a way that would continue to serve the interests of the colonial power. It may seem curious that Mill implied that the Natives themselves would not be consulted in accumulating knowledge about local colonial conditions, for he did insist that qualified Natives be appointed to all administrative and governmental positions "for which they are fit," though without "appointing them to the regular service." Mill's utilitarian reason for this restriction was that Natives were not to be "considered for the highest service" for "if their promotion stopped short while that of others went on, it would be more invidious than keeping them out altogether." And as Europeans, rationally superior, were to be the appeal of last resort, Natives' ascension was naturally delimited.[14] James Mill seemed to project onto the Natives of the colonies the same utilitarian paternalism with which he treated his son, and John Stuart never managed to shake this paternal(istic) framing.[15]

However, even in their administrative advance, the Natives (here Indian) were to be "Indian in blood and colour, but English in tastes, in opinions, in morals and in intellect."[16] Blood may run thicker than water, but it was to be diluted by a cultural solution. Cultural colonialism mediates racial inferiority, culture replacing biology as the touchstone of racial definition. Accordingly, English was to be the language of administration, the local vernacular to be used only to convey rules and regulations to the local population. Far from "creating the conditions for the withering away of their rule,"[17] Mill (even if inadvertently) was instrumental in identifying and administering the sort of conditions that would perpetuate indirect rule, postcolonial control from afar without the attendant costs.

D

Mill's argument for benevolent despotism failed to appreciate that neither colonialism nor despotism is ever benevolent. Benevolence here is the commitment to seek the happiness of others.[18] But the mission of colonialism is exploitation and domination of the colonized generally, and Europeanization at least of those among the colonized whose class position makes it possible economically and educationally.[19] And the mandate of despotism, its conceptual logic, is to assume absolute power to achieve the ruler's self-interested ends. Thus colonial despotism could achieve the happiness of colonized Others only by imposing the measure of Europeanized marks of happiness upon the other, which is to say, to force the other to be less so. Mill's argument necessarily assumed superiority of the despotic, benevolent or not; it presupposed that the mark of progress is (to be) defined by those taking themselves to be superior; and it presumes that the ruled will want to be like the rulers even as the former lack the cultural capital (ever?) quite to rise to the task. Mill's ambivalence over the inherent inferiority of "native Negroes," even as he marked the transformation in the terms of racial definition historically from the inescapable determinism of blood and brain size to the marginally escapable reach of cultural determination, has resonated to this day in liberal ambivalence regarding racial matters.

Liberalism's racially mediated meliorism and commitment to a moral progressivism translates into an undying optimism that its racist history will be progressively overcome, giving way ultimately to a standard of nonracialism. Yet this standard nonracialism [sic] is imposed upon the body politic at the cost of the self-defined subjectivity of the traditionally dominated. Liberalism's response to matters of race in the face of the fact that race matters amounts to denying or ignoring race, paternalistically effacing a self-determined social subjectivity from those who would define themselves thus without imposing it on others. This erasure in the name of nonracialism rubs out at once the history of racist invisibility, domination, and exploitation, replacing the memory of an infantilized past with the denial of responsibility for radically unequal and only superficially deracialized presents. Divested of a historically located responsibility, the relatively powerful in the society are readily able to reinstate the invisibility of the subject positions of the presently marginalized: savages becomes the permanently unemployable, the uncivilized become crack heads, the lumpenproletariat the underclass, Distressed Needlewomen become sweated labor, poor Irish peasants turn into distressed defaulting family farmers and, well, "Niggers" become "Negroes," or blacks scarcely disguised beneath the seemingly benign nomenclature. For every Mill of yesteryear there is today a William Bennett or a Gary Becker, and for every Carlyle a Dinesh D'Souza.

Between Mill's "Negro" and Carlyle's "Nigger," then, lies the common thread of racist presumption and projection, bald and vicious on the one hand, polite and effete on the other, but both nevertheless insidious and odious. Better in utilitarian terms to have a Mill, perhaps, for at least one gets the sense that it is possible to enlighten and thus transform such a person. With a Carlyle one knows clearly and openly what resistance to racisms is up against, what it has to confront and in some circumstances to avoid; with a Mill, a promoter of abolition is at once a barrier to it. This exchange between two leading English public intellectuals of their day reveals in the final analysis, then, that structural and discursive transformation necessary for resisting racisms are deeply related to subjective expression. Ultimately, it makes abundantly apparent that a combined commitment to changing minds and to changing conditions is crucial.

NOTES

1. Eugene August, ed., *Carlyle,* The Nigger Question *and Mill,* The Negro Question (New York: Appleton Century Crofts, 1971). All parenthetical page references in the text are to this edition.

2. August includes in his little volume an editorial in a London newspaper of the day, *The Inquirer,* protesting Carlyle's claims.

3. This is Fanon's cutting characterization: Frantz Fanon, *Black Skin White Masks* (London: Paladin, 1970), 79.

4. August, *Carlyle,* xvii.

5. Laura Ann Stoler, *Race and the Education of Desire* (Durham, N.C.: Duke University Press, 1995).

6. John Stuart Mill, *Principles of Political Economy* (London: Longmans, 1909), 971.

7. Mill, *Principles,* 189–90.

8. Gyozo Fukuhara, "John Stuart Mill and the Backward Countries," *Bulletin of University of Osaka Prefecture,* series D: Sciences of Economy, Commerce and Law, 3 (1959), 64–75.

9. John Stuart Mill, *Autobiography,* ed. Harold Laski (London: Longmans, 1924), 72.

10. John Stuart Mill, *Considerations on Representative Government,* in *Collected Works,* vol. 19, *Essays on Politics and Society,* general editor J. Robson et al. (Toronto: University of Toronto Press, 1977), 563.

11. See George D. Bearce, Jr., "John Stuart Mill and India," *Journal of the Bombay Branch of the Royal Asiatic Society* 29, no. 5 (1954), 74–75.

12. Mill, *Principles,* 749.

13. John Stuart Mill, *Parliamentary Papers* 30, (1852–1853), 313–14.

14. Mill, *Parliamentary Papers,* 324–25.

15. See also S. V. Pradhan, "Mill on India: A Reappraisal," *Dalhousie Review* 56, no. 1 (Spring 1976), 5–22.

16. Mill, quoted in H. Sharp, *Selections from Educational Records* 1, 1781–1839 (1920), 116.

17. Abraham L. Harris, "John Stuart Mill: Servant of the English East India Company," *Canadian Journal of Economics and Political Science* 30, no. 2 (May 1964), 201.

18. See Henry Sidgwick, *The Methods of Ethics,* 7th ed. (Indianapolis: Hackett, 1981), 239.

19. See Frantz Fanon, *A Dying Colonialism* (London: Pelican Books, 1970), 17.

7

Empire, Race, Euro-centrism: John Stuart Mill and His Critics

Georgios Varouxakis

Of all vulgar modes of escaping from the consideration of the effect of social and moral influences on the human mind, the most vulgar is that of attributing the diversities of conduct and character to inherent natural differences.

J. S. Mill, *Principles of Political Economy*

Mill was a racist.

Stewart Justman

Discriminations must be made between one kind of cultural work and another when it comes to involvement in imperialism; so we can say, for example, that for all his illiberalism about India, John Stuart Mill was more complex and enlightened in his attitudes to the notion of empire than either Carlyle or Ruskin (Mill's behaviour in the Eyre case was principled, even retrospectively admirable).

Edward Said

For those who celebrate Mill as a champion of progressive, liberal values it is tempting to emphasize his stand on slavery and the civil war in the United States, the Governor Eyre controversy in Jamaica, and the Irish question, and downplay or ignore altogether his work at the India House. After all, Mill did take a leadership role in many prominent public battles. He supported 'liberal' causes and he often stood in opposition to the policies of his own government. He was certainly outspoken when he perceived abuses of British power, but he did not doubt the legitimacy of British hegemony over non-Europeans. While Mill's efforts on behalf of the British Empire are discomforting, they should not be surprising. In many ways, he was a product of his time. Just because he was 'ahead of his time' on many social issues, we cannot expect him to have been an enlightened thinker on all of them. Perhaps Mill should have known better. He was often sensitive to the interests of those who were oppressed and excluded from social, political, and cultural participation. His actions on behalf of the rights of women, the poor, and minorities was, for the most part, respectable and commendable. Although Mill's basic position on colonialism and the spread of civilization was problematic, it is important not to let his shortcomings undermine everything else that he fought to achieve.

Don Habibi

This chapter comes to revise and complement an earlier article, which I had published in 1998 in *Utilitas*, entitled "John Stuart Mill on Race."[1] In that piece I did indeed "ignore altogether [Mill's] work at the India House"—to use the words of the author of the last quote above. Given, however, that it was not my intention to "celebrate Mill as a champion of progressive, liberal values," I did not succumb to the temptation "to emphasize his stand on slavery and the civil war in the United States, the Governor Eyre controversy in Jamaica, and the Irish question" either (among these very significant incidents or issues related to Mill's thought and political activism I only briefly used some of his comments on the Irish to corroborate my argument). Rather than refer to these well-known manifestations of Mill's sensitivity to the plight of the underdog, I chose there to focus strictly on his theoretical statements on the issue of "race" and its purported influence on "national character." That choice of focus led also to the decision to leave aside Mill's views on colonialism and his involvement in the East India Company, which, though certainly related to his views on "race," are broader issues. What I propose to do here is both to address interpretations and perspectives different from mine on Mill's attitude towards "race" and to broaden my examination with a consideration of Mill's overall attitude toward non-European peoples, which, obviously, will take the discussion to issues such as colonialism and the British Empire.

As I argued in the earlier article, Mill, although his use of the discourse of his time has misled many a commentator to accuse him of outright racism, or at the very least of heavy reliance on racial explanations, was, in fact, in the forefront of attempts to discredit racial theories and their deterministic as well as inegalitarian implications. Especially from the middle of the nineteenth century onward, Mill went out of his way to discard racial theories and to assert the idea of "mind over matter"—as he put it himself[2]— in terms of how national characters are formed or can be altered and improved. Very far from accepting racial determinism, Mill took the lead in fighting what he saw as the increasingly unpalatable deterministic applications to which theories about race were being put with the sanction of purportedly "scientific" theories. National character was malleable for Mill, who believed in the "astonishing pliability" of human nature and was therefore hopeful about the prospects opened up by the study of the factors affecting its formation. On all sorts of issues or occasions, such as the mental capacities of blacks, slavery, the American Civil War, the Governor Eyre controversy, the question of Irish "backwardness" and disaffection, and many more, Mill consistently as well as militantly stood up against claims to the effect that there were racially determined inequalities of capacities or even permanent and unalterable differences. He argued persistently and vociferously that environmental and historical causes could account amply for most existing apparent differences among human groups and that proper education, adequate institutions, and human will and endeavor could alter beyond any recognition what were supposed to be the innate characteristics of various human groups.

As much as it may surprise some of his late-twentieth- (and early-twenty-first-) century critics, who see him as a "racist," Mill stood accused exactly of the opposite charge in his own time. It was a commonplace of mid-Victorian review articles (some of them being written by respectable—albeit idiosyncratic—liberals such as John [Lord] Acton or James Fitzjames Stephen) to attack Mill (either directly or indirectly through criticizing his professed disciple, H. T. Buckle or, more often, both of them together) for having deprecated the importance of "race" as an explanatory tool.[3] In the same context, it is not accidental at all that the founder and first president of the *Anthropological Society of London*, "ardent racialist"[4] James Hunt, repeatedly chose Mill as his main target.[5] In mid-Victorian Britain, it was Mill who was seen as the leading influence behind the rejection, by some, of the increasingly prevalent view that "race" was an all-important explanatory category.[6]

The issue of "race" in the nineteenth century was a particularly complex one.[7] Use of terms such as "race" was quite casual and did not always correspond with consistent opinions that would be called "racist" today.[8] Having said this, implicit acceptance of racial determinism does not make racial determinism less real. In any case, however, things became more and more explicit from the middle of the nineteenth century onward. Scientific theories, interpretations or adaptations of Darwinism, and a general attempt to imitate science in the realm of social and moral issues were not the least of the reasons. An additional major contribution seems to have been made by the impact of the failure of the revolutions of 1848 on the continent of Europe. For, as young Walter Bagehot put it, shortly after the culmination of the failure of 1848 with Louis Napoleon Bonaparte's *coup d'état* of December 1851, "the events of 1848 have taught thinking persons . . . that of all . . . circumstances

. . . affecting political problems, by far and out of all question the most important is *national character*." Why was this so? According to Bagehot, "in that year the same experiment—the experiment, as its friends say, of Liberal and Constitutional Government—as its enemies say of Anarchy and Revolution—was tried in every nation in Europe—with what varying futures and differing results!" The effect of those events had been "to teach men—not only speculatively to know, but practically to feel," how absurd it was to expect the same kind of institutions to be suitable or possible for different national characters. The formation of national character is "one of the most secret of marvellous mysteries." On this issue, the only thing that was certain was that all men and all nations have a character, "and that character, when once taken, is, I do not say unchangeable—religion modifies it, catastrophe annihilates it—but the least changeable thing in this ever-varying and changeful world." Races exhibited the same physical traits and characters for centuries or even millennia. And in a metaphor that should give believers in the malleability of national characters the shivers, the young Bagehot opined: "There are breeds in the animal man just as in the animal dog. When you hunt with greyhounds and course with beagles, then, and not till then, may you expect the inbred habits of a thousand years to pass away, that Hindoos can be free, or that Englishmen will be slaves."[9] Even more explicitly, Edinburgh anatomist and arch-racialist Robert Knox, author of *The Races of Man* (1850), who had complained of the failure to appreciate the importance of race in Britain in the 1840s, came to regard 1848 and its aftermath as a turning point. As Catherine Hall has put it: "By 1850, however, when the book was published, the revolutions of 1848, Knox believed, had clarified to the world at large how race had something to do with the history of nations."[10] It may not be accidental, therefore, that it was exactly from 1850 (starting from his response to Carlyle's "Occasional Discourse on the Negro Question" of December 1849) onward that Mill emerges as more and more vociferous in his denunciation of racial theories.[11]

What needs to be stressed is the extent to which Mill's position was a minority position in the second half of the nineteenth century. Compared to contemporaries such as Matthew Arnold, John (Lord) Acton, Karl Marx, Thomas Carlyle, John Ruskin, Charles Kingsley, James Fitzjames Stephen, historians of the school of E. A. Freeman, to say nothing of most anthropologists of the day, Mill emerges as the leading voice of the antiracist camp.[12] At a time when the attribution of the traits of "national characters" to "race" was a matter of course, the attempt to discredit racial theories was most eagerly and influentially undertaken by Mill, his avowed disciple H. T. Buckle (author of the ambitious *History of Civilization in England*)[13] and, among scientists, Thomas Henry Huxley (who "considered a subject such as human heredity to be a scientific matter from which he personally would draw no political or non-scientific conclusions").[14]

And yet, Mill is still regularly being accused of pandering to racial-biological explanations even by highly sophisticated observers.[15] In a work that demonstrates an excellent grasp of Mill's near-obsession with progressiveness versus stationariness, and which offers a number of valid criticisms of Mill's attitude toward what he saw as "backward" peoples, Uday Singh Mehta proffers an assertion that would leave one with the impression that Mill was an *exceptionally* ardent racialist: "Here John Stuart Mill is a surprising exception. He invests race with far greater seriousness than most of his liberal contemporaries, who generally view it as a catchall term that loosely designates what might be called cultural difference." Instead, Mehta contends that Mill "elaborates the term through the biological notion of 'blood.' Hence for example in the *Considerations on Representative Government* (chaps. 16, 18) he draws what he takes to be the crucial distinction in terms of readiness for representative institutions by reference to 'those of our blood' and those not of our blood."[16] Mehta is apparently misled into interpreting this as proof of reliance on the biological factor by Mill's use of language. What Mill actually means when he talks of colonists "of our blood" is their cultural traits, coming from the mother country, the metropolis. He does not use "blood" literally. As I have argued in my earlier article on the subject,[17] by the time he wrote *Representative Government* at any rate, Mill would have no truck whatsoever with biological race and blood as political categories but rather, on the very contrary, fought strenuously and vociferously against such uses by others. However, as I stressed in that same article, his use of the language of his time—including references such as the one adduced by Mehta, or others pointed out by myself in *Representative Government* itself[18]—has in some cases compromised his very arguments, to a certain extent, and, moreover, has led later critics to interpret his whole discourse as no better than that of the racists he was fighting against.

Mehta is in good company. Vincent Pecora has argued, referring to Mill's account of the causes of "Chinese stationariness" in *On Liberty*—in contradistinction to the salutary "diversity" that had preserved Europe from the same plight[19]—that "it is hard not to understand this result as a product of innate racial disposition, for it is only an unexplained and seemingly natural 'diversity of character and culture' that, with proper nurturing, will save European nations and individuals from a similar fate."[20] This is a clear misconstruction of what Mill wrote not only in that very text in *On Liberty*, but also in *Representative Government*,[21] his second (1840) review of Tocqueville's *Democracy in America*,[22] or his two reviews of Guizot's historical works.[23] Mill does not talk of any "unexplained and seemingly natural 'diversity of character and culture.'" On the very contrary, his whole point in all the texts in question was that the diversity to which he, following Guizot,[24] attributed what he saw as Europe's "progressiveness" was not innate or natural to Europeans but rather the result of historical accident and that there would always be a serious danger of its disappearing if Europeans ever were to believe that it was natural to them and took it for granted (his message was that they would have to strive to preserve it through being vigilant against any power, class, value, or idea that threatened to become too preponderant and eliminate the struggle and competition that had kept up diversity in modern Western Europe). This is what he wrote in his second review of Tocqueville's book:

> It is not in China only that a homogeneous community is naturally a stationary community. . . . It is profoundly remarked by M. Guizot, that the short duration or stunted growth of the earlier civilizations arose from this, that in each of them some one element of human improvement existed exclusively, or so preponderatingly as to overpower all the others; whereby the community, after accomplishing rapidly all which that one element could do, either perished for want of what it could not do, or came to a halt, and became immovable. It would be an error to suppose that such could not possibly be our fate. In the generalization which pronounces the "law of progress" to be an inherent attribute of human nature, it is forgotten that, among the inhabitants of our earth, the European family of nations is the only one which has ever yet shown any capability of spontaneous improvement, beyond a certain low level. *Let us beware of supposing that we owe this peculiarity to any necessity of nature, and not rather to combinations of circumstances, which have existed nowhere else, and may not exist for ever among ourselves.*[25]

To accuse the thinker who warned fellow Europeans to "beware of supposing that [they owed] this peculiarity to any necessity of nature . . ." or to say that he presented diversity "as a product of innate racial disposition"[26] is to completely miss the point.

However, the fact that Mill did not present what he saw as evident European superiority "as a product of innate racial disposition" does not change the fact that he did speak of European civilization as being superior because it was "progressive." Does this make him a racist? David Theo Goldberg thinks that it does. In an article which discusses the Mill-Carlyle debate of 1849–1850 (following the publication of Carlyle's "Occasional Discourse on the Negro Question"), Goldberg's main claim is that, despite appearances, the two main opponents in this debate were both racist, the only difference being that Carlyle's contribution to the debate represented "colonialism's vicious recourse to neo-scientific racism," while Mill's was characteristic of "liberalism's polite racism." According to Goldberg, "Here then are to be found the two prevailing pillars of nineteenth century racial theory." Carlyle "represented the bald claim to the 'Negro's' inherent inferiority articulated by racist science of the day"; Mill, on the other hand, "was the principal spokesman for the European's historically developed superiority, though . . . he temperantly acknowledged the influence of ancient Egyptians on the Hellenic Greeks."[27] I think that the two things are separate and that the term "racism" is not appropriate to describe Mill's attitude; "Euro-centric" would do. When he comes to the concrete discussion of Mill's response to Carlyle (in "The Negro Question," published in the next issue of the same periodical where Carlyle's "Occasional Discourse" had been published—*Frazer's Magazine*), Goldberg claims that "it was Carlyle's call to re-institute slavery to which Mill principally objected in his response. This perhaps is predictable, given Mill's longstanding and well-known commitment to abolition." Thus, "Mill's critical concern with Carlyle's racist sentiment was only secondary and much more understated." This is debatable. Mill spent a lot of space in his article attacking Carlyle for his disregard for "the analytical examination of human nature" and his failure to apply the mode of analytical examination "to the laws of the formation of character" which had led Carlyle to "the vulgar error of imputing every difference which he finds among human beings to an original difference of nature."[28] It was not slavery that Mill focused on but rather the deeper theoretical and epistemological issues involved in Carlyle's facile assumptions about black people's inherent inferiority. As Mill put it:

> What the original differences are among human beings, I know no more than your contributor, and no less; it is one of the questions not yet satisfactorily answered in the natural history of the species. This, however, is well known—that spontaneous improvement, beyond a very low grade,—improvement by internal development, without aid from other individuals or peoples—is one of the rarest phenomena in history; and whenever known to have occurred, was the result of an extraordinary combination of advantages; in addition doubtless to many accidents of which all trace is now lost. No argument against the capacity of negroes for improvement could be drawn from their not being one of these rare exceptions.[29]

Moreover, in a statement that could be seen as—to an extent—an assertion of "Afro-centrism" *avant la lettre*, as it were, Mill concluded: "It is curious withal, that the earliest known civilization was . . . a negro civilization. The original Egyptians are inferred from the evidence of their sculptures, to have been a negro race: it was from negroes, therefore, that the Greeks learnt their first lessons in civilization."[30] Even such a statement—more or less unthinkable for the vast majority of Mill's contemporaries—does not satisfy Goldberg, though: "Yet Mill's superficial bow to what has become an Afrocentric cornerstone barely hid beneath the surface the polite racism of his Eurocentric history. Contingent racism is still a form of racism—not so usual, not so bald, not so vituperative, and polite perhaps, but condescending nevertheless even as it is committed to equal opportunity." For Goldberg, his interpretation of Mill as a "polite" racist "is borne out by placing Mill's response to Carlyle in the context of Mill's views on development, modernization, and race." According to Goldberg, Mill's belief that Europeans were developed and civilized, whereas non-Europeans were undeveloped and less civilized, a difference defined by Mill in terms of a people's capacity "to enable and promote representative self-government and individual self-development," or, "[i]n short, in terms of its capacity for autonomy and good government," and his conclusion that a "benevolent despotism" imposed on nondeveloped countries by the more developed was appropriate, mean that Mill was not that better than Carlyle: "Mill's ambivalence over inherent inferiority of 'native Negroes,' even as he marked the transformation in the terms of racial definition historically from the inescapable determinism of blood and brain size to the marginally escapable reach of cultural determination has resonated to this day in liberal ambivalence regarding racial matters."

It is here that I disagree with people like Goldberg. Mill's thought was indeed Euro-centric, and, despite his efforts to be open-minded, he did show himself deplorably ignorant and prejudiced about non-European cultures, not least those of the Indian Peninsula. And his belief that a benevolent despotism was a legitimate mode of governing those he called "barbarians" (provided its aim be to "civilize" them and thereby prepare them for self-government) was paternalistic and based on assumptions that we cannot accept today.[31] However, this does not render him a "racist." I object to the use of the terms "racist" and "racism" to designate all sorts of people and attitudes with which those who use these terms today disagree or which they find exclusionist or prejudiced, etc. There are plenty of more accurate terms to describe each of these attitudes. But "racism" should be reserved for the attitudes of those who believed in the all-importance of biologically transmitted characteristics and in the existence and great significance of inherent traits that are there to stay, with all the deterministic implications of such beliefs. This does not mean that there are no problems with attitudes like Mill's or that he should not be criticized for his pronouncements on the non-European colonized peoples. All I am saying is that we should not confuse these other reproachable attitudes with "racism," thereby impeding the understanding of where the problem is in each case.

Besides my disagreement with the rather promiscuous use of the term "racist" evinced in the writings of many scholars, I also wish to take issue with some of the comments made in recent years about the nature and extent of Mill's celebration of European "superiority," to say nothing of accusations that he was too ethno-centric or Anglo-centric. In a widely discussed article entitled "Decolonising Liberalism," as well as in his more recent book on multiculturalism, Bhikhu Parekh has treated J. S. Mill as the epitome of the liberal tradition with regard to the issues he discusses ("Since the liberal case was best represented by J. S. Mill. . . , I shall concentrate on him").[32] According to Parekh, "From time to time Mill . . . came pretty close to the crude racism of his time, but by and large he managed to avoid it." He concedes that, unlike the racists, Mill "insisted that the non-Europeans once had their glorious periods and were not entirely inferior, that the Europeans too had their dark ages and were not naturally superior, and that the differences between them had a non-biological explanation." Yet, Parekh goes on to claim that Mill's own explanation of the differences between the Europeans and the non-Europeans was "muddled." According to Parekh's reading: "For Mill the East had become stationary because it lacked individuality. That was so because it had fallen under the sway of despotic customs, and that in turn was due to bad forms of government and social structures. As to why and how the latter came into existence, he had no answer." This is not exactly so. Mill did have an answer to the question, an answer he had found in François Guizot's historical works. I am not arguing that the answer in question was necessarily as historically accurate or unproblematic as Mill or Guizot would have one believe; nor is Parekh wrong in accusing Mill of having "disposed of thousands of years of the arbitrarily homogenized East." All I am arguing is that Mill did have an answer and an argument—that was more straightforward than Parekh would have us believe—regarding the causes of what he saw as Europe's "progressive" civilization and the reasons for its differences from what was the case in "the East." Parekh comments: "Having disposed of thousands of years of the arbitrarily homogenized East, Mill went on to explain why Europe was able to come out of its backward past unaided." Then Parekh gives a long quote from Mill's *On Liberty*:

> What is it that has hitherto preserved Europe from this lot? What has made the European family of nations an improving, instead of a stationary portion of mankind? Not any superior excellence in them, which, when it exists, exists as the effect not as the cause; but their remarkable diversity of character and culture. Individuals, classes, nations, have been extremely unlike one another; they have struck out a great variety of paths, each leading to something valuable; and although at every period those who travelled in different paths have been intolerant of one another, and each would have thought it an excellent thing if all the rest could have been compelled to travel his road, their attempts to thwart each other's development have rarely had any permanent success, and each has in time endured to receive the good which the others have offered. Europe is, in my judgement, wholly indebted to this plurality of paths for its progressive and many-sided development.[33]

After having quoted the above text, Parekh went on to comment, among other things: "Mill's explanation raised more questions than it answered. He did not explain . . . why and when [Europe's] people began to develop the love of diversity. He did not explain either why the presence of different classes should by itself cultivate and sustain the love of diversity when similar social differences in India, China and elsewhere did not."[34] Apparently, Parekh has missed Mill's point. Mill never wrote (either here, in *On Liberty*, or in any of the other texts where he discussed Europe's "progressiveness" and the "diversity" that had led to it) that Europeans developed a love of diversity. Nor did he speak of "the presence of different classes" as alone responsible for the outcome which he was describing (as Parekh explicitly says). What Mill said, rather, in several works, was that an astonishing array of different social, cultural, religious, and political groups, values, ideas and centers of power or influence kept up a continuous struggle for predominance in Europe, all of them wishing to preponderate exclusively and annihilate all the rest to extinction. According to Mill (again, following Guizot), a certain degree of diversity and struggle had existed also in Eastern societies (India, Egypt, China) as well as in ancient Greece, and this parallel existence of different "elements of improvement" and the concomitant struggle among them had resulted in significant progress and achievements in civilization. However, at some—relatively early—point in the history of those societies, one element, value, idea, or class managed to become victorious in the struggle and preponderate exclusively, annihilating all the others and therefore ending the diversity and antagonism that had existed before. Following this development, the societies in question either perished, as happened to Greece, once that one victorious element of improvement (in Greece's case, democracy) had exhausted the good it was able to offer, or froze and became stationary for centuries (as India and Egypt, according to Guizot, and China as well, according to Mill and his British contemporaries, for whom China was the paradigmatic cautionary tale against stationariness). In contrast to this plight, Europe was more fortunate, in the sense that a stormy struggle among all sorts of elements, values, ideas, centers of power and influence, nations, religions, and classes was kept up unabated, thanks to the fortunate fact (accident) that none of them was successful in the attempt to prevail completely.[35] In other words, we are again faced with the idea discussed earlier à propos of Pecora's criticisms of Mill. I am not saying that this is an accurate account of the historical record, that the latter is not much more complicated, or that Guizot's account is not rather too schematic. What I am saying is that Mill's argumentation was not what Parekh argues it was, and his explanation was not as incoherent and incomplete as Parekh would have us believe.

Following other criticisms of Mill's attitude toward the French-Canadians,[36] Parekh also discusses critically Mill's attitude toward India. The younger Mill's attitude toward, and involvement with, India is a long story, already the subject of important works by people more competent to deal with it than myself, and I cannot enter it here in detail.[37] I will, however, refer to one of the points made by Parekh, as it is characteristic of the fallacies and confusions that still surround discussions of these issues. After accusing Mill (unfairly, as I have argued elsewhere)[38] of having approved of Lord Durham's assimilationist proposals for the French-Canadians, Parekh goes on to discuss Mill's own Indian policy recommendations and role:

Just as Lord Durham wanted the French Canadians to become English, Macaulay wanted the Indians English in all respects save the colour of their skin. Liberals in other parts of the British empire felt the same way about the indigenous ways of life and thought. *Drawing their inspiration from Mill* they wondered why people should "blindly" adhere to their traditions and customs, and why the colonial rulers should not use a subtle mixture of education and coercion to get them to adopt the liberal ways of life and thought.[39]

Reading this, one is more or less bound to assume that Mill and Macaulay were at one in wishing to anglicize the Indians, even that Macaulay might have "[drawn] inspiration from Mill." This is grossly unfair, to the extent that the fundamental disagreements between the younger Mill and Macaulay on exactly the latter's anglicization policy proposals constitute one of the major *causes célèbres* in the history of he East India Company. Lumping them together in the above statement does not help our understanding of the internal disagreements within liberal thought on imperialism.[40] Quite similar misrepresentations have occurred when the profound differences between Mill and people like James Fitzjames Stephen are obscured, as they usually are.[41] As Julia Stapleton has noted, "Mill's orientalist sympathies and his concern for the 'internal culture' of the native people of India produced a model of imperial rule that was starkly opposed to the authoritarian prescriptions of Stephen."[42] These differences have been fully brought out by Lynn Zastoupil.[43]

When all is said and done, Mill's position is perhaps best summarized in a recent brief reference to these issues by Alan Ryan: "Mill undoubtedly held views about the Indian people that were both prejudiced and ignorant; he was altogether too quick off the mark in describing them as slavish, indolent, and superstitious." "But," continues Ryan, "he was not racist. Given the environmentalist prejudices of the psychological theories on which he had been brought up, he could only believe that, however slavish, indolent, or superstitious Indians might be, it required only a different environment to induce most of them to become self-governing, rational, and energetic. It was the task of the Company to create that environment, to the extent that it was possible to do it." Having said that: "If not a racist, however, he was most certainly an imperialist in the sense in which liberals of his stripe could hardly help being imperialists." Thus, Mill "believed in progress, and although he did not believe that we have a natural right to go around civilizing people against their will, he had no particular qualms about taking advantage of situations in which we can improve other people." Yet, there was a world of difference between Mill's imperialism and that of most of his contemporaries: "Unlike imperialists whose goal was the greater glory of the imperial power, Mill envisaged self-abolishing imperialism; if it was justified it was as an educative enterprise, and if successful its conclusion was the creation of independent liberal-democratic societies everywhere, at which point there would be no further imperial powers."[44] This is not bound to make him popular with many, as it means that Mill "turns out to be at odds with almost everyone from democrats who regard all forms of colonialism with abhorrence to imperialists who deplore Mill-like pandering to dissident natives."[45]

Do the above remarks exonerate Mill? Not necessarily, and my aim here is not to classify him as one of the "good guys" or the "bad guys," but rather to try to contribute toward understanding him and establishing where he stood. Don Habibi's recent assessment of Mill is apposite in this respect: "The key to understanding Mill lies in recognizing the value he places on human growth. . . . He accepted the consequentialist justification that a well-administered colonial system would ultimately maximize happiness. This was unmistakably clear to him when compared to the alternatives." Because, according to Habibi, if we are to attain to a fair assessment of Mill's justification of British colonialism, "we must keep in mind what colonial rule displaced and what surrender to unruly nationalistic groups would entail, as well as the likelihood that other European and Asian powers would step up their efforts to dominate or colonize." Thus, "in the case of India, English rule provided the most enlightened path to progress and independence. As far as Mill was concerned, he had good reasons to believe that if the English had not subjugated the subcontinent, others would have—without the effectiveness, commitment to modernization, and good intentions of the East India Company. The masses enjoyed greater opportunities for improvement and hopes for the future than they would have under the Portuguese, Moguls, local despots, etc." Therefore, he continues, "to understand Mill, we must make an effort to understand the historical context and the world as he saw it." Yet, "unfortunately, numerous commentators demonstrate a superficial understanding of Mill's position and do not give him a fair assessment." Very simply: "During his lifetime, practically no one from Western Europe questioned the notion that their cultures were more advanced than all other contemporary cultures."[46]

Instead of offering all sorts of anachronistic readings or criticisms of Mill because he was not sufficiently "politically correct," by our standards today, it is more important to understand what exactly he was trying to do, how he perceived the world, and what we can learn from all this. Mill's failure to challenge the consensus concerning Western superiority is not that surprising, given the time during which he lived and wrote. What I find quite telling is something else. Mill, as I have argued elsewhere, was particularly conscious of the dangers of ethno-centrism. He was fanatically opposed to it and made strenuous, genuine and sustained efforts to overcome ethnocentric ways of perceiving the world.[47] And yet, for all this, his attitude toward non-European peoples shows the limitations of his achievement in this respect. But the conclusion from this is not what most commentators on these issues would have us believe: that Mill, the paragon of liberalism, was a narrow-minded racist and the like. Mill was, arguably, the most open-minded, the most cosmopolitan and the least parochial of mid-Victorian political thinkers.[48] And yet, his open-mindedness did not reach far enough. This is very important for what it shows about the limitations not of Mill in particular but rather the limitations of the time, of Victorian Britain's elites' *Weltanschauung* and of their discourses. It may also show a thing or two about the dangers inherent in being the world's greatest power and the degree of self-consciousness, vigilance, and sensitivity required on behalf of those who find themselves in that position.

NOTES

1. Georgios Varouxakis, "John Stuart Mill on Race," *Utilitas* 10, no. 1 (1998): 17-32.

2. John Stuart Mill, *The Collected Works of John Stuart Mill* [hereafter: *CW*], general editor F. E. L. Priestley and subsequently John M. Robson, 33 vols (Toronto and London, University of Toronto Press, 1963-91).

3. In a review of the first volume of H. T. Buckle's *History of Civilization in England*, Acton comes to the point where "Mr Buckle declares . . . that 'original distinctions of race are altogether hypothetical' . . . ; in support of which view that eminent positivist Mr. Mill is very properly quoted." This was, in Acton's view, a "great absurdity": "For the same race of men preserves its character, not only in every region of the world, but in every period of history, in spite of moral as well as physical influences." Acton, "Buckle's Philosophy of History" (1858), in: John Emerich Edward Dalberg-Acton, First Baron Acton, *Selected Writings of Lord Acton*, ed. J. Rufus Fears, 3 vols. (Indianapolis: Liberty Classics, 1985-88), III, 457–58, 449. Cf. James Fitzjames Stephen, "History of Civilization in England. By Henry Thomas Buckle. Vol. I. London: 1857," *Edinburgh Review* 107 (1858): 465–512; James Fitzjames Stephen, "History of Civilization in England. By Henry Thomas Buckle. Volume the Second. London: 1861," *Edinburgh Review* 114 (1861): 183–211; Matthew Arnold, *The Complete Prose Works of Matthew Arnold*, ed. R. H. Super, 11 vols. (Ann Arbor: University of Michigan Press, 1960-1977), III, 353; Lionel Trilling, *Matthew Arnold* (London: G. Allen and Unwin, 1974), 235.

4. See John W. Burrow, *Evolution and Society: A Study in Victorian Social Theory* (Cambridge: Cambridge University Press, 1968), 118–36 (especially 121, 130).

5. See James Hunt [anon.], "Race in Legislation and Political Economy," *The Anthropological Review* 4 (1866): 113–35; Ronald Rainger, "Race, Politics, and Science: The Anthropological Society of London in the 1860s," *Victorian Studies* 22 (1978): 51–70; Varouxakis, "Mill on race."

6. Besides Varouxakis, "Mill on Race," Mill's exceptional place in the antiracist cause has recently been highlighted in an article by Peter Mandler: "Mill's influence was again paramount. He was about as clear in his rejection of biological race as it is possible to get." And Mandler goes on to cite the quote from Mill's *Political Economy* about the vulgarity of "attributing the diversities of conduct and character to inherent [natural] differences," which features in the Epigraph of this article (Peter Mandler, "The Consciousness of Modernity? Liberalism and the English 'National Character,' 1870–1940," in *Meanings of Modernity: Britain from the Late-Victorian Era to World*

War II, ed. Martin Daunton and Bernhard Rieger [Oxford: Berg, 2001], 124). Mandler also emphasizes the close connection between Mill's *System of Logic* and Buckle's *History of Civilization in England* (1857–1861) (ibid., 122, 124). For an appreciation of Mill's distance from racists like Carlyle from a different perspective see: Catherine Hall, "Competing Masculinities: Thomas Carlyle, John Stuart Mill and the Case of Governor Eyre," in *White, Male and Middle Class: Explorations in Feminism and History* (Cambridge: Polity, 1992): 255–95; and Catherine Hall, *Civilizing Subjects: Metropole and Colony in the English Imagination 1830–1867* (Cambridge: Polity, 2002), 352.

7. See Douglas A. Lorimer, "Race, Science and Culture: Historical Continuities and Discontinuities, 1850–1914," in *The Victorians and Race*, ed. Shearer West (Aldershot, England: Scolar Press, 1996): 12–33; Peter Mandler, "'Race' and 'Nation' in Mid-Victorian Thought," in *History, Religion and Culture: British Intellectual History 1750–1950*, ed. Stefan Collini, Richard Whatmore, and Brian Young (Cambridge: Cambridge University Press, 2000): 224–44; Christine Bolt, *Victorian Attitudes to Race* (London: Routledge and Kegan Paul, 1971); George Watson, *The English Ideology: Studies in the Language of Victorian Politics* (London: Allen Lane, 1973); Frederic E. Faverty, *Matthew Arnold the Ethnologist* (Evanston, Ill.: Northwestern University Press, 1951); John W. Burrow, *The Crisis of Reason: European Thought, 1848–1914* (New Haven and London: Yale University Press, 2000); Maurice Mandelbaum, *History, Man and Reason: A Study in Nineteenth-Century Thought* (Baltimore: The Johns Hopkins University Press, 1971); Paul B. Rich, *Race and Empire in British Politics*, 2nd ed. (Cambridge, England: Cambridge University Press, 1990); George W. Stocking, Jr., *Race, Culture, and Evolution: Essays in the History of Anthropology* (Chicago: University of Chicago Press, 1968); Robert J. C. Young, *Colonial Desire: Hybridity in Theory, Culture and Race* (London and New York: Routledge, 1995).

8. See, for instance, George W. Stocking's remarks on Leslie Stephen's use of "race": George W. Stocking, Jr., *Victorian Anthropology* (New York: Free Press, 1987), 138–39. For the confusion and lack of precision that characterizes the use of the type of race not just in common parlance but also among specialists, see Michael Banton, *Racial Theories* (Cambridge, England: Cambridge University Press, 1987), xii–xv, 29–32.

9. "On the New Constitution of France, and the Aptitude of the French Character for National Freedom" (1852), in Walter Bagehot, *The Collected Works of Walter Bagehot*, ed. Norman St John-Stevas, 15 vols. (London: The Economist, 1965–86), IV, 48–50. If we compare statements such as these with what Bagehot came to write a couple of decades later, in his most scientifically ambitious work, *Physics and Politics* (1872), it is obvious that in 1852 he stressed the fixity of national characters much more than he was to do in the later work. When he wrote *Physics and Politics*, besides the possible benefit of older age Bagehot was equipped with Darwinian theory which in his hands offered ways in which to explain the formation and changes of national character without recourse to racial explanation. In fact, in *Physics and Politics*, Bagehot explicitly rejects fashionable biological explanations of the formation of national character (see Mandler, "'Race' and 'Nation,'" 234; cf. Georgios Varouxakis, *Victorian Political Thought on France and the French* [Basingstoke, England, and New York: Palgrave, 2002], 115–22). On the significance of *Physics and Politics* see: H. S. Jones, *Victorian Political Thought* (Basingstoke, England, and London: Macmillan; New York: St. Martin's Press, 2000), 67; Stefan Collini, Donald Winch, and John W. Burrow, *That Noble Science of Politics: A Study*

in Nineteenth-Century Intellectual History (Cambridge: Cambridge University Press, 1983), 164.

10. Catherine Hall, "The Nation Within and Without," in *Defining the Victorian Nation: Class, Race, Gender and the Reform Act of 1867*, ed. Catherine Hall, Keith McClelland, and Jane Rendall (Cambridge: Cambridge University Press, 2000), 179–233, p. 192. Knox has been called Gobineau's British counterpart (Zeev Sternhell, "Racism," in *The Blackwell Encyclopaedia of Political Thought*, ed. David Miller et al., [Oxford: Blackwell, 1987], 414), and "an almost hysterical racialist," who had asserted (in *The Races of Man: A Philosophical Inquiry into the Influence of Race over the Destiny of Nations*, 1852) that "race is everything; literature, science, art—in a word, civilization, depends on it" (Burrow, *Evolution and Society*, 130). Cf. Nancy Stepan, *The Idea of Race in Science: Great Britain 1800–1960* (Basingstoke, England: Macmillan, 1982), 43.

11. Varouxakis, "Mill on Race."

12. For more on the indulgence in racial explanation on the part of these and other thinkers see: Varouxakis, *Victorian Political Thought*, 103–30 and passim. Cf. Hall, "Competing Masculinities;" Faverty, *Matthew Arnold*; Diane Paul, "'In the Interests of Civilization': Marxist Views of Race and Culture in the Nineteenth Century," *Journal of the History of Ideas* 42 (1981): 115–38; Bernard Semmel, *The Governor Eyre Controversy* (London: MacGibbon and Kee, 1962).

13. For more on Buckle see: Bernard Semmel, "H. T. Buckle: The Liberal Faith and the Science of History," *British Journal of Sociology* 27 (1975): 370–86; Mandler, "'Race' and 'Nation'"; Mandler, "The Consciousness of Modernity?"

14. Rainger, "Race, Politics, and Science," 65. Cf. T. H. Huxley, "Emancipation—Black and White," *Reader* 5 (1865): 561–62; Adrian Desmond, *Huxley* (London: Penguin Books, 1998).

15. Besides the cases examined in this paper, for earlier examples see: E. D. Steele, "IV. J. S. Mill and the Irish Question: Reform and the Integrity of the Empire, 1865–1870," *The Historical Journal* 13 (1970): 419–50; Bruce Mazlish, *James and John Stuart Mill: Father and Son in the Nineteenth Century* (London: Hutchinson, 1975), 407. Cf. Justman, *The Hidden Text*, 122–24.

16. Uday Singh Mehta, *Liberalism and Empire: A Study in Nineteenth-Century British Liberal Thought* (Chicago and London: The University of Chicago Press, 1999), 15 n22. For other instances where Mehta says or implies that J. S. Mill indulged in racial thinking, cf. ibid., 70, 73.

17. Varouxakis, "Mill on Race."

18. Varouxakis, "Mill on Race," 28–31.

19. Mill, *CW*, XVIII, 273–74.

20. Vincent P. Pecora, "Arnoldian Ethnology," *Victorian Studies* 41 (1997–1998): 355–79, 372.

21. Mill, *CW*, XIX, 458–59.

22. *CW*, XVIII, 197.

23. Georgios Varouxakis, "Guizot's Historical Works and J. S. Mill's reception of Tocqueville," *History of Political Thought*, no. 20 (1999), 292–312.

24. See Varouxakis, "Guizot's Historical Works."

25. Emphasis added: Mill, *CW*, XVIII, 197.

26. Pecora, "Arnoldian Ethnology," 372.

27. See Theo Goldberg's contribution to this volume.

28. Mill, "The Negro Question," *CW*, XXI, 93.

29. Cf. David Hume, "Of national characters" (1748): "I am apt to suspect the negroes, and in general all the other species of men . . . to be naturally inferior to the whites. There scarcely ever was a civilized nation of any other complexion than white, nor even any individual, eminent either in action or speculation. No ingenious manufacturers amongst them, no arts, no sciences." (Emphasis added). David Hume, "Of National Characters," in David Hume, *Political Essays*, ed. Knud Haakonssen (Cambridge, England: Cambridge University Press, 1994), 86n.

30. *CW*, XX1, 93.

31. For one of the most sustained and sophisticated recent critiques of Mill in these respects see: Mehta, *Liberalism and Empire*, pp. 97–114 and passim. See also: Beate Jahn, "Barbarian Thoughts: Imperialism in the Philosophy of John Stuart Mill," *Review of International Studies*, 31 (2005), forthcoming. Cf. also Michael Levin, *J. S. Mill on Civilization and Barbarism* (London: Routledge, 2004).

32. Bhikhu Parekh, "Decolonizing Liberalism," in Aleksandras Shtromas, ed., *The End of "Isms"? Reflections on the Fate of Ideological Politics after Communism's Collapse* (Oxford: Blackwell, 1994), 85-103; Bhikhu Parekh, *Rethinking Multiculturalism: Cultural Diversity and Political Theory* (Basingstoke and London: Macmillan, 2000).

33. Mill, *CW*, XVIII, 273-74.

34. Parekh, "Decolonizing Liberalism," 89–90.

35. Mill, *CW*, XX, 268–70. For a fuller analysis of this idea and textual evidence from several of Mill's works see: Varouxakis, "Guizot's Historical Works," 296–305.

36. I have taken issue with Parekh regarding those in: Georgios Varouxakis, *Mill on Nationality* (London and New York: Routledge, 2002), 14–19.

37. See, from an extensive literature: Lynn Zastoupil, *John Stuart Mill and India* (Stanford, Calif.: Stanford University Press, 1994); Martin I. Moir, Douglas M. Peers, and Lynn Zastoupil, eds., *J. S. Mill's Encounter with India* (Toronto: University of Toronto Press, 1999); Trevor Lloyd, "John Stuart Mill and the East India Company," in *A Cultivated Mind: Essays on J. S. Mill Presented to John Robson*, ed. Michael Laine (Toronto: University of Toronto Press, 1991); A. L. Harris, "John Stuart Mill: Servant of the East India Company," in *John Stuart Mill: Critical Assessments*, ed. John Cunningham Wood, 4 vols. (1987), IV, 207–25; Eric Stokes, *The English Utilitarians and India* (Delhi: Oxford University Press, 1982 [1959]); Mehta, *Liberalism and Empire*. For related issues see also: Javed Majeed, *Ungoverned Imaginings: James Mill's History of British India and Orientalism* (Oxford: Clarendon Press, 1992); Duncan Forbes, "James Mill and India," *Cambridge Journal* 5 (1951): 19–33; J. H. Burns, "The Lights of Reason: Philosophical History in the Two Mills," in *James and John Stuart Mill: Papers of the Centenary Conference* ed. John M. Robson and Michael Lane (Toronto: University of Toronto Press, 1976), 3–20; Fred Rosen, "Eric Stokes, British Utilitarianism and India," in *J. S. Mill's Encounter with India*, ed. Martin I. Moir, Douglas M. Peers, and Lynn Zastoupil (Toronto: University of Toronto Press, 1999), 18–33; Brian Gardner, *The East India Company* (New York: McCall Publishing Company, 1971); R. N. Ghosh, "John Stuart Mill on Colonies and Colonisation," in *John Stuart Mill: Critical Assessments*, ed. John Cunningham Wood, 4 vols. (1987), IV, 354–67; John M. Robson,

"Civilization and Culture as Moral Concepts," in *The Cambridge Companion to Mill*, ed. John Skorupski (Cambridge: Cambridge University Press, 1998), 338–71.

38. Varouxakis, *Mill on Nationality*, 14–19.

39. Emphasis added: Parekh, "Decolonizing Liberalism," 91.

40. See more in Zastoupil, *Mill and India*; Alexander Brady, "Introduction," in John Stuart Mill, *Essays on Politics and Society*, vol. 18 of *The Collected Works of John Stuart Mill* (Toronto: University of Toronto Press, 1977), xlvi–li.

41. Fred Rosen has recently argued cogently that many of the confusions regarding the attitude of the British utilitarians towards India are due to the fact that the scholar who pioneered the study of the subject in the second half of the twentieth century, Eric Stokes, took James Fitzjames Stephen to be much more paradigmatic and much more representative of classical utilitarianism than he in fact was. See Rosen, "Eric Stokes," 19, 28–30.

42. Julia Stapleton, "James Fitzjames Stephen: Liberalism, Patriotism, and English Liberty," *Victorian Studies*, no. 41 (1998), 252.

43. Zastoupil, *Mill and India*, 201–7 and passim. Mehta discusses the differences between "the Orientalists" and the "Anglicists" (Mehta, *Liberalism and Empire*, 89), but no mention is made of where John Stuart Mill stood.

44. Mill was perceived as "the great supporter of Indian independence in the East India House." Gardner, *The East India Company*, 238; cf. Habibi, *John Stuart Mill*, 212 n43.

45. Alan Ryan, "Introduction," in Martin I. Moir, Douglas M. Peers, and Lynn Zastoupil (eds), *J. S. Mill's Encounter with India* (Toronto: University of Toronto Press, 1999), 3–17 (pp. 15–16).

46. Habibi, *John Stuart Mill*, 184–5, 202. Habibi goes on to illustrate his claim with the oft-used (and yet well-chosen) example of the (strikingly disparaging) attitudes of Marx and Engels toward the peoples of Africa and Asia (and, one could add, the Balkans) as well as their emphatic endorsement of European colonialism.

47. See Varouxakis, *Mill on Nationality*, especially pp. 94–110; Varouxakis, *Victorian Political Thought*, passim.

48. I have to stress "mid-Victorian," because people like Bentham or Burke can be said to have done remarkably better. They came from an earlier, more cosmopolitan time, though. See, in particular, Jennifer Pitts's article in this volume on Bentham; also, Jennifer Pitts, "Empire and Social Criticism: Burke, Mill, and the Abuse of Colonial Power," paper presented at the 2002 Annual Meeting of the American Political Science Association, 29 August–1 September 2002. As for a later generation, see, notably, Bart Schultz's and David Weinstein's contributions to this volume. Some late Victorian thinkers displayed a vigorous and militant anti-imperialism. For a few comments in this respect regarding Herbert Spencer and Frederic Harrison, see: Georgios Varouxakis, "'Patriotism,' 'Cosmopolitanism' and 'Humanity' in Victorian Political Thought," *European Journal of Political Theory*, vol. 5, no. 1, forthcoming (first issue of 2006).

8

Chairing the Jamaica Committee: J. S. Mill and the Limits of Colonial Authority

J. Joseph Miller

On July 9, 1866 John Stuart Mill was unanimously elected chairman of the Jamaica Committee. For the following two years, Mill's was the public face of the committee's attempts to prosecute Governor Edward Eyre of Jamaica for murder. Mill pursued Eyre with a passion that many of his contemporaries found to be at odds with his reputation as a cold logician. Mill's spirited public pursuit of Eyre roused much of the British middle class against him, leading ultimately to a furious campaign to unseat Mill in Parliament. That campaign proved effective, as Mill lost what had long been a safe seat in liberal Westminster.[1] One cannot help but wonder what it is about the Eyre controversy that drove Mill's crusade against Eyre even in the face of increasingly hostile public opinion. Jennifer Pitts has suggested that Eyre's actions in Jamaica shook Mill's faith in benevolent colonialism and that Mill aggressively pursues Eyre as a bad apple that, if left unchecked, might spoil the bunch.[2]

In this paper, I suggest a more charitable reading of Mill's colonialism. I will argue that Mill pursues Eyre not as a matter of abstract justice but rather as a matter of policy: Eyre's actions, Mill thinks, are the antithesis of good British colonial policy. Indeed, for Mill Eyre represents not so much a single bad administrator but rather the personification of a type of colonialism that Mill rejects. Eyre's actions are indicative of an arbitrary colonialism that exploits the colonized for the benefit of the colonizers. For Mill, though, one of the chief functions of a good government is the improvement of its citizens; that function applies to all sorts of governments, both domestic and colonial. Eyre's actions were a fundamental violation of the aim of government and as such were the essence of despotism. That Eyre had to be punished for his actions seemed obvious to Mill; failure to take a definitive stand against Eyre's

155

behavior would be tantamount to endorsing despotism for the sake of despotism. Mill envisioned a world full of self-determining nations trading freely to the betterment of all involved and argued that that vision could be achieved only if the British colonized, and improved through an enlightened despotism, those parts of the world containing people unable either to be self-determining or to see the value of free trade.

The facts of the Morant Bay Rebellion are fairly well known. On October 11, 1865, a local riot resulted in the deaths of a justice of the peace, fifteen members of his militia, and several rioters. The incident led to sporadic rioting throughout Morant Bay. On hearing of the events in Morant Bay, Governor Edward John Eyre placed the entire district under martial law. The proclamation remained in effect for a month, during which time soldiers killed 439 blacks, flogged more than 600 people (including women and children), and burned roughly 1,000 houses. Martial law, together with the hangings, floggings, and burnings, continued throughout the month, despite the fact that Brigadier Nelson, the officer in charge of the operations against the rebels, reported as early as October 13, that he found all to be quiet in Morant Bay.

Two days after imposing martial law, Eyre concluded that the riot had in fact been a planned rebellion, one organized by George William Gordon, an outspoken black member of the legislature, and a man whom Eyre had earlier described as "the most consistent and untiring obstructor of the public business in the House of Assembly."[3] Eyre issued a warrant for Gordon's arrest on October 16, holding that Gordon was morally guilty of inciting the rioting. Immediately upon learning of the warrant, Gordon surrendered to the local authorities in Kingston, where he had been throughout the rioting and where civil law remained in effect. Eyre had Gordon transported to Morant Bay, where he was convicted of high treason by court-martial and hanged on October 23.

These sobering findings, chronicled in the 1866 "Report of the Jamaica Royal Commission,"[4] together with the refusal of the Conservative government to press charges against Eyre led to Mill's involvement with the Jamaica Committee, a group formed to bring Eyre to justice. Indeed, Mill, who was just beginning his term in Parliament as the member for Westminster, regarded the prosecution of Eyre to be the most important issue before Parliament in its 1866 session, claiming in a letter that "the two great topics of the year will be Jamaica and Reform," adding later that "there is no part of it all, not even the Reform Bill, more important than the duty of dealing justly with the abominations committed in Jamaica."[5] Mill's insistence on bringing criminal charges against Eyre led to the resignation of Charles Buxton as chairman of the Jamaica Committee and resulted in Mill's being elected to that post.[6]

Mill's efforts to prosecute Eyre on criminal charges, though successful in having the governor removed from his office, ended with the case twice being thrown out of court. Later, the government granted Eyre a pension and paid his legal fees. Mill, though disgusted with the behavior of the government, nevertheless believed that some good had come out of the affair, writing in the *Autobiography* that the Committee had at least demonstrated "that there was at any rate a body of persons determined to use all the means which the law afforded to obtain justice for the injured" and that the Committee's efforts had ensured that "Colonial Governors and other persons in authority will have a considerable motive to stop short of such extremities in future."[7]

Given the brutal facts of Eyre's case, one might reasonably wonder why Eyre received such favorable treatment from Parliament, the courts, and the public in general. That such sympathy was given in the face of near-universal acknowledgement that Eyre did indeed continue to have people court-martialed, flogged, and hanged well after all active rebellion had ceased particularly calls out for some explanation. While a full treatise on British attitudes toward Eyre is beyond the scope of this essay, I will sketch at least some of the underlying reasons offered by Eyre's supporters, for those reasons help to shed light on Mill's arguments for prosecuting Eyre.

First, a bit of background: two events, both only nominally connected to Jamaica, helped to shape Victorian attitudes toward the rebellion in Morant Bay. Although it had taken place nearly a century earlier (1791-1803), the English still vividly recalled the Haitian struggle for independence, a struggle which saw revolutionaries summarily executing all persons of European descent. The British had, of course, abolished slavery in 1833, but the English citizenry could not help but know that there would be much festering resentment among the more than 400,000 blacks in Jamaica toward the largely absentee English plantation owners and toward the English colonial government. The second incident was the Sepoy Mutiny of 1857–1858, in which the sepoys in the British army mutinied against the East India Company. In their quest to establish the last Mogul emperor as ruler of all India, the rebel sepoys were responsible for murdering numerous European (mostly British) civilians. The rebellion took nearly a year to put down and led to numerous changes in British colonial policy in India, most notably the effective dismantling of the East India Company.

For the middle class and the aristocracy of Britain, the Haitian revolution symbolized the potential explosiveness of unrest in the West Indies, while the Sepoy Mutiny brought home the frightening truth that rebellion could strike even the mighty (and for a colonial power, relatively benevolent) British Empire. Those truths, together with an unfortunate and long-entrenched racism, led to much support for Eyre from the aristocracy and from much of the middle class.[8] Somewhat surprisingly, Eyre also received support from many of Britain's leading men of letters. Thomas Carlyle, John Ruskin, Charles Dickens, Alfred Tennyson, and Charles Kingsley all were supporters of Eyre. Men such as these argued that Eyre had acted in a way that saved Jamaica for the empire. Ruskin, for instance, argued in defense of Eyre's execution of Gordon that since it is perfectly lawful to kill an individual who has invaded your property simply on the suspicion that said person might harm you, then why

for the safety, not of your own poor person, but of sixteen thousand men, women, and children, confiding in your protection, and entrusted to it; and for the guardianship not of your own stairs and plate-chest, but of a province involving in its safety that of all the English possessions in the West Indies—for these minor ends it is not lawful for you to take a single life on suspicion, though the suspicion rest . . . on experience of the character and conduct of the accused during many previous years.[9]

Carlyle offered a similar metaphor to defend the "excessive" floggings and hangings, claiming that it was "as if a ship had been on fire; the captain, by immediate and bold exertion, had put the fire out and been called to account for having flung a bucket or two of water into the hold beyond what was necessary. He had damaged some of the cargo perhaps, but he had saved the ship."[10] The accounts of Ruskin and Carlyle were echoed by Jamaican landowners and by British peers, most of whom denounced the rebels as lazy and uneducated while holding up the governor as the man who had single-handedly saved Jamaica for Queen and Empire.[11]

For those arguing in Eyre's defense, preserving colonies for the empire was a colonial governor's first duty. Eyre had done what was necessary to protect Jamaica for the queen. Indeed, the stories of atrocities committed by both the sepoy mutineers in 1857 and by the rebels in Jamaica "had convinced much of the public that only by weighty force, crushingly exercised, would it be possible to maintain control over the semi-educated, barbarous, coloured races of the Empire."[12] Preserving the empire would, in other words, require that the overseas colonies employ measures that would never be tolerated were they used in England itself.

The importance of Britain's colonies was not lost on those on the other side of the Eyre controversy, the Jamaica Committee. Indeed, Mill himself in the last chapter of *Considerations on Representative Government* offers several arguments in favor of retaining the empire, arguing that the empire helps to ensure universal peace, protects portions of the world from being annexed by less beneficent foreign governments, keeps markets open, and adds weight to Britain's position in the international community.[13] But members of the Jamaica Committee, together with their working-class allies, did not buy into the idea of one standard of treatment for the English and another for nonwhite natives. Indeed, as many working-class leaders saw things, the laborers of England had much in common with the rebels in Jamaica, both groups finding themselves frustrated in their attempts to gain the franchise and to secure better wages and safer working conditions. An open-air meeting held on August 30, 1866, organized and attended primarily by working-class Londoners, linked Eyre to British aristocratic oppression, with one speaker claiming that all aristocrats were opposed to individual rights and always ready to support oppression. A subsequent meeting on September 3 saw a jury of 10,000 workingmen try and burn in effigy Governor Eyre for his crimes in Jamaica.

Joining with the working classes in denouncing Eyre were middle-class radicals, many of them Britain's leading economists and scientists. Joining Mill on the Jamaica Committee were, among others, Charles Darwin, Thomas Huxley, Charles Lyell, and Herbert Spencer. Although many members of the committee were quite outspoken in their attacks on Eyre, Mill was widely known to be the driving force behind the Jamaica Committee, having almost single-handedly persuaded the committee that securing Eyre's dismissal as governor should be only a prelude to pressing forward with criminal charges against the former governor. That Mill pursued Eyre with a Javertian relentlessness earned for Mill the reputation of a "persecutor" of the unfortunate Eyre, a reputation that still lingers among Eyre sympathizers.[14] Interestingly, though, Mill was moved less by a desire to bring Eyre to justice then by what he saw as an important question of constitutional law.[15] Indeed, for Mill personally, the main issue at stake was "whether the British dependencies, eventually perhaps Great Britain itself, were to be under the government of law, or of military license."[16] Mill was, in other words, moved to his relentless prosecution of Eyre not so much out of a sense of justice to those whom Eyre wrongly killed and flogged[17] but rather as a matter of foreign policy. As Mill himself writes:

> At all events, while the world is as full of crime as it is, I do not suppose that however strong my feelings about it, I should have considered myself as peculiarly called upon to interfere against him [Eyre]. But I do consider myself as an Englishman called upon to protest against what I believe to be an infringement of the laws of England; against acts of violence committed by Englishmen in authority, calculated to lower the character of England in the eyes of all foreign lovers of liberty; against a precedent that could justly inflame against us the people of our dependencies; & against an example calculated to brutalize our own fellow countrymen.[18]

Here Mill argues that prosecuting Eyre is not simply a matter of bringing the governor to justice; rather, for Mill the Eyre case serves as a *casus belli* for reforming British foreign policy.[19] Eyre was, in the words of one member of the Jamaica Committee "simply the personification of wrong,"[20] a specific instance of a more general problem that needed to be addressed.

Mill's views were shared by much of the Jamaica Committee. Herbert Spencer, for instance, asked in his autobiography how "cultivated Englishmen should not have perceived that the real question at issue was whether free institutions were to be at the mercy of a chief magistrate."[21] Another committee member, Frederic Harrison, wrote a series of letters to the *Daily News* arguing that "English law is of that kind, that, if you play fast and loose with it, it vanishes. . . . What is done in a colony today may be done in Ireland tomorrow, and in England hereafter."[22] Harrison went on to object to the idea that different standards should apply to white Englanders and black Jamaicans.

The attitude of Mill, Spencer, and Harrison is reflected in the official position of the Jamaica Committee. The 1866 "Statement of the Jamaica Committee" sets forth the committee's two main purposes. First, the members desire to show that the execution of British citizens must always be governed by law and not by the personal decisions of the executive branch. The authors of the statement argue that citizens of Britain would have their lives changed for the worse if their lives and liberties are guarded only by the executive government rather than by the force of law.[23] Second, the members of the committee hope to limit the jurisdiction of martial law generally and of courts-martial specifically. Committee members argue that courts-martial are often made up of untrained officers with little or perhaps even no knowledge of the law or of criminal procedures and who are "inflamed, probably, by the passions of the crisis" and that as such courts-martial are not equipped to dispense justice at all.[24] A later progress report, written by the committee in 1868 and issued to members of the committee, summed up the aims of the committee in three parts: "To obtain a judicial inquiry into the conduct of Mr. Eyre and his subordinates; to settle the law in the interest of justice, liberty and humanity; and to arouse public morality against oppression generally, and particularly against the oppression of subject and dependent races."[25] Both the 1866 and 1868 statements make clear that prosecuting Eyre is important insofar as a successful prosecution would effectively establish the limits of colonial authority.

What is perhaps most surprising about the Governor Eyre controversy is the fact that Eyre's supporters and detractors seem, on the face of it, to have chosen the wrong sides. The economists and scientists of the Jamaica Committee were denounced even in their own time as unsentimental, concerned only with hard facts and dismissive of sentiment, lampooned by Dickens as the Scrooges and the Gradgrinds of the world. The Eyre Defence Committee, on the other hand, included most of the prominent poets and writers of the day, social reformers who extolled sentiment above reason. Yet the poets and writers sided with Eyre's use of brute strength against the oppressed. Strongly influenced by Carlyle's advocacy of hero worship and his fear of chaos and disorder, men like Dickens and Ruskin saw Eyre as a heroic savior of order and empire. Prominent members of the Eyre Defence Committee ridiculed Eyre's opponents for pursuing justice at the expense of empire abroad while tacitly consenting to much of the human misery being caused by *laissez faire* capitalism at home.[26]

Members of the Jamaica Committee, on the other hand, rejected utilitarian arguments for preserving the empire at the cost of a few individuals, arguing instead for colonial reform. Especially surprising, at least on a surface reading, is to find Mill leading the charge against Eyre. Critics of Mill made much of supposed inconsistencies between Mill's attitudes toward Eyre and his utilitarianism. Conservative periodicals such as *Punch* and *The Times* were merciless in their attacks on Mill, both for matters of consistency and for a supposed extremism that seemed at odds with Mill's reputation as an imperturbable logician. Shortly after Mill's unsuccessful reelection campaign in 1868, *The Times* commented on a public exchange of letters between Mill and Priscilla McLaren in which Mill expresses disappointment that some women had supported Eyre, blasting Mill for, in John Robson's words, "his utter failure to practice the tenets that his writings had made his supporters expect."[27] Later, the same editorial accuses Mill of a "vehement, narrow partisanship, and apparent inability to see a redeeming point in a political adversary"[28] (a charge that Mill denies in the *Autobiography*).[29] Indeed, at the height of his unpopularity, Mill reports receiving "abusive letters" and even threats of assassination anonymously in the post. Attacks on the consistency of Mill's thought are frequently a product of serious misunderstandings of Mill's arguments, sometimes deliberate and sometimes not. Thomas Beggs, a contemporary of Mill, complains that Mill's opponents took extracts from Mill's books

> which without the context, were made to read very differently to the author's intention. Nothing but blank pages could save an author under such treatment. The walls were covered with them, and it was the stock article of the canvassers. Some of them carried about with them printed matter, which it was alleged Mr. Mill had written, but took care not to let this pass out of their hands.[30]

Modern supporters of Eyre commit the same mistakes. Geoffrey Dutton, hardly an expert on Mill's moral philosophy, nonetheless attempts to discredit Mill as confused or inconsistent, offering a lengthy quotation from *Utilitarianism* in his Eyre apology, *The Hero as Murderer*, and noting that Mill claims there:

> With many, the test of justice in penal infliction is that the punishment should be proportioned to the offence; meaning that it should be exactly measured by the moral guilt of the culprit (whatever be their standard for measuring guilt): the consideration, what amount of punishment is necessary to deter from the offence, having nothing to do with the question of justice, in their estimation: while there are others to whom that consideration is all in all; who maintain that it is not just, at least for man, to inflict on a fellow-creature, whatever may be his offences, any amount of suffering beyond the least that will suffice to prevent him from repeating, and others imitating, his misconduct.[31]

Dutton argues that Eyre can be interpreted as following Mill's guidelines in punishing Gordon, being certain of Gordon's moral guilt and offering the punishment that Eyre believed to be the only way of deterring actions like Gordon's. Eyre himself argues that his was an attempt to send "an immediate and signal example" that would "strike terror and thereby deter the black population from attempting to raise the standard of rebellion in other districts."[32] Dutton claims, with some evidence, that Eyre acted in good faith and charges Mill with a sort of blind and irrational vindictiveness in his pursuit of Eyre.[33]

Understanding Mill's opposition to Eyre inevitably leads to a discussion of his views on colonialism and on the function of governments generally. Any reading of Mill's theoretical justifications of colonialism must begin with his commitment to the harm principle. While the harm principle ostensibly rules out colonialism, Mill weakens the principle with his famous qualification, arguing, "It is, perhaps, hardly necessary to say that this doctrine is meant to apply only to human beings in the maturity of their faculties."[34] Those not in the maturity of their faculties include children, the mentally incompetent (i.e., the insane), and "those backward states of society in which the race itself may be considered as in its nonage."[35] For such societies, "Despotism is a legitimate mode of government in dealing with barbarians, provided the end be their improvement, and the means justified by actually effecting that end."[36] Mill goes on to argue that liberty applies only to those who are capable of being improved by reason and arguments; those who lack such capacities need enlightened despots to rule them. Despotism should not be a permanent state, though; as Mill explains,

> as soon as mankind have attained the capacity of being guided to their own improvement by conviction or persuasion (a period long since reached in all nations with whom we need here concern ourselves), compulsion, either in the direct form or in that of pains and penalties for non-compliance, is no longer admissible as a means to their own good, and justifiable only for the security of others.[37]

Mill is at least theoretically willing to accept a double standard: Europeans and those of European descent are to be governed by the harm principle, while members of "barbarian" races are to be governed by benevolent despotism. Mill's argument here is that some nations simply are not ready for democratic self-rule, a position that does have at least some merit; the utter failure of democracy in the modern states that Britain and France created from the shards of the Ottoman Empire might serve as a case in point. Mill maintains that such nations are best served by a benevolent despotism, but it must be a despotism aimed at developing a populace that is capable of self-determination.[38]

Mill's distinction between Europeans and "barbarians" is a troubling one, for it bears some rather significant racist connotations. At best, Mill's distinction between European and barbarian societies rests upon a crude sociology, one in which every non-European society is deemed, almost by definition, to be incapable of real liberty, regardless of the details of that society's particular social, economic, or political status.[39] Indeed, in his essay on non-intervention, Mill explicitly grants "civilized peoples, members of an equal community of nations, like Christian Europe," full protection from aggression but denies that same protection to "barbarians."[40] Mill, not unlike many others of his class in 1868, is all too willing to assume Kipling's "white man's burden." Indeed, Mill is quick to accept that non-Europeans require a benevolent despotism if they are to progress to a more enlightened state even while arguing that women and Irish peasants fall short of the standards of European males only because they are hindered by institutional structures. He argues at length that removing those institutional hindrances will suffice to bring women and the Irish into the mainstream without any necessity for a lengthy educative process.[41] Interestingly, only women and the Irish seem to merit this sort of status; the remainder of the "barbarians" require significantly more help to reach a "civilized" state.

Mill's attitudes toward non-Europeans do not derive from the racist undertones that plague the thinking of so many of his contemporaries. In objecting to Carlyle's inflammatory claims in "The Negro Question" that blacks are born servants of whites, Mill argues,

> It is by analytical examination that we have learned whatever we know of the laws of external nature; and if he [Carlyle] had not disdained to apply the same mode of investigation to the laws of the formation of character, he would have escaped the vulgar error of imputing every difference which he finds among human beings to an original difference of nature.[42]

Nonetheless, Mill agrees with Carlyle that blacks generally are less capable than Europeans, comparing blacks to trees that grew in poor soil or poor climate or that might have suffered from exposure, storms or disease. Such human beings require outside intervention to be improved; in Mill's words,

> Spontaneous improvement, beyond a very low grade,—improvement by internal development, without aid from other individuals or peoples—is one of the rarest phenomena in history; and whenever known to have occurred, was the result of an extraordinary combination of advantages; in addition doubtless to many accidents of which all trace is now lost.[43]

Mill holds that non-European societies have, at least at times, achieved a very high state of civilization. In *On Liberty*, for example, Mill notes the Chinese as a race that once valued individuality but that stagnated when it ceased to do so.[44] Similarly, in "The Negro Question," Mill asserts (probably incorrectly, we now know) that the original Egyptians—teachers of the Greeks—were black and that as a consequence, Western civilization is perhaps descended from an earlier black civilization. I think it is clear that while Mill does not hold race itself to be indicative of ability (i.e., Mill denies that there are intrinsic reasons why non-Europeans would all be "barbarians"), he does apparently hold that, as a matter of historical accident, by the 1860s all non-Europeans turn out to be "barbarians."

Despite the obvious role that race plays in the Governor Eyre controversy (a fact noted by almost every other contributor to the debate, including Eyre himself), Mills writings on the affair remain curiously silent on matters of race.[45] Jennifer Pitts suggests that Mill's failure to address the ways in which the Eyre affair was specifically a problem of race and colonialism indicates "either a blindness to the peculiar injustices of colonial rule or a determination not to consider them."[46] Noting that in all of Mill's major speeches on Jamaica he never once makes reference to more general questions of race or of colonialism, Pitts argues that Mill "seems to have avoided following any line of inquiry . . . that might suggest that small, white ruling classes governing large populations of disfranchised non-European subjects were prone to abuses that had to be understood in terms of colonial power."[47]

In marked contrast to the other major players in the Governor Eyre debate, Mill focuses his public arguments exclusively on the rights of British subjects to be free from the dangers of martial law. Mill's arguments here are pragmatic, following fairly straightforwardly from his utilitarianism. The pragmatic argument is a two-part argument: first Mill argues that Eyre's actions were in fact illegal, and, second, he argues that allowing actions of the type Eyre performed to go unchecked could have negative repercussions for all British citizens. In his speech to Parliament on July 31, Mill claims that officials who declare martial law must be accountable after martial law ceases for actions that they performed under martial law. Martial law, Mill continues, is not the suspension of all law; rather, martial law is the imposition of military law. Military law may be different from civil law, but it still is law. Eyre, Mill argues, violated the strictures of martial law and thus committed criminal actions. Punishing those criminal acts is of paramount importance to the Empire. After all, Mill argues,

> If persons in authority can take the lives of their fellow subjects improperly, as has been confessedly done in this case, without being called to a judicial account, and having the excuses they make for it sifted and adjudicated by the tribunal in that case provided, we are giving up altogether the principle of government by law, and resigning ourselves to arbitrary power.[48]

And such will be the case not just in the colonies. Mill writes in his *Autobiography* that the abuses of authority in Jamaica could, if unchecked, eventually apply to Britain itself.[49] Mill's speech to the Jamaica Committee urging its members to prosecute Eyre for murder adopts a similar line: failure to prosecute Eyre sets a horrible precedent, one that could well affect the liberties of Britain itself.[50] Indeed, for Mill, law and liberty are inextricably linked and ought never to be dissevered.[51] Law, considered as a set of constraints upon the actions of others, is necessary to liberty.[52] The gist of the pragmatic argument, then: fail to uphold the law and English liberty will be in jeopardy.

Although Mill does on occasion admit privately to worries about systematic abuses of colonial power,[53] his public arguments are all variations on the pragmatic argument given above. Pitts's criticism of Mill as being willfully blind to the inherent dangers of colonialism is, to a great extent, predicated upon Mill's strange refusal to consider publicly that race played an important role in Eyre's actions in Jamaica. Pitts concludes that the events of Morant Bay inspired Mill to such an impassioned attempt to prosecute Eyre largely because Eyre's actions were a direct challenge to Mill's general faith in benevolent colonialism. Thus, rather than seeing Eyre's actions as evidence of a deeper problem with colonialism, Mill treated the governor as a criminal responsible for abusing a perfectly good system. Pitts closes by characterizing Mill's reaction to Eyre as a "willful not seeing" of the coercive effects of colonialism and charging Mill with "a failure of moral and political judgment."[54]

While I agree with Pitts that Mill does not recognize the systematic dangers inherent in colonialism, I disagree with her assessment of Mill as a sincere but, in some respects, oblivious defender of liberal colonialism. In what follows, I suggest a more charitable interpretation of Mill's reaction to Eyre, one that looks past his public pragmatic arguments and examines the theoretical roots of his commitment to colonialism, a commitment that follows as the logical extension of his theory of government generally.[55] Mill reacts so vehemently toward Eyre, then, not because Eyre challenges Mill's principles of colonialism but rather because Eyre is an affront to the very purposes of good government.

Besides his pragmatic arguments, Mill offers two distinct types of justification for colonialism, one economic and one cultural. These dual arguments are given their first full articulation in the *Principles of Political Economy*. There Mill argues that the undeveloped world suffers from a weakness of industry and an ineffective desire to accumulate. He offers several means for improvement:

> first, a better government: more complete security of property; moderate taxes; a more permanent . . . tenure of land. Secondly, improvement of the public intelligence: the decay of usages or superstitions which interfere with the effective implementation of industry; and the growth of mental activity, making the people alive to new objects of desire. Thirdly, the introduction of foreign arts . . . and

the inclusion of foreign capital, which renders the increase of production no longer exclusively dependent on the thrift or providence of the inhabitants themselves, which it places before them a stimulating example.[56]

Taking for granted that "barbarian" nations will require the assistance of Europeans if they are to develop, Mill offers here suggestions both economic and cultural for improvement. Economically, Mill claims, undeveloped countries require foreign capital and better economic laws. Culturally, citizens of undeveloped nations require mental development.

The economic argument for colonialism is grounded in Mill's concerns about the dangers of surplus capital at home.[57] Mill reasoned, following Edward Gibbon Wakefield, that Britain produced more capital than it could profitably invest at home. Surplus capital would produce a decline in profit, for with a stable population in place, surplus capital will raise labor costs and thus lower profits. Combining surplus capital with an increasing population results in a greater demand for food; increased food demand leads to the use of inefficient land for growing crops, which in turn leads to higher food prices, higher wages, and again, lower profits. In either case, declining profits lead to decreased investment which results in a stationary economy. Mill suggests that a stationary economy might be good at some point when it can be combined with a controlled population and a just distribution of wealth, but he claims that such a time is still well in the future.

Mill's answer to the problem of surplus capital is for England to engage in more foreign trade and foreign investment. Colonialism provides a way of increasing foreign trade and investment while at the same time reducing the population at home, both of which have the effect of raising wages for those remaining.[58] Additionally, financing emigration would require some of the surplus capital, allowing the remaining capital to be invested at home with higher profits. The capital used to finance emigration would not simply be lost; rather, it would be useful in establishing colonies that become exporters of inexpensive agricultural products, helping to keep profits up at home. Britain could then invest its capital at home to create manufactured products which it could subsequently sell abroad to pay for the import of agriculture and at home, thanks to the increased employment and wages of those remaining in Britain. Mill concludes that colonialism is an economic windfall; indeed, argues Mill, "the more capital we send away, the more we shall possess and be able to retain at home."[59]

Mill's cultural argument for colonialism takes a different form: rather than arguing for the benefits accruing to Britain through colonialism, the cultural argument examines the benefits that colonialism has on those who are colonized. And for Mill, one of the chief benefits of colonialism is that it prepares the colonized for eventual self-rule. Like Bentham, Mill agrees that people are the best judge of their own interests and thus ought, in principle, to rule themselves. In her essay in this volume, Pitts argues that Bentham holds that "people as they are are quite capable of participation under a system of good laws,"[60] adding that, for Bentham, the chief danger of democracy is abuse by a class of ruling elites. Pitts argues quite powerfully that Bentham's adherence to the principle that utilitarians must take into account actual people's actual preferences commits him to a powerful anticolonialism.

Unlike Bentham, Mill, echoing the worries that James Madison expresses in the *Federalist Papers*, greatly fears the "tyranny of the majority," arguing that an uneducated and unenlightened majority will, through shortsightedness and misguided self-interest, tend to enact laws that ultimately harm the entire society. Mill's writings on representative government are aimed predominantly at conservatives, many of whom objected to extending the franchise out of a fear that doing so would, in the words of Carlyle, amount to "the calling in of new supplies of blockheadism, gullibility, bribeabilty, amenability to beer and balderdash."[61] Mill is not immune to the perception common to Victorian intellectuals that the average working-class person—whatever the country of his origin—was possessed of a low character. Mill thus argues for limits on the amount of influence and power that the majority can actually wield.[62] The severity of those limits depends significantly on exactly how uneducated and unenlightened that majority might happen to be. Citizens of "civilized" nations are to govern themselves according to the harm principle, with the power of the majority held in check via the mechanisms of plural or proportional voting. Citizens of "barbarian" nations require the more active constraints of a benevolent despotism.

Mill specifically outlines several criteria for determining whether or not a society qualifies as "civilized." In his 1836 essay "Civilization," Mill offers two different definitions of "civilization," claiming that it can refer on the one hand to countries that are "further advanced in the road to perfection; happier, nobler, wiser" and on the other hand to "that kind of improvement only, which distinguishes a wealthy and powerful nation from savages or barbarians."[63] Mill devotes the remainder of the essay to a consideration of the latter type of civilization, enumerating the various traits such a civilization would have. Necessary characteristics of civilized nations include having dense populations living in cities or towns who carry on commerce, manufacture, and agriculture, jointly defend themselves in war, and who regulate and administer their daily lives by law. Mill claims that such "elements exist in modern Europe, and especially in Great Britain" but does not specifically mention any other part of the world that qualifies as civilized.[64] Mill echoes that refrain throughout his writings, arguing consistently that British colonies that are populated mainly by those of European descent (i.e., Canada, Australia, New Zealand, South Africa) are different from those whose inhabitants are mainly non-European (e.g., India, and central Africa).[65] Those colonies of "European race" should "possess the fullest measure of internal self-government," an idea that Mill had championed during his time as a Philosophic Radical.[66]

Mill is far from clear on the issue of whether Jamaica (or the West Indies generally) count as "civilized European" or as "barbarian" nations. In the *Principles of Political Economy*, Mill actually argues that the West Indies generally should not be regarded as colonies at all but rather as "outlying agricultural or manufacturing establishments belonging to a larger community," "a place where England finds it convenient to carry on the production of sugar, coffee, and a few other tropical commodities."[67] Calling the West Indies colonies would be much the same as calling Manchester a colony had it happened to be located on a rock in the North Sea. Thus, Mill reasons, trade with the West Indies is not really external trade at all; the islands really are just outlying parts of Britain herself, more akin to York or to Cornwall than to India or South Africa.

Mill oversaw seven editions of the *Principles*, making substantial revisions to some later versions. He does not, however, alter his claims about the West Indies in any of those versions. But whatever their status economically, Mill does not regard the West Indies to be politically a part of Great Britain, at least not in the same way that Manchester is part of Great Britain. Mill explicitly rejects any proposal to treat foreign colonies as part of a federal system, and nowhere does he argue for treating the West Indies politically in the same way that one would treat Birmingham or York.[68] He does not, for instance, think that Jamaica should have a member returned to Parliament, nor does he insist that the office of governor is an inappropriate one. Thus we are left to conclude that, despite Mill's claims about the economic status of the West Indies in the *Principles*, Mill nonetheless views British holdings in the West Indies as colonies at least for the purposes of political administration. That still leaves the question, then, of what status Mill ascribes to the colony of Jamaica: "European" or "barbarian."

As a factual matter, Jamaica in 1865 had considerable home rule; the constitution of Jamaica, granted by Charles II in 1662, provided for both an appointed council to assist the governor and an elected assembly that had the sole power to issue bills of appropriation. The governor did not have the power to override the legislative branch, meaning that, in effect, the island was responsible for its own governance.[69] Essentially, in 1865, Jamaica had exactly the status that Mill argued belongs to "European" colonies. That assembly was not, however, truly representative, considering that out of a population of 440,000 only 1,903 people were qualified to vote. In effect, 2,000 Europeans made all of the decisions for more than 400,000 blacks.[70] Mill objects to this arrangement, writing in an 1865 letter to Rowland Hazard that

[w]hat has just taken place in Jamaica might be used as a very strong argument against leaving the freedmen to be legislated for by their former masters. . . . It

seems not unlikely that England will have to make a clean sweep of the institutions of Jamaica, and suspend the power of local legislation altogether, until the necessary internal reforms have been effected by the mother country.[71]

Contrary to Mill's claims in the *Principles* that the West Indies should be thought of as another part of Britain itself, it seems clear from this passage that Mill does indeed regard Jamaica to be a colony and one that is, moreover, unfit at present for home rule.[72]

If Jamaica is to be regarded as a "barbarian" nation, it will require a benevolent despotism. But that despotism must be aimed at the improvement of Jamaicans, with the eventual goal of preparing the colony for home rule. Colonial governments should thus aspire to educate and improve their citizens. That Mill should hold education to be a central goal of colonial governments is unsurprising; indeed, for Mill, the educative role of government is its primary responsibility whatever the level of its citizens' development. Consider, for example, Mill's claim in *Representative Government* that "the first element of good government, therefore, being the virtue and intelligence of the human beings composing the community, the most important point of excellence which any government can possess is to promote the virtue and intelligence of the people themselves."[73] Mill goes on to argue, "We may consider, then, as one criterion of the goodness of a government, the degree in which it tends to increase the sum of good qualities in the governed, collectively and individually."[74] And still later in the same chapter Mill claims that the foundation of government "consists partly of the degree in which they promote the general mental advancement of the community, including under that phrase advancement in intellect, in virtue, and in practical activity and efficiency."[75] Mill seems pretty clearly to argue that one of the two most important roles of government is that of educating its citizens, both intellectually and morally.

Although Mill's arguments about the educative role of government refer specifically to the government of Great Britain, there is reason to think that Mill meant these ideas to apply to all governments, including colonial governments.[76] Mill argues that in uncivilized colonies, a colonial despotic government is justified "if it is the one which in the existing state of civilization of the subject people, most facilitates their transition to a higher stage of improvement."[77] The improvement of the "uncivilized" natives is the only reason to justify despotic action. When despotic policies do no more to promote improvement than native despotisms had done, "the rulers are guilty of a dereliction of the highest moral trust which can devolve upon a nation: and if they do not even aim at it, they are selfish usurpers, on a par in criminality with any of those whose ambition and rapacity have sported from age to age with the destiny of masses of mankind."[78] Even those governments in uncivilized colonies must refrain from despotism that does nothing to improve the natives and set them on their way to self-determination. Thus Mill finds it perfectly consistent to support phasing out the rajas as rulers of India through the auspices of the East India Company[79] while deploring the "monstrous excesses" committed by British troops in repressing the Indian mutiny, excesses that did nothing to advance Indian civilization.[80]

In "civilized" colonies such as Canada and Australia, governments are not permitted to be despotic, but they still must play an educative role. Perhaps Mill's most telling discussion of the proper role of colonial government comes in his 1838 defense of Lord Durham's activities in Canada. Indeed, Mill, who was instrumental in persuading Parliament to adopt the principles of Lord Durham's Report, thus setting the stage for Canadian home rule, argued that "a new era in the colonial policy of nations began with Lord Durham's Report."[81] Mill's position on Durham is thus instructive in understanding what Mill took to be an ideal colonial policy.

Lord Durham left England for Canada in 1837 in the wake of minor rebellions in the colony. At the time, Canada was divided into sections, an arrangement originally intended to pacify Canada but by 1837, one that had the effect of destroying any sense of national unity. In Quebec, a large French majority grew increasingly discontent with British rule, while in Ontario, emigrants from the United States, who were accustomed to democracy, grew restless under colonial rule. Much of Canada suffered from archaic economic laws and from corrupt and inefficient oversight of land distribution. Finally, in 1837, small rebellions broke out in several different provinces, prompting a minor crisis in Britain. The Americans were eager to welcome Canada into their federal system, and the British were wary of sending money and troops to quell yet another rebellious North American colony. The government decided to send a new colonial governor, one who it hoped might salvage Canada without the need for costly military intervention. Hoping to solve two problems at once, the government dispatched Lord Durham, a radical in Parliament who was a vocal critic both of the government and of its colonial policies.[82]

Immediately upon arrival in Quebec, Durham faced the challenge of dealing with the 160 rebels imprisoned after the unsuccessful rebellions. Durham's solution was to offer amnesty to most of the rebels, excepting only twenty or so of the ringleaders, whom Durham banished to Bermuda. Durham then began setting up committees to investigate the various grievances of the rebellious Canadians. In freeing rebels and moving to investigate their complaints, Durham appeared to his opponents in Britain to have completely sided with the rebels; his ordinances were overturned by Parliament, and he resigned his position a mere six months after his arrival. Upon his departure, Durham constructed what has become known as "Durham's Report," in which he outlined his plans for the administration of Canada, plans that include reuniting the various provinces, addressing Canada's many administrative woes, and establishing home rule.[83]

For his part, Mill found much to praise in Durham's Report. In "Lord Durham's Return," Mill eulogizes the measures Durham outlines, claiming that Durham's four most important programs were "all of first-rate importance, all such as ought to have been given." Those measures, in Mill's words, were

> free municipal institutions: not only the grand instrument of honest local management, but the great "normal school" to fit a people for representative government, and which have never yet existed in Canada. . . . The second measure was a comprehensive scheme of general education. The third was a Registry Act, for titles to landed property. The fourth was for the commutation of feudal tenures in Montreal, where they are peculiar, and peculiarly obnoxious to the English population.[84]

Mill goes on to quote some of Durham's future plans for Canada, all of which impressed Mill favorably; those plans included

> "large and solid schemes of colonization and internal improvement," a "revision of the defective laws which regulate real property and commerce," the introduction of "a pure and competent administration of justice," the "eradication of the manifold abuses engendered by the negligence and corruption of former times, and so lamentably fostered by civil disunions."[85]

Durham's project, then, involved three parts: implementing home rule for Canada, providing an education so as to prepare Canadians for self-government, and extending economic reforms to better the colonists.

Despite the similarities of their respective crises (disaffected minorities, outdated and harmful economic policies, minor rebellions), Eyre and Durham offer strikingly different responses. Rather than addressing the concerns of disaffected Jamaicans, Eyre consistently sided with the aristocratic planters looking only to exploit former slaves.[86] Rather than setting forth programs for educating Jamaicans and preparing them for self-determination, Eyre illegally court-martialed an elected member of his assembly. Rather than providing amnesty for minor participants in the rebellion, Eyre allowed his soldiers to hang hundreds and flog hundreds more, often without even a trial to determine real guilt. In short, Durham attempted to restore peace by making British Canada something that its citizens would prefer to fight for rather than rebel against. Eyre, on the other hand, restored peace by unleashing his soldiers and allowing them to terrorize the population for a full month.

If Durham represents, for Mill, ideal colonial behavior, then Mill's vehemence toward Eyre is less surprising, for Eyre's actions lie at the opposite end of the spectrum from Durham's. Indeed, on Mill's account, Eyre doubly fails in his duties. First, Eyre has committed numerous crimes: murdering Gordon, officially sanctioning his soldiers to murder hundreds of others, endorsing illegal courts-martial, and overseeing brutal treatment of many completely innocent British citizens. And second, Eyre has performed all of these actions simply to maintain Jamaica as part of the empire. On Mill's account, the British are not to keep colonies simply for the sake of having colonies. Colonies are justified provided certain criteria are met. "Civilized" colonies provide practical economic and political benefits and should be kept as part of the empire as long as the colonists themselves consent to that arrangement.[87] "Uncivilized" colonies are justified only if their governing bodies administer them with the ultimate purpose of educating the inhabitants to be self-determining. Eyre fails as a colonial governor regardless of the level of Jamaica's civilization. Citizens of "civilized" colonies may choose whether or not to remain part of the empire; no colonial governor is permitted to wield despotic power to preserve a "civilized" colony for the crown. But even if Jamaica is not a "civilized" colony, Eyre still would be required to implement measures to educate and improve the citizens of Jamaica. Martial law, courts-martial, hangings, floggings, and executions of one's political opponents hardly seem tactics calculated to educate and improve native citizens.

On my reading, Mill pursues Eyre not simply because Eyre threatens a colonial system whose weaknesses Mill refuses to acknowledge. Rather, Eyre represents a particular vision of colonialism (arbitrary despotism wielded only to the advantage of the colonizer) that is fundamentally at odds with Mill's considered conception of colonialism. As Mill himself says, the fact that Eyre has committed great injustices against Jamaican blacks is bad, but probably not bad enough by itself to motivate Mill to action.[88] The real problem is that Eyre carries with him the authority of the British crown. When Eyre acts, his actions carry with them the imprimatur of official government policy. The message that Eyre's particular actions sent was completely at odds with what Mill believed British colonial policy should be. For Mill, governments are to improve their citizens; colonial despotism is acceptable only for "uncivilized" colonies, and there that despotism must still be aimed at preparing the people for self determination. Eyre acts despotically for the sake of maintaining despotic rule; it is no wonder that Mill argues so forcefully against such a precedent.

Mill has thus offered two arguments for colonialism. His economic argument puts forth the claim that colonialism leads to improved economic standing for the colonists, for the natives of the area being colonized, and for the citizens at home. His cultural argument maintains that colonialism is valuable for its ability to "civilize" the natives, preparing them eventually for full self-determination; despotism in "uncivilized" colonies is acceptable provided that it has laying the groundwork for democracy as its ultimate end. Colonial governments, then, must enforce policies calculated to achieve both of these ends; governments must enact policies ensuring the economic well-being of all parties involved and they must also educate and improve their citizens. For Mill, those who—like Eyre—attempt to abuse colonial authority, who resort to despotism for the sake of despotism while failing to improve the lives of their charges, should face the full weight of British law. Mill's position, then, is that colonial governments ought to (a) protect the rights of their citizens, and (b) establish fair economic policies within a context of free and open trade, and (c) prepare its citizens to engage productively in the modern world.

NOTES

All citations to Mill's works will include an abbreviated title as well as volume and page numbers from the *Collected Works of John Stuart Mill* (Toronto, 1963-91). The following abbreviations will be used: A—*Autobiography*; ; C—"Civilization"; CRG—*Considerations on Representative Government*; E&I—"England and Ireland"; WNI—"A Few Words on Non-Intervention"; LDR—"Lord Durham's Return"; NQ—"The Negro Question"; OL—*On Liberty*; PPE—*Principles of Political Economy* SJC[1866]—"Statement of the Jamaica Committee [1866]"; SJC[1868]—"Statement of the Jamaica Committee [1868]"; SW—*Subjection of Women*; U—*Utilitarianism*. I will give the location and date of Mill's public speeches, and the addressee and date of all letters.

1. For detailed account of Mill's losing election in 1868 and the role that the Eyre controversy played in that defeat, see Bruce Kinzer, Ann P. Robson, and John M. Robson, *A Moralist in and out of Parliament: John Stuart Mill at Westminster, 1865–1868* (Toronto: University of Toronto Press, 1992), esp. chap. 7.

2. See Pitts, "Legislator of the Word," in this volume. See also "Empire and Social Criticism: Burke, Mill and the Abuse of Colonial Power," unpublished manuscript. I am extraordinarily grateful to Professor Pitts for allowing me to quote from her in-progress work on Mill and colonialism. I have learned much both from her writing and from our ongoing discussions. Her comments on earlier versions of this paper have proved invaluable.

3. Edward John Eyre to Edward T. Cardwell, May 17, 1865, in *Colonial Office Papers*, 137, 391.

4. See "Report of the Jamaica Royal Commission," *Parliamentary Papers*, 1866, XXX, 489–531.

5. Mill, "Letter to William Fraser Rae, 14 December 1865," XVI, 1126.

6. For Mill's account of the events leading to his installation as chair of the Jamaica Committee, see Mill, I, 281–82.

7. Mill, *A*, I, 282.

8. In *Civilising Subjects*, Catherine Hall traces British attitudes toward race from the general sympathy of British citizens toward nonwhites in the 1830s (the great period of abolitionism) to the vicious racism of the 1860s. Hall argues that by the 1860s, racism had come to be a dominant feature of British society. See Catherine Hall, *Civilising Subjects* (Chicago: University of Chicago Press, 2002).

9. John Ruskin, letter to the *Daily Telegraph*, quoted in Bernard Semmel, *Jamaican Blood and Victorian Conscience: The Governor Eyre Controversy* (Boston: Houghton Mifflin Company, 1963), 111.

10. Thomas Carlyle to James Anthony Froude, quoted in Semmel, *The Governor Eyre Controversy*, 106.

11. See, for example, Semmel's excellent account of the Southampton reception for Eyre, one of the first formal gatherings of Eyre's supporters. Of course not all of Eyre's defenders offered such defenses. Lord Cardigan, himself infamous for flogging British soldiers, was only too happy to praise Eyre as the man who flogged thousands of Jamaican blacks. Defenders like Cardigan accepted the picture of Eyre as a sadistic and cruel oppressor of natives and argued that that attitude was exactly the right one for a colonial governor to adopt. See Semmel, *The Governor Eyre Controversy*, esp. 81–101.

12. Semmel, *The Governor Eyre Controversy*, 131.

13. Mill, *CRG*, XIX, 565–56.

14. See for instance Geoffrey Dutton's highly sympathetic biography of Eyre, *The Hero as Murderer* (Sydney: William Collins, Ltd., 1967). Dutton is merciless in his denunciation of Mill as uninformed, naïve, and monomaniacal.

15. Mill in fact notes that he had read Eyre's *Journals of Expeditions of Discovery into Central Australia* with great interest and that he had formed a good impression of Eyre as a result. But Mill also expresses a deep disdain for and disgust with Eyre after the Jamaica incident, claiming that he holds Eyre in contempt for refusing to allow a public hearing on his actions. So whether Mill is in fact motivated only by a concern for law and order or whether he is at least partly motivated by his contempt for Eyre the man is up for some debate. Still, given Mill's actual arguments, the principle of charity suggests that we take Mill at his word: the pursuit of Eyre was about establishing legal precedent for limiting colonial authority.

16. Mill, *A*, I, 281

17. That is not to say that Mill was not at all concerned with the specific actions that Eyre performed. He remarks in both the *Autobiography* and in a letter to David Urquhart that he is in fact concerned to secure justice and equal treatment for people of all races, but he maintains that that concern is less important than establishing the limits of the law. See Mill, *A*, I, 281, and "Letter to David Urquhart, 4 October 1866," XVI, 1205.

18. John Stuart Mill, "Letter to William Sims Pratten, June 9, 1868," XVI, 1411.

19. Bernard Semmel, in *The Governor Eyre Controversy* (Boston: Houghton Mifflin Company, 1963), actually argues that most of the members of the Jamaica Committee "were determined to make effective use of the events in Jamaica to further their overall political principles and objectives," 64.

20. Quote from Peter Taylor, speech given at the July 9, 1866, special meeting of the Jamaica Committee, quoted in Semmel, *The Governor Eyre Controversy*, 70.

21. Herbert Spencer, *An Autobiography*, vol. 2, (London: Williams and Norgate, 1904), 168.

22. Frederic Harrison. *Martial Law, Six letters to "The Daily News"* (London: The Jamaica Committee, 1867), quoted in Semmel, *The Governor Eyre Controversy*, 131.

23. Mill, SJC[1866], XXI, 423.

24. Mill, SJC [1866], XXI, 424.

25. Mill, SJC [1868], XXI, 433.

26. See Semmel, *The Governor Eyre Controversy*, 105–22.

27. Kinzer, Robson, and Robson, *A Moralist in and out of Parliament*, 271.

28. *The Times*, December 23, 1868.

29. Mill, *A*, I, 278–79.

30. Thomas Beggs, *The Times*, November 21, 1868, 5. Beggs makes these comments specifically in reference to Mill's reelection to Parliament in 1868. The complaint, though, is hardly new; much of Mill's parliamentary career consisted of his defending his practices as being consistent with his theoretical writings.

31. Quoted in Dutton, *The Hero as Murderer*, 326.

32. Eyre to Cardwell, January 1866, *Parliamentary Papers*, 1866, vol. 30, 3–18.

33. See Dutton, *The Hero as Murderer*, esp. 324–400. Not surprisingly, Mill himself explicitly rejects the sort of argument Dutton offers in defense of Eyre. In arguing before Parliament, Mill takes on the argument that Eyre firmly believed Gordon to be guilty of instigating the Morant Bay rebellion. Citing both the St. Bartholomew's Day Massacre and the Reign of Terror, Mill points out that many who break the law do so believing that they are fully justified (see "Mr. Mill's Speech on Mr. Buxton's Motion, 31 July 1866," XXVIII, 105–113). Mill argues that Robespierre seemed sincerely to believe that the aristocrats he helped to execute really were criminals; for all his sincerity and for all of his (perhaps) good intentions, Robespierre was nonetheless still a criminal. Mill concedes in an August 3 address to Parliament that Eyre may well be a person of outstanding character, but he maintains that Eyre is still a criminal; that Eyre acted in good faith is simply an insufficient justification for Eyre's behavior (see "Speech on the Extradition Treaties Act, 3 August 1866," XXVIII, 117).

34. Mill, *OL*, XVIII, 224.

35. Mill, *OL*, XVIII, 224.

36. Mill, *OL*, XVIII, 224.

37. Mill, *OL*, XVIII, 224.

38. Again, to take an example not available to Mill, one could argue that, justified or not, the United States' benevolent despotism in Japan after World War II did create a thriving democracy out of an environment that had previously been almost totally unsuited for a democratic government. Interestingly, as I write these words, American troops are invading Iraq with a purported intention that one can only suppose Mill might have approved, namely that of making Iraq suitable for democracy.

39. I am grateful to Professor Pitts for pointing out this line of argument. I am deeply in her debt for the following discussion of race in Mill's attitudes toward colonialism.

40. Mill, FNI, XXI, 118-9.

41. See Mill, SW, XXI, 277–78.

42. Mill, NQ, XXI, 93

43. Mill, NQ, XXI, 93.

44. See Mill, *OL*, XVIII, 273–74.

45. Mill's oversight here might be partially intentional. He remarks in the *Autobiography* that "to bring English functionaries to the bar of a criminal court for abuses of power committed against negroes and mulattoes, was not a popular proceeding with the English middle classes" (*A*, I, 219). Thus some of Mill's neglect of the race issue might simply be a matter of strategy.

46. Jennifer Pitts, "Empire and Social Criticism," 19.

47. Pitts, "Empire and Social Criticism," 25

48. Mill, "Speech on Buxton," XXVIII, 107–78.

49. Mill, *A*, I, 281.

50. Cited in Semmel, *The Governor Eyre Controversy*, 70

51. "Introduction to Goldwin Smith Lecture, 4 February 1867," XXVIII, 130–31.

52. Mill, *OL*, XVIII, 220.

53. See, for instance, his October 4, 1866, letter to David Urquhart (XVI, 1205–6) and his June 9, 1868, letter to William Sims Pratten (XVI, 1411).

54. Pitts, "Empire and Social Criticism," 32.

55. There is, I think, good evidence for holding the view that Mill's public statements regarding Eyre might not be synonymous with his theoretical justification for his position. Consider, for instance, Mill's public statements, while in Parliament, in favor of the Reform Bill. Although Mill does, on several occasions, mention his general commitments both to the single transferable vote (the Hare scheme) and to female suffrage, his major speeches on the subject are not reformulations of his arguments from *Considerations on Representative Government*. Although by no means a gifted politician, Mill was savvy enough to throw his support behind reform measures that were likely to pass even when they were not what he might have preferred. Mill's speeches on those occasions bowed to the political realities of moving bills through Parliament; the content of such speeches was not philosophical but was rather pragmatic, aimed at moving Parliament to act in a certain way, and strategically chosen as the best method for accomplishing that task. (For a first-rate account of Mill's activities on reform while in Parliament, see Kinzer, Robson, and Robson, *A Moralist in and out of Parliament*, esp. chaps. 3 and 4. It thus seems not unreasonable to suggest that Mill might have adopted a similar strategic position with respect to Eyre; knowing of the racist attitudes he would confront, Mill chose the pragmatic argument outlined above rather than the theoretical justification I will offer below.

56. Mill, *PPE*, III, 186–67.

57. Mill, *PPE*, III, 733–46.

58. Mill, *PPE*, III, 745–46.

59. Mill, *PPE*, III, 746.

60. Jennifer Pitts, "Legislator of the World? A Rereading of Bentham on Colonies," *Political Theory* 31, no. 2, 224.

61. Thomas Carlyle, "Shooting Niagara: And After?" *Centenary Edition of the Works of Thomas Carlyle* (New York: Charles Scribner and Sons, 1909), 9.

62. While I agree with Pitts's assessment that "Mill was concerned to bring about a 'readiness' for representative government in the bulk of the population," I fear that she gives short shrift to Mill's commitment to participation. Both competence and participation play central roles in Mill's political thinking. Dennis Thompson, who first articulates these principles in Mill, argues that the principles are in tension with one another, with each acting to limit the other (Dennis Thompson, *John Stuart Mill and Representative Government* [Princeton: Princeton University Press, 1976], esp. chaps. 3 and 5). I argue elsewhere that the principles of competence and participation actually work in concert for Mill, such that neither competence nor participation realizes its full value without the presence of the other. See my "J. S. Mill on Plural Voting, Competence, and Participation," *History of Political Thought* 24, no. 3 (Winter 2003), 647–67.

63. Mill, C, XVIII, 119.

64. Mill, C, XVIII, 120–21.

65. Mill's one exception to this general pattern concerns Ireland. Though Ireland was not a colony but rather a proper part of the United Kingdom, Mill maintained that Ireland would be better off were it administered as a "barbarian" colony. Mill argued repeatedly that the Irish were not ready for home rule and needed a benevolent despotism to prepare them for self-determination. See Mill, E&I, VI.

66. Mill, *CRG*, XIX, 563. Of particular interest here are Mill's *Westminster Review* articles "Lord Durham's Return" and "Radical Party and Canada," both written in 1838, which argue for the return of full self-rule to Canada. Mill in fact spends considerable time praising Durham's decisions as the only way of preserving a government that are not dependent upon brute force. See John Stuart Mill. "Lord Durham's Return." VI, 445–64. and "Radical Party and Canada," VI, 407–35. I will discuss Mill's position on Durham at length below.

67. Mill, *PPE*, III, 693.

68. Mill, *CRG*, XIX, 564–65.

69. Interestingly, after the Morant Bay rebellion, Eyre managed to persuade the assembly that blacks would soon be enfranchised and thus would win control of the legislature. The assembly voted to abolish itself and petitioned London to make Jamaica a crown colony controlled directly by the governor. In Mill's terms, the Jamaican Assembly voted away its "civilized" status and accepted instead the treatment Mill accorded to "barbarian" nations. See Semmel, *The Governor Eyre Controversy*, 34–55.

70. Semmel, *The Governor Eyre Controversy*, 35

71. John Stuart Mill to Rowland G. Hazard, 15 November 1865, XVI, 1117.

72. It is worth noting that, when confronted with a similar question regarding mistreatment of Maoris by New Zealander colonists, Mill does not suggest the suspension of home rule in New Zealand. Rather, he argues that the matter is an internal affair for New Zealanders. He asks in an 1866 letter, "Is it possible for England to maintain an authority there for the purpose of preventing unjust treatment of the Maoris, and at the same time allow self government to the British colonists in every other respect? How is that one subject to be kept separate, and how is the Governor to be in other things a mere ornamental frontispiece to a government of the colony by a colonial Cabinet and Legislature, and to assume a will and a responsibility of his own, overruling his cabinet and legislature wherever Maoris are concerned?" (John Stuart Mill to Henry Samuel Chapman, January 7, 1866, XVI, 1136.) That Mill would suggest that a Maori rebellion and subsequent mistreatment of Maoris by New Zealanders is an internal matter while arguing that Eyre's abuse of blacks in Jamaica is cause for abolishing home rule in that colony would seem to indicate that Mill regards Jamaica to be a fundamentally different type of colony.

73. Mill, *CRG*, XIX, 390.

74. Mill, *CRG*, XIX, 390.

75. Mill, *CRG*, XIX, 392.

76. One might object to the aptness of the analogy between government in Britain and government in the colonies. After all, by enfranchising the citizens of Britain, Mill gives them some veto authority over the government set up to educate them. Thus, the coercive power that teachers (in this case, the government) naturally possesses

over their students (the citizens) are held in check by the the students' power to change teachers. Citizens of colonies—particularly the citizens of "uncivilized" colonies—have no such power. That disanalogy is important, but, I think, not fatal. In Mill's political thinking, protecting the majority from the ruling elite is never one of his main concerns. Although he does occasionally echo Bentham's arguments about democracy best representing people's own interests, Mill mostly argues for political participation on the merits of its educative powers. Mill is actually far more concerned about abuse of power by the majority than he is about abuse of power against the majority. While it is true that Mill places much faith in the moral virtue of educated elites, that faith is not limited to colonial settings. Perhaps because of this faith, Mill seems not to be especially concerned with providing the majority with mechanisms to protect them from the ruling class. For Mill, then, the fact that participation provides British "students" some protection from their "teachers" is an unintentional side-effect and not necessarily even a virtue of the system; the safety net provided to British citizens is, in some sense, an accidental one. That Mill fails to provide a similar safety net for colonists is not, I think, a devastating blow to the analogy.

77. Mill, *CRG*, XIX, 567.

78. Mill, *CRG*, XIX, 567–68.

79. See Mill's defense of the East India Company's actions presented in "Memorandum of the Improvements during the Last Thirty Years." Mill presented this paper as an introduction to the *Petition of the East India Company* against the transfer of power from the Company to the Crown in 1858. Mill expresses similar views in "Non-Intervention" (XXI, 111ff) and in an 1859 letter to Alexander Bain (XV, 646). Mill, somewhat naively, likewise praised the actions of the United States in offering large sums of money for "the purpose of civilizing the [American] Indians, concluding that "The conduct of the United States towards the Indian tribes has been throughout not only just, but noble." (Unheaded article in the *Examiner*, January 9, 1831, XXIII, 236.)

80. See Mill's letters to William W. Ireland [June 22, 1867], (XVI, 1282), and to David Urquhart [October 4, 1866], (XVI, 1205). See also his "The Petition of the East India Company," XXX, 81–82.

81. Quoted in Kenneth Miller, "John Stuart Mill's Theory of International Relations," *Journal of the History of Ideas* 22: 4 (Oct.-Dec. 1961), 507n.

82. See the account in Michael St. John Packe, *The Life of John Stuart Mill* (New York: Macmillan Company, 1954), 224–34.

83. See John George Lambton, Earl of Durham, "Report on the Affairs of British North America, for the Earl of Durham," *Parliamentary Papers* XVII, 1839, 1–690.

84. Mill, LDR, VI, 457.

85. Mill, LDR, VI, 457.

86. See Semmel, *The Governor Eyre Controversy*, 29–39.

87. Mill, *CRG*, XIX, 563–65.

88. See note 18 above.

9

The Early Utilitarians, Race, and Empire: The State of the Argument

H. S. Jones

To the best of my knowledge this book is the first systematic study of the relationship between utilitarianism and the concept of race, and the reason is clear: the conventional assumption was that utilitarianism simply had no concept of race. This assumption had its origins in the ideas of nineteenth-century critics of utilitarianism. These critics—they might be romantics, historicists, nationalists, or proto-racists—held that utilitarianism took individuals and their interests as the building blocks of social and political theory, was oblivious to the historical determinants of "human nature" and hence left no room for a strong conception of nationhood and nationality, let alone a biologically grounded deterministic conception of race. The Italian patriot Mazzini, for instance, maintained that the English were too utilitarian a people to grasp the significance of the concept of nationality,[1] and the Christian socialist F. D. Maurice observed that the Benthamites, lacking any sense of nationality, treated all "national distinctions" as mere accidents which should be discarded as quickly as possible.[2] The Edinburgh anatomist Robert Knox identified "the hard-handed, spatular-fingered Saxon utilitarian" as a type that offered "the sternest opposition" to the kind of racial determinism Knox pioneered in Britain.[3]

In the later Victorian period utilitarianism was often accused of being an anachronism, and its supposed indifference to history and its insensitivity to national character were among its anachronistic qualities. This, for instance, was the perspective adopted by one of the earliest historians of utilitarianism, Sir Leslie Stephen, who held that the impact of Darwinism made unhistorical conceptions of society or of human nature untenable: utilitarianism was therefore, for Stephen, one of the victims of the Darwinian revolution in Victorian intellectual history.[4] Stephen was explicitly critical of both J. S. Mill

179

and his follower, the historian of civilization H. T. Buckle, for their refusal to accept that national characters might be determined by race. "The sound doctrine that we can only learn by experience what are the differences between men" became, in Mill and Buckle, "the doctrine that all differences are superficial, and therefore the man always the same."[5]

From this point of view, however much J. S. Mill in particular might have sought to accommodate the insights of romanticism and historicism, the utilitarians broadly remained faithful to the "civilizational perspective" of the Enlightenment, and this whole tradition, though it might be convicted of Eurocentrism, was consistently resistant to explicitly racial or strongly national modes of argument. Utilitarianism and race theory represented alternative and incompatible projects for the scientific study of society. This is why, as Georgios Varouxakis notes, Mill was much criticized by self-styled scientific racists such as James Hunt of the Anthropological Society of London for being oblivious to the scientific potential of the concept of race.[6] Contemporaries sometimes get these things wrong, of course, but in spite of the growing prestige then enjoyed by racial arguments, Mill never sought to defend himself against these criticisms by asserting that race was, after all, at the heart of his outlook.

Mill, it should be explained, was attached to a hierarchical model of scientific explanation which held that, if the empirical generalizations formulated by a relatively "concrete" branch of investigation such as sociology were to count as scientific, they must be capable of being deduced from the laws of a more abstract science; specifically, in this case, the universal laws of mind.[7] Although Mill sought to understand, by means of his projected science of ethology, the way in which history impacted on human nature to form national character, his ultimate conviction was that human nature was malleable in accordance with universal laws of psychology. Hence there could be no question of a social science founded on the idea of race. Mill was attached to the hierarchical model in large part because it had the potential to challenge those who confused conventional inequalities with natural differences. In his polemic with Carlyle on "the negro question," Mill defended the "analytical examination of human nature" against Carlyle's "vulgar error" of imputing every actual difference among human beings to "an original difference of nature."[8]

In an important and stimulating contribution to the debate on the place of nationalism and nationality in Victorian thought and culture, Peter Mandler has depicted the weakness of ideas of race and nation as an important aspect of British intellectual exceptionalism in the nineteenth century. For Mandler, even the liberal Anglicans, who were prominent exponents of German modes of thought and vocal critics of utilitarianism, remained attached to a "civilizational perspective," which posited an essentially uniform human nature, whereas continental thinkers were more inclined to

Herder's view that (as Mandler epitomizes it) "different nations had essentially different moral natures."[9] In historiographical terms, Mandler self-consciously sets out to defend an established interpretation of mid-Victorian thought against its recent critics. He notes that historians such as Catherine Hall and Robert Young, both influenced by postcolonial modes of thought, have suggested that "even at mid-century English thought was profoundly imbued with strong concepts of race and nation."[10] This, according to Mandler, is a misinterpretation. As he has argued more recently, it depends on attaching exaggerated importance to some little-read texts such as Knox's book.[11]

So is there anything more to be said about utilitarianism and the idea of race than that they historically stood, and perhaps logically stand, in opposition to each other? In the remainder of this short epilogue I propose to consider what light the essays collected here shed on this question. Two principal issues arise here: on the one hand, the implications of utilitarianism for empire, and, on the other, the relationship between what Mandler terms the "civilizational perspective" and the idea of race.

UTILITARIANISM AND EMPIRE

In historiographical terms, it is the awakening of interest in the racial foundations of colonial ideology—chiefly under the influence of postcolonial theory—that has led historians to reconsider the relationship between the utilitarians and ideas of race. It has long been noticed that some of the most prominent of the utilitarians were trenchant defenders of the imperial project, perhaps because empire provided, so to speak, a laboratory in which their belief in the plasticity of human nature could be put to the test. This was the thrust of Eric Stokes's now classic account of *The English Utilitarians and India*, which evoked the tension in British rule in India between traditional Indian society and a utilitarian liberalism which pursued a civilizing mission aiming to expunge "the physical and moral distance separating East and West."[12] The implication was that the utilitarians' imperialism rested on their insensitivity to cultural difference: because they took the interests of "man," and not those of the Englishman or the Indian, as the measure of moral right, they showed little interest in the preservation of cultural identities, which they tended to regard as obstacles to rational reform. A mechanical and universalistic mode of thought thus underpinned both the utilitarians' indifference to race as a fundamental factor in history and political theory and their sympathy for European imperialism. Broadly speaking, this interpretation is echoed by Mehta's recent study of *Liberalism and Empire*, which argues that as a general rule it was liberals and progressives who sought to justify imperial rule. The utilitarians feature especially prominently in Mehta's account, which contrasts Bentham, the Mills, and Macaulay on the one hand with conservative critics of empire such as Burke.[13]

Today the prevalent view is that imperial rule is almost by its very nature rooted in constructions of racial "otherness" and in ideas of racial superiority and inferiority. There is therefore an unwillingness to accept that prominent servants of empire such as the two Mills were also free of racial bias, which is why the foundations of their colonialism have come to be subjected to more intense historiographical scrutiny. But, as the essays collected here indicate, the result has not been to elucidate a single coherent utilitarian theory of empire but instead to show that the utilitarians differed surprisingly widely in their approach to empire. Consider the relationship between utilitarianism and liberal imperialism. The ideological underpinnings of nineteenth-century British imperialism, and especially of the phenomenon known as "liberal imperialism," have been the focus of some important historical work in recent years, in part because of the fashionable postmodernist tendency to highlight the authoritarian potential of abstract and universalistic liberalism. To that degree the historiographical orthodoxy has been reinforced, for utilitarianism has long been seen—at least since Halévy—as a potentially authoritarian version of liberalism.[14] But the essays collected here highlight the diversity of utilitarian approaches to the question of empire. The relationship between utilitarianism and liberal imperialism was by no means as direct as we might be inclined to infer from the prominent role played by both James Mill and his son in the governance of British India through the East India Company. In her powerful revisionist account, Jennifer Pitts shows that Bentham, while not wholly free of ambiguity, was for the most part a trenchant critic of empire rather than its apologist. For that matter, as Javed Majeed indicates, James Mill himself had an ambivalent attitude toward empire: like Bentham, he tended to regard imperialism as economically wasteful, although this critique was qualified by the possibility that empire could serve as a testing ground for progressive ideas before they were implemented in the metropolis. Indeed, little seems to have separated Bentham from James Mill, but quite a lot separated James Mill from his son. Bentham and the elder Mill both held that, for the colonizer, the costs of empire greatly outweighed the benefits, and both agreed, therefore, that dependencies should be emancipated where there was no substantial difference in degree of civilization between colonizer and colonized, for in such cases the colonized, granted independence, would be capable of achieving progress under their own steam. There was more equivocation where the colonial relationship was perceived as one between civilized and barbarian: James Mill, notably in his *History of India*, endorsed the duty of the civilized to rule the barbarian until such time as the latter became capable of self-government, whereas it is the originality of Pitts's essay that she highlights the recurrent strand of moral critique that ran alongside the better known economic critique of empire in Bentham's thought and that led him to be suspicious even of the benefits of colonial rule of "barbarian" peoples.

Of the major utilitarians, it was J. S. Mill who was the first to develop a more or less unqualified defence of empire. As Eileen Sullivan has put it, the younger Mill

> inherited a liberal tradition which was primarily anti-imperialist. He served as an intellectual leader in the transformation of this tradition into a justification for a complex empire. Mill actually wrote the first important fully developed liberal defense of nineteenth-century English imperialism.[15]

Mill was more forthright than his utilitarian predecessors in asserting the civilizational legitimation for imperial rule. The logic of this argument is well summarized in Mehta's study of *Liberalism and Empire*. For the utilitarians, the utility principle ("the greatest happiness of the greatest number") was the ultimate criterion on all ethical and legal issues. But the utilitarians were also attached to a range of other, "secondary," principles, such as *laissez faire* and representative government, which they held generally conduced to the maximization of happiness. But James Mill accepted tentatively, and J. S. Mill more explicitly, that a certain level of civilization was required for these secondary principles to be valid. This was the argument that the younger Mill developed most explicitly in *Considerations on Representative Government*, where he maintained that a people who "have still to learn the first lesson of civilisation, that of obedience" would not be suited to representative government and would be better governed despotically, provided always that the aim of the despotic rule was to prepare the people for ultimate self-government, in accordance with the principle that "a people of savages should be taught obedience, but not in such a manner as to convert them into a people of slaves."[16] In *On Liberty* he had been just as forthright: "Despotism is a legitimate mode of government in dealing with barbarians, provided the end be their improvement, and the means justified by actually effecting that end. Liberty, as a principle, has no application to any state of things anterior to the time when mankind have become capable of being improved by free and equal discussion."[17]

As Sullivan and, in this volume, J. Joseph Miller demonstrate, Mill also differed still more radically from his utilitarian predecessors in arguing for the possible benefits of empire for the colonial power itself, although it not clear that he regarded that as a legitimation for empire in the absence of a moral underpinning.

RACISM AND ENLIGHTENMENT UNIVERSALISM

In the essay previously mentioned, Peter Mandler draws a sharp distinction between the civilizational tradition on the one hand and racial determinism on the other. By contrast, the thrust of David Theo Goldberg's argument in his contribution to this volume is to suggest that the two traditions of thought are not as far apart as Mandler implies: both, he asserts, are imbued with "racist" assumptions, the only difference being that the racism of the former is "polite and effete," whereas the latter's is "bald and vicious"; but both are "insidious and odious."[18] Varouxakis takes issue with Goldberg, and other postcolonial pundits, on precisely this point, arguing that while J. S. Mill can unproblematically be convicted of Eurocentrism, to call him a racist is to confuse rather than to clarify our understanding. In my view Varouxakis has definitively refuted the surprisingly resilient belief that Mill had recourse to racial explanations in history and political thought. As an historical argument, Goldberg's thesis does not hold water. He focuses on a debate which pitted Mill, as a civilizational liberal, in direct confrontation with Carlyle, the racial determinist. This debate provides a clear illustration of Mandler's two traditions of thought at work, and it is at best counterintuitive to construe the debate as revealing Mill's hidden racism. And in fact Goldberg's evidence is curiously slight. He makes a lot of Mill's use of the term "The Negro Question" and asserts that this term "indicates Mill's presumption that . . . blacks are a problem." This assertion seems both linguistically and historically insensitive. On the one hand, a question is not a problem. On the other hand, the Victorians had a habit of reifying a cluster of related issues into a "Question"—the Irish Question and the Schleswig-Holstein Question, of course, but also the Education Question and the Suffrage Question. This usage did not imply that anyone was to blame for posing the question, and "education" was not necessarily any more of a "problem" than the "negro" was. And Mill was, in the first place, responding to Carlyle's "Occasional Discourse on the Negro Question," and was taking up Carlyle's construction of "the Negro Question" in order to rebut it.

But Goldberg's argument is not straightforwardly historical and is not readily open to empirical refutation. For the most part, his case against Mill is not that he invoked racial distinctions but that he did not: he denied or ignored race "in the face of the fact that race matters," which amounted to "paternalistically effacing a self-determined social subjectivity from those who would define themselves thus."[19] So Goldberg is arguing that a theory which is race-blind on principle will tend, in effect, to benefit the advantaged over the disadvantaged race, because self-conscious racial identity (or "subjectivity") is a weapon that oppressed races need but their oppressors do not. In this respect Goldberg's argument is evidently closely related to the familiar postmodernist critique of the so-called Enlightenment project. Utilitarianism, it seems, inherited the universalist bias of Enlightenment philosophy and deployed a unitary rather than a plural conception of civilization. "Civilization" in practice meant Western values, and the rhetoric of "progress" served as a tool for the imposition of those values on the rest of the world.

Whether Enlightenment thought was really universalist in this sense, and whether universalism is as vulnerable to this line of critique as its critics suppose, are large questions which are beyond the scope of this short contribution. But I do want to make two points about the relevance of this line of criticism to the question of utilitarianism and race.

The first point is that whereas it is largely true at the beginning of the twenty-first century that self-conscious racial subjectivity is a weapon to be used by the oppressed against their current or former oppressors, this was hardly the case in the nineteenth century. Then, race theory was commonly deployed in support of colonial despotism, as the involvement of Carlyle and others in the Governor Eyre controversy demonstrated. J. S. Mill's stance on colonialism may not satisfy our standards of political correctness, but the political bite of his race-blindness was powerfully progressive in its time.

Secondly, the argument advanced for regarding J. S. Mill as a "racist" is remarkably similar to the case for saying that he was not really a feminist, whatever he and his contemporary opponents might have thought. Barbara Caine, for instance, has argued that Mill was notably dismissive of the possibility that women, because of their particular experience as mothers and household managers, might have a distinctive contribution to make to civic life. She asserts that Mill held that men embodied "the universal standard of human excellence" and that his case for women's enfranchisement rested on the potential of women to emulate that standard.[20] Similarly, the case for regarding Mill as a racist depends on the belief that his "civilizational perspective" betrayed on an unspoken assimilation of "civilization" to white European civilization: the white European, then, embodied the universal standard of human excellence. This enabled Mill to defend imperial rule in the name of a civilizing mission rather than of racial superiority, but, for Goldstein, that civilizing mission was nevertheless imbued with racism, just as, for Caine, Mill's "feminism" was imbued with patriarchal assumptions.

Mill was a consistent believer in the importance of "nurture" rather than "nature" in shaping the character of individuals and of groups. He was therefore remarkably impervious to arguments that invoked natural differences of race or sex, and he had a strong suspicion that the function of such arguments was usually to undermine the case for equal treatment by public institutions. At the same time, and for fundamentally similar reasons, he was unsympathetic to "equal but different" arguments: that is, arguments for equality founded on the distinctive qualities of the oppressed. Mill tended to believe that oppression made people oppressed, not that it made people good in a distinctive way. Postcolonial thinkers are not wrong to see in him a fundamental antagonist of the thesis that the oppressed are vouchsafed with a uniquely valuable insight into their condition. So the case against Mill—best articulated in this volume by Jennifer Pitts—is, in effect, the case of the radical emancipationist against the liberal emancipationist: he did not appreciate the extent to which his understanding of what emancipation must entail was itself rooted in relations of domination. But as Pitts herself indicates, this is a critique of Mill and not of the utilitarian tradition as a whole.

NOTES

1. Peter Mandler, "'Race' and 'Nation' in Mid-Victorian Thought," in Stefan Collini, Richard Whatmore, and Brian Young, eds., *History, Religion, and Culture: British Intellectual History 1750–1950* (Cambridge: Cambridge University Press, 2000), 229; cf also Denis Mack Smith, *Mazzini* (New Haven and London: Yale University Press, 1994), 23, 28–29.

2. F. D. Maurice, *The Kingdom of Christ* (London: Macmillan, 3rd ed., 1883), i, 221–22.

3. Robert Knox, *The Races of Men: A Fragment* (London: Renshaw, 1850), v.

4. Noel Annan, *Leslie Stephen: The Godless Victorian* (New York: Random House, 1984), 202–3; Leslie Stephen, *Social Rights and Duties* (London: Sonnenschein, 1896), i, 57–58, 79–80; Leslie Stephen, *The English Utilitarians* (London: Duckworth, 1900), ii, 336, and iii, 442, where he draws attention to James and John Stuart Mill's imperviousness to any notion of evolution.

5. Leslie Stephen, *The English Utilitarians* iii, 282–83, 355–56.

6. Georgios Varouxakis, "Empire, Race, Euro-centrism: J. S. Mill and His Critics."

7. Alan Ryan, *The Philosophy of John Stuart Mill*, 2nd ed. (Houndmills: Macmillan, 1987), 156–57.

8. Quoted by J. Joseph Miller, "Chairing the Jamaica Committee: J. S. Mill and the Limits of Colonial Authority."

9. Mandler, "'Race' and 'Nation,'" 228.

10. Mandler, "'Race' and 'Nation,'" 224.

11. Peter Mandler, "The Problem with Cultural History," *Cultural and Social History* 1 (2004): 96–103.

12. Eric Stokes, *The English Utilitarians and India* (Oxford: Oxford University Press, 1959), esp. xiii.

13. Jennifer Pitts's essay in this volume should be read as a corrective to Mehta's remarks about Bentham. See Uday Singh Mehta, *Liberalism and Empire: A Study in Nineteenth-Century British Liberal Thought* (Chicago and London: University of Chicago Press, 1999), esp. 2–3.

14. This view is contested, in relation to Bentham, by Frederick Rosen, *Jeremy Bentham and Representative Democracy: A Study of the Constitutional Code* (Oxford: Oxford University Press, 1983).

15. Eileen Sullivan, "Liberalism and Imperialism: J. S. Mill's Defense of the British Empire," *Journal of the History of Ideas* 44 (1983), 599.

16. John Stuart Mill, "Considerations on Representative Government," in *Essays on Politics and Society* II, ed. J. M. Robson, vol. XIX of *The Collected Works of John Stuart Mill* (London: University of Toronto Press, 1977), 415 and 396.

17. John Stuart Mill, "On Liberty," in *Essays on Politics and Society* I, ed. J. M. Robson, vol. XVIII of *The Collected Works of John Stuart Mill* (London: University of Toronto Press, 1977), 224.

18. Goldberg.

19. Goldberg.

20. Barbara Caine, *Victorian Feminists* (Oxford: Oxford University Press, 1992), 37–38.

10

Imagining Darwinism

David Weinstein

INTRODUCTION

Herbert Spencer (1820-1903) is typically, though quite wrongly, considered a coarse social Darwinist. After all, Spencer, and not Darwin, coined the infamous expression "survival of the fittest," leading G. E. Moore to conclude erroneously in *Principia Ethica* (1903) that Spencer committed the naturalistic fallacy. According to Moore, Spencer's practical reasoning was deeply flawed insofar as he purportedly conflated mere survivability (a natural property) with goodness itself (a nonnatural property).

Roughly fifty years later, Richard Hofstadter devoted an entire chapter of *Social Darwinism in American Thought* (1955) to Spencer, arguing that Spencer's unfortunate vogue in late nineteenth-century America inspired Andrew Carnegie, John D. Rockefeller, Jr., and William Graham Sumner's visions of unbridled and unrepentant capitalism. For Hofstadter, Spencer was an "ultra-conservative" for whom the poor were so much unfit detritus. His social philosophy "walked hand in hand" with reaction, making it little more than a "biological apology for laissez-faire."[1] And more recently, Peter Singer has echoed Hofstadter's assessment, insisting that Spencer "who was more than willing to draw ethical implications from evolution, provided the defenders of laissez-faire capitalism with intellectual foundations that they used to oppose state interference with market forces."[2] Citing Hofstadter, he repeats Spencer's influence on Carnegie and Rockefeller. But just because Carnegie interpreted Spencer's social theory as justifying merciless economic competition, we should not automatically attribute such justificatory ambitions to Spencer. Otherwise, we risk uncritically reading the fact that Spencer happened to influence popularizers of social Darwinism into our interpretation of him. We risk falling victim to what Skinner perceptively calls the "mythology of prolepsis."

Spencer's reputation has never fully recovered from Moore and Hofstadter's interpretative caricatures, as Singer's remarks reveal, thus marginalizing him to the hinterlands of intellectual history, though recent scholarship has begun restoring and repairing his legacy. Happily, in rehabilitating him, some scholars have begun to appreciate not just how fundamentally utilitarian his political theory was but how principled and progressive it occasionally could be.

The history of political thought is forever being rewritten as we necessarily reinterpret its canonical texts and occasionally renominate marginalized thinkers for canonical consideration. Changing philosophical fashions and ideological agendas invariably doom us to reconstructing incessantly our political philosophical heritage. For instance, Isaiah Berlin's understandable preoccupation with totalitarianism induced him to read T. H. Green and Bernard Bosanquet as its unwitting accomplices insofar as both purportedly equated freedom with dangerously enriched, neo-Hegelian fancies about self-realization. Regrettably, this ideological reconstruction of new liberals like Green and Bosanquet continues largely unabated.[3] But as our ideological sensitivities shift, we can now begin rereading them with changed prejudice, if not less prejudice. And the same goes for how we can now reread other marginalized, nineteenth-century English liberals like Spencer. As the shadow of European totalitarianism wanes, and eugenics along with it, the lens through which we do intellectual history changes and we can more easily read our Spencer as he intended to be read, namely as a utilitarian liberal.

Like J. S. Mill, Spencer struggled to make utilitarianism authentically liberal by infusing it with a demanding principle of liberty and robust moral rights. He was convinced, like Mill, that utilitarianism could accommodate rights with independent moral force and yet remain genuinely consequentialist. Subtly construed, utilitarianism can effectively mimic the very best deontological liberalism.

But unlike Mill, Spencer's liberal utilitarianism mimicked deontological liberalism more faithfully. Spencer not only held that basic moral rights were indefeasible contrary to Mill. He also insisted that this very indefeasibility made any form of imperialism, no matter how well intentioned and seemingly benign, illiberal, and thus unethical.

SPENCER'S LIBERAL UTILITARIANISM

Spencer was a social evolutionist without question but he was never crudely social Darwinist. He was a liberal utilitarian first who traded heavily in evolutionary theory in order to explain how our liberal utilitarian sense of justice emerges.

Though a utilitarian, Spencer took distributive justice no less seriously than Mill. For him as for Mill, liberty and justice were equivalent. Whereas Mill equated fundamental justice with his liberty principle, Spencer equated justice with equal liberty, which holds that the "liberty of each, limited by the like liberty of all, is the rule in conformity with which society must be organized."[4] Moreover, for Spencer as for Mill, liberty was sacrosanct, ensuring that his utilitarianism was equally a bona fide form of liberalism. For both, respect for liberty also just happened to work out for the utilitarian best all things considered. Indefeasible liberty, properly formulated, and utility were therefore fully compossible.

Now in Spencer's case, especially by *The Principles of Ethics* (1879-93), this compossibility rested on a complex evolutionary moral psychology combining associationism, Lamarckian use-inheritance, intuitionism, and utility. Pleasure-producing activity has tended to generate biologically inheritable associations between certain types of actions, pleasurable feelings, and feelings of approval. Gradually, utilitarianism becomes intuitive.[5] And wherever utilitarian intuitions thrive, societies tend to be more vibrant as well as stable. Social evolution favors cultures that internalize utilitarian maxims intuitively. Conduct "restrained within the required limits [stipulated by the principle of equal freedom], calling out no antagonistic passions, favors harmonious cooperation, profits the group, and, by implications, profits the average of individuals." Consequently, "groups formed of members having this adaptation of nature" tend "to survive and spread"[6] Wherever general utility thrives, societies thrive. General utility and cultural stamina go hand in hand. And general utility thrives best where individuals exercise and develop their faculties within the parameters stipulated by equal freedom.[7]

In short, like any moral intuition, equal freedom favors societies that internalize it and, ultimately, self-consciously invoke it. And wherever societies celebrate equal freedom as an ultimate principle of justice, well-being flourishes and utilitarian liberalism spreads.

Spencer likewise took moral rights seriously insofar as properly celebrating equal freedom entailed recognizing and celebrating basic moral rights as its "corollaries." Moral rights specify equal freedom, making its normative requirements substantively clearer. They stipulate our most essential sources of happiness, namely life and liberty. Moral rights to life and liberty are conditions of general happiness. They guarantee each individual the opportunity to exercise his or her faculties according to his or her own lights, which is the source of real happiness. Moral rights cannot make us happy but merely give us the equal chance to make ourselves happy as best we can. They consequently promote general happiness indirectly. And since they are "corollaries" of equal freedom, they are no less indefeasible than the principle of equal freedom itself.

Basic moral rights, then, emerge as intuitions too, though they are more specific than our generalized intuitive appreciation of the utilitarian prowess of equal freedom. Consequently, self-consciously internalizing and refining our intuitive sense of equal freedom, transforming it into a principle of practical reasoning, simultaneously transforms our emerging normative intuitions about the sanctity of life and liberty into stringent juridical principles. And this is simply another way of claiming that general utility flourishes best wherever liberal principles are seriously invoked. Moral societies are happier societies and more vibrant and successful to boot.

Though Spencer sometimes labels basic moral rights "natural" rights, we should not be misled, as some scholars have been, by this characterization. Spencer's most sustained and systematic discussion of moral rights occurs in the concluding chapter, "The Great Political Superstition," of *The Man versus the State* (1884). There, he says that basic rights are natural in the sense that they valorize "customs" and "usages" that naturally arise as a way of ameliorating social friction. Though conventional practices, only very specific rights nevertheless effectively promote human well-being. Only those societies that fortuitously embrace them flourish.

Recent scholars have misinterpreted Spencer's theory of rights, because, among other reasons, they have no doubt misunderstood Spencer's motives for writing *The Man versus the State*. The essay is a highly polemical protest, in the name of strong rights as the best antidote, against the dangers of incremental legislative reforms introducing socialism surreptitiously into Britain. Its vitriolic antisocialist language surely accounts for much of its sometimes-nasty social Darwinist rhetoric, which is unmatched in Spencer's other writings notwithstanding scattered passages in *The Principles of Ethics* and in *The Principles of Sociology* (1876-96).[8]

Spencer's liberal utilitarian credentials are therefore compelling, as his 1863 exchange of letters with Mill further testifies. Between the 1861 serial publication of *Utilitarianism* in *Fraser's Magazine* and its 1863 publication as a book, Spencer wrote Mill, protesting that Mill erroneously implied that he was anti-utilitarian in a footnote near the end of the last chapter, "Of the Connection between Justice and Utility." Agreeing with Benthamism that happiness is the "ultimate" end, Spencer firmly disagrees that it should be our "proximate" end. He next adds:

> But the view for which I contend is, that Morality properly so-called—the science of right conduct—has for its object to determine how and why certain modes of conduct are detrimental, and certain other modes beneficial. These good and bad results cannot be accidental, but must be necessary consequences of the constitution of things; and I conceive it to be the business of moral science to deduce, from the laws of life and the conditions of existence, what kinds of action necessarily tend to produce happiness, and what kinds to produce unhappiness. Having done this, its deductions are to be recognized as laws of con-

duct; and are to be conformed to irrespective of a direct estimation of happiness or misery.[9]

Specific types of actions, in short, necessarily always promote general utility best over the long term though not always in the interim. While they may not always promote it proximately, they invariably promote it ultimately or, in other words, indirectly. These action types constitute uncompromising, normative "laws of conduct." As such, they specify the parameters of equal freedom. That is, they constitute our fundamental moral rights. We have moral rights to these action types if we have moral rights to anything at all.

Spencer as much as Mill, then, advocates indirect utilitarianism by featuring robust moral rights. For both theorists, rights-oriented utilitarianism best fosters general happiness because individuals succeed in making themselves happiest when they develop their mental and physical faculties by exercising them as they deem most appropriate, which, in turn, requires extensive freedom. But since we live socially, what we practically require is equal freedom suitably fleshed out in terms of its moral right corollaries. Moral rights to life and liberty secure our most vital opportunities for making ourselves as happy as we possibly can.

Spencer's liberal utilitarianism, however, differs from Mill's in several respects, including principally the greater stringency that Spencer ascribed to moral rights. Indeed, Mill regarded this difference as the fundamental one between them. Mill responded to Spencer's letter professing allegiance to utilitarianism, observing that he concurs fully with Spencer that utilitarianism must incorporate the "widest and most general principles" that it possibly can. However, in contrast to Spencer, Mill protests that he "cannot admit that any of these principles are necessary, or that the practical conclusions which can be drawn from them are even (absolutely) universal."[10]

RATIONAL VERSUS EMPIRICAL UTILITARIANISM

Spencer referred to his own brand of utilitarianism as "rational" utilitarianism, which he claimed improved upon Bentham's inferior "empirical" utilitarianism. And though he never labeled Mill a "rational" utilitarian, presumably he regarded him as one.

One should not underestimate what "rational" utilitarianism implied for Spencer metaethically. In identifying himself as a "rational" utilitarian, Spencer distanced himself decidedly from social Darwinism, showing why Moore's infamous judgment was misplaced. Responding to T. H. Huxley's accusation that he conflated good with "survival of the fittest," Spencer insisted that "fittest" and "best" were not equivalent. He agreed with Huxley that though ethics can be evolutionarily explained, ethics nevertheless preempts normal struggle for existence with the arrival of humans. Humans invest evolution with an "ethical check," making human evolution qualitatively different from nonhuman evolution. "Rational" utilitarianism constitutes the most advanced form of "ethical check[ing]" insofar as it specifies the "equitable limits to his [the individual's] activities, and of the restraints which must be imposed upon him" in his interactions with others.[11] In short, once we begin systematizing our inchoate utilitarian intuitions with the principle of equal freedom and its derivative moral rights, we begin "check[ing]" evolutionary struggle for survival with unprecedented skill and subtlety. We self-consciously invest our utilitarianism with stringent liberal principles in order to advance our well-being as never before.

Now Henry Sidgwick seems to have understood what Spencer meant by "rational" utilitarianism better than most, although Sidgwick did not get Spencer entirely right either. Sidgwick engaged Spencer critically on numerous occasions. The concluding of Book II of *The Methods of Ethics* (1907), entitled "Deductive Hedonism," is a sustained though veiled criticism of Spencer.[12]

For Sidgwick, Spencer's utilitarianism was merely seemingly deductive, even though it purported to be more scientific and rigorously rational than "empirical" utilitarianism. However, deductive hedonism fails, because, contrary to what deductive hedonists like Spencer think, no general science of the causes of pleasure and pain exists, ensuring that we will never succeed in formulating universal, indefeasible moral rules for promoting happiness. Moreover, Spencer only makes matters worse for himself in claiming that we can nevertheless formulate indefeasible moral rules for hypothetically perfectly moral human beings. First of all, in Sidgwick's view, since we cannot possibly imagine what perfectly moral humans would look like, we could never possibly deduce an ideal moral code of "absolute" ethics for them. Secondly, even if we could somehow conceptualize such a code, it would nevertheless provide inadequate normative guidance to humans as we find them with all their actual desires, emotions, and irrational proclivities.[13] For Sidgwick, all we have is utilitarian common sense, which we can, and should, try to refine and systematize according the demands of our changing circumstances.[14]

Sidgwick, then, faulted Spencer for deceiving himself in thinking that he had successfully made "empirical" utilitarianism more rigorous by making it deductive and therefore "rational." Rather, Spencer was simply offering just another variety of "empirical" utilitarianism instead. Nevertheless, Spencer's version of "empirical" utilitarianism was much closer to Sidgwick's than Sidgwick recognized. Spencer not only shadowed Mill substantively but Sidgwick methodologically.

In the preface to the sixth edition of *The Methods of Ethics* (1901), Sidgwick writes that as he became increasingly aware of the shortcomings of utilitarian calculation, he became ever more sensitive to the utilitarian efficacy of common sense "on the ground of the general presumption which evolution afforded that moral sentiments and opinions would point to conduct conducive to general happiness. . . ."[15] In other words, common sense morality is a generally reliable, right-making decision procedure because social evolution has privileged the emergence of general happiness-generating moral sentiments. And whenever common sense fails us with conflicting or foggy guidance, we have little choice but to engage in order-restoring, utilitarian calculation. The latter works hand in glove with the former, forever refining and systematizing it.

Now Spencer's "empirical" utilitarianism works much the same way even though Spencer obfuscated these similarities by spuriously distinguishing between "empirical" and supposedly superior, "rational" utilitarianism. Much like Sidgwick, Spencer holds that our common sense moral judgments derive their intuitive force from their proven utility-promoting power inherited from one generation to the next. Contrary to what "empirical" utilitarians like Bentham have mistakenly maintained, we never make utilitarian calculations in an intuition-free vacuum. Promoting utility is never simply a matter of choosing options, especially when much is at stake, by calculating and critically comparing utilities. Rather, the emergence of utilitarian practical reasoning begins wherever our moral intuitions breakdown. Moral science tests and refines our moral intuitions, which often prove "necessarily vague" and contradictory. In order to "make guidance by them adequate to all requirements, their dictates have to be interpreted and made definite by science; to which end there must be analysis of those conditions to complete living which they respond to, and from converse with which they have arisen." Such analysis invariably entails recognizing the happiness of "each and all, as the end to be achieved by fulfillment of these conditions."[16]

"Empirical" utilitarianism is "unconsciously made" out of the "accumulated results of past human experience," eventually giving way to "rational" utilitarianism which is "determined by the intellect."[17] The latter, moreover, "implies guidance by the general conclusions which analysis of experience yields," calculating the "distant effects" on lives "at large."[18]

In sum, "rational" utilitarianism is critical and effectively empirical rather than deductive. It resolutely though judiciously embraces indefeasible moral rights as necessary conditions of general happiness, making utilitarianism rigorously and uncompromisingly liberal. And it was also evolutionary, much like Sidgwick's. For both Spencer and Sidgwick, utilitarian practical reasoning exposes, refines and systematizes our underlying moral intuitions, which have thus far evolved in spite of their underappreciated utility. Whereas Spencer labeled this progress toward "rational" utilitarianism, Sidgwick more appropriately called this "progress in the direction of a closer approximation to a perfectly enlightened [empirical] Utilitarianism."[19]

Notwithstanding the undervalued similarities between their respective versions of evolutionary utilitarianism, Spencer and Sidgwick nevertheless parted company in two fundamental respects. First, whereas for Spencer, "rational" utilitarianism refines "empirical" utilitarianism by converging on indefeasible moral rights, for Sidgwick, systematization never ceases. Rather, systematizing common sense continues indefinitely in order to keep pace with the vicissitudes of our social circumstances. The best utilitarian strategy requires flexibility and not the cramping rigidity of unyielding rights. In effect, Spencer's utilitarianism was too dogmatically liberal for Sidgwick's more tempered political tastes. And nowhere does Spencer's dogmatism divulge itself more strikingly then in his uncompromising opposition to imperialism, as we shall shortly see. Spencer detested imperialism, whereas Sidgwick and J. S. Mill embraced it, however reluctantly, and however much in keeping, despite themselves, with the disciplining spirit of their times.

Second, Spencer was a Lamarckian, while Sidgwick was not. For Spencer, moral faculty exercise hones each individual's moral intuitions. Being biologically (and not just culturally) inheritable, these intuitions become increasingly authoritative in succeeding generations, favoring those cultures wherever moral common sense becomes more uncompromising all things being equal. Eventually, members of favored societies begin consciously recognizing, and further deliberately refining, the utility-generating potency of their inherited moral intuitions. "Rational," scientific utilitarianism slowly replaces common sense, "empirical" utilitarianism as we learn the incomparable value of equal freedom and its derivative moral rights as everyday utilitarian decision procedures.[20]

ANTI-IMPERIALISM

In her contribution to this collection, Jennifer Pitts argues that while Bentham's successors were not vehemently anti-imperialist, Bentham was. For instance, Bentham regarded colonies as poor investments that fueled militarism at home. They were not happiness-maximizing for either metropole or colony. In her view, later Benthamites warmed to colonialism in keeping with increasing general enthusiasm for it.[21] According to Bart Schultz in his contribution, even Sidgwick fell victim to these enthusiasms despite his utilitarian principles and skepticism about racial categories. The changing context of the professional circles in which he moved inside and outside of Cambridge compromised his cosmopolitanism under the weight of "white man's burden." Whereas for Pitts, scholars have regrettably read Bentham out of context by reading into him the altered, unflattering views of those who followed in his name, for Schultz, scholars have read Sidgwick out of context by not sensitizing themselves to the pressures of these very same altered views in which he labored.

Now Spencer managed to resist these pressures perhaps, in part, because he never moved in circles like Sidgwick's Cambridge or worked for India House as James and J. S. Mill did. More than that of James Mill, J. S. Mill or Sidgwick, Spencer's anti-imperialism was categorical, making him the more faithful successor to Bentham at least on this score. And this is most ironic, given Spencer's unflattering, though undeserved, reputation. Spencer, then, was not just another liberal utilitarian, contrary to the received view. He was, in addition, a liberal utilitarian who seems to have taken his liberalism more seriously than the rest in terms of his unwavering and indignant opposition to Britain's global empire. Though he became increasingly pessimistic about imperialism's decline, he never foreswore his nearly visceral hostility to it.[22]

Spencer attributed the rise of modern imperialism to several regrettable motives. In *Social Statics*, he ascribes colonialism to missionary activity and an "insatiate greediness—a mere blind impulse to clutch whatever lies within reach" that, in turn, encourages the erroneous belief that an "increase of estate is manifestly equivalent to an increase in wealth."[23] Colonialism is commercially unsound, because, by securing captive markets for their products, metropoles inadvertently invest capital and utilize labor inefficiently at home.[24]

By the time he began writing *The Principles of Sociology*, the European "scramble for Africa" had begun as France and Britain began converting informal empire into formal empire. Imperial political annexation replaced colonial manipulation. According to Spencer, this most unfortunate transformation stemmed from Britain's military having grown too large, causing it to be deployed belligerently rather than defensively as was proper. In particular, excess military capacity fueled self-fulfilling misadventures in the colonies. Informal colonial penetration invariably bred disorder and unrest which, in turn, favored formal political annexation given the excess military wherewithal to impose it:

> In Sherbo our agreements with native chiefs having brought about universal disorder, we send a body of soldiers to suppress it, and presently will allege the necessity of extending our rule over a larger area. So again in Perak. A resident sent in to advise becomes a resident who dictates; appoints as sultan the most plastic candidate in place of one preferred by the chiefs; arouses resistance which becomes a plea for using force; finds usurpation of the government needful; has his proclamation torn down by a native, who is thereupon stabbed by the resident's servant; then (nothing being said of the murder of the native), the murder of the resident lead to outcries for vengeance, and a military expedition establishes British rule.[25]

Spencer's analysis of how informal empire tends ineluctably to degenerate into formal political seizure is prescient for the way it anticipates Fieldhouse's theory of imperialism. According to Fieldhouse, England and France stumbled into becoming imperial powers in Africa in the nineteenth-century as colonialism produced political instability in colonies, which then led to military intervention followed by imperial annexation.[26]

Other factors contribute to the rise of modern imperialism according to *The Principles of Sociology*. These included love of glory and parliamentary and press jingoism. Parliament and the press had become jingoistic because they had fallen into the hands of men who Spencer describes as admiring Achilles six days a week and Christ only on the seventh.[27]

Imperialism, in turn, rebarbarized all of English society by reimporting the spirit of Achilles. As early as *Social Statics*, Spencer denounced colonialism for infringing the property rights of citizens by burdening them with excess taxation required for maintaining distant colonies. Furthermore, colonialism violated the rights of colonists by dictating to them. The British empire could be made just only by making all its dependencies "integral parts of one empire, severally represented in one united assembly commissioned to govern the whole." Like J. S. Mill, Spencer nevertheless dismisses transforming the British empire into a global democracy as impractical. Uniting the empire under one grand legislature would be like "proposing that the butcher should superintend the classification of the draper's goods, the draper draw up a tariff of prices for the grocer, and the grocer instruct the baker in making bread."[28]

One of Spencer's last essays, "Imperialism and Slavery," bemoans with loathing, pessimistic resignation the rebarbarizing consequences of imperialism.[29] The essay opens denouncing imperialism as embodying the most barbaric of sentiments, namely submission. Imperial powers say to indigenous populations: "You shall submit. We are masters and we will make you acknowledge it." He then complains that imperialism "invariably entails on the master himself some form of slavery more or less pronounced." Echoing Hegel, he says:

> Here is a prisoner with hands tied and cord around his neck (as suggested by Assyrian bas reliefs) being led home by his savage conqueror, who intends to make him a slave. The one, you say, is captive and the other free? Are you quite sure the other is free?. . . . He must be himself tied to the captive while the captive is tied to him. . . . In various ways, then, he is no longer completely at liberty; and these ways adumbrate in a simple manner the universal truth that the instrumentalities by which the subordination of others is effected, themselves subordinate the victor, the master, or the ruler.[30]

Imperialism, in short, is an exercise in national self-definition. By making others "acknowledge" one's mastery over them, imperialism constitutes a pathological self-referencing.

Spencer's anti-imperialism followed from the underlying normative distinction he drew between unjust "offensive" versus just "defensive" wars. As long as the "world continues to be occupied by peoples given to political burglary," wars of defense remained regrettably justifiable.[31] And insofar as Spencer sometimes characterized imperialism as a form of "political burglary," we can safely assume that he regarded it as unjust "offensive" warfare, as the following acerbic comment from "Patriotism," another late essay, testifies:

> Some years ago I gave expression to my own feeling—anti-patriotic feeling, it will doubtless be called—in a somewhat startling way. It was at the time of the second Afghan war, when were invading Afghanistan. News had come that some of our troops were in danger. At the Athenaeum Club a well-known military man—then a captain but now a general—drew my attention to a telegram containing this news, and read it to me in a manner implying the belief that I should share his anxiety. I astounded him by replying—When men hire themselves out to shoot other men to order, asking nothing about the justice of their cause, I don't care if they are shot themselves![32]

Spencer's anti-imperialism was most uncompromising. It was at least as radical as Bentham's and more radical than James Mill's, J. S. Mill's, or Sidgwick's. Many readers will find this no less surprising than the potent similarities between Mill and Spencer's versions of liberal utilitarianism argued for earlier. Yet it is the dissimilarities between Spencer and Mill's versions of liberal utilitarianism that explain Spencer's more radical anti-imperialism and, hence, generate our second source of surprise.[33]

As we have seen, Spencer tried to accommodate utility with *indefeasible* rights as opposed to merely strong, yet ultimately *defeasible*, rights as with Mill. Hence, anti-imperialism followed naturally for Spencer. Cultural differences deprive basic moral rights of none of their normative force. The universality and indefeasibility of rights leave no room for imperialism, no matter how loose, benevolent, or well intentioned. Indefeasible universal rights exclude treating members of other cultures as if they were children even if for their own good. Presumably, for Spencer, respecting the rights of members of foreign cultures maximizes their overall, long-term happiness, just the way a liberal, rights-respecting society maximizes the overall, long-term happiness of its own citizens. But even though liberal utilitarian cultures have no business violating the rights of anyone whether at home or abroad, we still might wonder why they should not intervene in nonliberal utilitarian cultures that fail to respect the rights of their own citizens? Why should Spencerian-style liberal utilitarianism not justify liberal imperialism after all? Mere geographic boundaries, it would seem, cannot constitute a source of independent moral force for liberal utilitarians, especially those who take moral rights so extraordinarily seriously.[34]

EXCURSUS

Allan Gibbard has suggested that, for Sidgwick, in refining and systematizing common sense, we transform "unconscious utilitarianism" into "conscious utilitarianism." We "apply scientific techniques of felicific assessment to further the achievement of the old, unconscious goal."[35] Spencer's liberal utilitarianism was comparable moral science. Sidgwick, however as noted earlier, aimed simply at "progress in the direction of a closer approximation to a perfectly enlightened Utilitarianism." Spencer, by contrast, had more grandiose aspirations for repairing utilitarianism. Merely moving toward "perfectly enlightened Utilitarianism" was scientifically underambitious. Fully "enlightened" and juridically inflexible, liberal utilitarianism was conceptually accessible and perhaps even politically practicable.

Spencer, then, merits greater esteem if for no other reason than that Sidgwick, besides Mill, took him so seriously as a fellow utilitarian worthy of his critical attention. Unfortunately, contemporary intellectual history has been less kind, preferring a more convenient and simplistic narrative of the liberal canon that excludes him.

Spencer's liberal utilitarianism was bolder and arguably more unstable than either Mill's or Sidgwick's. He followed Mill investing utilitarianism with robust moral rights, hoping to keep it ethically appealing without forgoing its systemic coherence. While the principle of utility retreats to the background as a standard of overall normative assessment, moral rights serve as everyday sources of direct moral obligation, making Spencer no less an indirect utilitarian than Mill. But Spencer's indirect utilitarianism is more volatile, more logically precarious, because Spencer burdened rights with indefeasibility while Mill made them stringent but nevertheless overridable depending on the magnitude of the utility at stake. For Spencer, we never compromise basic rights, at home or abroad, let the heavens fall. But for Mill, the prospect of collapsing heavens would easily justify appealing directly to the principle of utility at the expense of respect for moral rights.

Now, critics of liberal utilitarianism from William Whewell (1794-1866) to David Lyons more recently have taken Mill and subsequent liberal utilitarians to task for trying to have their utilitarian cake and eat their liberalism too. As Lyons argues with great effect, by imposing liberal juridical constraints on the pursuit of general utility Mill introduces as a second normative criterion with independent "moral force" compromising his utilitarianism. He risks embracing value pluralism if not abandoning utilitarianism altogether. And if Mill's liberal utilitarianism is just value pluralism in disguise, then he still faces the further dilemma of how to arbitrate conflicts between utility and rights. If utility trumps rights only when enough of it is at stake, we must still ask how much enough is enough. And any systematic answer we might give simply injects another normative criterion into the problematic logic of our liberal utilitarian stew, since we have now introduced a third higher criterion that legislates conflicts between the moral force of the principle of utility and the moral force of rights.[36]

If these dilemmas hold for Mill's liberal utilitarianism, then the implications are both better and worse for Spencer. Though for Mill, utility always trumps rights when enough of the former is in jeopardy, with Spencer, fundamental rights always trump utility no matter how much the latter is imperiled. Hence, Spencer does not need to introduce surreptitiously supplemental criteria for adjudicating conflicts between utility and rights, because rights are indefeasible, never giving way to the demands of utility or disutility no matter how immediate and no matter how promising or how catastrophic. In short, for Spencer, basic moral rights always carry the greater practical (if not formal) moral force. Liberalism always supersedes utilitarianism in practice no matter how insistently Spencer feigns loyalty to the latter. But such feigned loyalty has its merits, namely, obdurate hostility to imperialism regardless of how paternalistically gentle its guise.

Naturally, one can salvage this kind of utilitarianism's authenticity by implausibly contending that indefeasible moral rights always (meaning literally without exception) work out for the utilitarian best over both the short and long terms. As Wayne Sumner correctly suggests, "absolute rights are not an impossible output for a consequentialist methodology."[37] While this maneuver certainly rescues the logical integrity of Spencer's version of liberal utilitarianism, it does so at the cost of considerable commonsense credibility. And even if it were miraculously true that respecting rights without exception just happened to maximize long-term utility, empirically demonstrating this truth would certainly prove challenging at best. Moreover, notwithstanding this maneuver's practical plausibility, it would seem to cause utilitarianism to retire to a "residual position" that is indeed hardly "worth calling utilitarianism."[38]

Whether Spencer actually envisioned his liberal utilitarianism this way is unclear. In any case, insofar as he also held that social evolution was tending toward human moral perfectibility, he could afford to worry less and less about whether liberal utilitarianism was a plausible philosophical enterprise. Increasing moral perfectibility makes secondary decision procedures like basic moral rights unnecessary as a utility-promoting strategy. Why bother with promoting general utility indirectly once we have learned to promote it directly with certainty of success? Why bother with substitute sources of stand-in obligation when, thanks to having become moral saints, utilitarianism will fortunately always do? But moral perfectibility's unlikelihood is no less plausible than the likelihood of fanatical respect for basic moral rights always working out for the utilitarian best.[39] In any case, just as the latter strategy causes utilitarianism to retire completely for practical purposes, so the former strategy amounts to liberalism entirely retiring in turn. Hence,

Mill's version of liberal utilitarianism, notwithstanding its imperialism, must be deemed more compelling and promising for those of us who remain stubbornly drawn to this problematical philosophical enterprise.

CONCLUSION

The received view of Spencer tells a different story than the one I have been telling. According to it, Spencer was the nineteenth century's foremost social Darwinist. Therefore, he must have been an imperialist too. And he surely could not have been a utilitarian, especially a liberal utilitarian as fashionable still as J. S. Mill.[40]

This essay has taken up the double and related tasks of demonstrating that Spencer was not some crude social Darwinist or an imperialist, let alone a racist imperialist. Rather, he was so vehemently anti-imperialist precisely because he was so radically liberal utilitarian. Even if we find the latter unpersuasive, it nevertheless explains what otherwise seems such a surprising and inimitable stance about foreign policy for a purported social Darwinist. Happily, the history of political thought is not always the accommodating supplicant for those who insist on narrating more reassuring fancies about our intellectual debts and legacies.

Spencer's liberal utilitarianism has much to recommend for it despite its unconventional features and implausible implications. Even more than Mill, he suggests how liberal utilitarians can attempt to moderate utilitarianism in other ways, enabling it to retain a certain measure of considerable ethical appeal. Spencer's utilitarianism wears its liberalism not only by constraining the pursuit of utility externally by deploying robust moral rights with palpable independent moral force. It also, and more successfully, shows how utilitarians can liberalize their utilitarianism by building internal constraints into their maximizing aims. If, following Spencer, we make our maximizing goal distribution-sensitive by including everyone's happiness within it so that each individual obtains his or her fair share, then we have salvaged some kind of consequentialist authenticity while simultaneously securing individual integrity too. We have salvaged utilitarianism as a happiness-promoting, if not a happiness-maximizing, consequentialism. Because everyone is "to count for one, nobody for more than one," not just as a resource for generating utility but also as deserving to experience a share of it, no one may be sacrificed callously without limit for the good of the rest.[41] No one may be treated as a means only but must be treated as an end as well. And this goes for humans everywhere, which is why imperialism, whether traditional or neo, is so fundamentally objectionable.

Spencer's liberal utilitarianism also has much to recommend for it simply for its much undervalued importance in the development of modern liberalism. If Mill and Sidgwick are critical to making sense of our liberal canon, Spencer is no less critical. If both are crucial for coming to terms with Rawls particularly, and consequently with post-Rawlsianism generally, as I strongly believe both are, Spencer surely deserves better from recent intellectual history. Intellectual history is one of the many ways we narrate our cultural identity. What a shame when we succumb to scholarly laziness in doing intellectual history just because such laziness both facilitates meeting the pedagogical challenges of teaching the liberal tradition and answering our need for a coherent philosophical identity. Unfortunately, we do not need to travel far and wide to distant, enchanting lands to find our cultural "others" when we can make them up so readily from within.

NOTES

The first half of this essay draws extensively from my entry, "Herbert Spencer," The Stanford Encyclopedia of Philosophy (Winter 2002), Edward N. Zalta ed., plato.stanford.edu/archives/win2002/entries/spencer/.

1. Richard Hofstadter, *Social Darwinism in American Thought* (Boston: Beacon Press, 1955), 41, 46.
2. Peter Singer, *A Darwinian Left* (New Haven and London: Yale University Press, 1999), 11.
3. Quentin Skinner, "A Third Concept of Liberty," *London Review of Books*, April 4, 2002, 16.
4. Herbert Spencer, *Social Statics* (Robert Schalkenbach Foundation, 1970), 79.
5. In his earlier, preevolutionary *Social Statics* (1851), Spencer explained ethical development by combining moral sense, psychology, and phrenology. See D. Weinstein, *Equal Freedom and Utility* (Cambridge: Cambridge University Press, 1998), ch. 2. Also see R. M. Young, *Mind, Brain and Adaptation in the Nineteenth Century* (Oxford: Oxford University Press), 1970.
6. Herbert Spencer, *The Principles of Ethics* (Indianapolis: Liberty Classics, 1978), ii: 43.
7. For a recent, and not entirely dissimilar, account of the evolution of morality that appeals to the convergence of utility and fitness maximization, see Alexander Rosenberg, "The Biological Justification of Ethics: A Best-Case Scenario," in *Darwinism in Philosophy, Social Science and Policy* (Cambridge: Cambridge University Press, 2000), 132–36.
8. See, in particular, Hofstadter, *Social Darwinism*, 40–41, for an egregious misinterpretation of Spencer that runs together interpreting him as a social Darwinist and a proponent of traditional natural rights. For a more recent example that wrongheadedly attributes natural rights to Spencer, see John Offer, "Introduction," in *Herbert Spencer: Political Writings*, ed. John Offer (Cambridge: Cambridge University Press, 1994), xxv–vi. Also see Spencer, *The Principle of Ethics*, vol. ii, 1978, 195, for Spencer's account of basic moral rights as emergent, indefeasible conventions. For an

example of crude Darwinism, see Herbert Spencer, *The Man versus the State* (Indianapolis: Liberty Classics, 1981), 113–14, where Spencer condemns poor-law reform for compelling "diligent and provident" citizens "to pay that the good-for-nothings might not suffer." Moreover, those "who are so sympathetic that they cannot let the struggle for existence bring on the unworthy the sufferings consequent on their incapacity or misconduct, are so unsympathetic that they can, deliberately, make the struggle for existence harder for the worthy, and inflict on them and their children artificial evils in addition to the natural evils they have to bear!" And for an example of more of the same in *The Principles of Ethics*, see Herbert Spencer, *The Principles of Ethics*, ii: 409.

9. Herbert Spencer, *An Autobiography* (London: Watts, 1904), ii,: 88–89. Spencer considered his letter of clarification to Mill important, because he reprinted it partially in *The Principles of Ethics* and fully in *An Autobiography*. In *The Principles of Ethics*, he adds that traditional utilitarians follow Bentham in wrongly failing to deduce from "fundamental principles, what conduct *must* be detrimental and what conduct *must* be beneficial" (vol. i, 92).

10. David Duncan, *The Life and Letters of Herbert Spencer* (London: Methuen and Co.), 108. Also see the second footnote that Mill appended to the last chapter of *Utilitarianism* in response to Spencer's letter of complaint where Mill says: "With the exception of the word 'necessarily,' I have no dissent to express from this [Spencer's] doctrine; and (omitting that word) I am not aware that any modern advocate of utilitarianism is of a different opinion." See J. S. Mill, *Utilitarianism*, in *The Collected Works of John Stuart Mill*, ed. John M. Robson (Toronto: University of Toronto Press, 1969), x: 258.

11. For Huxley's accusation that Spencer's moral reasoning is fallacious because it commends the "gladiatorial theory of existence," see his controversial 1893 Romanes Lecture, "Evolutionary Ethics," in T. H. Huxley, *Evolution and Ethics and Other Essays* (New York: D. Appleton and Co., 1929), 80–82. Also see Herbert Spencer, "M. De Laveleye's Error," in *Various Fragments* (New York: D. Appleton and Co., 1898), 116. Spencer, vol. I, 1901: 125–28.

12. Also see Henry Sidgwick, "Mr. Spencer's Ethical System," *Mind* 5 (1880) and Henry Sidgwick, *Lectures on the Ethics of T. H. Green, Mr. Herbert Spencer and J. Martineau* (London: Macmillan, 1902), for more of Sidgwick's assessment of Spencer. For Spencer's 1881 response to Sidgwick, see, for instance, appendix E, in Spencer, *The Principles of Ethics*, vol. ii. Also see D. Weinstein, "Deductive Hedonism and the Anxiety of Influence," *Utilitas* 12, no. 3 (2000), for Spencer's undervalued role in Sidgwick's thinking.

13. See especially, Henry Sidgwick, *The Methods of Ethics*, 7th ed. (Indianapolis: Hackett Publishing Co., 1981), 467ff.

14. For Sidgwick's moral theory, see Jerome Schneewind, *Sidgwick's Ethics and Victorian Moral Philosophy* (Oxford: Oxford University Press, 1977). Also see the special issue of *Utilitas*, November 2000, commemorating the hundredth anniversary of Sidgwick's death.

15. Sidgwick, *Methods*, xxiii.

16. Spencer, *The Principles of Ethics*, i: 204.

17. Spencer, *The Study of Sociology* (Ann Arbor: University of Michigan Press, 1969), 279ff.

18. Spencer, *The Man Versus*, 162–65.

19. Sidgwick, *Methods*, 455.

20. See Sidgwick, *Lectures*, 138ff. for his rejection of Lamarckianism. D. G. Ritchie likewise rejected Spencer's Lamarckianism, in an effort to overstate his differences with Spencer. Ritchie was an evolutionary, liberal utilitarian for whom, following Spencer, utilitarian practical reasoning superseded moral intuitionism as prudent "rational selection" replaced fortuitous natural selection as the mechanism driving social progress and well being. For Ritchie's criticisms of Spencer, see especially D. G. Ritchie, *The Principles of State Interference, Collected Works of D. G. Ritchie*, ed. Peter P. Nicholson (Bristol: Thoemmes Press, 1998), vol. i. Also see D.Weinstein, "Vindicating Utilitarianism, *Utilitas* 14, no. 1 (2002), 83–90 for a detailed discussion of the overlooked parallels between Spencer and Ritchie. See Sandra M. Den Otter, *British Idealism and Social Explanation* (Oxford: Oxford University Press, 1996), 93–98, for the received view of Spencer vs. Ritchie. And see Weinstein, *Equal Freedom*, 1998, 26–29, for Spencer's critical exchange with August Weismann about the plausibility of Lamarckianism.

21. In *Ungoverned Imaginings: James Mill's* The History of British India *and Orientalism* (Oxford: Clarendon Press, 1992), Javed Majeed interprets James Mill's views on imperial rule in India more generously. For Majeed, James Mill was "not in any way racist," even though he sometimes seemed an "ambivalent" anti-imperialist (138, 190).

22. See especially "Government Colonialism," in Spencer, *Social Statics*, for Spencer's optimism about imperialism disappearing.

23. Spencer, *Social Statics*, 321.

24. Spencer invokes McCulloch's authority on this score. He adds that colonialism is further damaging because it compels metropoles to important goods and raw materials from their dependencies that might otherwise be obtained more cheaply elsewhere. Also see Spencer's still earlier (1842) "The Proper Sphere of Government," in *The Man versus the State*, 219–20.

25. Herbert Spencer, *The Principles of Sociology* (New York: D. Appleton and Co., 1897), i: 602–3. Also see vol. iii, 584, where Spencer says: "Resistance to an intruding sportsman or a bullying explorer or disobedience to a Resident, or even refusal to furnish transport-coolies serves as sufficient excuse for attack, conquest, and annexation. Everywhere usual succession runs thus: Missionaries, envoys to native rulers, concessions made by them, quarrels with them, invasions of them, appropriations of their territories. . . . The policy is simple and uniform—bibles first, bombshells after." See, too, Spencer, "To Kentaro Kantaro," August 26, 1892, in *Life and Letters*, 321–23. Kantaro was a Japanese cabinet minister who earlier sought Spencer's advice regarding Japanese foreign policy toward the West. In response, Spencer insists that Westerners be prohibited from purchasing or leasing property, engaging in coastal trade or intermarrying. Otherwise, conflicts will inevitably occur, which Western governments will interpret as provocations. Military forces will then be sent to establish order, eventually causing all of Japan, like India had already, to fall to outside subjugation. And see Spencer, "To J. Ashley Cooper," June 20, 1893, *Life and Letters*, 328, where he recommends that colonists should be left to fend for themselves as this would compel them to live more amicably with indigenous populations. Responding to Cooper's invitation to join a committee advocating British colonial federation, Spencer replies that this would encourage "aggressive action on

the part of the colonies, with a still more active appropriation of territories than is present going on." See, as well, Spencer, "The Proper Sphere," 221–25, where he claims that emigrants forgo their citizenship and therefore their rights to protection that come with it. Furthermore, unprotected emigration causes local populations to be treated better as was the case in the settlement of Pennsylvania. Finally, see Spencer, *Social Statics*, 330, where Spencer holds that colonial violence is exacerbated by "prize money" colonial commanders can expect to earn by fomenting quarrels with natives and by civil administrators for whom deepening colonial control promises "more births and quicker promotions."

26. See D. K. Fieldhouse, *Economics and Empire: 1830–1914* (Ithaca: Cornell University Press, 1973), esp. part 4. As Fieldhouse says there, "In the most general terms it must be concluded that Europe was pulled into imperialism by the magnetic force of the periphery" (463).

27. Spencer, *The Principles of Sociology*, ii: 632. According to Spencer in "Representative Government—What Is It Good For?" *Essays: Scientific, Political and* Speculative (London: Williams and Norgate, 1901), ii: 303, England's military was much too overrepresented in Parliament. Hobson likewise attributed imperialism, in part, to glory seeking and press jingoism.

28. Spencer, *Social Statics*, 320–21.

29. For another example of Spencer's deepening pessimism regarding imperialism, see Spencer, "To M. D. Conway," July 17, 1898, *Life and Letters*, 410, where Spencer laments: "Now that the white savages of Europe are overrunning dark savages everywhere—now that the European nations are vying with one another in political burglaries—now that we have entered upon an era of social cannibalism in which the strong nations are devouring the weaker—now that national interests, nation prestige, pluck, and so forth are alone thought of, and equity has utterly dropped out of thought, while rectitude is scorned as 'unctuous,' it is useless to resist the wave of barbarism. There is a bad time coming, and civilized mankind will (morally) be uncivilized before civilization can again advance." For more of Spencer's later despair, see Spencer, *An Autobiography*, i: 441–42.

30. Herbert Spencer, "Imperialism and Slavery," *Facts and Comments* (London: Norgate and Williams, 1902), 112–13. Spencer also speculates that Britain's empire has cost the average British taxpayer 13 and ½ days' worth of extra taxation per year. And insofar as for Spencer, taxation is labor done for the state, imperialism means unnecessary political enslavement. For other discussions imperialism and rebarbarization, see Spencer, *The Man versus*, 174–75; Spencer, *The Principles of Ethics*, ii: 320, and Spencer, "To the Hon. Auberon Herbert," September 30, 1888, *Life and Letters*, 284.

31. Spencer, *The Principles of Ethics*, ii: 88. Spencer regarded war as initially adaptive: "While conceding that without these perpetual bloody strifes, civilized societies could not have arisen, . . . we may at the same time hold that such societies having been produced, the brutality of nature in their units which was necessitated by the process, ceasing to be necessary with the cessation of the process, will disappear." See Spencer, *The Principles of Sociology*, ii: 242. Also, see 286, where he claims, "Cooperation in war is the chief cause of social integration."

32. Herbert Spencer, "Patriotism," *Facts and Comments*, 90. Spencer adds that some might conclude that soldiers could therefore decide for themselves as to

whether a war was just or not, resulting in the breakdown of the military. He responds that this applies to "aggressive" wars only thus begging the rhetorical question. In 1881, Spencer helped found the "Anti-Aggression League," which was established to combat British imperialism. In a letter soliciting John Bright's support, Spencer insisted that the League's guiding principle was "non-aggression" rather than "non-resistance." By abandoning its colonies, Britain would not forgo its right to resist aggression. And by resisting imperialism, indigenous populations were simply invoking it. For Spencer's letter to Bright, see Spencer, "To John Bright," July 2, 1881, *Life and Letters*, 221. The League had little impact and soon collapsed. Spencer attributed its failure to Rousseavian realism: "While continental nations were bristling with arms, and our own was obliged to increase its defensive forces and simultaneously foster militant sentiments and ideas, it was out of the question that an Anti-Aggression League could have any success." See Spencer, *An Autobiography*, ii: 378.

33. Both Spencer and Mill agreed that liberal, free-trading societies tended to be inherently pacific because they were less likely to violate the principle of non-intervention. Mill nevertheless held that non-intervention did not apply to how "civilized" nations were entitled to treat "barbarous" nations. (Presumably, for Mill, non-intervention nevertheless holds for how "barbarous" nations must treat "civilized" ones.) According to Mill in "A Few Words on Non-Intervention," *The Collected Works of John Stuart Mill*, ed. John M. Robson (Toronto: University of Toronto Pres, 1984), xxi: 118–19, "To suppose that the same international customs, and same rules of international morality, can obtain between one civilized nation and another, and between civilized nations and barbarians, is a grave error, and one which no statesman can fall into, however it may be with those who, from a safe and unresponsible position, criticize statesmen." Uncivilized societies "have no rights as a *nation*, except a right to such treatment as may, at the earliest possible period, fit them for becoming one." Or even worse, as Mill infamously remarks in "On Liberty," vol. xviii, 224, the uncivilized are children who should consider themselves lucky to be ruled by a benevolent "Akbar or a Charlemagne." But also see Mill, "A Few Words," 119, where he says that the uncivilized nonetheless deserve to be treated according to the "universal rules of morality between man and man." Presumably, Mill means that insofar as the uncivilized are childlike, the moral limitations that apply to how adults may treat children equally apply to how metropoles treat indigenous inhabitants. See, too, J. S. Mill, "Considerations on Representative Government," vol. xix, 571, where Mill condemns colonists for treating native populations as "mere dirt under their feet: it seems to them monstrous that any rights of the natives stand in the way of their smallest pretensions." Finally, see J. S. Mill, "To A. M. Francis," May 8, 1869, *Collected Works*, ed. Francis E. Mineka and Dwight N. Lindley (1972), xvii: 1599, where Mill anguishes: "But the common English abroad—I do not know if in this they are worse than other people—are intensely contemptuous of what they consider inferior races, & seldom willingly practise any other mode of attaining their ends with them than bullying & blows." Mill and Spencer also differed over whether Britain should emancipate its colonies with Spencer, as we have seen, favoring immediate and complete emancipation and Mill favoring colonial federation with Britain responsible for foreign policy even for colonies like Australia. And though Spencer rejected such

thin federated imperialism, he nevertheless hoped that a genuinely democratic, pacific "federation of higher nations" might somehow and someday emerge.

34. To insist that Spencer was anti-imperialist is not to deny that he shared bigoted attitudes commonplace among Victorians toward non-Western cultures. Like Bentham, James Mill, J. S. Mill and Sidgwick, he often referred to Africans, South Pacific islanders, etc., as "primitives" inferior in rationality and industriousness. Yet, he sometimes viewed many "primitives" as morally superior: "What a pity these Heathens cannot be induced to send missionaries among the Christians!" See Spencer, *The Principles of Sociology*, ii: 642.

35. Allan Gibbard, "Inchoately Utilitarian Common Sense: The Bearing of a Thesis of Sidgwick's on Moral Theory," in *The Limits of Utilitarianism*, ed. Harlan B. Miller and William H. Williams (Minneapolis: University of Minnesota Press, 1982), 72.

36. For a historical overview of liberal utilitarianism's critics, many of whom have recently repeated unknowingly what earlier ones had already said, see Weinstein, *Equal Freedom*, "Introduction." For favorable accounts of Millian liberal utilitarianism, see John Gray, *Mill on Liberty: A Defence* (London: Routledge and Kegan Paul, 1983) and Jonathan Riley, *Liberal Utilitarianism: Social Choice Theory and J. S. Mill's Philosophy* (Cambridge: Cambridge University Press, 1988). Gray has more recently recanted his defense of Mill in particular, and liberal utilitarianism in general, in John Gray, "Mill's and Other Liberalisms," in *Liberalisms: Essays in Political Philosophy* (London: Routledge and Kegan Paul, 1989).

37. W. L. Sumner, *The Moral Foundations of Rights* (Oxford: Oxford University Press, 1987), 211.

38. Bernard Williams, "A Critique of Utilitarianism," in *Utilitarianism: For and Against*, ed. J. C. C. Smart and Bernard Williams (Cambridge: Cambridge University Press, 1973), 135.

39. Spencer was clearly overly sanguine in expecting that social evolution was morally perfecting. But his perfectionism was grounded, as I have suggested, in his conviction that "empirical" utilitarianism was gradually and relentlessly giving way to "rational" utilitarianism, which his embrace of Lamarckianism encouraged. If our acquired mental and moral talents were inheritable no less than our physical ones, then, so Spencer believed, succeeding generations would become increasingly motivated to act by utilitarian reasons as well as increasingly capable of making the requisite utilitarian calculations.

40. For a rejection of the cogency of such revisionist claims, see Mark Francis's unforgiving review of my book-length study of Spencer in *The History of Political Thought* 23, no. 2 (2002), 348–51.

41. For Mill's confused rendering of this infamous dictum, which has so often wrongly been attributed to Bentham thanks to Mill in part, see Mill, *Utilitarianism*, 257–58. Mill interprets this dictum inconsistently. One the one hand, he says that it means the "equal claim of everybody to happiness," which implies that everyone rightfully deserves, as a matter of distributive justice, some equal measure of happiness. On the other hand, he claims that it "involves an equal claim to all the means of happiness," which implies much less, namely that everyone rightfully deserves equal opportunities to make themselves happy. He also says in his long footnote about Spencer that this principle "may be more correctly de-

scribed as supposing that equal amounts of happiness are equally desirable, whether felt by the same or by different persons." This rendering is more disturbing, suggesting that *only* states of happiness have value whereas individuals have derivative value only as means to happiness. Only the second version is authentically liberal and fits comfortably with what Mill and Spencer mostly had in mind as liberal utilitarians.

11

Sidgwick's Racism

Bart Schultz

There may be Elements of English Politics, or of American, or of French or Prussian; but the elements of general politics, if cast into general considerations, must either be quite colorless or quite misleading.

Woodrow Wilson, review of Sidgwick's *Elements of Politics*

I share to the full the general disillusionment of political idealists, perhaps all the more fully that I am spending my time in trying to finish a book on the Theory of Politics, with a growing conviction that the political results of the coming generation will be determined by considerations very unlike those that come to the pen of a theoretical person writing in his study.

Sidgwick to A. J. Patterson, December 27, 1889.

THE CONCERN

Henry Sidgwick (1838-1900) has often been identified as the third greatest of the classical utilitarians, after Bentham and J. S. Mill, though some have persuasively claimed that his masterpiece, *The Methods of Ethics* (1874), actually ranks as the fullest and most philosophically sophisticated defense of the classical view to be found anywhere. In any event, there can be little doubt that Sidgwick deserves his place in the canon of philosophical ethics, a place secured in recent decades by the importance accorded the *Methods* by such luminaries as John Rawls, J. B. Schneewind, and Derek Parfit.

Curiously, however, scholarship on Sidgwick has been somewhat narrowly conceived, when compared to that on Bentham and Mill. Much of the commentary on Sidgwick's work has focused on the *Methods*, been analytical

211

rather than historical, and been concerned more with this or that ethical argument rather than with the overall ethical and political position that Sidgwick articulated. This is a somewhat ironic fate, one that has made for an unfortunately blinkered reception of his legacy.

Like Mill, Sidgwick sought to reshape human sentiment to foster a sense of sympathetic unity with humanity. But unlike Mill, he thought the foundation of utilitarianism was wobbly and that an intuitionistic epistemology was needed to defend it or any other ethical view. Ultimately, however, Sidgwick did not believe that he or anyone else had succeeded in providing such a defense, since, as he saw it, in the absence of a theological harmonization of the moral universe, rational egoism and the greatest happiness principle appeared to be in a stand-off, with each as rational as the other, but sometimes in conflict. Although he shared Mill's emphasis on "internal sanctions" involving the cultivation of sympathetic character, Sidgwick thought that, short of a theistic postulate, there were serious limits to how far any harmonization of interest and duty could go. In many respects, then, Sidgwick was someone who believed that what Mill had called an age of transition had inexorably warped itself into an age of crisis, with no adequate substitute for the orthodox religious faith that was often feared to be crumbling. And he feared the results of this crisis, hoping against hope that some new substitute for religion could be found to bolster the social order.

It was this sense of crisis, I believe, that led Sidgwick to mask some of his more controversial and troubling views, such that the racist and Euro-centric subtexts of his work are often very difficult to discern, particularly when focusing exclusively on the *Methods*. Indeed, even the better, more historical and comprehensive efforts to come to terms with Sidgwick's views on the fate of civilization have failed to seriously consider his views on such issues as race and imperialism. As the other contributions to this volume demonstrate, there is a vital, growing body of research on Bentham and Mill on the culture of imperialism, and such research explores in detail the conceptions of race, civilization, nationality, and national character to be found in early utilitarianism. Strangely, there has been virtually no such work on Sidgwick. The best-known works covering his larger political perspective—such as James Kloppenberg's *Uncertain Victory*, Christopher Harvie's *The Lights of Liberalism*, or Stefan Collini's contributions to the collections *Essays on Henry Sidgwick* and *Henry Sidgwick*—debate the ways in which Sidgwick evolved (or devolved) from a Millian form of academic liberalism, to liberal unionism, to more free-floating political independent, often supporting the policies of his Tory brother-in-law, the future prime minister Arthur Balfour. Kloppenberg tries to place Sidgwick as a figure in the "via media," the broad, international sweep toward progressivism that the late Victorian era witnessed; Collini, by contrast, tends to emphasize how in "English terms, he may have been an early example of a type which became more familiar by

the mid-twentieth century: the socially well-connected don, one who made
a career by attaining eminence in a branch of scholarship, but one whose social experience gave him both the confidence and the means of access to
contribute directly and indirectly to the policy-making process, largely by-
passing general public debate."[1] And yet nowhere in these works is there a
simple, direct confrontation with the orientalist thesis, to the effect that the
British culture of imperialism depended on racial—and racist—constructions
of subject populations, as this might bear on Sidgwick.

This is all the more puzzling given that it is of course roundly admitted
that, following the Indian Mutiny of 1857 and the Darwinian revolution, constructions of race became a much more significant feature of scientific and
political discourse among the Victorians. That is, Sidgwick's mature philosophical life, unlike Bentham's or Mill's, fell wholly within the Darwinian and
post-mutiny era, when "race," however variously and absurdly conceived,
was a very prominent feature of the intellectual landscape. If he owed a great
debt to the earlier utilitarians, it is nonetheless natural to wonder how he
might have modulated their views under these very different ideological
conditions.

Simply put, then, the question animating this essay is: was Sidgwick a
"racist," in some meaningful sense of the term? Unfortunately, the answer
would seem to be a qualified "yes."

To get at this question, it is essential to look beyond the *Methods* to consider Sidgwick's other writings, particularly such works as *The Elements of
Politics* (first edition, 1891) and the posthumous *The Development of European Polity* (1903). But beyond that, it is also crucial to consider other
sources as well, particularly Sidgwick's correspondence. For Sidgwick's major academic works were cast in a remarkably abstract mode, often ascend-
ing to high principle with little illustration of what, concretely, he actually
had in mind when he used, for example, the expression "the lower races."
Again, this was, to be sure, part of his analytical method, a self-conscious effort to achieve agreement on principle that might not be forthcoming if the
implications were spelled out for going political disputes. In short, his academic books often call for a certain decoding, in order to understand just
how he would have fleshed out his more abstract claims.

What follows is a sketch of some of the historical figures and contexts—
only some—that illustrate this claim about Sidgwick's often hidden assumptions. I have sought to confront the question of racism as squarely as possible, treating it partly in isolation from the issues of imperialism and
colonialism. After all, even if Victorian imperialist thinking was often bol-
stered by racist stereotypes, there were non-racist imperialists and anti-imperialist racists about during Sidgwick's lifetime.[2] My main concern is
whether Sidgwick harbored racist tendencies; the further question of how
these may have informed his theorizing about empire and colonialism is

important, and a few of the links are set out, though the complexities of late Victorian imperialist thinking are hardly broached. If much of what follows has a provocative tone, that is meant as a deliberate corrective to the alarming silence about this side of Sidgwick's life.

GOVERNMENT HOUSE UTILITARIANISM—IN THEORY

It is best to begin by sketching out some of the reasons for holding that Sidgwick was often less than candid in his publications and public pronouncements, and this for somewhat elitist reasons, however philosophically reflective they may have been. Some contemporary philosophers have found it very difficult to recognize this aspect of Sidgwick's philosophizing.

Thus, in his 1971 essay on "Natural Law, Skepticism, and the Methods of Ethics," after beginning with some remarks on how Kant's method for discovering what morality requires "is a method that everyone can use," J. B. Schneewind explains:

> I take the label "method of ethics" from the work of Henry Sidgwick. A method of ethics, he says, is any rational procedure by which we determine what it is right for an individual to do or what an individual ought to do. Since the moralists I want to consider do not all think of morality as rational, I shall broaden the notion by saying that a method is any systematic or regular procedure, rational or not, by which we determine what morality requires.
>
> Sidgwick does not say who the "we" are who make use of a method of ethics. Are "we" theorists or bystanders or members of a privileged social group who determine what others are to do? Or is a method something every normal adult uses, even if she is not aware of it as such and could not explicitly formulate it? If Sidgwick meant the latter, as I think he did, then it is worth noting that he simply took it for granted that everyone is in possession of some adequate method or other.[3]

Clearly, much swings on the details here, since if the ordinary person has an unconscious method that he or she could not explicitly formulate or explain, the theorists or members of a privileged social group might for all practical purposes be able to call the shots by way of conscious practical guidance. What "degree of publicity" did Sidgwick have in mind here? Schneewind has never really pressed the question, but he has clearly been drawn to a charitable interpretation, making Sidgwick out as at least as much of a moral democrat as Kant was. This is evident from another essay, his 1993 "Classical Republicanism and the History of Ethics," which reaches the comforting conclusion that:

> Mill and Sidgwick revised utilitarianism in ways that distance it from classical republicanism. They tried to show, as Bentham did not, how normal adults can

see for themselves what morality requires in daily life. They also tried to show how each person could be moved to act morally, regardless of legislatively engineered sanctions. Both thus aimed at explaining how utilitarianism could be the morality of autonomous moral agents; and their shift in direction seems to have been accepted without question in recent utilitarian theorizing.[4]

Strangely, Schneewind does not, in these pieces, stress the Sidgwick that he so painstakingly revealed in his classic book, *Sidgwick's Ethics and Victorian Moral Philosophy*[5]—namely, the Sidgwick who was essentially dualistic and only qualifiedly utilitarian. But he does, in an oddly offhand way, effectively develop the Kantian reading presented at length in the book, by way of showing how both Sidgwick and Mill were in effect qualifying utilitarianism by resort to considerations of moral autonomy, the view that any normal adult can see for him or herself, without benefit of moral experts, what morality essentially requires in daily life.

Wonderful as it would be to cast Sidgwick in this role as moral democrat, no such reading can work, at least in any clear and straightforward way. The crucial problem was set out with characteristic wit by Bernard Williams, in his essay "The Point of View of the Universe: Sidgwick and the Ambitions of Ethics," a piece that originated as the Sidgwick Memorial Lecture of 1982, delivered at Newnham College, Cambridge, an institution that Sidgwick and his wife Eleanor virtually founded. Williams highlighted some singularly provocative passages in the *Methods*, such as the following, in which Sidgwick's defense of utilitarian indirection goes so far as to become a defense of the possibility of utilitarianism being an esoteric morality reserved for people competent enough to deploy its method effectively:

> The Utilitarian conclusion, carefully stated, would seem to be this; that the opinion that secrecy may render an action right which would not otherwise be so should itself be kept comparatively secret; and similarly it seems expedient that the doctrine that esoteric morality is expedient should itself be kept esoteric. Or if this conclusion be difficult to maintain, it may be desirable that Common Sense should repudiate the doctrines which it is expedient to confine to an enlightened few. And thus a Utilitarian may reasonably desire, on Utilitarian principles, that some of his conclusions should be rejected by mankind generally; or even that the vulgar should keep aloof from his system as a whole, in so far as the inevitable indefiniteness and complexity of its calculations render it likely to lead to bad results in their hands.[6]

Williams's infamous gloss reads:

> On this kind of account, Utilitarianism emerges as the morality of an elite, and the distinction between theory and practice determines a class of theorists distinct from other persons, theorists in whose hands the truth of the Utilitarian justification of non-Utilitarian dispositions will be responsibly deployed. This

outlook accords well enough with the important colonial origins of Utilitarianism. This version may be called "Government House Utilitarianism." It only partly deals with the problem [of theory and practice], since it is not generally true, and it was not indeed true of Sidgwick, that Utilitarians of this type, even though they are theorists, are prepared themselves to do without the useful dispositions altogether. So they still have some problem of reconciling the two consciousnesses in their own persons—even though the vulgar are relieved of that problem, since they are not burdened with the full consciousness of the Utilitarian justification.[7]

Although Williams was not working up his interpretation as a direct critique of Schneewind's, his essay effectively amounts to that. As he went on to observe, other ethical theories "might at least satisfy one test which . . . Sidgwick's notably and confessedly failed (though he seems not to have regarded it as a failing), the test of being *open*; the requirement, that is to say, that if the theory in question governs the practice of a given group, then it must be possible for everyone in that group to know that it does. Rawls's theory, for instance, reasonably introduces, and itself passes, this test."[8] The test in question is of course cast by Rawls as a publicity requirement, and as such acknowledged as a fundamental element of the Kantian approach. As Kant formulated it in *Perpetual Peace*: "All actions affecting the rights of other human beings are wrong if their maxim is not compatible with being made public."

Williams does not, unfortunately, note the complications that arise from Sidgwick's esotericism being conjoined with Sidgwick's dualism, but it is safe to say that rational egoism could also enthusiastically endorse the esoteric way, should that have the best consequences for the agent.

At any rate, for all of its Kantian sympathies, or because of them, *Sidgwick's Ethics* failed to recognize these passages in the *Methods* for the provocation that they were: "Sidgwick thinks that while contradictory moral beliefs cannot both be correct it may be advantageous at times to have conflicting opinions held by different social groups—one is reminded here of John Stuart Mill's passionate defence of diversity of opinion—and so it may be best that one person should commit an act, for which he is condemned by a segment of society."[9] Sidgwick himself couched his points with such inoffensive allusions. But, after reading Williams, the reader who confronts these passages is more apt to be reminded of the involvement of the Mills in the imperial rule of India than of any Millian defense of diversity in the domestic context. Or, if the reader has happened to read Sidgwick's later collection of essays, *Practical Ethics* (1897), of such claims as the following:

> I admit cases in which deception may legitimately be practiced for the good of the person deceived. Under a physician's orders I should not hesitate to speak falsely to save an invalid from a dangerous shock. And I can imagine a high-

minded thinker persuading himself that the mass of mankind are normally in a position somewhat analogous to that of such an invalid; that they require for their individual and social well-being to be comforted by hopes, and spurred and cured by terrors, that have no rational foundations. Well, in a community like that of Paraguay under the Jesuits, with an enlightened few monopolizing intellectual culture and a docile multitude giving implicit credence to their instruction, it might be possible—and for a man with such convictions it might conceivably be right—to support a fictitious theology for the good of the community by systematic falsehood.[10]

Schneewind has never explained how, on a Sidgwickian conception of a method of ethics, the "docile multitude" of moral invalids—in effect Sidgwick's (slanderous) depiction of native Americans—was supposed to be at some level deploying a method of ethics with the best of the Jesuits.[11] Nor was Williams adding a bit of nasty wit when he described the conflict as, for Sidgwick, that between the theorist and the vulgar. Sidgwick regularly resorted to such terms when describing the mass of humanity. "The vulgar," "the sensual herd," "savages"—his correspondence, especially, is simply littered with such condescending terms.

Admittedly, in those passages from *Practical Ethics*, Sidgwick immediately goes on to say that such tactics of "pious fraud" would not work in modern England, "where everyone reads and no one can be prevented from printing." Still, the flavor of these remarks, which have to do with practical efficacy rather than philosophical principle, hardly resonates with Kant on matters of lying and publicity. Plato's noble lie, so beloved by the philosopher imperialists, would be more like it. And as I shall presently urge, Sidgwick was in truth not at all averse to esotericism at home as well as abroad, particularly with respect to religion, sexuality, and race. In practice, "pious fraud" was a highly relevant, pressing concern for him, not something reserved for distant lands and ages.

Williams's debunking of any reading of Sidgwick that stresses his faith in the moral capacities of ordinary people has been given an interesting twist by Margaret Urban Walker, in her feminist critique of Sidgwick, *Moral Understandings*. For Walker, Sidgwick's *Methods* is "a carefully reasoned operator's manual for the scientific utilitarian ethic in the hands of an elite." It is this elite, "people in positions of political or administrative power," who "are at once most in need of a systematic view, because they are responsible for whole systems." They "are most likely to be able to put such a view into practice . . . because their power opens workings of that system to them at will, from places of privilege which most mothers will never enter, or even get a clear view of." Thus, Sidgwick "judiciously counsels the wise few to take care for such matters as lost power and credibility, negative moral kickbacks of utilitarian attempts at moral reform that are not matched by hoped-for gains, and possible unsavory impacts on the utilitarian operative's own character." Rather than say, with Sidgwick, that the sincere utilitarian would likely be an "eager politician," Walker suggests that "historically and practically" the "tendency was likely to be the other way around."[12]

To be sure, neither Williams nor Walker even tries to back up such claims about Sidgwick's imperialist tendencies by providing evidence about his political views, theoretical or practical. Thus, Walker's feminist critique does not so much as remark that Sidgwick was generally recognized as a Millian feminist, one who devoted an extraordinary amount of time and effort—and money—to the cause of higher education for women. Like the very theorists she criticizes, she sticks to the philosophical debate focusing on the *Methods*. Yet her critique does, like Williams's, at least point to the serious need for further work on political issues in Sidgwick's life and work, to bring out just how given Sidgwick was to various forms of esotericism. Again, as it transpires, esotericism was virtually second nature to him. And this becomes rather clearer once we ask, as Walker urges us to ask, just what kind of audience Sidgwick was addressing and why.

VERY PIOUS FRAUD

Doubtless it is one of the odder paradoxes arising from Sidgwick's life and work that he enjoyed, during and after his lifetime, a reputation for extraordinary honesty and candor, while he was in fact busily theorizing and implementing an esoteric morality. Even Williams observes that there "was quite a strong tendency, at least in liberal circles, to regard Sidgwick as rather saintly. This was a response in particular to his intellectual honesty, to be found both in the marked scrupulousness of the argument of *The Methods of Ethics*, and also in his resignation of his Fellowship because he could not subscribe sincerely to the Thirty-Nine Articles."[13] Of course, what Williams does not explain is how Sidgwick admittedly went on to keep "strict silence" with regard to his deeper religious doubts, out of the conviction that public morality, at that time and place, still very much required the religious buttress. Hence, for utilitarian reasons, he did not want to do anything to further the decline of popular religious belief, though he would in private be open to considering such issues when raised by philosophically inclined minds already given to doubt. As he put it to an old friend:

> the reason why I keep strict silence now for many years with regard to theology is that while I cannot myself discover adequate rational basis for the Christian hope of happy immortality, it seems to me that the general loss of such a hope, from the minds of average human beings as now constituted, would be an evil of which I cannot pretend to measure the extent. I am not prepared to say that the dissolution of the existing social order would follow, but I think the danger

of such dissolution would be seriously increased, and that the evil would certainly be very great.[14]

But Sidgwick did not simply stick to negative inaction on this matter, since after all, his most beloved discussion society, the Cambridge Apostles, was really in many respects a subversive organization long before the Cambridge spies came along; in Sidgwick's day it was out to undermine, typically in a behind the scenes way, the hold of orthodox Anglican religion on such social institutions as Oxbridge.[15] Thus, with religion as with morals, what was appropriate for the educated elite was one thing, but what was appropriate for the vulgar public was something else. And Sidgwick's feminist reformism was rather akin to his religious reformism in its cautious vanguardism that might even try to keep the pace of reform slow out of fear of a public backlash resulting from openness.

Still, as these particular examples should suggest, Sidgwick's esoteric elitism often amounted to a form of vanguardism that was as skeptical of the abilities of real world social elites—landed aristocrats, religious conservatives, etc.—as it was of the general public, whose literacy was, even in the later Victorian era, hardly something to take for granted. One might say that Sidgwick was an educational reformer who recognized how far genuine education had to go at all levels of society. Neither Williams nor Walker manage to indicate, or so much as hint at, just how critically distanced Sidgwick was from the religious and political status quo, which like Mill he often blasted for its "stupid conservatism"—even if Arthur Balfour was his brother-in-law.

Yet in at least one very worrisome respect—namely, on the matter of race—Sidgwick may have been more reflective of his milieu than a philosopher with his critical acumen should have been. As Edward Said has so often and persuasively argued, the late Victorian era was not simply the age of imperialism but the age of an imperialism that legitimated itself in large measure through racist constructions of the populations being subjugated. However incoherent such racial constructions may have been—and it is manifest that they were deeply absurd—it was race, in some sense, as much as class or mere difference, that underlay much of imperialist thinking at the height of the British empire. Such is Said's "orientalist" thesis.[16]

Now, it is the possible applicability of Said's thesis to Sidgwick that is so profoundly troubling, and so hard to make out from the *Methods*. One of the characters that looms large in Said's account is Sir John Seeley, author of the infamous *The Expansion of England*, which became a virtual textbook for the new imperialist thinkers of the late Victorian period. Seeley, as it turns out, was a much admired friend and colleague of Sidgwick's, and Sidgwick in fact edited and introduced his posthumous *Introduction to Political Science*, never suggesting that there was anything substantially wrong with Seeley's main claims on behalf of the empire. Yet Seeley was one of the intellectual architects of the age of empire, the one who, with Sidgwick, helped to turn Cambridge into something of a school for statesmen, in competition with Benjamin Jowett's Balliol College, Oxford.

This connection, which is not even mentioned in Schneewind's work on Sidgwick, is in itself suggestive of how Sidgwick might well have viewed much of the world as fitting the model of Paraguay under the Jesuits, with a none too generous view of common-sense morality with a different complexion. He apparently managed to lull his skeptical conscience to sleep when it came to the matter of England's civilizing mission, from time to time letting drop some statement to the effect that naturally enough his countrymen might have to "commit acts which cannot but be regarded as aggressive by the savage nations whom it is their business to educate and absorb."[17] Nor was it only a question of "savage" nations. He would also remark on how the only remaining civilization that it was left to the British to "overcome"—his word—was that of the Chinese. Although he was quite cosmopolitan, and in fact famous as a champion of international law, Sidgwick envisioned the growth of international law as occurring through the lead and disproportionate influence of the "Concert of Europe."

But as remarked, my present purpose is to focus on a few specific issues concerning race, as a preliminary to any larger consideration of Sidgwick's contribution to imperialist thinking, though with sufficient material to indicate how his racism did figure in his theoretical work. And I would like to focus mainly on Sidgwick's views of blacks, since it is in this connection that his failings emerge with special clarity.

Although Sidgwick scrupulously avoids the word in his published works, in his political correspondence he now and then casually uses the "N word"—"nigger." Thus, in a letter to Lord Lytton, the former Viceroy of India, he sets about explaining the importance of recognizing the difference between matters of international comity and strict international duty, concluding: "I mean, at least, that U.S.A. took this view of the treatment of British niggers by South Carolina in 1849-51, for the Federal Government is constitutionally bound to punish 'offences against the law of nations.'" And in a letter to his close friend James Bryce, the Oxford academic and statesman who sent the drafts of his *The American Commonwealth* to Sidgwick for review, he remarked of Bryce's prognostications about the future of the United States: "Only people of European origin appear to be contemplated in this forecast. Is the nigger no longer a problem, and is the Mongolian played out?"[18]

It would be a serious mistake to generously wave aside such usage as excusable ancestral innocence, perhaps the result of the good natured but bumbling academic having read Mark Twain. Sidgwick had in fact read Mark Twain, but the problem is deeper. As is well known, Sidgwick's post-Darwinian era was actually witnessing a sharp increase in racist thinking, and this in ways that the previous generation—including Mill, Maine, and other influences on Sidgwick—found offensive even at the time. Recall how Mill had responded to Carlyle's virulently racist "The Nigger Question" with his piece on "The Negro Question."[19] And recall too how Sidgwick was careful not to employ such terms in his published work, suggesting that he knew full well that there was nothing innocent about them. In fact, in one of his more astonishingly manipulative tactics, he actually manage to publish a review essay dealing with Charles Henry Pearson's *National Life and Character*[20] that failed to so much as note that the book's central thesis concerned the dire future potential for racial conflict, with the "inferior" races threatening white supremacy. Although he criticized the book sharply, Sidgwick also called it "the most impressive book of a prophetic nature which has appeared in England for many years."[21] Pearson's prophecies "always rest on a simply empirical basis, and only distinguish themselves from the common run of such forecasts by the remarkably wide and full knowledge of relevant historical facts which the writer shows, and the masterly skill with which the facts are selected and grouped. His predictions are almost always interesting and sometimes, I think, reach a degree of probability sufficient to give them a real practical value."[22]

Pearson was a friend and for a time a Cambridge colleague of Sidgwick's. An admirer of Nietzsche and Ibsen who had moved to Australia and there fanned fears about the "Yellow Peril" (the threat posed by Chinese immigrant laborers), he was emphatic in his expressions of concern about nonwhite races. Thus, in lamenting the limitations of going policies, he complained in his book that "the transportation of an inferior race, like the negroes of the United States, to a country where they would be harmless, is too vast, and of too uncertain benefit, to be readily attempted."[23]

Indeed, Pearson's book was concerned to make such arguments as the following, in which Mill's worries about the loss of cultural vitality get transmuted into a Nietzschean mode, not that one would ever guess it from Sidgwick's review:

> Summing up, then, we seem to find that we are slowly but demonstrably approaching what we may regard as the age of reason or of a sublimated humanity; and that this will give us a great deal that we are expecting from it—well-ordered polities, security to labour, education, freedom from gross superstitions, improved health and longer life, the destruction of privilege in society and of caprice in family life, better guarantees for the peace of the world, and enforced regard for life and property when war unfortunately breaks out. It is possible to conceive the administration of the most advanced states so equitable and efficient that no-one will even desire seriously to disturb it. On the other hand, it seems reasonable to assume that religion will gradually pass into a recognition of ethical precepts and a graceful habit of morality; that the mind will occupy itself less and less with works of genius, and more and more with trivial results

and ephemeral discussions; that husband and wife, parents and children, will come to mean less to one another; that romantic feeling will die out in consequence; that the old will increase on the young; that two great incentives to effort, the desire to use power for noble ends, and the desire to be highly esteemed, will come to promise less to capable men as the field of human energy is crowded; and generally that the world will be left without deep convictions or enthusiasm, without the regenerating influence of the ardour for political reform and the fervour of pious faith which have quickened men for centuries past as nothing else has quickened them, with a passion purifying the soul. It would clearly be unreasonable to murmur at changes that express the realization by the world of its highest thought, whether the issue be good or bad. The etiolated religion which it seems likely we shall subside upon; the complicated but on the whole satisfactory State mechanism, that will prescribe education, limit industry, and direct enjoyment, will become, when they are once arrived at, natural and satisfactory. The decline of the higher classes as an influence in society, the organization of the inferior race throughout the Tropical Zone, are the natural result of principles that we cannot disown if we would. It would be impossible for a conservatively-minded monarch to reconstruct the nobility of the eighteenth century in the twentieth; and even now no practical statesman could dream of arresting Chinese power or Hindoo or negro expansion by wholesale massacres. The world is becoming too fibreless, too weak, too good to contemplate or to carry out great changes which imply lamentable suffering. It trusts more and more to experience, less and less to insight and will.[21]

In Nietzschean fashion, Pearson frets endlessly about the fate of a society of weak men, a society that "has no purpose beyond supplying the day's needs, and amusing the day's vacuity." What has such a society "to do with the terrible burden of personality?" But there "seems no reason why men of this kind should not perpetuate the race, increasing and multiplying till every rod of earth maintains its man, and the savour of vacant lives will go up to God from every home."

The precise nature of the human predicament, according to Pearson, has everything to do with race:

Even during historical times, so-called, the world has mostly been peopled by races, either like the negro very little raised above the level of brutes, or at best, like the lower-caste Hindoo and the Chinaman, of such secondary intelligence as to have added nothing permanent to our stock of ideas. At this moment, though the civilized and progressive races have till quite recently been increasing upon the inferior types, and though the lowest forms of all are being exterminated, there seems, as we have seen, good warrant for assuming that the advantage has already passed to the lower forms of humanity, and indeed it appears to be a well-ascertained law that the races which care little for comfort and decency are bound to tide over bad times better than their superiors, and that the classes which reach the highest standard are proportionally short-lived. Nay, so profusely is life given in excess of what we can account the efficient use

made of it, so many purposeless generations seem to pass away before humanity is in travail of a prophet or a thinker, that some inquirers have actually defined the method of creation as a law of waste.[25]

Pearson bleakly consoles the reader with invocations of the Norse "twi-
light of the gods" as the possible future, when, although there may be a "tem-
porary eclipse of the higher powers," even the losing struggle is a kind of
vindication.

Pearson's basic position, as Sidgwick later described it in a festschrift in his
honor, was that if the "Liberal ideal of open competition were maintained,
the human world would gradually become mainly yellow, with a black band
round the tropics, and perhaps an aristocratic film of white on the surface!"[26]
At points, Pearson seemed to be vaguely regretting that genocide was politically incorrect, in dealing with "the lower races." At any rate, in describing
the commonsensical position that he finds too complacent, he explains that:

> No one, of course, assumes that the Aryan race—to use a convenient term—can
> stamp out or starve out all their rivals on the face of the earth. It is self-evident
> that the Chinese, the Japanese, the Hindoos, if we may apply this general term
> to the various natives of India, and the African negro, are too numerous and
> sturdy to be extirpated. It is against the fashion of modern humanity to wish that
> they should suffer decrease or oppression. What is assumed is that the first three
> of these races will remain stationary within their present limits, while the negro
> will contribute an industrial population to the states which England and Ger-
> many will build up along the Congo or the Zambesi. The white man in these
> parts of the world is to be the planter, the mine-owner, and manufacturer, the
> merchant, and the leading employee under all these, contributing energy and
> capital to the new countries, while the negro is to be the field-hand, the com-
> mon miner, and the factory operative. Here and there, in exceptional districts,
> the white man will predominate in numbers, but everywhere he will govern and
> direct in virtue of a higher intelligence and more resolute will.[27]

There is simply no way in which Sidgwick could have been innocently
unaware of what he was doing when he published a review of this work that
criticized its method while trumpeting its importance and censoring its leading racist claims. This may not be quite on a par with the Heidegger problem, but it is a very bad performance for a moral philosopher. Moreover,
what one witnesses here is simply the application of a principle actually formulated in the *Methods*—namely, that, as a footnote on page 488 of the fifth
edition puts it, "it would be commonly thought wrong to express in public
speeches disturbing religious or political opinions which may be legitimately
published in books."[28] Political speeches, or the more popular periodical
press, were one thing, academic tomes another. And Sidgwick was so cautious that even his books tended to put matters in a colorlessly abstract way,
while yet somehow or the other insinuating the point. This was the form of

esotericism that he both theorized and practiced. As in the case of religion, he did not want to be personally responsible for contributing to the instability—potentially violent instability—of the social order.

For my part, it was precisely when trying to understand Sidgwick's ideas in their philosophical context by reading the books to which he kept referring that the question of his racism began to loom. Pearson was one case in point; Bryce was another. Sidgwick was even closer to Bryce, who also enthusiastically praised Pearson's work and was instrumental in getting it published. Sidgwick gave Bryce extensive comments on the proofs of *The American Commonwealth*, and Bryce returned the favor by giving Sidgwick much feedback on the proofs of *The Elements of Politics*. It was in this connection that Sidgwick used the term "nigger," in the letter quoted earlier. And when one turns to Bryce's *American Commonwealth*, one finds that it is, if not as rabidly alarmist as Pearson's work, nonetheless fundamentally racist. Apparently in response to Sidgwick's prodding, Bryce developed his account in a way that is positively shot through with racist stereotypes masquerading as analyses of "national character." For Bryce, it was a serious mistake to grant the American negro political equality, in the aftermath of the civil war. And as he elaborates:

> Against the industrial progress of the Negro there must be set two depressing phenomena. One is the increase of insanity, marked since emancipation, and probably attributable to the increased facilities which freedom has given for obtaining liquor, and to the stress which independence and education have imposed on the undeveloped brain of a backward race. The other, not unconnected with the former, is the large amount of crime. Most of it is petty crime, chiefly thefts of hogs and poultry, but there are also a good many crimes against women. Seventy per cent of the convicts in Southern jails are Negroes; and though one must allow for the fact that they are the poorest part of the population and that the law is probably more strictly enforced against them than against the whites, this is a proportion double to that of their numbers.[29]

Bryce, in a word, virtually defines the expression "blaming the victim," and he goes on to talk about the developing problem of "race repulsion" in the United States and elsewhere:

> Even at the North, where the aversion to Negro blood is now less strong, "miscegenation," as they call it, is deemed such a disgrace to the white who contracts it that one seldom hears of its occurrence. Enlightened Southern men, who have themselves no dislike to the black race, justify this horror of intermarriage by arguing that no benefit which might thereby accrue to the Negroes could balance the evil which would befall the rest of the community. The interests of the nation and of humanity itself would, in their view, suffer by such a permanent debasement of the Anglo-American race as would follow. Our

English blood is suffering enough already, they say, from the intrusion of inferior stock from continental Europe; and we should be brought down to the
level of San Domingo were we to have an infusion of Africa added.[30]

Bryce finds this a powerful line of argument and continues by allowing that
it "is the argument to which reason appeals. That enormous majority which
does not reason is swayed by a feeling so strong and universal that there
seems no chance of its abating within an assignable time." He hopes for future progress, for the repression of lynching and other evils, but he is not op-
timistic about overcoming the color line or finding alternatives to the de facto
forms of apartheid to be found in both the United States and Africa.[31]

Sidgwick did not, despite his greater skepticism, effectively distance himself from such views. He pronounced Bryce's book a "great work," and it
clearly influenced him profoundly. Buried deep in the text of *The Elements
of Politics* is a footnote that explains: "Of course if it should become clear
that the social amalgamation of two races would be debasing to the superior
race, or otherwise demonstrably opposed to the interests of humanity at
large, every effort ought to be made to carry into effect some drastic and permanent measures of separation."[32] To his credit, Sidgwick did admit that the
case had not yet been made for such permanent segregation in any real
world context, and he was consistently skeptical of pseudo-scientific claims
about the relative effects of nature versus nurture. Still, this was the rare case
in which he was not skeptical enough. His Millian sensibilities and critical
abilities could and should have led him to blast Bryce and Pearson in the
way that Mill had blasted Carlyle. Instead, he affirmed their positions as very
serious possibilities and sought to stage-manage the debate to keep it from
alarming the races and classes whose abilities were in question. In the context of his times, he could safely assume that his message would reach only
the right parties.

What this case in point helps to illustrate is just how right Walker is to urge
that we must ask, as Sidgwick asked, "For whom are the labors of moral
philosophers and the accounts that these labors produce? What are moral
philosophers imagining as the social realization of the views they propose
and defend? If moral philosophy answers a need or has a use, whose need
is this and where is moral philosophy used?"[33] Indeed, this is especially true
of the utilitarians in general and Sidgwick in particular, at least if one wants
to come to terms with the questions of his elitism, racism, etc. It is clearly appropriate to wonder just how tight the intellectual linkage between his philosophizing and his politicizing might have been.

Moreover, even if Sidgwick were as much of a Kantian as Schneewind suggests, the question of his racism would not go away. After all, Kant himself
can aptly be described as a racist, despite his cosmopolitanism and case for
moral democracy, which was in crucial respects carefully qualified in racial

terms. As Robert Bernasconi has shown, in a brilliant essay, Kant, among other things, "warned, with reference to Europeans breeding with either Native Americans or Blacks, that race mixing degrades 'the good race' without lifting up 'the bad race' proportionately." And Kant's racism was a much more integral part of his philosophical system than, say, Hume's. It has only been with the Rawlsian revolution that the more sinister side of the Kantian legacy has been effectively erased from intellectual history, in a manner not unlike the erasure of Sidgwick's more problematic sides.[34]

INTERNATIONAL "MORALITY"

As the above references to Kant might suggest, to come to terms with the question of Sidgwick's racism, much more needs to be said about his various accounts of the progress of civilization, and about how his views on race were reflected in his views on colonialism, imperialism, war, and international morality. Clearly, the terms "progress," "civilization," and "culture" played no small role in all of Sidgwick's major works, and it would be impossible to confront the limitations of his position without considering just what significance he attached to them. That he long regarded the crown of culture as "philosophy," in a fairly exalted sense of the enterprise, does not quite convey how he employed that notion when considering such matters as British rule in India and South Africa—or Ireland and Australia, for that matter.

Given the long history of utilitarian involvement in India, it is striking how little Sidgwick has to say about the issue, how focused he always remained on European civilization. Indeed, much of what Sidgwick has to say on all race-related subjects is to be found in the chapters of the *Elements* on "Principles of International Duty," "The Regulation of War," "International Law and Morality," and "Principles of External Policy," which cover a much wider range of issues as well. In these chapters, he argues that the general principles of international duty are "abstinence from aggression and observance of compact," rather in parallel with the individualistic principle of governmental nonpaternalism. He allows that, for all the differences that may arise over particular rules meant to interpret or apply these principles, still "the general principles on which these rules are avowedly based, are of much wider application" and there "seems to be no class of societies—civilized, semi-civilised, or savage—in dealing with which a civilized State can be exempted from the obligation to observe these principles, unless it has adequate grounds for expecting that they will be violated on the other side." But he does believe that in dealing "with uncivilized or semi-civilised communities difficult questions arise as to the interpretation of the duty of abstinence from aggression, and the manner in which it is to be reconciled with the legitimate claim of civilized communities to expand into unoccupied territory, and their alleged right—or even duty—of spreading their higher type of social existence."[35]

The claim that colonization was the vehicle for utilitarian policy in this respect was something of a fixture of Sidgwick's thought. As early as 1861 he had written to his close friend Henry Graham Dakyns:

> I forget whether you agree with Mill's population theory. I think the way he blinks the practical morality of the question is the coolest thing I know. And I know many cool things on the part of your thorough-going theorists. I believe in "Be fruitful and multiply." I think the most crying need now is a better organized colonization. To think of the latent world-civilisation in our swarms of fertile Anglo-Saxon pauperism.[36]

A follow-up letter flatly states: "Colonization is unanswerable, I think; if not, please answer it."

Of course, Sidgwick was the first to admit that England was the great colonizer, and he appreciated the complex forms it had taken. In a broadly sympathetic review of Cairnes's *Essays*, he especially complimented the one on "Colonisation," which

> Presents very effectively in sharp outline and impressive contrast the three states of English colonization: the first period, closed by the war of American Independence, when the aims of colonization were commercial, while in other matters the habits and genius of our race produced an unwatched and half-unwarranted freedom of self-government; the second period, of Colonial-Office control and convict settlement; the third period, initiated 'by an event as obscure as the War of Independence was famous,' the formation of the Colonisation Society in 1830. Mr. Cairnes . . . dwells with justifiable pride on the success of this latter movement, certainly one of the most remarkable triumphs of constructive theorizing that English history has to show.[37]

He does allow, however, that there was a serious setback with the "bursting of the Wakefield bubble," the early bankruptcy of South Australia and Wakefield's failures in New Zealand. Still, he concludes that "we may fairly attribute the present prosperity of Australia and New Zealand to the Colonisation Society of 1830."

Yet ultimately, Sidgwick's considered views on colonization were neither so simple nor so sanguine:

> Experience, however, seems to show that, generally speaking, taking into account the risk of conflict with aborigines and of collisions with other civilized states, the cost of founding a colony will outweigh any returns obtainable to the public treasury of the mother country; and that the extra cost cannot be thrown on the colonists, since, so long as the colony is weak, it is too poor to bear it,

while, when it has grown richer, it will also have grown stronger, and will refuse
to pay. Still . . . even where colonization is a bad investment from the point of
view of public finance, it may still be remunerative in one way or another to the
community as a whole.[38]

At least on the economic side, Sidgwick would seem to follow more
closely the skeptical approach to colonies prevalent in Smith and eighteenth-
century political economy, such as Turgot's, according to which the economic gains to be had from colonies are doubtful or at least highly variable
from case to case.[39] He allows the possibility that "substantial gains are likely
to accrue to the conquering community regarded as an aggregate of individuals; through the enlarged opportunities for the private employment of capital, the salaries earned in governmental service, and especially, in the case
of a commercial community, through the extended markets opened to
trade."[40] Similarly, he thinks they may be of doubtful help in terms of war
and national defense, noting that the British possession of India is if anything
a handicap in this respect, though there may be exceptional cases.

But, having thus set out this mass of qualifications and warnings about the
inconclusiveness of the arguments to come, Sidgwick proceeds to engage
with the issues of the relations between "civilized" and other states, introducing his discussion with some fatuous remarks about immigration and emigration in the case of the United States:

As between old fully-peopled States like those of Western Europe and civilized
States like the American, with a large amount of unoccupied land, the transfer
of population tends to be more extensive and one-sided; the old States—even
when they are growing in numbers and wealth—send to the newer countries a
considerable excess of both over what they receive. When, however, emigration
takes place from civilized States into regions uninhabited except by savage
tribes—whose political organization would hardly be held to justify the name of
"States"—it is in modern times normally combined with extension of the territory of the State from which it takes place, and may be regarded as a process of
Expansion of the community as a whole.[41]

The term "colonization," Sidgwick explains, generally refers to "the occupation by a civilized community of regions thinly inhabited by uncivilized
tribes; in which, accordingly, even supposing the 'aborigines' to be treated
with equity and consideration, there is room for a new population of immigrants far exceeding the old in numbers."[42] Recognizing, however, that this
does not apply to all cases, and that some colonization has involved conquest of not so thinly populated areas, Sidgwick also lays down the following general strictures:

The case is different when the conquered, though not uncivilized, are markedly
inferior in civilization to the conquerors. Here, if the way that led to the con-

quest can be justified by obstinate violation of international duty on the part of
the conquered, the result would generally be regarded with toleration by impartial persons; and even, perhaps, with approval, if the government of the conquerors was shown by experience to be not designedly oppressive or unjust;
since the benefits of completer internal peace and order, improved industry, enlarged opportunities of learning a better religion and a truer science, would be
taken—and, on the whole, I think, rightly taken—to compensate for the proba-
ble sacrifice of the interests of the conquered to those of the conquerors, whenever the two came into collision.[43]

It is here, in fact, in cases along these lines, that Sidgwick finds some of the
more remunerative factors involved in colonization:

there are sentimental satisfactions, derived from justifiable conquests, which
must be taken into account, though they are very difficult to weigh against the
material sacrifices and risks. Such are the justifiable pride which the cultivated
members of a civilized community feel in the beneficent exercise of dominion,
and in the performance by their nation of the noble task of spreading the highest kind of civilization; and a more intense though less elevated satisfaction—
inseparable from patriotic sentiment—in the spread of the special type of civilization distinctive of their nation, communicated through its language and
literature, and through the tendency to imitate its manners and customs which
its prolonged rule, especially if on the whole beneficent, is likely to cause in a
continually increasing degree.[44]

Sidgwick labels this process "spiritual expansion," to contrast it in part
with the "physical expansion which takes place when the conquered region
is so thinly populated as to afford room for a considerable immigration of the
conquerors." He mentions the French in Algeria as an apparent case in point
of this spiritual expansion, and his argument certainly recalls the language of
Seeley in *The Expansion of England*.

In a revealing note, Sidgwick observes that it is often difficult "to estimate
the force of the desire for national expansion,—including the desire of cultivated minds to spread the special type of civilization which they enjoy—as
distinguished from the more primitive impulse to the amelioration of the emigrants' condition." He goes on to remark on the peculiar relationship between Great Britain and the United States, observing that despite their economic and political rivalry, "if we derive any satisfaction from the expansion
of the English race, and of the English type of civilization as communicated
through its language, literature, and law, the prosperous growth of the community inhabiting the United States must be regarded as the most important
means to this end—and perhaps more important than if the colony had remained in political connexion with England." In one of his better forecasts,
he allows that "if any existing language should ever become the one common language of civilized man it will probably be English: and the chief

cause of this result, if it should be brought about, will probably be the growth and commercial pre-eminence of the United States."[45] Thus, the Sidgwickian twist: spiritual expansion may actually be at odds with the expansion of empire (or the British Empire, at any rate).

There are also some particularly revealing remarks in Sidgwick's discussion of colonization in the case where the immigrants move into thinly populated territory occupied by "savages" in political organizations that are not quite "states." What principles of international duty are to apply, given that Sidgwick denies that this form of expansion can be legitimately curtailed in the interests of preserving the way of life of the native populations? As he puts it:

> It remains to speak of the management of the relations between civilized settlers and the uncivilized tribes inhabiting the district into which immigration takes place—commonly called the "aborigines." It is not without hesitation that I venture to touch this question, as I can only treat it in a very brief and general way; while any student of the history of European colonization must be profoundly impressed with its difficulty. What a well-informed writer [Merivale], by no means unduly sentimental, called the "wretched details of the ferocity and treachery which have marked the conduct of civilized men in their relations with savages," forms one of the most painful chapters in modern history; all the more painful from the frequent evidence it gives of benevolent intentions, and even beneficent efforts, on the part of the rulers of the superior race. At present in England there is a general agreement that the wellbeing of the uncivilized first-comers, found in regions colonized by civilized men, should be earnestly and systematically kept in view by the governors of these latter; and that the "aborigines" should be adequately compensated for any loss that they may suffer from the absorption of their territory—and ultimately of themselves—by the expanding civilized societies. It is therefore permissible to hope that in the future some closer approach may be made to the realization of this ideal than has been made in the past.[46]

Sidgwick did at least show some anxiety about his treatment of this subject. In a letter to Bryce, complaining about his slow progress, he explained that "there is a horrid new chapter on 'Principles of External Policy' which has been giving me trouble for weeks: I am trying to find something judicious to say on the treatment of 'aborigines' but have not yet succeeded." Bryce, in response, stated: "The greatest difficulty about the aborigines question seems to be the question of their lands—as to which there are many American [duties?] but none that clear up the practical perplexities of reconciling justice with the 'progress of civilization.'"[47]

As Sidgwick sees it, one cental issue—a very Pearsonian one—concerns the difference between colonies "where the manual labour can be and will be supplied by the civilized race," versus those where the "civilized" race "can only supply capital and superior kinds of labour."

In the first case the main difficulties of the problem are likely to be transient; the incoming tide of civilized immigration will gradually modify or submerge the barbarism of the aborigines; so that ultimately the question, how to deal with such of them as may survive without becoming really fit for civilized work, will sink into a part of the general question of dealing with the incapable and recalcitrant elements found in all civilized communities. But in its early stages the collision of races is likely to be more intense in colonies of this class; since the process of settlement inevitably involves more disturbance of the economic conditions of the life of the aborigines.

On the other hand, in colonies where the superior race does not supply the manual labour, the difficulties of governing a community composed of elements very diverse in intellectual and moral characteristics must be expected to last indefinitely longer; but there is no stage at which the conflict of interests need be quite so acute as in the former.[48]

Sidgwick holds that the former case has been more important historically, but that "its importance is rapidly diminishing, and in most of the territories open to the future expansion of civilized European States, manual labour is likely to be mainly performed by non-European races." He also tries to downplay the significance of his remarks, explaining that he will not discuss either case in detail, but only "indicate briefly the nature of the problems that arise and the principles *prima facie* applicable to them, in accordance with the general view of politics taken in the present treatise." Incredibly, he goes on to state that he will "not attempt to distinguish between the international duty and the interest of the civilised nation aiming at expansion," because he believes that "here, as elsewhere, duty and interest are mostly coincident," though he could not demonstrate this in all cases. But he would have it understood that he has always in view, "as the ultimate end, the aggregate happiness of all the human beings concerned, civilised and uncivilized—native or imported." If it "does not seem possible—even if it were desirable—to check the expansion of civilised Europe," then "the problem of regulating and governing composite social aggregates, with a civilised minority superimposed on a semicivilised majority, must be regarded as one of the most important proposed for European statesmanship in the proximate future."[49]

Thus, having done his best to recognize the realities of European expansion, stress the importance of the issue, and profess the inadequacy of his treatment of it, Sidgwick finally brings himself to issue some broad statements of principle. On the matter of the "civilised State" claiming supreme control over the territory in question:

It would be going too far to say that no exercise of power over these latter is justifiable, unless the general consent of the persons subjected to it may be presumed from agreements formally made by their chiefs or on some other adequate ground. But we may say that no serious interference of the civilised government with the aborigines should take place without such evidence of consent, except under circumstances which afford a special justification for it;—as (e.g.) when the civilised State has been victorious in a war provoked by the aggression of the inferior race, or when the interference is necessary for the security of its own subjects in the exercise of rights that they may fairly claim, or to protect the natives from the evils of intercourse with the most lawless and degraded elements of civilised society. Further, the claim of sovereignty should not be understood to carry with it any obligation to interfere with the laws and customs of the aborigines, even when opposed to civilised morality. Such interference should be regulated by an unprejudiced regard for the social wellbeing of the tribes subjected to it; which might be seriously impaired by the sudden abolition even of pernicious customs.[50]

This shows at least a trace of cultural sensitivity, as well as the recognition that the "civilised society" may not be all that civilized. Futhermore, Sidgwick insists that in

regulating the relations between aborigines and settlers, the care of Government will be specially needed to prevent the interests of the former from being damaged through the occupation of land by the latter. We may lay down that the aborigines should never be deprived of any definite rights of property without full compensation; and that, so far as possible, such rights should be only ceded voluntarily. I cannot, indeed, hold that compulsory transfer is in principle inadmissible; since I cannot regard savages as having an absolute right to keep their hunting-grounds from agricultural use, any more than an agricultural occupant in a civilised State has a right to prevent a railway from being made through his grounds. Still, compulsory deprivation should be avoided as far as possible, even where it may seem abstractly justifiable, on account of the violent resentment that it is likely to cause.[51]

Government may also have to control the sale and purchase of lands, in order to prevent the aborigines from being taken advantage of. Even when the aborigines may not have conceptualized their "property right," compensation should be made "for the loss of the utilities in the way of hunting, fishing, etc., which they have been accustomed to derive from such lands."

As for further restrictions on the free interaction between settlers and aborigines, these need to be worked out on a case by case basis, the familiar examples of the "prohibition of the sale of intoxicating liquors, and the prohibition of the sale of firearms" being in principle defensible. Sidgwick goes further, suggesting that "in some cases a more complete separation of races, and a more thorough tutelage of the inferior race, would seem to be temporarily desirable." But he hastens to add that it is "hardly likely that this kind of artificial isolation can ever be more than partially successful," and that "such measures should generally be regarded as essentially transitional, and only adopted—if at all—in order better to prepare the aborigines for complete social amalgamation with the colonising race." It is in this connection that he allows, in the footnote discussed earlier, that there has been no proof adequate to support the conclusion that "the social amalgamation of two races would be debasing to the superior race," though if it were clearly demonstrable permanent forms of separation would be justifiable.[52] As was so often the case, Sidgwick's verdict on the issue—in this case, "race degradation"—would seem to be: clearly undecided. But this time his agnosticism has a sinister side. The "method of isolation," increasingly popular in medical discourse dealing with such matters as moral insanity, has its counterpart in racial policy.

Furthermore, the government must insure that the punishment of crimes against the settlers proceed "within the limits of strict justice," though the crucial object is less to achieve "pedantic adhesion to the forms of civilised judicial procedure" and more to "impress the intellect of the aborigines with the relation between offence and punishment." On the matter of education, however, Sidgwick is insistent that the aborigines are owed much more than mere "industrial education." The educational task "should include all kinds of instruction required to fit the inferior race to share the life of civilised mankind. In particular, though the religion of the settlers should not be compulsorily imposed on the natives, every encouragement should be given to the effort of missionaries to teach it. Experience seems to show that the potency of such teaching as an instrument of civilization varies very much in different cases, but few will doubt the desirability of allowing full scope to its application."[53] Finally, Sidgwick argues that:

One of the most indisputable services that—as we may hope—the expansion of civilised States is destined to confer on uncivilized humanity is the abolition of the evils of enslavement, and of the wars and raids that have enslavement for their object; and, ultimately, of the condition of slavery. But it may often be expedient that this latter result should be only gradually attained: while, on the other hand, even where the status of slavery is formally excluded by law, special restrictions on freedom of contract between natives and settlers are likely to be required in the case of contracts of service; since, if such contracts are left unrestricted, there is some risk that the inferior race may be brought too completely into the power of private employers. This point is of course peculiarly important in the case of colonies in which the superior race cannot or will not undertake the main part of the manual work required: in this case the demand of the capitalist employer for a steady supply of reliable labour led modern civilization in its earlier stage back to the institution of slavery in an extreme form: and prompts even now to longing aspirations after some system of compulsory labour, which shall have the economic advantages of slavery without its evils. But I know no ground for thinking that such a system can be devised: and should accordingly deprecate any attempt to approximate to it. I do not therefore infer—as some have inferred—that contracts of long duration ought to be prohibited altogether; but only that they ought to be carefully supervised and closely watched. The need for this vigilance arises equally—it may be even greater—when the labourers in question are not natives, but aliens belonging to a lower grade of civilization; at the same time there are strong economic reasons for introducing labour from abroad in colonies of this class, where the natives are either not sufficiently numerous or wanting in industrial capacity.[54]

Such is the inconclusive close of Part I of the *Elements*. Sidgwick returns to the topic in Part II only one more time, briefly, in a chapter on "Federal and Other Composite States." There he reiterates his conviction that the mother country must take a hand in regulating relations between colonists and aborigines, since the "greater impartiality that may be reasonably attributed to the home government seems to render it generally desirable that the management of the aborigines should not be regarded as an 'internal affair' of the colony, so long as there is any serious danger of a conflict of races or persecution of the inferior race."[55] More painfully, however, he also adds some further discussion of the case "where the manual labour can never be in the main supplied by the superior race: since here the composite character of the population must be regarded as permanent unless the races blend."

> To a society so constituted the governmental structure sketched in the *preceding* chapters is *prima facie* unsuited: but the extent and nature of the modifications that should be introduced into it must vary very much with the degree of civilization actually reached by the inferior race, and its apparent capacity for further improvement. It will be difficult to prevent a simple oligarchy of the superior race from being tyrannical: on the other hand, it seems a desperate resource to give equality of electoral privileges to members of the inferior race while admittedly unfit to control the operations of the government, in the mere hope that experience may in time educate them up to a tolerable degree of fitness. So long as the composite society presents this dilemma, it will probably conduce to its wellbeing as a whole that the colony should remain a dependency; so that, even where the business of government is mainly left in the hands of the colonists, the control of the central government may prevent or mitigate any palpable oppression of the inferior race.[56]

These statements are obviously explosive.

What can be said on behalf of Sidgwick's arguments? The better points of his analysis, insofar as there are any, reflect the critical skepticism evident in other departments of his work. Against the rising tide of neo-Darwinian racism, he holds out an agnostic claim that no seriously "debasing" inherent racial differences have been scientifically demonstrated. Against the rising tide of British imperialism, he urges that spiritual expansion may not necessarily take the form of extended empire and that although colonization is generally a good thing, the rights of the "semi-civilised" and aboriginal peoples must be protected—especially from the less than impartial colonists themselves. Indeed, he recognizes how abysmally cruel the treatment of native populations has been, by the "civilised" states, even when statesmen were well intentioned, and he thinks of denying independence as in part a measure to ensure that the exploitation by the colonists is not perpetuated. And against any educational program that would merely underwrite the inferior social and economic position of the "lower races," he demands full educational opportunity to share the benefits of "civilization," the "better religion" and "truer science" that he rather presupposed it represented.

Thus, colonization, in Sidgwick's eyes, might advance the general happiness of humanity, gradually undermining the prescientific superstitions and institutions—such as slavery and the slave trade—that mostly contributed to human misery. The model is the spread of education, rather than the spread of capitalism, the principles of which could not determine overall policy in this domain. Such an outlook is ultimately more cosmopolitan than nationalistic, though this is somewhat compromised by the weight given to European states in defining international duty. A very heavy educational responsibility fell on the home government.

But obviously, on the other side, one can only gasp at the naivete and fatuity with which Sidgwick designates unfamiliar peoples "semi-civilised" or "inferior" or "savage," with perfect insouciance consigning their ways of life to extinction. Given his own deeply skeptical attitude toward the Christian religion and his reformist concern to reduce the religious influence on higher education, how could he have been so calmly and Euro-centrically accepting of the "superiority" of his civilization? So easily forgiving of what in other contexts he sharply condemned as missionaries rushing out to preach what they did not know? And what did it mean, in practice, to be so warmly appreciative of the greater impartiality of the home governments, so that their benevolence was linked to maintaining British dependencies? "Spiritual expansion" is a very suspicious expression, even when Sidgwick fails, in his all too discreet way, to give it much concrete content.

Undeniably, one of the more frustrating features of Sidgwick's writings on this score is his abstract way of describing the issues, his intentionally steering clear of too much particular political reference, the better to foster agreement on principle. Just which peoples did he suppose to be "savage" and which "semi-civilised"? What was his list of the future cases where the colonists were unlikely to engage in manual labor? What did he mean by "race," and which "races" did he think would be conquered or fused? What did it mean to remain agnostic about the possible necessity of "permanent" segregation?

However, if one recalls in this connection his warm regard for the works of Bryce and Pearson, and his casual use of racial epithets to refer to blacks (including black citizens of the United States), his concerns about "manual labour" and the possibility of "race degradation" appear very sinister indeed. He was theorizing the very possibilities that Bryce and Pearson addressed in much more concrete and overtly racist terms.

Indeed, Bryce's work, especially, could helpfully be taken as providing something of a key for interpreting Sidgwick's more abstract accounts. It is here that one finds the issues of national character, manual labor, and "debasement of the race" versus fusion raised, and the problem of the color line in the United States used as a unique way of categorizing the various forms of interaction between different populations. In his account, the "coolies" and the "ryot" were industrious compared to the "Negro," and the "ancient and cultivated races" of India and China did not pose quite the same problems as the "savage" aboriginal populations of the Congo, the Australian wilderness, and the American West. These were the concrete examples behind Sidgwick's colorless arguments about race and colonization. Again, he knew Bryce's work well, having supplied him with extensive commentary on the proofs of *The American Commonwealth*, and the points that he did not query are as important as the ones he did, suggesting shared assumptions.

Moreover, as noted, Sidgwick actually played a role in stimulating Bryce's extended meditations of the subject of race. Recall the line quoted earlier, from the extensive correspondence that they maintained during the eighties, with Sidgwick complaining about Bryce only considering "people of European origin" in his forecasts. Another letter from October 1888 explains, "I enclose an extract from the Times of today about the nigger: it represents a view I have heard more than once expressed with much confidence: but I am glad to hear that the best authorities do not share it." This continues with the suggestion: "For 'antecedent theory' I should be inclined to suggest 'prevalent views of heredity': as I do not think that there [has] ever been any theory deserving the name of scientific which has professed to determine the relative influences of physical heredity and social environment."[57]

The painful dissonance that comes from finding Sidgwick so casually lapsing into offensive slang—slang that, like Bryce, he scrupulously avoided in his published works and that even Maine found offensive—while at the same time denying the very ground of the racism that Bryce describes (and represents) suggests just how deeply problematic and pervasive the racism of his cultural context was. Some might urge that one can convict Sidgwick of many failings—Euro-centrism, certainly, and also falling in with any number of ridiculous stereotypes that were legitimated under the rubric of "national character"—but not, on the face of it at least, of harboring fundamentally decided racist convictions appealing to hereditary inferiority, and this for much the same reason that it is difficult to convict Mill of harboring any such convictions.[58] But the evidence is more difficult to come to terms with. After all, Sidgwick did not think that science had established the reality of an afterlife, either, but he still hoped that it would and was often inclined to think the evidence pointed that way. Perhaps he took a roughly similar attitude toward the matter of hereditary racial differences? At any rate, for all the abstraction of his ethical and political theorizing, he rather plainly allowed that "race degradation" was a possibility that had to be taken seriously. The matter, for Sidgwick, was political, as well as personal.

GOVERNMENT HOUSE RACISM

Much more could be said, of course, about just how to apply Said's thesis to Sidgwick and his historical context, and about the difficulties that arise from the shifting meanings of "race" and "racism." My argument so far is only a sketch, one that could be filled in with details drawn from many further sources, sources that often highlight the way the old Benthamites and Millians compromised themselves when confronted with the emerging racism of the late Victorian era.

Consider, for example, A. V. Dicey, another friend and colleague of Bryce's—and of Sidgwick's. Dicey, an Oxford don and author of the classic *The Law of the Constitution*, wrote a very informative letter to Bryce on Christmas Day, 1901:

> Your subject for the Romanes Lectures which I am delighted to hear you are going to deliver is an excellent one. "The Contest Between Civilized and Uncivilised Races" is perhaps the most important of the time and will become more and more important as the century goes on and happily as yet it has not become a party question. Accidental circumstances have recently called my attention to it. There is a terrible danger that, as we cannot talk of human equality with the same confidence with which the best men of the 18th and earlier 19th century spoke of it, and as we are compelled to attach more importance than they did to race, we may come to give up faith in the truth, of which I think they had a firm hold, that the qualities which races have in common are at least as important as (I should say more important than) the characteristics in which they differ. Then the whole matter is complicated to my mind by the growth of an idea, which I think may be true that the races with different ideals and different moralities had best live apart. I cannot myself feel at all sure that the cry for a "White Australia" is not at bottom a sound one. But all I want at present to urge is the great advantage of your taking up this topic and dealing with it in your lecture.[59]

Dicey, the old Benthamite and ardent opponent of home rule for Ireland, here insists on the importance of race, expressing some doubts as to whether Pearson might not be right. This comes as part of a congratulatory message to Bryce for his willingness finally to tackle head on, in a *public* lecture, a subject that has not yet become a "party question," perhaps because leading representatives of all the parties could adopt a similar tone when it came to the "Contest" with "Uncivilised Races."

It is noteworthy, in this connection, that in the 1860s Sidgwick's close friend J. J. Cowell had softened him to the Southern cause in the American Civil War, which he tended to treat in legalistic terms as a matter of the right of secession and noninterference.[60] As in the case of the Boer War, in the late 1890s, Sidgwick often managed to discuss the conflict without serious consideration of the problems of racial justice involved—that is, without confronting the particulars of the "Contest" in question. Dicey, who had also read the drafts of Sidgwick's *Elements*, may well have had Sidgwick in mind when he wrote that letter to Bryce, knowing how Sidgwick, too, had worried about the question of race (albeit not in a public lecture).

Moreover, many of Sidgwick's favorite writers—who considerably influenced his accounts of ethics and politics—were profoundly racist. Mark Twain was less so than Walt Whitman,[61] but Alfred Lord Tennyson was perhaps even worse. Tennyson, the revered laureate and one of Sidgwick's favorite poets, made his convictions abundantly clear at an 1865 dinner party that included Gladstone and Sidgwick's very close friend John Addington Symonds, who described the conversation:

> They were talking about the Jamaica business—Gladstone bearing hard on Eyre, Tennyson excusing any cruelty in the case of putting down a savage mob. Gladstone had been reading official papers on the business all the morning and said, with an expression of intense gravity, just after I had entered, "And that evidence wrung from a poor black boy with a revolver at his head! . . ." Tennyson did not argue. He kept asserting various prejudices and convictions. "We are too tender to savages; we are more tender to a black than to ourselves." "Niggers are tigers; niggers are tigers," in *obligato, sotto voce*, to Gladstone's declamation. "But the Englishman is a cruel man—he is a strong man," put in Gladstone. My father illustrated this by stories of the Indian Mutiny. "That's not like Oriental cruelty," said Tennyson; "but I could not kill a cat, not the tomcat who scratches and miawls over his disgusting amours, and keeps me awake,"—thrown in with an indefinable impatience and rasping hatred. Gladstone looked glum and irate at this speech, thinking probably of Eyre.[62]

But for present purposes, some more telling evidence comes from Sidgwick's brother-in-law, the Tory politician Arthur Balfour, who had also been one of Sidgwick's first philosophy students and became a close colleague in the Society for Psychical Research. Intriguingly, Bryce the Liberal and Balfour the Conservative shared at least some of the presuppositions of the culture of imperialism, and they collectively suggest just how problematic and limited Sidgwick's political orbit could be. Both could sound a lot like Pearson.

When in 1908, former prime minister Balfour undertook to deliver the Henry Sidgwick Memorial Lecture at Newnham College, in honor of his late teacher and brother-in-law, he used the occasion to speak to the theme of "Decadence." The type of decadence he considered was that which infected the Roman Empire—"the decadence which attacks, or is alleged to attack, great communities and historic civilizations: which is to societies of men what senility is to man, and is often like senility, the precursor and the cause of final dissolution." This is the type of decadence, or degeneration, that occurs when "through an ancient and still powerful state, there spreads a mood of deep discouragement, when the reaction to recurring ills grows feebler, and the ship rises less buoyantly to each succeeding wave, when learning languishes, enterprise slackens, and vigour ebbs away."[63]

Balfour worried that Western European civilization might not be quite as lucky as the Roman Empire. If cultural advance in these states "is some day exhausted, who can believe that there remains any external source from which it can be renewed? Where are the untried races competent to construct out of the ruined fragments of our civilisation a new and better habitation for the spirit of man?" The inexorable conclusion, of course, is: "They do not exist; and if the world is again to be buried under a barbaric flood, it will not be like that which fertilized, though it first destroyed, the western provinces of Rome, but like that which in Asia submerged forever the last races of Hellenic culture." Thus, he would emphatically not infer that "when some wave of civilisation has apparently spent its force, we have a right to regard its withdrawing sweep as but the prelude to a new advance."

Of course, in conclusion, there is the requisite "hopeful" note:

We cannot regard decadence and arrested development as less normal in human communities than progress; though the point at which the energy of advance is exhausted (if, and when, it is reached) varies in different races and civilizations: that the internal causes by which progress is encouraged, hindered, or reversed, lie to a great extent beyond the field of ordinary political discussion, and are not easily expressed in current political terminology: that the influence which a superior civilisation, whether acting by example or imposed by force, may have in advancing an inferior one, though often beneficent, is not likely to be self-supporting; its withdrawal will be followed by decadence, unless the character of the civilisation be in harmony both with the acquired temperament and the innate capacities of those who have been induced to accept it: that as regards those nations which still advance in virtue of their own inherent energies, though time has brought perhaps new causes of disquiet, it has brought also new grounds of hope: and that whatever may be the perils in front of us, there are so far, no symptoms either of pause or of regression in the onward movement which for more than a thousand years has been characteristic of western civilisation.[64]

Balfour also makes a strong Sidgwickian case for science, as a new force on the horizon the advance of which is not easily explained, though he is of course not one to suppose that science could prove ultimately satisfying to the religious consciousness of ordinary people. Democracy, too, is addressed and finds its due place as a regulative force in at least some modern societies. But though the forward movement of humanity "may be controlled or checked by the many; it is initiated and made effective by the few," which was why it was a good thing that even in the advanced societies there was, in terms of mental capacity, "a majority slightly below the average and a minority much above it." He denies that "any attempt to provide widely different races with an identical environment, political, religious, education, what you will, can ever make them alike. They have been different and unequal since history began; different and unequal they are destined to remain through future periods of considerable duration."

Balfour's Sidgwick lecture found a very enthusiastic and receptive audience in the person of the president of the United States, the Bull Moose Progressive Teddy Roosevelt. Roosevelt, who had fond memories of Balfour as the ally who kept England from interfering in the Spanish-American War, heartily agreed with much of what his British friend had to say. He had "ugly doubts as to what may befall our modern civilisation" and thought it an "irritating delusion" that there would necessarily be forward progress, about which there was nothing inevitable or necessary. In writing to Balfour, Roosevelt explained, "It is equally to the interest of the British empire and of the United States that there should be no immigration in mass from Asia to Australia or North America. It can be prevented, and an entirely friendly feeling between Japan and the English speaking people preserved, if we act with sufficient courtesy and at the same time with sufficient resolution."[65]

As Kenneth Young has observed in his biography of Balfour, it was quite possibly this letter from Roosevelt that "decided Balfour early in 1909 to put some of his most cherished and far-seeing ideas on the future before the President. Among the Royal papers there is a very remarkable document headed 'The Possibility of an Anglo-Saxon Confederation,'" which was apparently sent to Roosevelt. In this, Balfour outlined the necessity of England and American confronting the twentieth century as firm allies, insisting that disarmament was a dream, that a few nations were bound to control the world, and that peace would come "only when these powers have divided the world between them." He worries about the expansion of Russia and Germany, but as for most of Africa, it will never be the home of whites, being already possessed by "many millions of an inferior black race with whom white men cannot live and work on equal terms," and besides "the climate is not suitable for hard manual labour." Thus, the "progressive races" might develop some commerce or military installations, but in the main, it "will be given over to the negro and, in the North East, to the Mohammedans." Still, such underpopulated areas as Australia and South Africa were desirable: "Not until these countries are more thickly populated than they are today can their future as Anglo-Saxon states be assured, unless they are protected by a power invincible at sea."

But Balfour's main point, as Young clearly demonstrated, was that the United States and Britain should federate to "be a more than equal counterpoise to the other great nations of the future and also partly in order to secure to them the undisputed possession and development of the still thinly populated areas of the world." Otherwise, they will end in conflict, of which no good will come. "If England and America do not federate, the history of the world will continue to be one of warfare, for a number of world powers will be competing for the supremacy," but if they unite, they will "be beyond attack."[66] That the warfare to come was beyond anything imaginable to the Edwardians suggests the limits of Balfour's vision. Still, needless to say, from this point England and the United States began that singularly intimate alliance that has so frequently led other nations and people of color to regard both with suspicion.

But the crucial point here is that the Tory leader was speaking directly to the Progressive leader and reinforcing the worst tendencies of both when it came to the "lower races," and this in terms that often overlapped with those of Bryce and Pearson. That so much of Balfour's vision was contained in his memorial lecture for Sidgwick is surely revealing. The deep-seated bigotry that it displays—a smug bigotry that must have been of fixture of Sidgwick's home life, when off at 4 Carlton Gardens, or Whittingehame, or Terling Place—cannot help but make one wonder whether Sidgwick himself could ever have been even agnostic about such matters. Balfour sounds very like an advocate of "spiritual expansion" who had read his Pearson and been tutored in the dangers of philosophical doubt—refusing, like Sidgwick, to let his philosophical doubts diminish his activism or make him "unpractical."

Curiously, and ironically, at precisely the time that Balfour was using the Sidgwick Memorial lecture as a bully pulpit to fan fears of decadence and pitch racist eugenics, Bryce was moving in a different direction, one that might have been more congenial to a Sidgwick living into the twentieth century. Later trips to the United States led Bryce to moderate his racism considerably, producing an additional chapter, "Further Reflections on the Negro Problem." Now, he regards the progress of blacks as indisputable, and if he allows that there is something to the claim that they are "inefficient" workers, the cause is, he argues, probably environmental: "All that can be said is that they are the natural result of the previous conditions, that he is less lazy in the United States than in the West Indies, and that he is improving steadily if slowly—improving in the way which is surest, viz., by his own exertions and by the example of a few of the best among his own race. A solid ground of hope lies in the fact that the evils described will naturally diminish as he grows more efficient, and that with the extension of agricultural and manual instruction, his labour will doubtless become more efficient."[67]

Bryce even goes on to say that W. E. B. DuBois's *The Souls of Black Folk* "presents in a striking manner the hardship of the coloured man's lot," and he concludes by asking, when "the sentiment of a common humanity has so grown and improved within a century as to destroy slavery everywhere, may it not be that a like sentiment will soften the bitterness of race friction also?"[68] Revealingly, he now has nothing but praise for the thirst for education that was so prevalent among African Americans.

Perhaps the best that can be said on Sidgwick's behalf, when it comes to the issue of racism, is that one call well imagine him going with Bryce in this way and becoming an admirer of DuBois. After all, he never fully converted to Balfour's Toryism, and he did find Pearson's work depressing. After the book appeared, Pearson sent Sidgwick a complimentary copy, to which gesture the latter replied:

> I am much obliged to you for sending me your book which I am reading with much interest. When I find myself too depressed by it, I console myself by thinking that sociology is not yet an exact science, so that the powers of prediction possessed by the wisest intellect are limited.
> I am glad to see that the reviews are giving you justice—so far as I see them.[69]

And of course, Pearson's claims had rested on the notion that it was often easier to forecast the big developments of social evolution, rather than the nearer and more specific future. "Fortunately," Sidgwick argued, concerning whether there really is any science of social dynamics worthy of the name, "there is a simple criterion of the effective establishment of a science—laid down by the original and powerful thinker who must certainly be regarded as the founder of the science of society, if there is such a science—the test of Consensus of experts and Continuity of scientific work." This criterion, derived in part from Comte, shows that "social science is not yet effectively constructed—at least so far as the department of 'social dynamics' is concerned—since it is certain that every writer on the subject starts *de novo* and builds on his own foundation."[70]

HOW RACIST?

The later Brycean note in Sidgwick is important, suggestive of the slightly more moderate, slightly more open and agnostic attitude that he might have harbored, amid a sea of racial prejudice. It is exceedingly strange to find treatises from this period, on these topics, sounding for the most part so detached about the subject of race, but that is how Sidgwick's works read, at least at points. And this makes the task of sorting out just how he conceptualized "race" difficult in the extreme. He did not live long enough to articulate the issues in public lectures, after the manner of Bryce and Balfour, and even if he had, he may well have resisted the temptation, out of fear of contributing to making the "Contest" a "party question."

Still, there are some intriguing passages in the posthumously published *The Development of European Polity*, a work that Sidgwick was close to finishing at the time of his death in August 1900. It was to be his more historical, inductive work in political theory/science, and if Sidgwick had any specific projections about the future of race relations, this would have been the place to put them.

Once again, however, Sidgwick's method of avoidance is much in evidence. There are no specific projections about racial conflicts to speak of, and in fact, China, India, Africa and even Australia are largely conspicuous by their absence from the narrative. Sidgwick does discuss the future of federation, with an eye to home rule, and there is much disputing with H. S. Maine over the evolution of patriarchy, custom, and law in ancient Greece and Rome. He does make the (for him) stock point that "competent judges hold that it might have prevented serious mistakes in our government of India, if the governing statesmen had had before their minds the historical development of land-tenure, as we now conceive it to have taken place in European countries." But there is little effort to demonstrate any serious familiarity with non-European states or any serious reliance on the concept of race, after the manner of Pearson.

Yet the reason for this is embedded in the very structure of the book. As Sidgwick explains in his opening chapter, he is going to confine his attention "mainly to the political institutions of the ancient Greeks and Romans, and of Western Europe and its colonies in post-Roman times." The rationale for this is:

> Though there are societies—groups of gregarious men—in which the "differentiation" into governors and governed is barely perceptible, such societies constitute a very insignificant portion of humanity: it is almost universally true that a man is a "political animal" in the sense of being either ruler or ruled, either obeying or constituting a government of some kind. But there is a sense in which *higher* political development has originated almost exclusively in, and is still mainly confined to certain portions of the white, or—as some still call it—Caucasian race. They alone have developed, along with the development of their civilisation, governing organs of which the members are accustomed "to rule and obey alternately"—whether (1) the supreme ruler is merely elected by the citizens for a limited time, and then gives up power and may be formally called to account for his exercise of it, or (2) the supreme rule is in whole or in part exercised collectively by a body of citizens meeting from time to time.
>
> In the history of political institutions these forms interest us most, not only as citizens of a modern West-European State, but as students of Political Science: just as the highest forms of life have a special interest for the biologist. I shall accordingly confine my attention mainly to the nations who have shown a

power of developing them. And among them the most important and conspicuous of those whose history is known to us are certainly the Greeks, Romans, and West-Europeans. They stand pre-eminent among the civilised portions of humanity as having developed, up to the highest point that their civilisation has yet reached, not only political *in*stitutions, but *con*stitutions and constitutional ideas and theories.[71]

Plainly, Sidgwick was here once again swimming in rather than examining the various prejudices of his times, since he knew nothing whatsoever about, say, the Iroquois Nation, the civilizations of Africa, and so on. Yet it is noteworthy that he did not appeal to any biologically reductionistic notion of race. *Development* in fact gives one of his clearest and most extensive statements on the subject:

Some explanation is required of these notions of "race" and "family of nations." Firstly, in speaking of the "white race," I do not mean to imply that there are four or five original stocks of human beings, distinguishable by colour and other marks, as "white," "brown," "yellow," and "black" races. In the present state of anthropology there is no ground for assuming any such original differences of stocks; and the physical differences actually existing are more numerous and complicated, and shade off into each other more gradually, than the popular nomenclature suggests. And since all varieties of human beings are zoologically of one species—inter-marriage between any two generally producing fertile offspring—the physical differences of race historically presented may be to an indefinite extent referable to crossing of breeds. A special instance of this is perhaps presented by the marked differences we find between the fair whites, prevalent in Northern Europe, and the dark whites prevalent in Southern Europe and parts of Asia;—as the latter are considered by leading anthropologists to be probably due to a crossing of the fair whites with a darker race. It is to be observed that this distinction cuts across that which Comparative Philology would lead us to draw between Aryan or Indo-Germanic and Semitic nations; and this illustrates another uncertainty in which the application of the notion of "race" is involved, from the difficulty of separating, among the mental characteristics that distinguish average members of different societies, what comes from physical heredity and what from social influence. In consequence of this affinities of language are a very imperfect guide to affinities of race. Hence, in speaking of the "Indo-Germanic family of nations," I must not be understood to imply that the nations thus grouped together are all physically derived from one stock; but only that they are connected with one ancient social group by a continuous social life, evidenced by continuity of language and at least partly due to continuity of race.

At the same time there are certain broad distinctions of physical race which have remained nearly permanent during the range of history. As Mr. Tyler says, on the wall-paintings at Thebes we can distinguish red-brown Egyptians, Ethiopians like those of the present day, captives from Palestine with the well-known Semitic profile, thick-lipped negroes, and fair-skinned Libyans. And these examples may remind us that civilisation is not a monopoly of the white race, in the widest sense of that term. "At the dawn of history, the leaders of culture were the brown Egyptians, and the Babylonians," whose language is not connected with any known language of white nations; while the yellow Mongoloid Chinese have been "for four thousand years or more a civilised and literary nation." The civilisation that spread round the Meditarranean was not originated by the dark whites—Phoenicians, Greeks, Romans—but only carried on by them. Still we may perhaps say that higher *political* civilisation, the capacity for developing constitutional government in a *civilised state*, belongs primarily to the white race; and mainly to branches of the white which speak an Indo-Germanic language, and therefore show a partial continuity of descent from one single original group.[72]

Sidgwick goes on to address the importance of climate and geography in shaping peoples, roughly following lines laid down by Bryce.

These distinctions between race, civilization, and political civilization would seem to be quite important for appreciating the particulars of Sidgwick's position. He had long been sharply critical of those who dogmatically pronounced on just where civilisation was to be found. Of special note is an 1872 review of Lord Ormathwaite's *Astronomy and Geology Compared*— one of the tartest things Sidgwick ever wrote—in which he complains of the "lucid and well-bred tediousness" of the "store of platitudes" by which the author attempts to challenge Darwin. But the "climax of complacent commonplaces" is only reached when Ormathwaite tries to show "how entirely progress and civilisation have been confined to the European branch of the human race." According to him, Asiatic nations "never seem to have been inspired by any of the loftier motives which animate Europeans"—they cannot "recognize among them patriotism, or honour, or moral principle" and seem never to have "possessed any body of works worthy to be termed a literature." For such ignorance Sidgwick can scarcely conceal his scorn, and only notes that "comment would be superfluous" and that on the "outside of the volume we find the stamp of a coronet, indicating a delicate appreciation of the intrinsic value of its contents." No doubt, Sidgwick admits, the "class of readers to which it is suited would really prefer the platitudes of a peer— even a recently created one—to those of a commoner; and we can assure them that the platitudes are not unpleasantly put." The problem with the book arises "entirely from the matter."[73]

Development nowhere rises to such a fiery assault on upper-class bigotry, but it does at least suggest that for all of his shortcomings, Sidgwick was struggling, at the end of his life, to recognize some of the difficulties surrounding the concept of race and went to some length to defend the cultural achievements of other civilizations. Bryce and Dicey were slightly surprised by the work. Eleanor Sidgwick had consulted both of them, and Leslie

Stephen, about the possibility of going ahead with its publication, and their responses were very positive. Bryce went so far as to write that in "the main principles or statements of fact there was nothing to differ from" and that he was especially impressed by Sidgwick's treatment of Rome, a subject on which he, Bryce, had written extensively.[74] Such remarks suggest again the value of interpreting Sidgwick's work in light of Bryce's, albeit the work of Bryce's that, like the Romanes lecture, came before his rethinking of the subject. But if Bryce could have been moved by DuBois, perhaps Sidgwick could have been as well.

Still, there can be no avoiding the conclusion that in various unfortunate respects, Sidgwick was too much a creature of his time. His often unthinking faith in the virtues of English civilization, his fatuous assumptions about "savage" and "semi-civilised" peoples, his offensive, casual use of racist epithets and talk of "inferior races"—all these are troublingly suggestive of just where he looked for his "moral experts." If some of his relatively more open-minded colleagues, such as Bryce, ended up being pleased when the members of the "lower races" proved themselves, they nonetheless harbored few doubts about who got to judge and who had to submit to the test. And Sidgwick himself said enough to allow us to understand why he did not say more—why, that is, he often chose not to speak out about such matters, or why he wove them into his political theorizing in abstract and agnostic terms.[75]

Philosophy only debases itself when it takes a too charitable or too protective approach to the past masters. To gloss over the racism of the past is to perpetuate it.

NOTES

1. Stefan Collini, "My Roles and Their Duties: Sidgwick as Philosopher, Professor, and Public Moralist, in *Henry Sidgwick*, ed. Ross Harrison (Oxford: Oxford University Press, 2001), 48.

2. David Weinstein, in his contribution to this volume, would appear to suggest that Herbert Spencer might be counted among the latter, though his claim may not mollify Spencer's critics.

3. J. B. Schneewind, "Natural Law, Skepticism, and Methods of Ethics," *Journal of the History of Ideas* 52 (April–June 1991), 289.

4. J. B. Schneewind, "Classical Republicanism and the History of Ethics," *Utilitas* 5 (November 1993), 207.

5. J. B. Schneewind, *Sidgwick's Ethics and Victorian Moral Philosophy* (Oxford: Oxford University Press, 1977). As I have argued elsewhere, this remarkable book gives a very Kantian, even Rawlsian, reading of Sidgwick. See Bart Schultz, "The *Methods* of J. B. Schneewind," *Utilitas* 16, no. 2 (July 2004), 146–67.

6. Henry Sidgwick, *The Methods of Ethics*, 7th ed. (London: Macmillan, 1907), 489–90.

7. Bernard Williams, "The Point of View of the Universe: Sidgwick and the Ambitions of Ethics," in *Making Sense of Humanity*, ed. Bernard Williams (New York: Cambridge University Press, 1995), 166.

8. Williams, "Point of View," 169.

9. Schneewind, *Sidgwick's Ethics*, 347.

10. Henry Sidgwick, *Practical Ethics: A Collection of Essays and Addresses* (London: Swan Sonnenschein & Co., 1898), 133–34.

11. In defense of his interpretation, Schneewind has urged, among other things, that Sidgwick might have had in mind equal *ability* to engage in moral deliberation, rather than equal moral *knowledge*, and moreover, that I need to do more to point up the philosophical interest of what might have been Sidgwick's personal failings. See J. B. Schneewind's, "Comments on the Commentaries," *Utilitas* 16, no. 2 (July 2004), 188–90. But I think that the material presented in the present essay, and in Schultz, *Henry Sidgwick, Eye of the Universe* (New York: Cambridge, 2004), rather strongly indicates that Sidgwick harbored serious doubts about the abilities of what he stigmatized as the "inferior races" to reason morally, and that this was, as in the case of Kant, not incidental to his philosophy. To read Sidgwick in his philosophical context, we must take care to contextualize rather than sanitize.

12. Margaret Urban Walker, *Moral Understandings: A Feminist Study of Ethics* (New York: Routledge, 1998), 43.

13. Williams, "Point of View," 154. He also notes that Bloomsbury went on to question this reputation.

14. Sidgwick and Sidgwick, *Memoir*, 357.

15. See for example the informative discussion in William Lubenow, *The Cambridge Apostles, 1820–1914* (New York: Cambridge University Press, 1998), esp. chap. 7.

16. See for example *Orientalism* (New York: Vintage Books, 1979). For a much publicized line of criticism, see David Cannadine, *Ornamentalism: How the British Saw Their Empire* (Oxford: Oxford University Press, 2001). As should evident, I have little sympathy for the nostalgic, neoconservative accounts of imperialism spawned in recent years. For an excellent brief critical review of developments in "Raj revivalism," etc., see Said, "Always on Top," a review of Catherine Hall's *Civilising Subjects* in the *London Review of Books*, March 20, 2003, 3–6. And Victor Kiernan's *The Lords of Human Kind* (London: Serif, 1969, 1995) remains an effective antidote to the sanitizing that usually accompanies "ornamentalist" accounts. There are, to be sure, important scholarly controversies surrounding Said's views, such as the degree to which he consistently takes a social constructionist approach to "race," in parallel with Foucault's approach to sexual identity. My line in this paper is suggestive of these controversies, though it scarcely does justice to them.

17. Henry Sidgwick, *Lectures on the Ethics of T. H. Green, H. Spencer, and J. Martineau*, ed. E. E. Constance Jones (London: Macmillan, 1902), 190. Given how often *Sidgwick's Ethics* does make reference to this work, it is all the more surprising that it could sidestep the question of Sidgwick's orientalism.

18. Both of these letters are reproduced in Schultz, *Henry Sidgwick*, chap. 7, and in Schultz, ed., *The Complete Works and Select Correspondence of Henry Sidgwick*, 2nd ed. (Charlottesville, Va.: InteLex Corp,. 1999).

19. Though it is far from clear that Mill can be exonerated of the charge of "polite" racism. See David Theo Goldberg's contribution to this volume, "Liberalism's Limits:

Carlyle and Mill on 'The Negro Question.'" For possible defenses of Mill, see the contributions by Georgios Varouxakis and H. S. Jones.

20. Charles Henry Pearson, *National Life and Character* (London: Macmillan, 1893).

21. Henry Sidgwick, "Political Prophecy and Sociology," *National Review* (December 1894), reprinted without change in Henry Sidgwick, *Miscellaneous Essays and Addresses*, ed. Eleanor Sidgwick and Arthur Sidgwick (London: Macmillan, 1904), 219.

22. Sidgwick, "Political Prophecy," 219.

23. Pearson, *Character*, 16–17.

24. Pearson, *Character*, 337–38.

25. Pearson, *Character*, 342.

26. W. Stebbing, ed., *Charles Henry Pearson: Memorials by Himself, His Wife, and His Friends* (London: Longmans, Green, and Co., 1900), 186.

27. Pearson, *Character*, 31.

28. Sidgwick, *Methods*, 488.

29. James Bryce, *The American Commonwealth* (Indianapolis: Liberty Fund, 1995), 1152–53. Bryce's work first appeared in 1888; the Liberty Fund edition carries an introduction by Gary McDowell that manages, like most commentary on Bryce, to completely evade the question of his racism.

30. Bryce, *American Commonwealth*, 1164.

31. Bryce also toured and wrote extensively about South Africa; see his *Impressions of South Africa*, 3rd ed. (New York: the Century Col., 1900) for further confirmation of these claims about his racism.

32. Henry Sidgwick, *The Elements of Politics* (London: Macmillan, 1891), 314.

33. Walker, *Moral Understandings*, 45.

34. See the extremely valuable essay by Robert Bernasconi, "Kant as an Unfamiliar Source of Racism," in *Philosophers on Race: Critical Essays*, ed. Julie K. Ward and Tommy L. Lott (Oxford: Blackwell Publishers, 2002), 145–66.

35. Sidgwick, *Elements*, 244.

36. Sidgwick and Sidgwick, *Memoir*, 66–67.

37. Henry Sidgwick, "Review of Cairnes's *Political Essays*," *Spectator,* November 8, 1873.

38. Sidgwick, *Elements*, 319.

39. As Jennifer Pitts shows, in her contribution to this volume, this was also Bentham's view.

40. Sidgwick, *Elements*, 312.

41. Sidgwick, *Elements*, 310.

42. Sidgwick, *Elements*, 314.

43. Sidgwick, *Elements*, 311.

44. Sidgwick, *Elements*, 313.

45. Sidgwick, *Elements*, 315.

46. Sidgwick, *Elements*, 322–23.

47. This exchange is reproduced in Schultz, *Henry Sidgwick*, 635; it takes place in autumn of 1889.

48. Sidgwick, *Elements*, 323.

49. Sidgwick, *Elements*, 323–24.

50. Sidgwick, *Elements*, 325.

51. Sidgwick, *Elements*, 325.

52. Sidgwick, *Elements*, 326.

53. Sidgwick, *Elements*, 327.

54. Sidgwick, *Elements*, 327–28.

55. Sidgwick, *Elements*, 550.

56. Sidgwick, *Elements*, 550.

57. This exchange is reproduced in Schultz, *Henry Sidgwick.*, 647. I have been unable to trace the "extract from the Times" to which Sidgwick refers.

58. On this, see Georgios Varouxakis, *Mill on Nationality* (London: Routledge, 2002), esp. chap. 3, as well as his contribution to this volume.

59. Dicey to Bryce, Bryce Collection, Modern Papers, Bodleian Library, Oxford.

60. Perhaps the familial cotton interests also inclined Sidgwick in that direction, though this is hard to say.

61. As David Reynolds notes in *Walt Whitman's America* (New York: Vintage Books, 1995), 470: Whitman "never said much about African-American suffrage, but when he did, his remarks were generally derogatory. In an essay on the suffrage question he sounded both nativist and racist: 'As if we had not strained the voting and digestive caliber of American Democracy to the utmost for the last fifty years with the millions of ignorant foreigners, we have now infused a powerful percentage of blacks, with about as much intellect and caliber (in the mass) as so many baboons.'" Whitman, the prophet of America and democracy, sounded rather more racist than Bryce.

62. Horatio F. Brown, ed., *Letters and Papers of John Addington Symonds* (New York: Scribner's, 1923), 1–2.

63. Included in Wilfrd Short, ed., *The Mind of Arthur James Balfour* (New York: George H. Doran Company, 1918), 92.

64. Short, *Balfour*, 97–98.

65. Quoted in Kenneth Young, *Arthur James Balfour: The Happy Life of the Politician, Prime Minister, Statesman, and Philosopher, 1848–1930* (London: G. Bell and Sons, 1963), 274–84.

66. Young, *Balfour*, 282–83.

67. Bryce, *American Commonwealth*, 1179.

68. Bryce, *American Commonwealth*, 1181, 1189.

69. Sidgwick to Pearson, February 8, 1893, Bodleain Library, Oxford. MS.Eng.Lett.d.190.175.

70. Sidgwick, "Political Prophecy," 224.

71. Henry Sidgwick, *The Development of European Polity*, ed. Eleanor Sidgwick (London: Macmillan, 1903), 9.

72. Sidgwick, *Development*, 12–13.

73. Henry Sidgwick, "Lord Ormathwaite's *Astronomy and Geology Compared*," *Athenaeum*, April 20, 1872.

74. See the correspondence concerning this contained in the Sidgwick Papers, Wren Library, Trinity College, Cambridge University, Add.Ms.c.104.26. Leslie Stephen also found nothing to which to object, and Dicey in fact praised the book as the only kind of historical work worth doing.

75. In an odd historical irony, one of the figures celebrated in DuBois's *The Souls of Black Folk* was the Cambridge-educated Alexander Crummell, the African-American

clergyman and missionary. When Crummell was receiving his Cambridge degree, a heckler called out "Three cheers for the Queen's nigger." A shout went up in response "Three cheers for Crummell," with the entire audience applauding in agreement. Crummell's champion was none other than Edward White Benson, future Archibishop of Canterbury and another brother-in-law of Henry Sidgwick, who had found in him his first mentor.

Index

abolition: Bentham on, 33; complexity of, 36–43; effects of, 48; Mill (J.S.) and, 129
abstraction, Sidgwick and, 213, 223, 235
active conception of happiness, 109; Aristotle on, 113; Bentham on, 112; Mill (J.S.) on, 115–17
Acton, John, 139–40, 149n3
adaptive preferences, 120–21
aesthetics, Mill (James) on, 97–101
Afghanistan, 199
ages of society: Bentham on, 74; Mill (James) on, 98
Allardt, Erik, 109
animals, Bentham on, 112, 119, 124n5
Anti-Aggression League, 207n32
anti-imperialism, Spencer and, 196–99
Anti-Slavery Society, 48
arête. See excellence
Aristotle: on happiness, 109–10, 113–15; on honesty, 124n4; on slavery, 37
Arnold, Matthew, 140
Asante, Molefi, 126
Ashanti, king of, 36
associationist psychology: Mill (James) on, 95, 97, 99; Spencer and, 191
August, Eugene, 125
Austin, J. L., 110

Australia: Bentham on, 66; Mill (J.S.) on, 132; Pearson and, 221
Auto-Icon, 83n16

Bagehot, Walter, 32n56, 139–40, 150n9
Bain, Alexander, 82n10, 178n79
Balfour, Arthur, 212, 219, 238–41
Balfour family, 26
Beggs, Thomas, 161, 175n30
Benson, Edward White, 250n75
Bentham, Jeremy, 6–15, 119; on colonialism, 167; and disregard for past, 86n69, 95–96; on happiness, 111–13; and hedonism, 100; and imperialism, 57–91; inconsistencies of, 13, 68; legacy of, 11–12, 58–60, 77–79, 120; legislative ambitions and limits of, 69–75; on Mill (James), 60, 68; on reform by force, 5; Russell on, 1–2; on slavery and slave trade, 33–56; supposed philistinism of, 84n21
Bentham Project, 7
Bentinck, William, 57
Berlin, Isaiah, 190
Bernasconi, Robert, 226
Biblical criticism, German, 99
blacks: Bryce on, 241–42; Mill (J.S.) and, 125–35; Sidgwick on, 220–21, 235

251

Bonaparte, Louis Napoleon, 139
Boralevi, Lea Campos, 6, 9–10, 34, 44, 54n77, 87n42, 87n45
Bosanquet, Bernard, 190
Bowring, John, 11, 60, 83n15, 84n18, 87n43
Brissot, J. P., and slavery, 40
British East India Company, 59; Bentham on, 67; Burke on, 94; Mill (J.S.) and, 130–31, 147–48, 170, 178n79
British empire: Bentham and, 64–66; and conservatism, 94–95, 103n11; and Eyre affair, 157–58; Mill (James) on, 101; Mill (J.S.) and, 158–59; and race, 173n8; and United States, 240–41; utilitarianism and, 57–62. *See also* imperialism
Brooks, Chris, 24–25
Bryce, James, 26, 220, 224, 230, 236, 245–46
Buckle, H. T., 139–40, 149n3, 180
Burke, Edmund, 21, 34, 68, 94, 182; and common law, 95
Burns, J. H., 89n69, 91n82
Burrow, John W., 30n23
Buxton, Charles, 156

Caine, Barbara, 185
Cairnes, J. E., 227
Cambridge Apostles, 219
Cambridge University, 215, 219–20
Canada, Mill (J.S.) on, 132, 170–71
capabilities approach, Mill (J.S.) and, 121
capitalism: Carlyle and, 126–27; social Darwinism and, 189
Carlyle, Thomas, 167; and Eyre affair, 157–58; on race, 137, 140
Carlyle-Mill debate on race, 125–35, 140, 142–43, 163, 180, 221
Carnegie, Andrew, 189
Catholics: Bentham on, 47; emancipation of, 98
censorial jurisprudence, 95
Charles II, king of Great Britain, 168
China: Mill (J.S.) on, 141–42, 163; Pearson and, 221; Sidgwick on, 220, 245

Chomsky, Noam, 3
Christianity: and abolition, 36, 40–41, 51n15; Bentham on, 55n80; Coleridge and, 98
civilization, 185; Balfour on, 238; Mill (J.S.) on, 77, 162–63, 167–68, 183; Roosevelt on, 240; Sidgwick on, 226, 228, 232–33, 235, 244–45
civil law: Bentham on, 43–45, 70–71; Mill (James) on, 94–95, 101; Mill (J.S.) on, 159–60, 165
Clarkson, Thomas, 36–38, 40
class: Mill (J.S.) on, 130; Sidgwick on, 245
classical utilitarianism, 1–5; definition of, 2
Claviere, Etienne, and slavery, 40
climate: Mill (J.S.) on, 163; Montesquieu and, 37–38
Clive, Robert, 98
Clough, A. H., 32n56
Coleridge, Samuel Taylor, 98–99; Mill (J.S.) on, 80
Collini, Stefan, 212
colonialism: Bentham and, 41–42, 58, 62–69, 80–81, 82n6, 85n28, 87n42; Mill (J.S.) and, 79–80, 129–33, 137–53, 155–78; Pitts on, 5–6; and racism, 125–26; Sidgwick and, 196, 226–37; Spencer and, 196–99
colonial rulers: Bentham on, 63–64; Mill (J.S.) on, 164–65
Committee for the Abolition of the Slave Trade, 38–39
common law tradition, 95
common sense, Spencer on, 195
communalism, 101
comparativism, 100; problems of, 95
compensation to slave traders: Bentham on, 35, 45; Pitt on, 34–35
competition: Mill (J.S.) on, 142, 146; Pearson on, 223
Condorcet, M. J. de Caritat, marquis de, and slavery, 40
conservatism, and British empire, 94–95, 103n11
contentment, Mill (J.S.) on, 116

contingent racism, 130, 143
Conway, Stephen, 82n6
Cooper, J. Ashley, 205n25
Corn Laws, abolition of, 1
corruption, Bentham on, 70–71, 74
cosmopolitan patriotism, 22
Cowell, J. J., 238
Crummell, Alexander, 250n75
culture: Mill (James) on, 95–96; Mill (J.S.) on, 133, 147, 165–67, 183; Sidgwick on, 226, 229; Spencer on, 199

Dakyns, Henry Graham, 227
Darwin, Charles: and Eyre affair, 159; theory of, Spencer and, 189–209
Darwin, Erasmus, 100
decadence, Balfour on, 238–39
deception, Sidgwick and, 216–26
deductive hedonism, Spencer on, 194
democracy: Balfour on, 240; Bentham and, 84n24; Mill (J.S.) on, 80, 146; Spencer on, 198
depression, Mill (J.S.) and, 110, 117–18
despotism, 133–34; Mill (J.S.) on, 58–59, 132, 144, 155, 162
Dewey, John, 3
Dicey, A. V., 28, 237, 245
dichotomies, Mill (J.S.) and, 78, 80
Dickens, Charles, 157
difference arguments, Mill (J.S.) and, 185–86
distributive justice, Spencer and, 191
diversity, Mill (J.S.) on, 141–42
Drescher, Seymour, 49
Drummond, William, 100
D'Souza, Dinesh, 126
dualism: Sidgwick and, 27; Sidgwick on, 215
Dube, Allison, 88n61
DuBois, W. E. B., 242, 250n75
Dumont, Etienne, 7, 29n13, 39, 41
Dundas, Henry, 69–70, 88n56
Dupuis, Charles François, 100
Durham, John George Lambton, earl of, 146, 170–71
Dutton, Geoffrey, 161–62, 175n33
Dworkin, Andrea, 121

economic arguments: for abolition, 33, 38, 43–44, 49; for colonialism, 62–64, 76, 96–97, 165–66, 228
education: Bentham on, 74; Mill (James) on, 95; Mill (J.S.) on, 132, 155, 169–70; Sidgwick and, 219, 233, 235
Egypt: Mill (J.S.) on, 126, 130, 143–44, 164; Sidgwick on, 244–45
elitism: Sidgwick and, 215–17, 219; utilitarianism and, 22–23
Elster, Jon, 120
Emancipate Your Colonies (Bentham), 41, 62, 64
emigration: Bentham on, 58; Mill (J.S.) on, 166; Roosevelt on, 240; Sidgwick on, 228
emotional states, and happiness, Mill (J.S.) on, 110, 117–20, 123
empire. *See* British empire; imperialism
empirical utilitarianism, Spencer and, 193–96
Engels, Friedrich, 153n46
English conception of happiness, 108–10
Enlightenment: and abolition, 37; and racism, 184–86
Epicureanism, 111
epistemology: intuitionistic, 212; Kantian, 97–98
equality, Mill (J.S.) and, 185–86
esotericism, Sidgwick and, 218–26
ethics: Sidgwick on, 214–15; Spencer on, 194
ethnocentrism, Mill (J.S.) and, 148–49
ethology, Mill (J.S.) on, 90n78, 91n82, 180
Eurocentrism: Mill (J.S.) and, 137–53; Sidgwick and, 212; term, 142; utilitarianism and, 180
evil pleasures: Aristotle on, 114; Bentham on, 112
evolution, Spencer on, 189–209
examination, Foucault on, 3
excellence: Aristotle on, 113; and happiness, 110; Mill (J.S.) on, 117; term, 123n3
expository jurisprudence, 95

Eyre affair, 20–21, 238; background of, 156–57; Mill (J.S.) and, 137, 155–78
Eyre Defence Committee, 160

Faulkner, Peter, 24–25
feminist theory: on Mill (J.S.), 107–24; on Sidgwick, 217–18
Ferguson, Adam, 76
Feuer, L. S., 90n81
Fieldhouse, D. K., 198
foreign policy, Mill (J.S.) on, 159
Fort William College, 94
Foucault, Michel, 2–3
Fox, Charles James, 34, 68
France: and abolition, 40; Bentham on, 62; Burke on, 94; Declaration of Rights, Bentham on, 42–43; Mill (J.S.) and, 119
Freeman, E. A., 140
free trade, Bentham on, 35–36

Gellner, Ernest, 17, 99
German biblical criticism, 99
Gibbard, Allan, 200
Gladstone, W. E., 238
Goldberg, David Theo, 18, 125–35, 142, 184–85
Gordon, George William, 156, 161–62, 172
Government House: and racism, 237–42; and utilitarianism, 214–18
government, Mill (J.S.) on, 131–32, 155, 165–66, 169–70
gradual emancipation: Bentham on, 44–45, 49–50; Society and, 48
Greece: Bentham on, 73; and happiness, 109–10; Mill (J.S.) on, 126, 130, 143–44, 146, 164; Sidgwick on, 243
Green, T. H., 25–26, 190
Guizot, François, 141–42, 145–46

Habibi, Don, 138, 148
Haitian revolution, and Eyre affair, 156–57
Halévy, Elie, 12, 61–62, 83n14
Hall, Catherine, 140, 173n8, 181

happiness: Aristotle on, 113–15; Bentham on, 111–13; characteristics of, 113; conceptions of, 108–10; Mill (J.S.) on, 107–24; Spencer on, 192
harm principle, 162, 167
Harrison, Frederic, 160
Harrison, Ross, 84n21
Hartley, David, 95, 97
Harvie, Christopher, 212
Hastings, Warren, 21, 66, 94
Hazard, Rowland, 168
Hazlitt, William, 86n39
Heber, Bishop, 67–68
hedonism: deductive, Spencer on, 194; radicalism and, 100
Herder, J. G. von, 181
Hinduism, Mill (James) and, 94
The History of British India (James Mill), 59, 75–76, 93–105
history, utilitarianism and, 179; Bentham and, 86n69, 95–96
Hodge, Arthur, 55n80
honesty, Aristotle on, 124n4
Hume, David, 152n25
Hunt, James, 139, 180
Huxley, Thomas Henry, 140, 193; and Eyre affair, 159

imagination: Coleridge on, 98; Mill (James) on, 97, 99–100
imperialism, 1–5, 23–24; Bentham and, 57–91; Bowring on, 60; Mill (James) and, 75–76, 93–105; Mill (J.S.) and, 76–81, 137–53; Pitts on, 5–6; Said on, 4–5; Sidgwick and, 226–37; Spencer and, 190, 196–99; utilitarianism and, 81n1, 93–105, 179–87; in Victorian era, 147
Imperialist League, 26
indefeasible rights, Spencer on, 199
India: Bentham and, 59–60, 67, 69–75; English beliefs on, 98; Mill (James) and, 75–76, 93–105; Mill (J.S.) and, 76–81, 131–32, 146–47; Sidgwick on, 226; Trevelyan on, 26
Indian Mutiny, 24; and Eyre affair, 156–57

indigenous peoples: Bentham on, 67;
Mill (J.S.) on, 133; Sidgwick on, 230,
232–33
international law, Sidgwick on, 220,
226–37
intuitionism, 25; Sidgwick and, 212;
Spencer and, 191, 195
Irish Question: Carlyle and, 126–27;
Mill (J.S.) and, 31n46, 139, 163,
177n65
Islam: Ashanti king on, 36; Bentham on,
45–46, 73–74; Mill (James) and, 94

Jahn, Beate, 152n31
Jamaica Committee: Mill (J.S.) and,
155–78; official position of, 160
Jamaica, home rule in, 168–69
Jones, H. S., 18, 179–87
Jones, William, 16; and Mill (James),
93–95, 99–100; and philology, 97;
and wealth of India, 98
Jowett, Benjamin, 220
jurisprudence, types of, 95
jury trials in India, Bentham on, 73–74
justice: Mill (J.S.) on, 121–22; Spencer
and, 191
Justman, Stewart, 137
just war, Spencer on, 199

Kant, Immanuel, 214; on publicity
requirement, 216; and racism,
225–26
Kantaro, Kentaro, 205n25
Kantian epistemology: Mill (James) and,
98; and utilitarianism, 97
Kelly, Paul, 33
Kingsley, Charles, 140, 157
Kinzer, Bruce, 31n46
Kipling, Rudyard, 27, 163
Klingberg, Frank J., 55n80
Kloppenberg, James, 212
Knight, Richard Payne, 100
knowledge, Mill (J.S.) on, 132–33
Knox, Robert, 140, 179

labor: Bryce on, 236; Sidgwick on,
230–31, 233. *See also* working class

Lafayette, Marie Joseph, marquis de,
and slavery, 40
Lamarck, J. B. de Monet, chevalier de,
196
language: Carlyle and, 125–26; Mill
(James) on, 97, 99; Mill (J.S.) and, 141;
Sidgwick and, 221, 224, 229–30, 236
Lansdowne circle, 40–41, 55n80
Lefkowitz, Mary, 126
legislation: Bentham and, 57–91, 95;
limits on, Bentham and, 69–75
Levin, Michael, 152n31
liberalism: and imperialism, 181–82; Mill
(J.S.) and, 121, 137–38, 144–45;
Spencer and, 190–93, 202–3
libertine tradition of radicalism, 100
liberty: Mill (J.S.) on, 162, 165; Spencer
and, 191–92
Locke, John: Bentham and, 44; and
slavery, 37
Long, Douglas, 33, 85n24
Lyell, Charles, 159
Lyons, David, 200
Lytton, Edward Robert, earl of, 27, 220

Macaulay, Thomas Babington, 147
Macfie, Alexander, 4
MacKinnon, Catharine, 108
Madison, James, 167
Maine, Henry Sumner, 26, 243
Majeed, Javed, 15–16, 93–105, 182,
205n21
male power, Mill (J.S.) on, 120–23
manavadharmasastra, 94
Mandler, Peter, 149n6, 180, 184
Maori people, 177n72
Marmontel, Jean François, 118–19,
124n6
marriage, Mill (J.S.) on, 122–23
Marshall, Alfred, 32n56
martial law, Mill (J.S.) on, 159–60, 164
Marx, Karl, 140, 153n46
Maurice, F. D., 179
Mazzini, Giuseppe, 179
McLaren, Priscilla, 161
Mehta, Uday, 84n22, 88n57, 89n69, 141,
181–82

Mill, Harriet Barrow, 117–18
Mill, James, 15–18; Bentham and, 60, 68; and Bentham's legacy, 11, 59–60; and Bentinck, 57; and imperialism, 59, 75–76, 93–105, 182–83; and John Stuart Mill, 59; and race, 182
Mill, John Stuart, 18–23; and Bentham's legacy, 12, 30n31, 77–79, 86n34, 120; and Carlyle and race, 125–35; on happiness, 107–24; and imperialism, 58–59, 61, 76–81, 183; inconsistencies of, 145, 161–62, 208n41; and Irish Question, 31n46, 139, 163, 177n65; and Jamaica Committee, 155–78; and James Mill, 59; legacy of, 147; and racism, 78–79, 125–35, 137–53, 162–63, 182, 184–85; and romanticism, 96, 110; versus Spencer, 190
Millar, John, 89n73
Miller, J. Joseph, 20–22, 155–78, 183
Miller, James, 3
Mirabeau, Honoré Gabriel Riqueti, comte de, 40–41, 62
mixing of races: Bryce on, 236; Kant on, 226; Pearson on, 223; Sidgwick on, 225, 237
Montesquieu, Charles Louis de Secondat, baron de, on slavery, 37–38
Moore, G. E., 28, 189
morality, Sidgwick and, 218–37
moral rights, Spencer and, 190–92, 195, 200–201
Morant Bay Rebellion, 156
mythology, Mill (James) and, 99–100

national character, 19-20; Bagehot on, 150n9; Bryce on, 224, 236; Mill (James) on, 99; Mill (J.S.) on, 77–78, 137–39; revolutions of 1848 and, 139–40; Stephen on, 179–80
Native Americans, Sidgwick on, 216–17
naturalism, Mill (J.S.) on, 130
natural rights: Bentham on, 34. *See also* moral rights
Nelson, brigadier, 156

Newnham College, Cambridge, 215, 238–39
New Zealand, 177n72
Nietzsche, Friedrich, 107, 109
noble lie, Sidgwick and, 216–26
non-intervention, utilitarians on, 207nn32–33
Nozick, Robert, 112
Nussbaum, Martha C., 18, 107–24

orientalism, 4, 219; Jones on, 93; Mill (J.S.) and, 147
Ormathwaite, lord, 245

pacifism, Bentham and, 82n6
pain, Bentham on, 111–12
pained virtue: Aristotle on, 114–15; Mill (J.S.) on, 116–17
pannomion, 57
panopticism, 3; definition of, 2
Panopticon, 2, 52n35, 65
Parekh, Bhikhu, 144–47
Parfit, Derek, 211
paternalism: Carlyle and, 127; Mill (James) and, 133; Mill (J.S.) on, 80, 144, 184
patriotism, cosmopolitan, 22
Patterson, A. J., 211
peace, Bentham on, 65–66
Peacock, Thomas Love, 98
Pearson, Charles Henry, 26, 221–22, 242
Pecora, Vincent, 141
philology, 97
pious fraud, 218–26; Sidgwick and, 216–17
Pitt, William, 34
Pitts, Jennifer, 5, 11–15, 18–21, 30n24, 57–91, 182; on Eyre affair, 155, 164–65
Place, Francis, 98
"Plan for an Universal and Perpetual Peace" (Bentham), 65–66
plantation subsidies, 126
Plato, 217
pleasure: Aristotle on, 114; Bentham on, 111–13; and happiness, 109–10; Mill (J.S.) on, 115; Spencer on, 191

post-colonial theory, and utilitarianism, 181

power: Bentham on, 47; Foucault on, 2–3; Mill (J.S.) on, 120–23, 132–33

Priam, luck of, 115, 117

Prichard, Henry, 109

Priestley, F. E. L., 19

private sphere, Mill (J.S.) and, 108

progress, 185; Mill (James) on, 76; Mill (J.S.) on, 131–32, 140–43, 145, 147–48, 162–63

property rights: Bentham on, 44–45; Spencer on, 198

Prosper, slave, 55n80

psychology: Mill (James) on, 95; Mill (J.S.) on, 180. *See also* associationist psychology

publicity requirement, 215–16; Sidgwick on, 216–17

public opinion: on abolition, 49; Bentham on, 63; and Eyre affair, 155–56; on Indian mutiny, 24

Quakers, and abolition, 38, 40, 51n15

race, 1–5, 27–28; Balfour on, 240–41; Bentham on, 72–73; British empire and, 173n8; Bryce and, 224, 241–42; Dicey on, 237; and Eyre affair, 155–78; Pearson on, 221–23; Sidgwick on, 244–45; term, 139, 150n8, 237; utilitarianism and, 179–87; in Victorian era, 125–26, 139–40, 180–81, 221

racism: Enlightenment universalism and, 184–86; Government House and, 237–42; Kant and, 225–26; Mill (J.S.) and, 78–79, 125–35, 137–53, 162–63, 182, 184–85; Sidgwick and, 211–50; term, 142, 144, 237

radicalism: and Eyre affair, 159; infidel, 100; libertine tradition of, 100

rationalism, Spencer and, 193–96

Rawls, John, 211, 216

reformism: Bentham on, 5, 41–42, 46–47, 58; Russell on, 1

religion: Balfour on, 240; Bentham on, 55n80; Coleridge and, 98; Mill (J.S.) on, 123; Sidgwick and, 212, 218–19; and slavery, 36–37, 48–49

respectability, Mill (James) and, 100

revolutions of 1848, and racism, 139–40

Rid Yourselves of Ultramaria (Bentham), 62

Ritchie, D. G., 25, 205n20

la Rochefoucauld, François, duc de, and slavery, 40

Rockefeller, John D., Jr., 189

romanticism: Mill (J.S.) and, 110; and utilitarianism, 96, 100

Rome, Sidgwick on, 243, 246

Romilly, Samuel, 7, 38–40

Roosevelt, Teddy, 240–41

Rosen, Frederick, 6–11, 33–56, 84n24, 153n41

Rousseau, Jean-Jacques, on slavery, 38

Roy, Rammohun, 73

Ruskin, John, 137, 140, 157–58

Russell, Bertrand, 1–2, 28

Ryan, Alan, 147

Said, Edward, 4–5, 28, 219–20; on Mill and race, 137

Schelling, Friedrich von, 98

Schneewind, J. B., 25, 211, 214, 217

Schultz, Bart, 1–32, 211–50

science: Balfour on, 238; Mill (J.S.) and, 138, 180; in Victorian era, 139

Scottish Enlightenment, Mill (James) and, 15–16, 76

secular liberalism: and abolition, 41, 48; and mythology, 100

Seeley, John, 26, 219–20

segregation, Sidgwick on, 225, 232–33

self-government: Bentham on, 63–64, 67; Mill (J.S.) on, 131, 144

Sen, Amartya, 120

Sepoy uprising. *See* Indian Mutiny

settler colonies, Bentham on, 58

sexuality: Mill (James) on, 100; Mill (J.S.) on, 120–21

Sharp, Granville, 40

Sidgwick, Eleanor, 215, 245–46

Sidgwick, Henry, 23–28, 200; and colonialism, 196; correspondence of,

213; and empirical utilitarianism, 195–96; late developments in work of, 242–44; and racism, 211–50; on Spencer, 194

Singer, Peter, 189

Skinner, Quentin, 190

slavery: Bentham on, 33–56; Carlyle on, 128–29; complexity of, 36–38; Mill (J.S.) on, 129–33; scale of, 48; Sidgwick on, 233; Spencer on, 198; term, 7, 47

slave trade, Bentham on, 33–56

Smith, Adam, 76; on colonies, 63; on slavery, 38, 49

social Darwinism, Spencer and, 189–209

socialism, Spencer and, 192

Société des Amis des Noirs, 40

Society for the Abolition of the Slave Trade, 36–37

Society for the Mitigation and Gradual Abolition of Slavery throughout the British Dominions, 48

Southey, Robert, 97

Spain, Bentham on, 62, 65

Spencer, Herbert, 23–28, 189–209; and Eyre affair, 159

Spivak, Gayatri, 5

Stapleton, Julia, 147

stationariness, Mill (J.S.) on, 140–41

Stephen, James Fitzjames, 12, 139–40, 147, 153n41

Stephen, Leslie, 88n55, 179–80, 245–46

Stocking, George, 5, 150n8

Stokes, Eric, 12, 57, 69, 153n41, 181

subjection, Mill (J.S.) on, 120

subjective expression, 134; in Victorian era, 185

sublime, Mill (James) on, 99

suffering, Bentham on, 112

Sullivan, Eileen, 83n13, 83n15, 85n30, 183

Sumner, Wayne, 201

Sumner, William Graham, 189

survival of the fittest, phrase, Spencer and, 189

Symonds, John Addington, 238

Taylor, Harriet, 117–19

Tennyson, Alfred, 157, 238

Thomas, Hugh, 36

Thomas, William, 81n1

Tocqueville, Alexis de, 141–42

Tooke, Horne, 97

Trevelyan, George, 26, 32n53

Turgot, Anne Robert Jacques, 228

Twain, Mark, 220, 238

Tylor, Edward Burnet, 244

unified government: Balfour on, 240–41; Bentham on, 65–66; Sidgwick on, 220

universalism, and racism, 184–86

universal jurisprudence, 95

utilitarianism: and British empire, 57–62; classical, 1–5; conscious versus unconscious, 200; early theorists of, and race and empire, 179–87; empirical, Spencer and, 193–96; Government House, 214–18; and history, 86n69, 95–96, 179; and imperialism, 81n1, 93–105, 181–83; and romanticism, 96, 100; Spencer and, 190–96, 202–3; variation in, 182

utility, definition of, 111

utility principle, 183; Bentham on, 111

Varouxakis, Georgios, 1–32, 90n80, 137–53, 180, 184

Victorian era: divisions of, 153n48; and imperialism, 4, 147; and race, 125–26, 139–40, 180–81, 221; Russell on, 1; Said on, 219–20

Villeneuve, Geoffroy de, and slavery, 40

virtue. *See* excellence

Volney, C. F. de C., 100

Voltaire, on slavery, 38

voting rights, Bentham on, 73–74

Wakefield, Edward Gibbon, 82n6, 166

Walker, Margaret Urban, 217

Walvin, James, 48

war, Spencer on, 199

Weinstein, David, 27–28, 189–209
Whewell, William, 19, 25, 200
Whitman, Walt, 238, 249n61
Wilberforce, William, 7, 34, 38–40, 52n35
Wilkes, John, 100
Williams, Bernard, 58–59, 215–16, 218
Williams, Eric, 49
Wilson, George, 39
Wilson, Horace Hyman, 93
Wilson, Woodrow, 211
Winch, Donald, 66, 85n28

women: Mill (James) on, 84n20; Mill (J.S.) and, 107–8, 117–23, 163
Wordsworth, William, 107, 109, 118, 124n4
working class: Carlyle on, 128–29; and Eyre affair, 158–59; Mill (J.S.) on, 167. *See also* labor

Young, Kenneth, 240
Young, Robert, 181

Zastoupil, Lynn, 147

About the Contributors

David Theo Goldberg is the Director of the system-wide University of California Humanities Research Institute and Professor of African American Studies and Criminology, Law, and Society at the University of California–Irvine. He is author, inter alia, of *The Racial State* (Blackwell, 2002), *Racist Culture: Philosophy and the Politics of Meaning* (Blackwell, 1993), and of *The Death of Race* (Oxford: Blackwell, forthcoming).

H. S. Jones is Senior Lecturer in History at the University of Manchester. He has published extensively on nineteenth-century political thought, British and French, including: *The French State in Question* (Cambridge University Press, 1993) and *Victorian Political Thought* (Macmillan, 2000).

Javed Majeed is currently at the School of English and Drama, Queen Mary, University of London. He is author of *Ungoverned Imaginings: James Mill's "The History of British India and Orientalism"* (Clarendon Press, 1992). He is also the coauthor, with Christopher Shackle, of *Hali's Musaddas: The Flow and Ebb of Islam* (OUP, 1997). He has a number of articles in journals and in edited books on colonial India. He is currently working on a book entitled *Autobiography, Travel, and Postnational Identity: Narratives of Selfhood in Gandhi, Nehru, and Iqbal*, to be published by Palgrave-Macmillan in 2006.

J. Jason Miller is Assistant Professor in the Department of Philosophy and Religion at the University of North Carolina, Pembroke, and has interests in Mill and in just war theory and military ethics. His recently published work includes "*Jus ad bellum* and an Officer's Moral Obligations: Invincible Ignorance, the Constitution, and Iraq," *Social Theory and Practice* 30:4 (October 2004). He is currently working on a Millian theory of humanitarian intervention.

Martha C. Nussbaum is the Ernst Freund Distinguished Service Professor of Law and Ethics in the Law School, Philosophy Department, and Divinity School at the University of Chicago. Her many works include *Hiding from Humanity: Disgust, Shame, and the Law* (Princeton University Press, 2004), *Upheavals of Thought: The Intelligence of Emotions* (Cambridge University Press, 2001), *Women and Human Development: The Capabilities Approach* (Cambridge University Press), and *Cultivating Humanity: A Classical Defense of Reform in Liberal Education* (Harvard University Press, 1997). She is currently completing a number of books, including *Frontiers of Justice: Disability, Nationality, Species Membership*.

Jennifer Pitts is an Assistant Professor of Politics at Princeton University. She is author of *A Turn to Empire: the Rise of Imperial Liberalism in Britain and France* (Princeton University Press, 2005), and the editor and translator of *Alexis de Tocqueville: Writings on Empire and Slavery* (Johns Hopkins University Press, 2001).

Frederick Rosen is Emeritus Professor of the History of Political Thought at University College London. For many years he was Director of the Bentham Project and General Editor of *The Collected Works of Jeremy Bentham*. He is author of numerous books and articles and his most recent book is *Classical Utilitarianism from Hume to Mill* (Routledge, 2003). He is currently working on a study of the thought of John Stuart Mill.

Bart Schultz is a Fellow and Lecturer in the Humanities and Humanities Collegiate Divisions and Special Programs Coordinator at the Graham School of General Studies at the University of Chicago. His works include *Essays on Henry Sidgwick* (Cambridge University Press, 1992), *The Complete Works and Select Correspondence of Henry Sidgwick* (InteLex Corp., 1999), and *Henry Sidgwick, Eye of the Universe: An Intellectual Biography* (Cambridge University Press, 2004). He is currently assembling *The Cambridge Companion to Henry Sidgwick* (Cambridge University Press, forthcoming).

Georgios Varouxakis is Senior Lecturer in the History Department of Queen Mary College, University of London. He is the author of *Mill on Nationality* (Routledge, 2002) and of *Victorian Political Thought on France and the French* (Palgrave, 2002) and has also published several articles on British and French political thought and on issues of political theory and nation-